COUPLES IN CONFLICT

COUPLES IN CONFLICT

Edited by

Alan Booth
Ann C. Crouter
Mari Clements
The Pennsylvania State University

Psychology Press
Taylor & Francis Group

New York   London

The final camera copy for this work was supplied by the editors.

First published by
Lawrence Erlbaum Associates, Inc., Publishers
10 Industrial Avenue
Mahwah, NJ 07430

First issued in paperback 2012

This edition published 2012 by Psychology Press

Psychology Press   Psychology Press
Taylor & Francis Group   Taylor & Francis Group
711 Third Avenue   27 Church Road
New York, NY 10017   Hove, East Sussex BN3 2FA

Psychology Press is an imprint of Taylor & Francis, an informa group company

Cover design by Kathryn Houghtaling Lacey

Library of Congress Cataloging-in-Publication Data

Couples in conflict / edited by Alan Booth, Ann C. Crouter,
Mari Clements.
        p. cm.
Includes bibliographical references and indexes.
   ISBN 0-8058-3545-8 (alk. paper)
   ISBN 978-0-415-64705-2 (Paperback)
   1. Marital conflict–United States. 2. Interpersonal conflict–
United States. 3. Married couples–United States–Psychology.
I. Booth, Alan, 1935– II. Crouter, Ann C. III. Clements, Mari.
   HQ535 .C69   2001
   306.872—dc21   2001023167
                                              CIP

Contents

Preface

Couple conflict is an important antecedent of domestic violence, ineffective parenting, and marital dissolution, phenomena that threaten the strong functioning of contemporary families and the adults and children living in families. As such, couple conflict is a topic of critical importance to family scholars and those charged with developing policies and programs in this area. Not all couple conflict is damaging, however. Indeed, a thread running through this volume is that constructive conflict and negotiation is beneficial for relationships. Together, the chapters in this volume provide a foundation for thinking about creative ways in which our society can work to prevent or minimize destructive couple conflict and to enhance couples' abilities to constructively handle their differences.

The chapters in this volume are based on the presentations and discussions from a national symposium on "Couples in Conflict" held at the Pennsylvania State University, November 1-2, 1999, as the seventh in a series of annual interdisciplinary symposia focused on family issues. The book is divided into four sections, each dealing with a different aspect of couple conflict. The first section addresses the question "What are the societal and bioevolutionary underpinnings of couple conflict?" Evolutionary psychologists Martin Daly and Margo Wilson make a case for why couple conflict may be the legacy of reproductive fitness strategies selected for over the course of human evolution. Drawing on several national data sets focused on homicides perpetrated by spouses or partners, they argue that women in cohabiting relationships are particularly at risk. Jay Belsky, a developmental researcher, elaborates on the evolutionary argument in his remarks. In contrast, clinical psychologist Rena L. Repetti cautions that there are many possible alternative explanations for the empirical data that Daly and Wilson present, including selection effects into and out of marriage and cohabitation. Demographer Frances K. Goldscheider concurs that contemporary Western culture offers a variety of explanations that are more parsimonious than is evolutionary theory.

In the second section of this volume, Thomas Bradbury, Ronald Rogge and Erika Lawrence— clinical psychologists whose research has focused on the longitudinal course of marriage— address the questions, "What are the interpersonal roots of couple conflict? What are the consequences for individuals and couples?" Bradbury et al. underscore the fact that couple conflict may not be the most important relationship process, and argue for the need to understand positive marital dynamics such as social support and cooperation. Steven R. H. Beach, a clinical psychologist, examines the way partners adjust their perceptions of themselves and their spouse and how these modifications influence whether potential conflict erupts or not. In a chapter that focuses more specifically on couple violence, Michael P. Johnson, a family sociologist, makes an important distinction between two types of couple violence: common couple violence and what he terms "patriarchal terrorism." The latter pattern typically involves a highly controlling male partner who uses violence and other forms of coercion to control his female partner. James V. Cordova, a clinical psychologist, asks how we can provide couples with information about their interactions that may help them prevent episodes of conflict or violence in the future. His Marriage Checkup is an example of one preventive approach.

The third section of the book focuses on children. E. Mark Cummings, Marcie C. Goeke-Morey, and Lauren M. Papp, all developmental scholars, address "What effects does couple conflict have on children? How do individual differences in children moderate these effects?" A central tenet of Cummings et al.'s chapter is that couple conflict has the most serious effect on children when it threatens their emotional security. Christy M. Buchanon, Michael Louca, and Robyn Waizenhofer, developmental psychologists, extend the picture by focusing on parental conflict in the context of divorce. Rand D. Conger, a family sociologist, puts couple conflict in a socioeconomic perspective, using family data drawn from rural Iowa and rural Georgia. John H. Grych, a clinical psychologist, focuses on how the type of conflict influences children's internalizing and externalizing behaviors.

The last section of the book is devoted to the issue of policies and programs that address couple conflict. Matthew R. Sanders, a clinical intervention researcher, shares the impressive efforts he and his University of Queensland colleagues have made to strengthen families and prevent psychopathology in children. Richard J. Gelles, a family sociologist, argues that intervention must be geared to the amount of violence and the factors that contribute to it. Theodora Ooms, a policy analyst and director of the Resources Center on Couples and Marriage Policy at the Center for Law and Social Policy, focuses attention on state and national policies that have implications for couple conflict and ways that states or the country as a whole could attempt to strengthen marriage. Finally, Robert E. Emery, a clinical psychologist, highlights the efficacy of mediation as a strategy to minimize couple conflict, particularly during the divorce transition. The book concludes with an essay by Chris Knoester and Tanya L. Afifi that pulls these four themes together and points to new directions for research and program efforts.

Acknowledgments

There are many to thank for assistance with the symposium. We are indebted to the Pennsylvania State University Population Research Institute; College of the Liberal Arts; College of Agricultural Sciences; Children, Youth and Families Consortium; Prevention Research Center; Center for Human Development and Family Research in Diverse Contexts; Department of Human Development and Family Studies; Department of Psychology; Department of Sociology; Crime, Law and Justice Program; and the National Institute of Child Health and Human Development for funding the symposium. The contributions of Kim Zimmerman, Kris McNeel, Sherry Yocum, Diane Mattern, and Erin Lesser in assisting with the administration of the symposium were invaluable. Special thanks to professors Paul Amato, Mari Clements, Catherine Cohan, and Keith Crnic for their excellent work in presiding over the four sessions, and for contribution to the flow of ideas during the sessions.

—*Alan Booth*
—*Ann C. Crouter*

I

What Are the Societal and Bioevolutionary Underpinnings of Couple Conflict?

1

The Evolutionary Psychology of Couple Conflict in Registered versus De Facto Marital Unions

Margo Wilson and Martin Daly

McMaster University, Department of Psychology

We have studied couple conflict primarily through the peculiar window afforded by homicide. This research has been premised on the notions that homicides, although rare and obviously extreme, frequently represent the culmination of conflicts whose substance is not so rare, and that factors associated with variation in the risk of being killed by one's partner are likely to be associated with variation in the prevalence and intensity of nonlethal couple conflict, too. If these premises are sound, then lethal violence holds two advantages as a conflict "assay": high face validity as a reflection of genuine conflict, and relatively minor problems of biased detection or reportage. In this chapter, we review findings about the epidemiology of spousal homicide, and also discuss evidence bearing on the premise that patterned variation in the incidence of lethal violence parallels variations in the much more prevalent phenomena of "normal" violence and coercive control. A pervasive theme is the importance of male sexual proprietariness as a motivational factor in severe couple conflict.

One major risk marker for spousal homicide is the legal status of the union. Wilson, Daly, and Wright (1993) reported, for example, that Canadian women incur a per capita risk of homicide at the hands of de facto husbands (i.e., cohabitant male partners, or "common-law husbands") that is about eight times that incurred by their registered marriage counterparts. In this chapter, we focus on the distinctions between de facto and registered marriage, in order to both explore possible reasons for this immense risk differential, and provide a framework for considering the more general issues of what couple conflict is about and what factors exacerbate or temper it. The theoretical framework that we find most helpful in pursuing these goals is that of evolutionary psychology.

EVOLUTIONARY PSYCHOLOGY AND INTERPERSONAL CONFLICT

"Evolutionary psychology" does not refer to a unitary, falsifiable theory. Like "social psychology" or "cognitive psychology," it refers to a field or approach, within which alternative theories vie (see, e.g., Bock & Cardew, 1997; Crawford & Krebs, 1998; Daly & Wilson, 1988, 1997, 1999; Gaulin & McBurney, 2001). If

3

we may define psychology as the science concerned with how brains/minds process information and generate behavior, then evolutionary psychology is simply the part of psychological science that is conducted with active attention to contemporary theory and research in evolutionary biology.

Brains/minds possess species-typical (albeit sexually differentiated) functional organization for the same reason that anatomy and physiology possess species-typical (albeit sexually differentiated) functional organization: because of the cumulative effects of a long history of Darwinian selection. From this uncontroversial proposition, we infer that theory and research in psychology and the social sciences would benefit from efforts to stay informed about theoretical and empirical developments in evolutionary biology. A great deal is known about the process of evolution by selection, and this knowledge affords numerous leads for fruitful investigation of its products, including human motives and emotions (Daly & Wilson, 1995).

The essence of the theory of evolution by selection, for present purposes, is that the basic attributes of any living creature, including the human animal, assumed their modern forms over evolutionary time because they contributed to reproduction and their own proliferation. More precisely, the "inclusive fitness" effects of an attribute consist of its average impact on the prevalence of copies of its carrier's particular genes in future populations, and because natural selection is differential reproductive success, attributes tend to evolve to be effective contributors to expected inclusive fitness. (*Expected* is used here in its statistical sense, and must also be interpreted to refer to outcome probabilities in ancestral environments, which contemporary environments may or may not resemble; see Daly & Wilson, 1999.) There is a theory of the foundations of self-interest implicit in this view: basic (nonidiosyncratic) likes and dislikes are means to the end of increasing expected inclusive fitness. Sugar is sweet because it signals nutrients needed for survival and reproduction. A mate's infidelity is painful because of the threats that it entailed for our ancestors' fitness.

From an evolutionary perspective, there are several kinds of close relationships that are qualitatively distinct in ways that cannot be summarized by simple dimensional constructs such as "closeness" or "intimacy" (Daly, Salmon, & Wilson, 1997; Emlen, Wrege, & Demong, 1995). More specifically, the relationship between mates in a sexually reproducing species is unique. The well-being and eventual reproduction of offspring contribute to both parents' fitness, and this fact can engender a unique commonality of interest: If personal reproduction (rather than collateral kin investment) is the main form of reproductive effort, and if mates reproduce monogamously, evolutionary reasoning suggests that the solidarity of long-term mates will evolve to exceed that of any other relationship, including even the closest blood kin, because the exigencies that affect one mate's fitness will generally have parallel effects on the other's (Alexander, 1987). Note the "ifs" in this proposition, however. Whereas genetic relatives necessarily share interests founded in correlated fitness, the solidarity of mates is more fragile because their fitness correlation has always been more fragile. The solidarity of mated couples is threatened by a number of interacting factors, including:

1. Temptations to abandon the present partner for another (exacerbated by sex differences in the lifespan trajectory of mate value).
2. Temptations to free-ride on the partner's investments in the couple's joint project (exacerbated by power asymmetries and by differential remating prospects or other opportunity asymmetries).
3. Nepotistic interests in distinct kindreds (the in-law problem).
4. Dependent offspring of prior unions (the stepchild problem).
5. Covert extra-pair mating (the cuckoldry problem).

The last of these is especially problematic, because it can abolish or even reverse the couple's expected fitness correlation. This consideration seems to explain the special status of adultery as a betrayal of the marital union, as well as the cross-cultural ubiquity of a double standard with respect to adultery's severity (Daly, Wilson, & Weghorst 1982).

MARITAL ALLIANCE:
THE CONTEXT OF COOPERATION AND CONFLICT

Around the world and throughout history, individual women and men have always entered into marriages: socially recognized alliances, indefinite in duration but ideally permanent, that entail sexual and other entitlements and duties, and that are deemed the appropriate or ideal context in which to produce and raise children to whom both partners have obligations (Flinn & Low, 1986; Goody, 1976; Murdock, 1967; van den Berghe, 1979). The cross-cultural universality of such practices suggests that marital alliance is an ancient arrangement that is in some sense instantiated in our evolved human nature. (The fact that alternative practices devised by utopian revolutionaries seem invariably to collapse amidst accusations of inhumanity and exploitation reinforces this conclusion.)

Marital alliance is not usefully defined in terms of the contemporary bureaucratic procedures that distinguish registered marriages from other cohabiting unions; consider the fact that marriages are transacted and celebrated in societies that lack government or any system of writing, as well as the long struggle between church and state over the entitlement to legitimize marriages. If there is a cross culturally applicable distinction corresponding to that between registered and de facto marriage in the modern West, the defining feature must be whether the union has been solemnized by a ceremony that legitimizes the partners' entitlements and obligations in the eyes of relatives and community members other than the partners themselves. This is not simply a matter of whether the couple has chosen to formalize their union in this way; the issue is often whether other interested parties are prepared to let the union be legitimized by ceremonial recognition.

In the contemporary West, we are inclined to see the mating game as a great marketplace of autonomous actors, but in kin-based societies and where power permits, people take a strong manipulative interest in the marital transactions of other people. One may even argue that this involvement of third parties is the primary feature that distinguishes human marriage from the mateships of other animals (Daly & Wilson, 2000). But although many writers have stressed that human marriages are economic unions or even political alliances between lineages, the reason why marriage exists has first and most basically to be understood in terms of its reproductive function. Marital transactions in traditional societies are negotiated exchanges in which the families of the bride and groom are deeply concerned about value received for value given. Where bridewealth flows from the groom's family to the bride's (as it does in a substantial majority of traditional societies), its magnitude is tied to the bride's fertility (Borgerhoff Mulder, 1995); and in those few societies in which dowry flows in the opposite direction, it is expended to marry a daughter into a social standing in which she will have higher-status sons and more grandchildren than would otherwise have been possible (Gaulin & Boster, 1990).

Evolutionists argue that offspring are cherished because they are the principal vehicles of parental fitness, but that the interests of parents and their children overlap only in part because their fitnesses are only correlated, not identical (Trivers, 1974). Daughters are reproductive and productive resources that parents have been only too pleased to treat as trade goods, and the marital futures of children of both sexes can be pawns in political transactions. The extensive role of kin in the arrangement and conduct of marriages multiplies the potential conflict domains. A particularly striking example of manipulative arranged marriages was the practice of *shim-pua* ("minor marriage") in Taiwan, in which parents acquired an infant girl as a bride for an immature son, and raised her to the role (Wolf & Huang, 1980). These future brides were often poorly treated as children, and their risk of dying before puberty was several fold greater than the risk incurred by their "adopting" in-laws' own daughters in the same households. Ironically, *shim-pua* marriages were often barren; apparently, rearing together from infancy had killed sexual interest (Wolf, 1995).

Giving very young children in marriage was, of course, common in European history as well. In medieval England, for example, children could be "espoused" as early as 7 years of age, with the Christian Church sanctifying the commitment (Helmholtz, 1974; Ingram, 1987; Swinburne, 1686/1985). Concomitant exchanges of property were contracted at the espousal stage, and if one family opted out of the planned marriage, the other family had a grievance. Although the church did not deem the marriage complete until sexual consummation after puberty, an aggrieved family could launch ecclesiastical court proceedings to recover damages. In England prior to 1563, marriages were arranged by parents with little interference from outside authority; conflicts concerning marital affairs were generally adjudicated by church courts. State registration was established in 1563 to prevent marriage by elopement from undermining parents' entitlement to arrange their children's marriages and to thwart bigamists, a problem that had formerly been contained by the Church's practice of publishing banns (announcement of parties' intention to marry) but which was a growing problem as the populace became more mobile (Stone, 1977; Trumbach, 1984); de facto bigamy must have remained a problem in customary unions, as it is to this day. Marriage registration and "poor laws" instituted about the same period were intended to reduce the costs of economic assistance to abandoned wives and mothers that the local communities were unable or reluctant to provide. Children born to abandoned or widowed women in "registered" marital unions enjoyed public recognition and state benefits to which children born to "unwed" mothers were not entitled until the twentieth century.

Behind these practices was a contract. When a man took a wife, he relinquished the right to take another, and the woman and any children that the union produced gained some claim on his property. But his proprietary entitlements were even clearer, including a right of exclusive sexual access and extensive rights to control the actions and the fates of both wife and children. These legal implications of marriage have been withering for many decades, but in a piecemeal fashion that varies in many details among nations and smaller jurisdictions within nations. Children's legal entitlements are seldom conditional on the marital status of the mother now, and many limitations on the freedom of married women have been lifted, including the doctrine of "unity of personality" (which denied wives legal standing as persons distinct from their husbands), the lack of entitlement to make financial transactions without husbands' approval, men's entitlement to "restrain" wives intent on leaving them by force, and a man's right to sue his wife's new partner for seduction or alienation of affection (Wilson & Daly, 1992a). Increased legal emphasis on the protection of personal autonomy has not always been to the benefit of wives, however, especially in the domain of divorce law reforms that have reduced financial support obligations to former partners. Some recent rulings (e.g., the Supreme Court of Canada's 1999 ruling in *Bracklow v. Bracklow*; see later discussion) indicate a renewed recognition of the need to protect vulnerable parties and hence a partial reversal of the trend toward treating obligation as revocable upon marital dissolution. In general, both sides in most recent debates about the ongoing changes in marital and family law profess a primary concern to protect the interests and autonomy of vulnerable parties, especially children.

With formal state-sanctioned rules in relatively democratic societies, the interests of some may go unrecognized, but at least the costs and benefits of different courses of actions are defined, as are the legal boundaries of one's entitlements and obligations. However, de facto marital unions have not typically been subject to standardized legal norms, and the interests of "wives" and "husbands" have not been well regulated, although very recent efforts to establish laws and

regulations for "registered partnerships" are intended to protect parties in dependent affectional relationships regardless of their sex or the partnership's
(dis)similarity to a traditional registered marriage (Bailey, 1999). A likely consequence of the precarious legal standing of unregistered unions is that the outcomes of conflict between de facto marriage partners are less predictable, or are
perceived as less predictable, than is the case for comparable conflicts in registered marriages, with the result that the bargaining power, intimidatory capability,
and relative social and economic status of the conflicting parties may be even
more consequential than in divorce proceedings or other registered marriage conflict negotiations. Furthermore, the solidarity and terms of the marital relationship
may have to be constantly negotiated rather than implicitly understood.

DIFFERENCES BETWEEN REGISTERED AND
DE FACTO MARITAL UNIONS

De facto unions now constitute a substantial proportion of all marital partnerships
in many developed countries, including Norway (Kravdal, 1999), Sweden (Bracher
& Santow, 1998), France (Léridon, 1990), New Zealand (New Zealand Department of Statistics, 1993), Australia (Bracher & Santow, 1988), Canada (Statistics
Canada, 1999), and the United States (Bumpass, Sweet, & Cherlin, 1991; Graefe
& Lichter, 1999;). Change has been rapid in some cases. In France, for example,
10% of the couples registering a marriage in 1970 had previously cohabited; just
10 years later, 50% had (Léridon, 1990). In some Latin American countries, consensual unions are almost as prevalent as registered marriages (DeVos, 1999) and,
in at least some cases, this has been true for decades (e.g., Glaser, 1999). In Canada,
the census has clearly distinguished registered from de facto marital unions only
since 1986; Fig. 1.1 shows that the proportion of the populace living in de facto

FIG. 1.1
**Number of De Facto Unions per 100,000 Women, or per 100,000 Men, in Each
Age Category in Canada in 1986, 1991, and 1996. Data from Statistics Canada
(1999).**

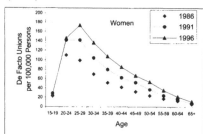
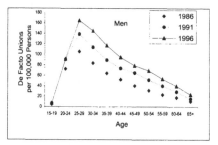

unions has since grown substantially, especially but not solely among young adults. In light of both rapid change and cross-national variability in the degree to which consensual unions are legitimate and institutionalized, generalizing about the distinctions between registered and de facto unions is obviously a risky business. Generalization is also perilous because de facto marriage is not a unitary phenomenon (DeVos, 1999; Landale & Fennelly, 1992; Léridon, 1990; Loomis & Landale, 1994; Schoen & Weinick, 1993); it encompasses "visiting unions," "trial" marriages, and partnerships scarcely distinguishable from registered marriages, which may even have been formalized ceremonially although not registered with civil authority— sometimes all of these variants occur in the same population. Nevertheless, we shall discuss ways in which de facto unions differ from registered marriages, because certain contrasts between the two appear to have some generality, at least in developed nations, and these distinctions appear to be relevant to differential levels of couple conflict.

One of the most important distinctions is that de facto unions are less likely to endure than registered marriages, and the participants know it. According to Nock (1995), one of the main distinctions between U.S. survey respondents in de facto versus registered unions is that the former perceive the "exit costs" to be lower. In a 1996 omnibus survey, cohabiting Norwegians without imminent plans for marriage nominated the greater difficulty of dissolving the relationship above all other rationales when asked why they were hesitant to marry; the expense of weddings ranked second (Kravdal, 1999). In Sweden, the greater stability of registered marriages is apparent even when the effects of childlessness are controlled (Hoehm & Hoehm, 1992, cited in Kravdal, 1997). Even in Latin America, where consensual unions are frequent and not at all deviant, DeVos (1999) reported that they have a higher rate of dissolution than registered marriages in each of nine countries. This is not just because de facto unions are more often childless. Landale and Hauan (1992) reported, for example, that 74% of children born to cohabiting couples in Puerto Rico had experienced the separation of their parents before their 10th birthdays compared to a figure (still remarkably high) of 50% born to couples in registered marriages.

The exit costs are lower for de facto unions because obligations are lower. Glaser (1999) noted, for example, that Costa Rican women are still disadvantaged financially in de facto unions, despite having recently gained maternity and health benefits from partners' insurance and the right to inherit from their partners' estates, because they still lack rights to property acquired during the union should it dissolve, and because the child support obligations of ex-de facto partners are not well enforced. Nevertheless, Glaser claimed that many women prefer de facto marriage because it is easier to terminate; registered marriage may provide a woman with more security, but at some perceived cost in autonomy.

In Canada, the obligations and exit costs of de facto and registered unions are in a state of flux. The Divorce Act of 1968 moved divorcing couples in the direction of division of assets and cessation of mutual obligation. De facto spouses did not enjoy similar entitlements until 1980, when the Supreme Court overturned a lower court ruling that had deprived a woman of all proceeds from the farm that she and her common-law husband had together developed (*Pettkuss v. Becker* [1980] 2 S.C.R. 834). The Divorce Act was revised in 1985, and a recent, much discussed Supreme Court ruling (*Bracklow v. Bracklow* [1999] S.C.R. March 25, 1999) interpreted the revised act as placing renewed limits on post-marital freedom, by imposing a continued duty of support on the ex-husband of a woman unable to work. Thus registered marriage in Canada entails at least the potential for an irreversible obligation to relieve economic hardship of an ex-spouse who is not reasonably capable of self-sufficiency. De facto marriage apparently does not, but in view of its increasing prevalence (Fig. 1.1) and concerns about discriminatory treatment of same-sex couples, the legal status of de facto unions is currently being evaluated with the aim of drafting legislation (e.g., Bailey, 1999; Ontario Law Reform Commission, 1993).

An evolutionary psychological perspective on sex differences suggests some possible outcomes that might follow from there being lower "exit costs" for de facto marriages. Many studies have shown that women and men prioritize somewhat different criteria when assessing persons of the opposite sex. Presumably because they assume the burden of gestation and postnatal child care and have done so throughout our evolutionary history, women tend to rank potential partners on the basis of economic and social status, whereas men's evaluation of women as marital prospects is less affected by their resource-accruing potential and more affected by attributes that were ancestral cues of health and fertility, including youth (Buss, 1994; Geary, 1998). It follows that conflict in marital unions is also sexually asymmetrical: Men are unable to deliver what women expect of them when they are poor and unemployed, whereas men's satisfaction and valuation of their wives is more dependent on youth, attractiveness, and fidelity.

The inclination to pursue multiple unions is also sexually differentiated. According to the anthropological record, wherever polygamy is legal, wealthy and powerful men tend to accumulate wives (Betzig, 1986), and even where monogamy is enforced, many men of means are serial polygamists and/or keep "mistresses" who may in effect be secondary de facto wives who bear children; women do not generally use wealth and power in this way. Evolutionists attribute this difference to the fact that the minimum cost of successful reproduction has always been lower for men, who neither gestate babies nor lactate, and the ceiling on potential reproduction has been higher, with the effect that polygamy was likely to enhance male fitness if it could be attained but was never as beneficial to female fitness. This is not to say, however, that women are monogamists "by nature," for although there is abundant evidence that they are less polygamously inclined than men, it is clear that they often do harbor such inclinations; why and when this is the case is the subject of considerable current interest (see, e.g., Gangestad & Simpson, 1990; Smith, 1984).

De facto unions are characterized by lesser commitment not only in the sense that they are relatively likely to dissolve, but also in the sense that even while cohabiting, the partners are not as likely to be faithful monogamists as registered marrieds. Forste and Tanfer (1996) reported results from a 1991 U.S. national survey of women: Among those in the age range 20 to 37, 20% of the women in de facto unions reported engaging in "sexual activity with other men" while living with their present partners, compared to just 4% of those in registered marriages. One possible interpretation is that women who choose not to marry are relatively unconcerned with convention more generally. Another is that women in de facto unions, recognizing their instability and unreliability, are more likely to be on the lookout for a change. But in either case, male concerns about the sexual fidelity of female partners constitute perhaps the most dangerous source of severe couple conflict, as further discussed later in this chapter, and these survey data suggest that men in de facto unions have substantially greater cause for such concern.

Besides having more extramarital affairs, common-law couples report higher rates of marital sex than do same-age couples in registered marriages (Bachrach, 1987; Call, Sprecher, & Schwartz, 1995). This would be predicted by any evolutionist familiar with recent work on "sperm competition." In various animal species in which females sometimes mate with more than one male, their mates respond to cues of such partner promiscuity by courting and copulating with the female more frequently themselves, and thereby increase their chances of siring her young (e.g., Birkhead & Møller, 1987). In this light, an active sex life cannot be interpreted as indicative of a low level of conflict.

Another important domain in which de facto unions tend to differ from registered marriages is with regard to children. On the one hand, de facto unions are more often childless (Léridon, 1990; Manning, 1995); indeed, cohabiting couples frequently decide to marry before starting a family (Bachrach, 1987; Léridon, 1990; Loomis & Landale, 1994; Manning, 1995). Children and the desire for children comprise one of the most salient distinctions between de facto and registered unions (Nock, 1995), and births to de facto couples are more often the results of unplanned pregnancies than is the case for registered unions (Bennett, Bloom, & Miller, 1995; Kravdal, 1997). On the other hand, although children of the union are rare in de facto households, children of former unions are relatively common. Survey data from various countries indicate that partners in common-law unions are more often in the status of stepparent to their partner's children than are their registered marriage counterparts (Brown & Booth, 1996; Bumpass, Raley, & Sweet, 1995; Bumpass, Sweet, & Cherlin 1991; Khoo, 1987; Léridon, 1990; Winkler, 1994). Graefe and Lichter (1999) concluded from a U.S. national panel survey that only 37% of those children born between 1979 and 1992 who had ever lived in a cohabiting family (estimated at 26% of all children) were the genetic offspring of the cohabiting couple.

Both of these contrasts provide further reason to believe that conflict will be more severe in de facto couples. As we noted at the outset, children in common create common cause, because couples who value the welfare of their young will

tend toward similar evaluations of hypothetical futures. However, children of previous unions create conflict, and there is abundant evidence that reconstituted families are disproportionately susceptible to problems ranging from lower marital satisfaction to violence (Daly & Wilson, 1996, 1998; Wilson & Daly, 1987). Messinger
(1976) asked remarried Canadians with children from previous marriages to rank
the areas of "overt conflict" in each marriage. "Children" and "money" topped the
list for the remarriages, but were hardly ever mentioned for the failed first marriages, and it was clear from the interviewees' elaborations that these two ostensibly distinct issues were really the same: The mother wanted more of the stepfather's
resources invested in her children than he was inclined to contribute. A variety of
studies have now shown that stepchildren, when compared to those living in
two-genetic-parent families of identical means and official marital status, are indeed the recipients of less parental investment (Anderson, Kaplan, Lam, & Lancaster,
1999; Anderson, Kaplan, & Lancaster, 1999; Biblarz, Raftery, & Bucur, 1997;
Bledsoe 1995; Case, Lin, & McLanahan, 1999; Marlowe 1999; Zvoch 1999), are
chronically stressed (Flinn & England, 1995; Thomson, Hanson, & McLanahan,
1994) and growth-retarded (Flinn, Leone, & Quinlan, 1999), and leave home early
(Davis & Daly, 1997; Mitchell 1994).

It appears that children from de facto families may be similarly disadvantaged.
They were more likely to be malnourished and stunted (low height for age) than
were children of registered unions in a study of child development in Brazil, Co-
lombia, and the Dominican Republic (Desai, 1992), for example, and although it
must be noted that De facto marriage is associated with low socioeconomic status
in these countries, an influence of the type of marital union on malnutrition was
still evident after controlling for SES. What has apparently never been assessed is
the extent to which the disadvantage incurred by children in De facto families is
attributable to the fact that so many are stepchildren, or indeed whether any
disdvantage would remain if the correlated effects of steprelationship and SES
were simultaneously controlled.

Finally, De facto unions often differ from registered marriages by being less
assortative (homogamous). In the United States, age disparity between the partners
is significantly smaller in registered unions, for example, and shared religious af-
filiation is significantly more prevalent (Forste & Tanfer, 1996; Schoen & Weinick,
1993). Lack of homogamy tends to be predictive of marital instability in registered
unions (Becker, Landes, & Michael, 1977; Heaton, 1984; Lehrer & Chiswick, 1993),
and it may be an important contributor to the higher rates of conflict and marital
dissolution in De facto unions. Conversely, couples who differ in age or religious
belief may remain unmarried because of a realistic perception that their relationship may not last. There is one possibly important exception to this pattern, however: De facto couples actually tend to be slightly more similar with respect to level
of education than do registered marrieds, a group that continues to include many
couples in which the husband's education exceeds the wife's (Forste & Tanfer,
1996; Schoen & Weinick, 1993). Education tends to enhance a man's marriage-

ability more than a woman's (e.g., Kravdal, 1999), perhaps because it increases earning power, which increases a man's desirability as a marriage partner more than it does a woman's (Buss, 1994). Indeed in some (but not all) developed nations, higher educational attainment is actually associated with lower rates of marriage (or later marriage) in women, the reverse of the correlation for men (Blossfeld & Jaenichen,1995; Thornton, Axinn, & Teachman, 1995). Unlike men, U.S. women have been reported to favor registered unions less as their earning power increases (Willis & Michael, 1994), which may indicate that they feel less need to tie themselves to husbands.

CONFLICT AND VIOLENCE IN REGISTERED AND DE FACTO MARITAL UNIONS

Systematic variation in the prevalence and intensity of marital violence should enable one to test hypotheses about the determinants of marital conflict, but violence is often hidden and detected cases may constitute a biased subset of the whole. For this reason, we have focused primarily on lethal violence, for which detection and reportage should be minimally biased. A number of factors that are predictable sources or correlates of marital conflict — including the wife's youth, a large age disparity, poverty, and the presence of children from prior unions — are associated with elevated risk of spousal homicide (Daly & Wilson, 1988; Daly, Wiseman, & Wilson, 1997; Wilson & Daly, 1993a; Wilson, Daly, & Wright, 1993; Wilson, Johnson, & Daly, 1995). Available evidence indicates that these same risk factors are also associated with elevated rates of nonlethal assaults on wives (Daly, Singh, & Wilson 1993; Wilson et al., 1995), supporting the premise that spousal homicide represents the tip of the iceberg of "normal" marital violence rather than an utterly disjunct phenomenon.

Evidence pertaining to the motives of spouse-killers tells a monotonous story. In samples of well-described uxoricides (killings of wives) from a diversity of cultures, it is consistently found that the great majority of the cases were ostensibly precipitated by the husband's conviction (well founded or not) that his wife was unfaithful and/or by her decision to end the relationship; a more generalized inability to control her may also be invoked (Chimbos, 1978; Daly & Wilson, 1988; Polk, 1994; Wilson & Daly, 1993a, 1996, 1998). Criminologists and police officers often attribute such cases to "jealousy," but we prefer to call these killers "proprietary," a word that implies a more encompassing mind-set, referring not just to the emotional force of one's desire for control and exclusivity, but also to feelings of entitlement and moral outrage (Wilson & Daly, 1992a).

Cases in which wives killed husbands are usually much rarer, although there are exceptions that we consider later in the chapter. However, killings of husbands, whether rare or common, are nowhere simply role-reversed versions of the more frequent uxoricides (Daly & Wilson, 1988; Wilson & Daly, 1992b). Men often hunt down and kill estranged wives, for example, but women hardly ever do likewise. Men kill wives as part of planned murder-suicides, but analogous acts by women are almost unknown. Men kill in response to revelations of wifely infidelity, but women almost never respond similarly. Men often kill wives after subjecting them to lengthy periods of coercive abuse and assaults; the roles in such cases are seldom reversed. Men perpetrate familicidal massacres, killing spouse and children together; women do not. Moreover, a large proportion of the spousal homicides perpetrated by wives, but almost none of those perpetrated by husbands, are self-defensive acts; when a wife kills her husband, the precipitating argument is again likely to have been one in which *he* accused *her* of infidelity, not the reverse (e.g., Chimbos, 1978). All of these sex-typed attributes of spousal homicide appear to have considerable cross-cultural generality.

The idea that uxoricides are in some sense motivated by husbands' concern to protect their proprietary entitlements may appear paradoxical. Yet, it is precisely the threat of loss or violation of these proprietary entitlements that seems to arouse violent inclinations directed at countering the threat: "If you ever leave me, I'll find you and kill you." When a wife is pursued and killed by a husband she has left, the killer's motive is clearly not merely to be rid of her, and many such killers explain their actions when apprehended or in suicide notes as a response to intolerable loss: "If I can't have her, then no one shall" (Wilson & Daly, 1993a). But if keeping her is really the killer's desire, then such murders, although often deliberate and even carefully planned, are anything but rationally instrumental. They are more plausibly interpreted as relatively rare maladaptive by-products of human passions: the dysfunctionally extreme manifestations of proprietary and violent inclinations whose lesser expressions are effective in coercive control.

A credible threat of potentially lethal violence is a powerful means of controlling others, and the frequent killings of estranged wives suggest that such threats by husbands are often sincere (Wilson & Daly, 1993b). Although uxoricide oversteps the bounds of utility, it is not clear that the same can be said of nonlethal wife abuse, and it is therefore noteworthy that the primary motives in wife beating are apparently the same as those precipitating uxoricides: adultery, jealousy, desertion, and male control (Brisson, 1983; Counts, 1990; Counts, Brown, & Campbell, 1992; Dobash & Dobash, 1979, 1984; Hilberman & Munson, 1978; Rounsaville, 1978). If the coercive use of violence is best understood as one means by which the proprietary claims of husbands are maintained, then such violence is likely to vary (both within and between communities or societies) in relation to indicators of the intensity of male sexual rivalry, cues of possible marital infidelity, various factors affecting the woman's attractiveness to potential rivals, her autonomy, and the costs of using violence (Wilson & Daly, 1993b). Some or all of these considerations may be relevant to the differential rates of violence in registered versus de facto marital unions.

Wilson, Daly, and Wright (1993) reported that Canadian women are slain by their partners at a much higher per capita rate in de facto marriages than in registered marriages. This contrast is not peculiar to Canada (see later discussion). Survey evidence indicates that nonlethal violence is also high in de facto unions. In 1993, Statistics Canada surveyed by telephone a national probability sample of Canadian women over 18 years of age, asking questions about the respondents' experiences of violence by partners and other men (Johnson & Sacco, 1995). Interviewees included 8,385 women residing with spouses, 88% in registered marriages and 12% in de facto unions. Assaults by their partners within the past year were reported by 9% of women in de facto unions, but only 2% of those in registered marriages (Wilson, Johnson, & Daly, 1995). Other surveys, conducted in other countries, have produced similar contrasts (Anderson, 1997; Lupri, Grandin, & Brinkerhoff, (1994; Stets, 1991; Williams, 1992).

There is also some evidence that violence may be more prevalent in de facto unions than in dating couples who are not cohabiting (Magdol, Mofitt, Caspi, & Silva, 1998). The comparison groups in this New Zealand study were similar with respect to average age but differed in other attributes that were also associated with the incidence of abuse, including age disparity and duration of the relationship. Whether the groups differed with respect to sexual fidelity and relationship commitment was not assessed. If violence were simply a manifestation of "mate guarding," we might expect it to be more prevalent when partners do not cohabit and monitoring is less continuous, but that is not necessarily the case; we suggest that the mix of a nascent sense of proprietary entitlement with perceived threats to male control and exclusivity may be especially conducive to the exercise of coercive violence against female partners.

Greater risk that one will be slain in a de facto union than a registered marriage applies not just to wives but also to husbands. In fact, the differential is typically even greater. Whereas de facto wives incur a homicide rate eight times higher than their registered marriage counterparts in Canada, for example, the corresponding ratio for male victimization is fifteen-fold (Wilson et al. 1993). Putting the same contrast differently, the proportion of spousal homicides that are committed by wives tends to be higher in de facto unions. This statistic — that is, the proportionate representation of wives as spouse-killers (or, in a simple transformation, the "sex ratio of spouse killing"; see Wilson & Daly, 1992b) — may itself be revealing of some subtle aspects of couple conflict.

The United States is exceptional in the high percentage of spousal homicides that are perpetrated by wives, who are the killers in over 40% of U.S. cases, but less than a quarter of those in Canada, Australia and Great Britain, and an even smaller percentage of those in other, non-Western societies (Wilson & Daly, 1992b). In U.S. cities with high homicide rates, such as Chicago and Detroit, slain husbands actually outnumber slain wives. This unusual form of "gender equity" in the United States is not new, does not extend to homicides other than spouse-killings, and cannot be explained by the availability of guns (Wilson & Daly, 1992b). Neither can it be taken to imply that women and men are similar in their motives or actions; the circumstantial differences between uxoricides and killings of husbands that we noted earlier evidently apply to U.S. cases no less than to countries in which wives rarely kill. Also consistent across countries is the fact that this proportionate representation of women as killers tends to be higher in de facto unions than in registered marriages (Table 1.1); this contrast is statistically significant ($p < .001$ by chi-square test) in each of the three largest samples (Chicago, Canada, England/ Wales).

Table 1.1
Numbers of Spousal Homicides and the Percent Perpetrated by Wives in Various Samples of All Cases Known to Police (Most of the killers are men, but the proportion perpetrated by women tends to be higher in *de facto unions than in registered marriages*)

	Registered Marriages		de Facto Marriages	
Data Set	N of Spousal Homicides	% Perpetrated by Wife	N of Spousal Homicides	% Perpetrated by Wife
Chicago, 1965-1989	916	47	790	55
NSW, Australia, 1968-1986	233	21	165	27
Canada, 1974-1992	916	21	690	34
England & Wales, 1977-1990	1198	17	347	27

Wilson and Daly (1992b) offered several hypotheses to explain these contrasts, but did not test them. One possibility is that couples in de facto unions are disproportionately poor or unemployed, and poor men, lacking other resources, are more physically coercive in marital conflict than are men of means. At the same time, poverty is likely to be associated with circumstances in which a man's presence is more costly than beneficial for his wife, especially if a "man in the house" rule means that his presence jeopardizes her welfare benefits (e.g., Darity & Myers, 1984). Women may then be less tolerant of abuse and readier to engage in violent retaliation. Data reported below indicate that de facto couples in Canada are not noticeably poorer than those in registered marriages, but this hypothesis may still have local relevance. Another possible reason why women might be readier to resort to dangerous conflict tactics in de facto unions concerns the protection of their children. The children in de facto unions are more likely to be stepchildren—the genetic offspring of the woman and a prior partner—than is the case in registered marriages (e.g., Bumpass et al., 1989; Khoo, 1987), and stepfathers assault their wards both physically and sexually at very much higher rates than do genetic fathers (Daly & Wilson, 1996).

There is no question that the presence of stepchildren is associated with marital conflict. Nonviolent manifestations include elevated rates of divorce in stepfamilies (Becker et al., 1977; White & Booth, 1985) and lower levels of marital satisfaction (Perkins & Kahan, 1979; Wilson & Daly, 1987). Moreover, women with children sired by previous partners have been found to be greatly overrepresented among both the clients of a battered women's shelter (Daly et al., 1993) and uxoricide victims (Brewer & Paulsen, 1999; Daly et al., 1997). Daly et al. (1997) estimated that such women were 12 times more likely to be killed by their partners in Hamilton, Canada, than were mothers whose children were all sired by the present partner. Whether stepfatherhood is associated with an even greater elevation in the risk that the man will be killed has yet to be determined, because homicide archives with sufficient numbers of cases to test this hypothesis do not contain the information needed to identify stepfamilies.

VICTIMIZATION OF WIVES AS A FUNCTION OF AGE

The differences in violence between registered and de facto unions cannot be attributed simply to differences in the age distributions of such unions, even though it is true that young adults are overrepresented in both de facto marriage and marital violence.

A wife's youth is one partial predictor of marital instability (Dumas & Péron, 1992; McKie, Prentice, & Reed, 1983), which may reflect the fact that young women can find new partners relatively easily. Youth is a major determinant of women's attractiveness to men (Borgerhoff Mulder, 1988; Buss, 1994; Kenrick & Keefe, 1992; Symons, 1979), and the younger a divorcee, the more likely she is to remarry (Glick & Lin, 1987; Trost, 1984). These considerations, plus their greater likelihood of still being childless, may make young wives more likely to terminate unsatisfactory marriages and more responsive to the attentions of men other than their husbands. For these reasons, we hypothesized that proprietary husbands might be especially likely to assault young wives (Daly & Wilson, 1988). Rates of uxoricide in Canada, the United States, England and Wales, and Australia are indeed maximal for the youngest wives and decline monotonically with age (Daly & Wilson, 1988; Mercy & Saltzman, 1989; Wilson & Daly, 1996; Wilson, Daly, & Scheib, 1997), and according to the 1993 Canadian survey of violence against wives, nonlethal assaults by husbands exhibit a similar decline with age of the wife (Wilson et al., 1995). Separating the influence of female age per se from that of correlated factors such as the husband's age, parity, and duration of the union is a formidable problem that awaits a satisfactory analysis, but there is some evidence that the wife's age is more relevant than the husband's, and that its influence persists when marital duration is controlled (Wilson et al., 1997).

When Daly and Wilson (1988) first reported that Canadian uxoricide rates declined as a function of wife's age, they also noted that the age pattern in common-law (de facto) unions was very different, rising to a peak in middle age. Figure 1.2 shows that this pattern, too, is not peculiar to Canada. What could account for these very different patterns of risk by age? One possibility is that the socioeconomic mix varies in such a way that the older the age category, the more de facto couples differ from registered marriage couples in means and class. This seems not to be the case, however, at least in Canada, where median household incomes of de facto couples are remarkably close to those of same-age registered-marriage couples in all age categories (Fig. 1.3).

FIG. 1.2

Uxoricide Rates in Registered and De Facto Unions in Canada (1974-1990), England and Wales (1977-1990), and New South Wales, Australia (1968-1986).

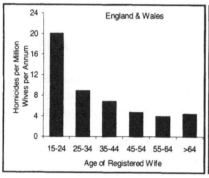 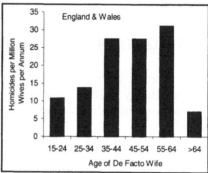

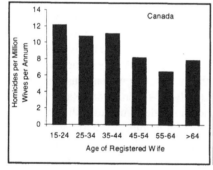 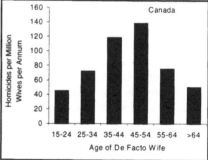

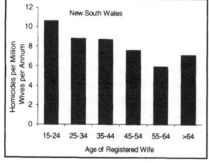 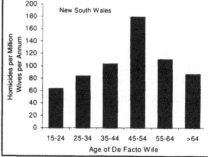

FIG. 1.3

Median Household Income in Registered and De Facto Marriages in Canada, 1990, in Relation to Age of Survey Respondent. Data from Statistics Canada (1990).

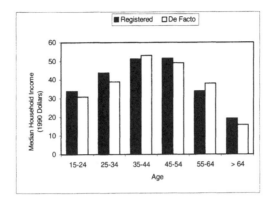

FIG. 1.4

Presence of Stepchildren in Registered and De Facto Marriages in Canada, 1990, in Relation to Age of Survey Respondent. Data from Statistics Canada (1990).

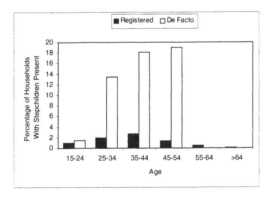

A more promising hypothesis is that middle-aged *de facto* couples are especially likely to be in conflict about the allocation of their joint resources to children of previous partners. Figure 1.4 shows that such couples are indeed the most likely to *have* coresiding minor children of prior unions, and that the prevalence of this risk factor rises with age in a pattern much like that of the homicide rate. In the homicide cases, "marital status" codings indicated that one or both partners were still legally married to someone else in more than half of the *de facto*, middle-aged couples. Unfortunately, information on the parties' reproductive histories and present household composition is not available.

CONCLUDING REMARKS

We have shown that the risk of uxoricide is much greater in de facto marital unions than in registered unions, and that the age patterns of risk are dramatically different, with young wives at greatest risk in registered unions and older wives at greatest risk in de facto unions (Fig. 1.2). These patterns are replicated in Canadian, British, and Australian data sets, and may apply widely, at least in developed nations. In Canada, household incomes change as a function of the couple's age, but there was no difference between registered and de facto marriages in this income pattern (Fig. 1.3) to help account for the different age-related patterns of lethal violence.

What may help explain these differences is conflicts related to the existence of children from prior unions, because the incidence of coresiding stepchildren peaks among middle-aged spouses of de facto unions (Fig. 1.4) much as the risk of uxoricide does. As far as we know, excess homicide risk in de facto unions, age patterns of uxoricide risk, their striking difference in registered versus de facto unions, and the possible relevance of the presence of stepchildren to these phenomena are findings and ideas that originated with ourselves, and they were all inspired by taking an evolutionary psychological view of couple conflict. In hindsight, one might say there is nothing very surprising about some of these statistical findings, but a great deal of research on violence against women and children had not identified these risk factors.

We must stress in conclusion that the distinction between de facto and registered marriage is a risk marker and not a causal variable. Some of the similarities and differences between these two types of marital union are reviewed here, and we propose that greater attention to the possible relevance of stepchildren to conflict, especially among middle-aged de facto couples, is warranted in the future. We also suggest that more attention to issues of commitment, sexual fidelity, and male efforts to exert control as women attempt to retain autonomy will be necessary for an improved understanding of why consensual unions are so often violent. Elucidation of the causal dynamics of marital conflict in de facto versus registered-married couples throughout the life course is of paramount concern as the popularity of de facto marriage increases.

We have studied couple conflict primarily through the window afforded by marital violence, especially lethal violence. We recognize that killing a spouse is a relatively rare outcome of extreme marital conflict compared with nonlethal assaults or termination of the relationship, and our assumption that these killings can be treated as the "tip of the iceberg" of "normal" marital conflict requires further scrutiny. This assumption is presently supported by similarities in motive, in context, and in demographic risk patterns for lethal and nonlethal assaults against wives in Canada, but risk patterns may not be identical in all details (Wilson et al., 1995). Further study of the differences between lethal and nonlethal risk patterns could elucidate important aspects of couple conflict, and may even contribute to the prediction of lethal risk among wives who have suffered assaults.

The evolutionary psychological perspective on marital conflict and violence that we have espoused assumes that the kinds of violent events discussed in this chapter are the outcome of the simultaneous activation of distinct psychological mechanisms and processes, especially inclination to use violence, resentment over investing in a rival's child, and the sense of entitlement associated with a proprietary view of a spouse. These separable aspects of the human psyche are sexually differentiated to varying degrees, with respect to their likelihood of being activated in certain contexts, and their predominance over alternative psychological reactions and perceptions associated with marital conflict. An evolutionary psychological perspective will be essential for further elucidation of the ways in which one's sex, age, marital and parental status, and social and economic standing all affect couple conflict and its consequences.

ACKNOWLEDGMENTS

We wish to thank Alan Booth, Nan Crowder, and Mari Clements for their many courtesies associated with organizing the Couples in Conflict conference. We also thank the Social Sciences & Humanities Research Council of Canada and the Natural Sciences & Engineering Research Council of Canada for financial support. We can be contacted by e-mail at wilson@mcmaster.ca and daly@mcmaster.ca.

REFERENCES

Alexander, R. D. (1987). *The biology of moral systems*. Hawthorne, NY: Aldine de Gruyter.

Anderson, K. G., Kaplan, H., Lam, D., & Lancaster, J. (1999a). Parental care by genetic and step fathers. II. Reports by Xhosa high school students. *Evolution and Human Behavior, 20*, 433-451.

Anderson, K. G., Kaplan, H., & Lancaster, J. (1999b). Parental care by genetic and step fathers. I. Reports by Albuquerque men. *Evolution and Human Behavior, 20*, 405-431.

Anderson, K. L. (1997). Gender, status, and domestic violence: An integration of feminist and family violence approaches. *Journal of Marriage and the Family, 59*, 655-669.

Bachrach, C. A. (1987). Cohabitation and reproductive behavior in the U.S. *Demography, 24*, 623-637.

Bailey, M. (1999). *Marriage and marriage-like relationships*. Report to the Law Commission of Canada, Ottawa.

Becker, G. S., Landes, E. M., & Michael, R. T. (1977). An economic analysis of marital instability. *Journal of Political Economy, 85*, 1141-1187.

Bennett, N. G., Bloom, D. E., & Miller, C. K. (1995). The influence of non-marital childbearing on the formation of first marriages. *Demography, 32*, 47-62.

Betzig, L. L. (1986). *Despotism and differential reproduction*. Hawthorne, NY: Aldine de Gruyter.

Biblarz, T., Raftery, A. E., & Bucur, A. (1997). Family structure and social mobility. *Social Forces, 75*, 1319-1339.

Birkhead, T. R., & Møller, A. P. (1987). *Sperm competition and sexual selection*. London: Academic.

Bledsoe, C. (1995). Marginal members: Children of previous unions in Mende households in Sierra Leone. In S. Greenhalgh (Ed.), *Situating fertility, anthropology and demographic inquiry* (pp. 130-153). Cambridge, UK: Cambridge University Press.

Blossfeld, H. P., & Jaenichen, U. (1992). Educational expansion and changes in women's entry into marriage and motherhood in the Federal Republic of Germany. *Journal of Marriage and the Family, 54,* 302-315.

Bock, G. R., & Cardew, C. (Eds.). (1997). *Characterizing human psychological adaptations* (Ciba Foundation Symposium 208). Chichester, UK: Wiley.

Borgerhoff Mulder, M. (1988). Kipsigis bridewealth payments. In L. Betzig, M. Borgerhoff Mulder, & P. Turke (Eds.), *Human reproductive behavior* (pp. 65-82). Cambridge, UK: Cambridge University Press.

Borgerhoff Mulder, M. (1995). Bridewealth and its correlates: Quantifying changes over time. *Current Anthropology, 36,* 573-603.

Bracher, M., & Santow, G. (1988). *Changing family composition from Australian life-history data.* Working Paper No. 6, Australian Family Project, Research School of Social Sciences, Australian National University, Canberra, Australia.

Bracher, M., & Santow, G. (1998). Economic independence and union formation in Sweden. *Population Studies, 52,* 275-294.

Brewer, V., & Paulsen, D. (1999). A comparison of U.S. and Canadian findings for uxoricide risk for women with children sired by previous partners. *Homicide Studies, 3,* 317-332.

Brisson, N. J. (1983). Battering husbands: A survey of abusive men. *Victimology, 6,* 338-344.

Brown, S. L., & Booth, A. (1996). Cohabitation versus marriage: A comparison of relationship quality. *Journal of Marriage and the Family, 58,* 668-678.

Bumpass, L. L., Raley, R. K., & Sweet, J. A. (1995). The changing character of stepfamilies: Implications of cohabitation and nonmarital childbearing. *Demography, 32,* 425-436.

Bumpass, L. L., & Sweet, J. A. (1989). National estimates of cohabitation: Cohort levels and union stability. *Demography, 25,* 615-625.

Bumpass, L. L., Sweet, J. A., & Cherlin, A. (1991). The role of cohabitation in declining rates of marriage. *Journal of Marriage and the Family, 53,* 913-927.

Buss, D. M. (1994). *The evolution of desire.* New York: Basic Books.

Call, V., Sprecher, S., & Schwartz, P. (1995). The incidence and frequency of marital sex in a national sample. *Journal of Marriage and the Family, 57,* 639-652.

Case, A., Lin, I.-F., & McLanahan, S. (1999). Household resource allocation in stepfamilies: Darwin reflects on the plight of Cinderella. *American Economic Association Papers and Proceedings, 89,* 234-238.

Chimbos, P. D. (1978). *Marital violence: A study of interspouse homicide.* San Francisco: R&E Research Associates.

Counts, D. (1990). Beaten wife, suicidal woman: Domestic violence in Kaliai, West New Britain. *Pacific Studies, 13,* 151-169.

Counts, D. C., Brown, J. K., & Campbell, J. C. (Eds.). (1992). *Sanctions and sanctuary: Cultural perspectives on the beating of wives.* Boulder, CO: Westview.

Crawford, C., & Krebs, D. (Eds.). (1998). *Handbook of evolutionary psychology.* Mahwah, NJ: Lawrence Erlbaum Associates.

Daly, M., Salmon, C., & Wilson, M. (1997). Kinship: The conceptual hole in psychological studies of social cognition and close relationships. In J. A. Simpson & D. T. Kenrick (Eds.), *Evolutionary social psychology* (pp. 265-296). Mahwah, NJ: Lawrence Erlbaum Associates.

Daly, M., Singh, L., & Wilson, M. (1993). Children fathered by previous partners: A risk factor for violence against women. *Canadian Journal of Public Health, 84,* 209-210.

Daly, M., & Wilson, M. (1988). *Homicide.* Hawthorne, NY: Aldine de Gruyter.

Daly, M., & Wilson, M. (1995). Discriminative parental solicitude and the relevance of evolutionary models to the analysis of motivational systems. In M. Gazzaniga (Ed.), *The cognitive neurosciences* (pp. 1269-1286). Cambridge, MA: MIT Press.

Daly, M., & Wilson, M. (1996). Violence against stepchildren. *Current Directions in Psychological Science, 5,* 77-81.

Daly, M., & Wilson, M. (1997). Crime and conflict: Homicide in evolutionary psychological perspective. *Crime and Justice, 22,* 251-300.

Daly, M., & Wilson, M. (1998). *The truth about Cinderella.* London: Weidenfeld & Nicolson.

Daly, M., & Wilson, M. (1999). Human evolutionary psychology and animal behaviour. *Animal Behaviour, 57,* 509-519.

Daly, M., & Wilson, M. (2000). The evolutionary psychology of marriage and divorce. In L. J. Waite (Ed.), *The ties that bind* (pp. 91-110). Hawthorne, NY: Aldine de Gruyter.

Daly, M., Wilson, M., & Weghorst, S. J. (1982). Male sexual jealousy. *Ethology and Sociobiology, 3,* 11-27.

Daly, M., Wiseman, K. A., & Wilson, M. (1997). Women with children sired by previous partners incur excess risk of uxoricide. *Homicide Studies, 1,* 61-71.

Darity, W. A., & Myers, S. L. (1984). Does welfare dependency cause female headship? The case of the black family. *Journal of Marriage and the Family, 46,* 765-779.

Davis, J. N., & Daly, M. (1997). Evolutionary theory and the human family. *Quarterly Review of Biology, 72,* 407-435.

Desai, S. (1992). Children at risk: The role of family structure in Latin America and West Africa. *Population and Development Review, 18,* 689-717.

DeVos, S. 1999. Comment of coding marital status in Latin America. *Journal of Comparative Family Studies, 30,* 79-93.

Dobash, R. E., & Dobash, R. P. (1979). *Violence against wives.* New York: Free Press.

Dobash, R. E., & Dobash, R. P. (1984). The nature and antecedents of violent events. *British Journal of Criminology, 24,* 269-288.

Dumas, J., & Péron, Y. (1992). *Marriage and conjugal life in Canada: Current demographic analysis.* Ottawa: Statistics Canada.

Emlen, S. T., Wrege, P., & Demong, N. J. (1995). Making decisions in the family: An evolutionary perspective. *American Scientist, 83,* 148-157.

Flinn, M. V., & England, B. (1995). Family environment and childhood stress. *Current Anthropology, 36,* 854-866.

Flinn, M. V., Leone, D.V., & Quinlan, R. J. (1999). Growth and fluctuating asymmetry of stepchildren. *Evolution and Human Behavior, 20,* 465-479.

Flinn, M. V., & Low, B. S. (1986). Resource distribution, social competition, and mating patterns in human societies. In D. I. Rubenstein & R. W. Wrangham (Eds.), *Ecological aspects of social evolution* (pp. 217-243). Princeton, NJ: Princeton University Press.

Forste, R., & Tanfer, K. (1996). Sexual exclusivity among dating, cohabiting, and married women. *Journal of Marriage and the Family, 58,* 33-47.

Gangestad, S. W., & Simpson, J. A. (1990). Toward an evolutionary history of female sociosexual variation. *Journal of Personality, 58,* 69-96.

Gaulin, S. J. C., & Boster, J. (1990). Dowry as female competition. *American Anthropologist, 92,* 994-1005.

Gaulin, S. J. C., & McBurney, D. H. (2001). *Psychology: An evolutionary approach.* Upper Saddle River, NJ: Prentice Hall.

Geary, D. C. (1998). *Male / Female: The evolution of human sex differences.* Washington, DC: American Psychological Association.

Glaser, K. (1999). Consensual unions in two Costa Rican communities: An analysis using focus group methodology. *Journal of Comparative Family Studies, 30,* 57-77.

Glick, P., & Lin, S.-L. (1987). Remarriage after divorce: Recent changes and demographic variations. *Sociological Perspectives, 30,* 162-179.

Goody, J. (1976). *Production and reproduction: A comparative study of the domestic domain.* Cambridge, UK: Cambridge University Press.

Graefe, D. R., & Lichter, D. T. (1999). Life course transitions of American children: Parental cohabitation, marriage, and single motherhood. *Demography, 36,* 205-217.

Helmholtz, R. H. (1974). *Marriage litigation in medieval England.* London: Cambridge University Press.

Hilberman, E., &. Munson, K. 1978. Sixty battered women. *Victimology, 2,* 460-470.

Ingram, M. (1987). *Church courts, sex and marriage in England, 1570-1640.* Cambridge, UK: Cambridge University Press.

Johnson, H., & Sacco, V. (1995). Researching violence against women: Statistics Canada's national survey. *Canadian Journal of Criminology, 37,* 281-304.

Kenrick, D. T., & Keefe, R. C. (1992). Age preferences in mates reflect sex differences in reproductive strategies. *Behavioral and Brain Sciences, 15,* 75-133.

Khoo, S.-E. (1987). Children in de facto relationships. *Australian Journal of Social Issues, 22,* 38-49.

Kravdal, Ø. (1997). Wanting a child without a firm commitment to the partner: Interpretations and implications of a common behaviour pattern among Norwegian cohabitants. *European Journal of Population, 13,* 269-298.

Kravdal, Ø. (1999). Does marriage require a stronger economic underpinning than informal cohabitation? *Population Studies, 53,* 63-80.

Landale, N. S., & Fennelly, K. (1992). Informal unions among mainland Puerto Ricans: Cohabitation or an alternative to legal marriage? *Journal of Marriage and the Family, 54,* 269-280.

Landale, N. S, &. Hauan, S. (1992). The family life course of Puerto Rican children. *Journal of Marriage and the Family, 54,* 912-924.

Lehrer, E. L., & Chiswick, C. U. (1993). Religion as a determinant of marital stability. *Demography, 30,* 385-404.

Léridon, H. (1990). Extra-marital cohabitation and fertility. *Population Studies, 44,* 469-487.

Loomis, L. S., & Landale, N. S. (1994). Nonmarital cohabitation and childbearing among black and white American women. *Journal of Marriage and the Family, 56,* 949-962.

Lupri, E., Grandin, E., & Brinkerhoff, M. B. (1994). Socioeconomic status and male violence in the Canadian home: A reexamination. *Canadian Journal of Sociology, 19,* 47-73.

Magdol, L., Moffitt, T. E., Caspi, A., & Silva, P. A. (1998). Hitting without a license: Testing explanations for differences in partner abuse between young adult daters and cohabitors. *Journal of Marriage and the Family, 60,* 41-55.

Manning, W. D. (1995). Cohabitation, marriage, and entry into motherhood. *Journal of Marriage and the Family, 57,* 191-200.

Manning, W. D., & Lichter, D. T. (1996). Parental cohabitation and children's economic well-being. *Journal of Marriage and the Family, 58,* 998-1010.

Marlowe, F. (1999). Showoffs or providers? The parenting effort of Hadza men. *Evolution and Human Behavior, 20,* 391-404.

McKie, D. C., Prentice, B., & Reed, P. (1983). *Divorce: Law and the family in Canada.* Ottawa: Statistics Canada (Catalogue No. 89-502E).

Mercy, J. A., & Saltzman, L. E. (1989). Fatal violence among spouses in the United States, 1976-1985. *American Journal of Public Health, 79,* 595-599.

Messinger, L. (1976). Remarriage between divorced people with children from previous marriages: A proposal for preparation for remarriage. *Journal of Marriage and Family Counseling, 2,* 193-200.

Mitchell, B. A. (1994). Family structure and leaving the nest: A social resource perspective. *Sociological Perspectives, 37,* 651-671.

Murdock, G. P. (1967). *Ethnographic atlas.* Pittsburgh: University of Pittsburgh Press.

New Zealand Department of Statistics. (1993). *New Zealand official yearbook 1993.* Auckland, NZ: Government of New Zealand.

Nock, S. L. (1995). A comparison of marriages and cohabiting relationships. *Journal of Family Issues, 16,* 53-76.

Ontario Law Reform Commission. (1993). *Report on the rights and responsibilities of cohabitants under the Family Law Act.* Toronto: Government of Ontario.

Perkins, T. F., & Kahan, J. P. (1979) An empirical comparison of natural-father and stepfather family systems. *Family Process, 18,* 175-183.

Polk, K. (1994). *When men kill.* Cambridge, UK: Cambridge University Press.

Rounsaville, B. J. (1978). Theories in marital violence: Evidence from a study of battered women. *Victimology, 3,* 11-31.

Schoen, R., & Weinick, R. M. (1993). Partner choice in marriages and cohabitation. *Journal of Marriage and the Family, 55,* 408-414.

Smith, R. L. (1984) Human sperm competition. In R. L. Smith (Ed.), *Sperm competition and the evolution of animal mating systems* (pp. 601-659). Orlando, FL: Academic.

Statistics Canada. (1990). General Social Survey, Cycle 5. (Data CD). Ottawa: Statistics Canada.

Statistics Canada. (1999). Age, sex, marital status and common-law status (Census Technical Report, Catalogue # 92-353-XIE). Ottawa: Ministry of Industry.

Stets, J. E. (1991). Cohabiting and marital aggression: The role of social isolation. *Journal of Marriage and the Family, 53,* 669-680.

Stone, L. (1977). *The family, sex and marriage in England, 1500-1800.* London: Weidenfeld and Nicolson.

Swinburne, H. (1686/1985). *A treatise of spousals, or matrimonial contracts.* London: Garland.

Symons, D. (1979). *The evolution of human sexuality.* Oxford, UK: Oxford University Press.

Thomson, E., Hanson, T. L., & McLanahan. S. S. (1994). Family structure and child well-being: Economic resources versus parental behaviors. *Social Forces, 73,* 221-242.

Thornton, A., Axinn, W. G., & Teachman, J. D. (1995). The influence of school enrolment and accumulation on cohabitation and marriage in early adulthood. *American Sociological Review, 60,* 762-774.

Trivers, R. L. (1974). Parent-offspring conflict. *American Zoologist, 14,* 249-264.

Trost, J. (1984). Remarriage in Sweden. *Family Relations, 33,* 475-481.

Trumbach, R. (1984). *Marriage, sex, and the family in England, 1660-1800.* New York: Garland.

van den Berghe, P. (1979). *Human family systems.* New York: Elsevier.

White, L. K., & Booth, A. (1985). The quality and stability of remarriages: The role of stepchildren. *American Sociological Review, 50,* 689-698.

Williams, K. R. (1992). Social sources of marital violence and deterrence: Testing an integrated theory of assaults between partners. *Journal of Marriage and the Family, 54,* 620-629.

Willis, R. J., & Michael, R. T. (1994). Innovation in family formation: Evidence on cohabitation in the United States. In J. Ermisch & N. Ogawa (Eds.), *The family, the market and the state in ageing societies* (pp. 9-45). Oxford, UK: Clarendon.

Wilson, M., & Daly, M. (1987). Risk of maltreatment of children living with stepparents. In R. J. Gelles & J. B. Lancaster (Eds.), *Child abuse and neglect: Biosocial dimensions* (pp. 215-232). New York: Aldine de Gruyter.

Wilson, M., & Daly, M. (1992a). The man who mistook his wife for a chattel. In J. H. Barkow, L. Cosmides, & J. Tooby (Eds.), *The adapted mind* (pp. 289-322). New York: Oxford University Press.

Wilson, M., & Daly, M. (1992b). Who kills whom in spouse killings? On the exceptional sex ratio of spousal homicides in the United States. *Criminology, 30,* 189-215.

Wilson, M., & Daly, M. (1993a). Spousal homicide risk and estrangement. *Violence & Victims, 8,* 3-15.

Wilson, M., & Daly, M. (1993b). An evolutionary psychological perspective on male sexual proprietariness and violence against wives. *Violence and Victims, 8,* 271-294.

Wilson, M., & Daly, M. (1996). Male sexual proprietariness and violence against wives. *Current Directions in Psychological Science, 5,* 2-7.

Wilson, M., & Daly, M. (1998). Sexual rivalry and sexual conflict: Recurring themes in fatal conflicts. *Theoretical Criminology, 2,* 291-310.

Wilson, M., Daly, M., & Scheib, J. E. (1997). Femicide: An evolutionary psychological perspective. In P. A. Gowaty (Ed.), *Feminism and evolutionary biology* (pp. 431-465). New York: Chapman & Hall.

Wilson, M., Daly, M., & Wright, C. (1993). Uxoricide in Canada: Demographic risk patterns. *Canadian Journal of Criminology, 35,* 263-291.

Wilson, M., Johnson, H., & Daly, M. (1995). Lethal and nonlethal violence against wives. *Canadian Journal of Criminology, 37,* 331-361.

Winkler, A. E. (1994). The determinants of a mother's choice of family structure: Labor conditions, AFDC policy or community mores? *Population Research and Policy Review, 13,* 283-303.

Wolf, A. P. (1995). *Sexual attraction and childhood association: A Chinese brief for Edward Westermarck.* Stanford, CA: Stanford University Press.

Wolf, A., & Huang, C. (1980). *Marriage and adoption in China: 1845-1945.* Palo Alto, CA: Stanford University Press.

Zvoch, K. (1999). Family type and investment in education: A comparison of genetic and stepparent families. *Evolution and Human Behavior, 20,* 453-464.

2

Marital Violence in Evolutionary Perspective

Jay Belsky

The Pennsylvania State University

Perhaps it is not unreasonable to wonder why a volume devoted to the topics of marital conflict—a phenomenon ubiquitous to marriage—and spousal violence— one that is all too frequent—begins with a chapter dealing with an event that, although occurring more often than anyone would desire, remains rather rare, namely spousal homicide. A reader may even wonder why psychologists who do not profess to be criminologists should choose to study homicidal violence between spouses and cohabiting partners at all. Is not wife-killing a horse of an entirely different color than nonlethal spousal violence and, especially, more run-of-the- mill marital conflict? According to Wilson and Daly's insightful evolutionary psychological analysis of lethal violence within legitimized and de facto unions, the answer to this query is clearly "not entirely," and perhaps even "not at all." In fact, these scholars convincingly argued that spousal homicide can be regarded as the tip of the family-violence iceberg which, from a scientific perspective, can serve as a window on much more frequent, but perhaps more difficult to study, nonlethal violence between couples, basically because homicide is so much more difficult to secret behind close doors.

LESSONS FROM THE STUDY OF THE ABNORMAL

The scientific strategy adopted by Wilson and Daly of using what might at first seem to be a phenomenon that is qualitatively different from less extreme versions of what may—but also may not—be related behavior has a long tradition not only within family studies, but also in the field of developmental psychopathology. For example, with regard to the former, I have argued for some time now that one of the benefits of studying the etiology of child abuse and neglect, beyond obvious concern with reducing this social problem, is that it can serve to illuminate the determinants of parenting more generally (Belsky, 1984, 1993; Belsky & Vondra, 1989). It was studies of the social isolation of maltreating parents, for example, that helped to highlight the role of social support in shaping parenting (e.g., Garbarino, 1977). Similarly, much interest in the intergenerational transmission of parenting derived from research indicating that maltreating parents were disproportionately likely to have been mistreated themselves as children (Kaufman & Zigler, 1989; Steele & Pollack, 1968).

For some time now, developmental psychopathologists have alerted developmentalists not particularly concerned with severe pathology that investigation of the abnormal can inform understanding of normal development (Cicchetti, 1984; Rutter & Garmezy, 1983). One of the best demonstrations that this is so also comes from the study of child abuse and neglect, as it was here that students of attachment theory first identified the disorganized attachment pattern (Main & Solamon, 1986). Now, even when studying samples of children who have not been subject to maltreatment, attachment researchers routinely assess this "pattern" of attachment, as well as the more familiar secure, avoidant, and resistant ones (Belsky & Cassidy, 1994). As a result, it is not only clear that children other than maltreated ones can develop disorganized attachments, but also that investigating abnormal populations can teach powerful lessons about more normative processes of development and functioning.

Brain scientists, of course, have recognized this for some time now, because they have a long tradition of studying unusual cases to advance understanding of the more everyday mind (Damasio, 1994). It was as a result of injuries to selected areas of the brain, in fact, that scientists first achieved insight into structure-function relations. The point to be made here is that in mining the topic of spousal homicide in order to illuminate spousal violence and marital conflict more generally, Wilson and Daly continued a long tradition of using, if you would, experiments in nature–of the kind one would never want to implement–to gain insight into more general family processes.

These scholars make their case for continuity between spousal conflict and violence and spousal homicide by noting the dramatic epidemiological similarities between the two forms of spousal conflict. To begin with, factors that predict marital conflict, most notably, a wife's youthfulness, age disparity between spouses, economic impoverishment, and especially the presence of stepchildren, also predict lethal violence between husbands and wives and cohabiting partners. Moreover, the motives for wife beating and wife killing appear to be the very same: adultery, jealousy, desertion, and male control. So probably are the motives for husband killing and nonlethal female violence against male partners, although Wilson and Daly did not mention this, namely, self-defense.

IS BIOLOGY DESTINY?

In addition to extending a long–standing tradition of using the study of extreme dysfunction (in this case, family dysfunction) to illuminate more frequent and less extreme forms of family functioning, Wilson and Daly endeavored to advance understanding of spousal violence by considering spousal violence from an evolutionary perspective. Central to such a perspective, as they noted, is the recognition that the fundamental goal of all living things, humans included, is to replicate their genes and leave descendants, either directly or indirectly, that is, through their own offspring or through collateral kin. Reproductive or inclusive fitness is, then, a kind of gravity of biological and thus psychological life.

Many resist biological and evolutionary analyses of human behavior, including behavior in families, in large part because of fears that an evolutionary analysis presumes that biology is destiny: What nature and especially natural selection has wrought cannot be changed. Although in some sense this is no doubt true, the fears of many social scientists reflect much more misunderstanding than intellectual sophistication. Indeed, it is my contention that rather than presuming that "biology is destiny," perhaps only an evolutionary perspective affords insight into overcoming biologically based proclivities. The metaphor of gravity provides a useful illustration of this point.

On the one hand, it is indisputable that by virtue of their biological design human beings simply cannot fly. As a result of the force of gravity and the nature of their quite limited aerodynamic design, humans would be ill advised to jump off cliffs in their natural condition if their desire was to travel like a bird. Gravity, among other things, makes it simply impossible—or so it would appear—for humans to achieve lift and flight. But the critical point to note is that this is by no means the case. And this is because once we *understand* the nature of gravity and thus of aerodynamics, flying becomes possible. In other words, instead of keeping us from flying, gravity—or at least our appreciation of it—was essential for the development of flying machines.

In the same way, then, that it would have been a mistake to conclude that the physics of the human body and gravity were destined to keep humans from flying, I think it is naive to regard evolutionary biology as destiny in the all–too–conservative way that many social scientists still do as we move into the twenty-first century. By understanding the gravitational force, if you would, of evolutionary biology, ways of circumventing those forces become theoretically possible—in the same way that understanding gravity enables one to circumvent constraints imposed by gravity. Rather than biology being destiny, then, an evolutionary-biological perspective may liberate us to engineer human relationships in ways that prevent family violence or many other human behaviors and activities that rightfully disconcert humanitarians around the world. Consider for a moment the possibility that an evolutionarily informed understanding of family conflict and lethal as well as nonlethal spousal violence could contribute to the reduction of family violence to such an extent that someday we could look back on those who naively claimed that an evolutionary analysis presumed that biology was destiny in the same way that we today look back on those who once claimed that humans would never be able to fly. Do we dare imagine a time when rates of spousal abuse are no higher than current rates of spousal homicide? Rather than presuming that biology is destiny, a central assumption of many who work from an evolutionary perspective is that if we are ever to succeed in preventing much behavior that we abhor, including spousal violence, we will need to appreciate—rather than deny and disregard—the gravitational forces of evolution on behavior.

MISUNDERSTANDING THE EVOLUTIONARY PERSPECTIVE

As Wilson and Daly made clear, evolutionary psychology—which is psychology informed by evolutionary theory—is not itself a theory. As a result, it is mistaken to complain, as some social scientists do, that it is not falsifiable. Neither for that matter is a life-span developmental perspective or a family–systems perspective. Rather, like these other frames of reference, evolutionary psychology is a perspective that fosters a variety of what Buss (1995) referred to as mid–level theories (e.g., theory of parental investment, theory of reciprocal altruism), derived from more general evolutionary theory, which themselves generate specific testable hypotheses that are eminently falsifiable. But just as important as recognizing that evolutionary psychology is not a theory itself, it is important to note that like many other perspectives on human development, it is probabalistic in its implications for human functioning. Thus, it is a fundamental error in thinking to believe that if one can show a single instance where humans behave in ways that clearly are at odds with their reproductive best interests, one has disproved evolutionary psychology or undermined an evolutionary perspective. Despite the fact that there are surely instances in which an expectation derived from social learning theory or attribution theory is not confirmed, especially in the case of a single individual, few would be inclined to jettison such theories on such a basis alone. But it is surprising how often this straw–man argument is wielded against evolutionary thinking. Rather than reflecting the astute critical posture it is often presumed to, such reasoning reflects instead classical head–in–the–ground thinking. If the subatomic physics to which all matter in the universe conforms tolerates indeterminancy and probabalism, it should be no surprise that the same is true of phenomena shaped by evolution. Indeed, given the long expanse of time on which evolutionary processes operate, it is principally as a result of probablistic consequences that natural selection works its magic. In the case of human behavior, then, exceptions to inherently probabalistic rules do not disprove these rules.

MARRIAGE IN EVOLUTIONARY PERSPECTIVE

Basic to an evolutionary perspective on the family, as Wilson and Daly made clear, is appreciation of the fact that marriage is first and foremost a social institution invented and designed to serve a reproductive function. Indeed, current thinking stipulates that the pair bond that in aboriginal, agricultural, industrial, postindustrial, and information-based societies takes the form of marriage (in one form or another) emerged in the ancestral history of our species as a means of promoting reproductive fitness (e.g., Chisholm, 1999; Lovejoy, 1981). Because of the increased caretaking demands placed on primate females once upright posture and limits on the design possibilities of the female birth canal promoted the early emergence of the human fetus from the womb, the challenge of sustaining a new-born life became much greater than it had been before such major changes took place in primate forms of life. Whereas before these evolutionary changes took place female primates could provide life–sustaining care to their mobile new-borns and infants while simultaneously securing the necessary nutrients to sustain their own lives, once these changes had occurred our evolutionary ancestors would have found themselves facing severe threats to their reproductive fitness had be-havioral accommodations not coincided with the physical changes. Put simply, the tasks of promoting an infant's development so that it could one day grow up to reproduce and of sustaining one's own life for purposes of providing support for one's progeny and/or for securing additional matings and conceptions would have been so difficult to master on one's own that some novel behavioral arrangement was required to make childbearing pay off reproductively for mother and father alike. It thus appears that tolerably stable pair bonds emerged as an evolutionarily strategic solution to challenges posed to reproductive fitness by the birthing of highly dependent and relatively helpless young. Such bonds both afforded a means of increasing paternal certainty, without which there would be little biological reason for parental investment on the part of males, while simultaneously increas-ing the resources available to the lactating mother and her young infant.

THE BIOLOGICAL COSTS OF MARRIAGE

What this evolutionary analysis of the origins of the human pair bond and even-tual marital systems perhaps does not make sufficiently clear is that the emer-gence of relatively stable and committed relationships between pair–bonded men and women also carried costs as well as benefits. Appreciation of the costs, espe-cially to men, may be essential if we are to understand so much of what motivates male desire to control females and thus so much spousal abuse. We begin, how-ever, by considering the case of females.

The Female Case

From the female's point of view, the price of support for herself and her child, which was received in exchange for increased paternal certainty on the male's part, was increased sexual exclusivity. Although it is the male of our species who is routinely depicted as not favoring sexual exclusivity, feminist evolutionary psy-chologists (Gowaty, 1992; Hrdy, 1997) have made it clear that matings with mul-tiple partners carry specific benefits to females as well as males. Perhaps most important is the opportunity to secure genes to mix with one's own that might be "better" than those provided by a relatively stable partner. By better we mean here genes that are more likely to engender future descendants. Thus, mating with a man who was stronger, a better provider, or simply more intelligent than her pair–

bonded partner, to cite but a few examples, became less feasible, even if not impossible, once pair bonding emerged as a central component of the human behavioral repertoire. By restricting matings with more varied men, pair bonding also reduced the likelihood of sperm competition, although by no means eliminated it entirely. As Baker and Bellis (1994) showed, the female reproductive tract seems designed to collect sperm from diverse partners to foster sperm competition so that the most viable would be most likely to fertilize the egg. By foregoing some, even if not all, mate diversification, and thus reducing sperm competition, reproductive degrees of freedom were lost to the average female primate with the evolution of pair bonding.

It is just these advantages to females of multiple partners that male sexual jealousy seems designed to defend against. And, as Wilson and Daly made eminently clear, it is sexual jealousy that seems at the heart of wife killing and much—if not most—domestic violence (Quinsey & Lalumiere, 1995). Because the costs of cuckoldry are so huge biologically, especially when duped men invest in offspring who are not their own, it is no wonder that for too many men "smoking gun" evidence of infidelity is not required to precipitate extreme action to coerce a woman to remain if she is threatening to leave or to discourage sexual behavior outside of the pair bond if she has been or is considering being unfaithful, or even if she is merely perceived to have been or to be considering being unfaithful.

In light of evidence from the study of human sperm competition that all sperm are not alike (Baker & Bellis, 1995), I have even come to wonder whether the strong emotion of male sexual jealousy may have evolved not only to stimulate mate-guarding behavior, which much male control is all about, but also to promote manufacture in the testes of what have now been identified as different types of sperm that serve different functions. Might it be the case, for example, that when males feel jealous the ratio actually changes of "egg–getting" sperm that play offensive roles within the female reproductive tract and "blocker" and "kamikaze" sperm that play defensive roles? As their name implies, egg–getters do the traditional work once attributed to all sperm of trying to get to the fallopian tube to fertilize the (hopefully) waiting egg. Blocker sperm have the job of establishing physical barriers (with their bodies) to prevent the egg–getting sperm of other males encountered in the female reproductive tract from succeeding in their mission. And, finally, it is the job of kamikaze sperm to seek out and destroy these enemies. However farfetched my speculation may seem that the ratio of these types of sperm could be affected by the evolved emotion of jealousy, the complex workings of the endocrine system in producing flight or fight behavior when fear is experienced cannot but lead me to wonder whether jeolousy could produce its own cascade of biological changes that serve the ultimate goal of promoting reproductive fitness. If nothing else is certain, it is that with enough time, mother nature in the form of natural selection has gone to great lengths to design living things to function in all sorts of ways that are, fundamentally, in their reproductive best interests.

The Male Case

When it comes to considering the costs of pair bonds, they may be even greater in the case of men than those considered earlier in the case of women. Perhaps the most fundamental difference between males and females from an evolutionary standpoint is that whereas the reproductive possibilities of females are theoretically and practically limited by pregnancy, lactation, menstruation, and menopause, those of men are virtually unlimited. Whereas the number of progeny that females can bear is severely restricted by their biology, in the case of men that is much less so. This is dramatically illustrated by considering the number of offspring that the most prolific woman in recorded history is known to have produced—32—in contrast to the 888 that the most prolific male is known to have produced (Hrdy, 1999). Now, of course, the reproductive success of most men does not come close to that of Ismail the Bloodthirsty, the Moroccan tyrant who holds the record for the most progeny. And, as well, it has to be acknowledged that the variance in male reproductive success is so much greater than that of females, because whereas virtually all females will reproduce, many males never get the chance.

Nevertheless, by restricting his mating possibilities exclusively to one partner, or at least mostly to one partner, the pair-bonded male who experiences heightened (although not perfect) paternal certainty in exchange for providing support for his partner and their offspring foregoes the theoretical possibility of multiple matings and thus the chance to sire offspring by many women. Not only do these foregone opportunities restrict his chances of diversifying the genes his genes get mixed with, but it also means that when his partner is not able to conceive—because of pregnancy, lactation, menstruation, or menopause—his chances of siring more offspring falls greatly.

DE FACTO MARITAL UNIONS

This analysis of some of the costs connected to with pair bonding begins to suggest why, as Wilson and Daly noted, the violence associated with de facto marital unions is greater than in the case of legitimized unions. Because commitment is reduced in the former relative to the latter, sexual and social defection occurs far more frequently. That is, the probability of sexual infidelity is increased, as is the probability of relationship break up. From a man's perspective in particular, these are the greatest threats to his reproductive interests. Because they stimulate jealousy and motivate the need for control, coercive tactics increase in frequency. Threats of violence and actual violence probably have been effective all too often in the course of human evolutionary history in promoting the reproductive fitness of males, so we find these behavioral options part of their arsenal for protecting their ultimate (i.e., reproductive) interests all over this supposedly modern world.

When other tactics fail, or when men have reason to believe that they will fail, these components of their behavioral repertoire are all too frequently exercised. And because many threatened women will behave in self–protective ways, and those with children who do not share genes with their current partner will endeavor to protect their progeny, defensive husband killing in de facto marital unions is heightened as well.

What Wilson and Daly's analysis of de facto unions have made clear, then, is that the rapid increase in such pair bondings over the past 30 years in the West is dangerous to women and children alike. Yet there is plenty of reason to suspect that this fact about cohabitation, which seems so obvious and reasonable once it is explained, remains a secret to most citizens in Western society. How many women know not only that there is increased risk of conflict with one's partner, but also of violence, including lethal violence, when they move in with a man to whom they are not married? And how many know that this seems to be especially the case when they bring children from previous relationships into such unions? If, as so many humanitarians like to say, children belong not just to their parents but to all of us, one can wonder whether social policy has failed women and children in a huge way by not standing more strongly against cohabitation. From this perspective, it seems ironic that it is the conservatives who are so concerned with the state of marriage in America who, at least in some respects, appear to be the true feminists.

CONCLUSION

Much popular writing about the abuse of spouses and cohabiting partners by males cast the issue only in moral terms of bad behavior. Without defending male violence against female partners, it seems useful to realize from whence the behavior that is so detestable comes. Evolution has designed living things to behave in ways that protect, if not enhance, their reproductive best interests, because it is reproductive fitness that life is, fundamentally, all about, not happiness, achievement, or existential insight. Because it has always been important for males to ensure that the progeny they may invest in are their own, and because females have always been a critical resource on which men are dependent to realize their reproductive interests, it should not be surprising that all sorts of ways have evolved so that males can serve those interests. The jealousy that motivates so much intimate violence represents one such evolved mechanism for promoting male reproductive success, perhaps when other strategies and tactics have failed. We may not like this fact, or its all-too-violent consequences, but that does not change the fact. Coming to grips with it, evolutionary psychologists argue, can enhance our ability to prevent spousal violence in the first place or remediate it once it has appeared. Denying the evolutionary basis of the strong emotional proclivities of men to serve their reproductive interests will only undermine efforts to reduce the scope of violence in legitimized and de facto marital unions. What needs to be understood, however, as stated earlier, is that such understanding is not an excuse for behavior we rightfully abhor. It is a fundamental intellectual mistake, then, to shoot the evolutionary-psychological messenger just because one does not like the message delivered. In their chapter, Wilson and Daly provided a most useful service in delivering a message that too many still resist hearing.

REFERENCES

Baker, R. R., & Bellis, M. (1995). *Human sperm competition.* London: Chapman & Hall.

Belsky, J. (1984). The determinants of parenting: A process model. *Child Development, 55,* 83-96.

Belsky, J. (1993). The etiology of child maltreatment: A developmental-ecological analysis. *Psychological Bulletin, 114,* 413-434.

Belsky, J., & Cassidy, J. (1994). Attachment: Theory and evidence. In M. Rutter & D. Hay (Eds.), *Development through life: A handbook for clinicians* (pp. 373-402). Oxford, UK: Blackwell.

Belsky, J., & Vondra, J. (1989). Lessons from child abuse: The determinants of parenting. In D. Cicchetti & V. Carlson (Eds.), *Current research and theoretical advances in child maltreatment* (pp. 153-202). Cambridge, UK: Cambridge University Press.

Buss, D. (1995). Evolutionary psychology: A new paradigm for psychological science. *Psychological Inquiry, 6,* 1-49.

Chisholm, J. (1999). *Death, hope and sex.* Cambridge, UK: Cambridge University Press.

Cicchetti, D. (1984). The emergence of developmental psychopathology. Child Development, 55, 1-7.

Damasio, A. (1994). *Descartes' error: Emotion, reason, and the human brain.* New York: Putnam.

Garbarino, J. (1977). The price of privacy in the social dynamics of child abuse. *Child Welfare, 56,* 565-575.

Gowaty, P. (1992). Evolutionary biology and feminism. *Human Nature, 3,* 217-249.

Hrdy, S. B. (1997). Raising Darwin's consciousness: Female sexuality and the prehominid origins of patriarchy. *Human Nature, 8,* 1-49.

Hrdy, S. B. (1999). *Mother nature.* New York: Pantheon.

Kaufman, J., & Zigler, E. (1989). The intergenerational transmissin of child abuse. In D. Cicchetti & V. Carlson (Eds.), *Current research and theoretical advances in child maltreatment* (pp. 129-150). Cambridge, MA: Cambridge University Press.

Lovejoy, C. (1981). The origin of man. *Science, 211,* 341-350.

Main, M., & Soloman, J. (1986). Discovery of insecure-disorganized/disoriented attachment pattern. In M. Yogman & T. Brazelton (Eds.), *Affective development in infancy* (pp. 17-46). Norwood, NJ: Ablex.

Quinsey, V., & Lalumiere, M. (1995). Evolutionary perspectives on sexual offending. *Sexual Abuse, 7,* 301-315.

Rutter, M., & Garmezy, N. (1983). Developmental psychopathology. In P. Mussen (Ed.), *Handbook of child psychology,* Vol. IV (pp. 775-911). New York: Wiley.

Steele, B., & Pollack, C. (1968). A psychiatric study of parents who abuse infants and small children. In R. Helfer & C. Kempe (Eds.), *The battered child syndrome* (pp. 101-137). Chicago: University of Chicago Press.

3

Men's Changing Family Relationships

Frances K. Goldscheider
Brown University

It is important to realize that both of the behaviors focused on in Wilson and Daly's chapter—cohabitation and stepparenting—have been experiencing extraordinarily rapid change in incidence. Hence, analyses of unchanging biological underpinnings of human behavior, even those with direct measurement of the biological markers (Booth & Dabbs, 1993; Udry, 1994), although informative, are unlikely to help us understand the dynamics involved in these phenomena currently.

There are innovators and followers in nearly every emerging social process, and these two groups are often are quite different. These differences are likely to mean that the processes linked with the early stages of a growing phenomenon, both as causes and as consequences, are likely to be unstable. As a result, the verities that emerge as early explanations and concerns, although they appear unchanging and normally become the basis of our theories, often are wrong fairly soon. The contexts have changed, at least in part because what was innovative is more routine. This should alert us to the importance of context, and to the ways it can shape the relationships we often take for granted.

I want to address the question of variation in context by examining two analyses I have been involved with that focus on the questions raised here today: cohabitation and stepparenthood. In each case, I can report that context, both in terms of history and national social structure, exerts powerful and differing effects. Let us begin with cohabitation. This is based on analyses I have been doing on changes in union formation in developed countries with Pierre Turcotte and Alex Kopp (Goldscheider & Turcotte, 1998; Goldscheider, Turcotte, & Kopp, 1999), using data from the Family and Fertility Surveys project (United Nations, 1996).

THE CHANGING DETERMINANTS OF COHABITATION

Our argument is that the increase in cohabitation is part of a constellation of family changes, often called the "second demographic transition" (van de Kaa, 1987), which are primarily the result of the ongoing gender revolution. The increase in equality in the adult lives of men and women has progressed unevenly. It was most apparent first in the public spheres of education (reflecting changes over a century), and of work outside the home, where change has been rapid primarily over the past 4 decades. Change has been much slower inside the family, which has been both reacting to the changes in women's roles outside the home and struggling to incorporate men within it more fully, but this process has barely begun, and we should not expect it to be complete for quite awhile.

Nevertheless, our theories about these changes are based primarily on the early stages of change: the move away from the separate spheres. The theorist most widely cited in this regard is the Nobel-Prize winning economist of the family, Gary Becker (1991). His economic theories, like those of sociologist Talcott Parsons (1949) before him, rest on the centrality for marriage of an extreme division of labor between men and women, with men working outside the home and women within—the context these theorists each grew up with in the first half of the twentieth century. Using the model of international trade, Becker viewed marriage as valuable only insofar as it is efficient, and it is most efficient when the partners specialize either in home or nonhome production, producing "gains to trade." Decreased specialization, such as occurs when women also work and/or men also care for children, reduces these gains and, Becker argued, should lead to delayed and/or nonmarriage. A simpler version that also derives from an earlier analysis of Becker's (1973, 1974) has been called the "independence hypothesis" (Ross & Sawhill, 1975), which posits that the ability to support themselves frees women from entering undesirable marriages. (Scholars making this argument usually fail to include the "undesirable" concept and assume either that marriage, per se, is necessarily undesirable to women or that there is nothing men are likely to do to make marriage more desirable. They also usually fail to include Ross and Sawhill's further derivation that increases in women's earnings also have an "income effect," making marriages both more feasible and more stable.)

Becker has been widely cited by those who postulate a causal link between the increase in female labor force participation and the rise in cohabitation and union instability, what has been called the "persuasive correlation" among trends (Cherlin, 1996). Hence, we ask, has the rise in female employment provided women the independence to avoid family roles, either by not entering them or leaving them voluntarily, or both? In particular, we examine whether and if so how the factors influencing union formation changed between the 1960s and the early 1990s. We consider four industrialized countries—the United States, Canada, Italy, and Sweden—and focus particularly on education, the central measure of human capital and, hence, the key to the independence hypothesis.

Table 3.1 presents the pattern of change in the effects of educational attainment on the probability that American, Canadian, Italian, and Swedish women enter cohabiting or marital unions. Change is tested by looking at interaction effects between educational levels and birth cohort. This allows us to observe the effects of educational attainment for each of four cohorts. These are presented as relative risk ratios. (The intermediate level of education in each cohort is the reference category.) Our emphasis is on whether and, if so, how the effects of education change, so that the coefficients show the effect of combining the coefficients for education and the interaction coefficients of education and cohort. This allows us to follow the trends over time in the effects of educational attainment on union formation. In each of these analyses, the effects of the other explanatory variables have been controlled.

Table 3.1
Changing Effect of Educational Attainment on Women's First Union Formation, by Union Type and Birth Cohort in Four Industrialized Countries

	Less Than High School	HS Diploma	College/University
		United States, 1995	
Marriage			
Before 1951	0.69	1	1.54
1951-1960	0.94 *	1	1.38
(1961-1970)	0.68 *	1	1.70 *
Cohabitation			
Before 1951	1.16	1	0.78
1951-1960	0.97	1	1.19
(1961-1970)	1.17 *	1	1.02
		Canada, 1995	
Marriage			
Before 1951	1.01	1	0.88
1951-1960	0.97	1	0.93
(1961-1970)	0.60 *	1	0.92
Cohabitation			
Before 1951	0.40 *	1	2.32 *
1951-1960	0.85	1	1.40 *
(1961-1970)	0.99	1	0.97
		Italy, 1995	
Marriage			
Before 1951	1.38 *	1	1.54 *
1951-1960	1.22 *	1	1.18
(1961-1970)	1.54 *	1	1.80 *
Cohabitation			
Before 1951	0.33	1	3.36
1951-1960	0.72	1	1.84
(1961-1970)	1.08	1	1.24
		Sweden, 1992	
Marriage			
Before 1951	1.63 *	1	1.64 *
1951-1960	1.23	1	0.88
(1961-1970)	1.50	1	1.07
Cohabitation			
Before 1951	0.84	1	2.02 *
1951-1960	1.05	1	1.39 *
(1961-1970)	0.87	1	1.15

* Coefficient significantly different from the level of schooling reference category within the cohort

Sources: 1995 National Survey of Family Growth, USA; 1995 General Social Survey, Canada; 1995 Fertility and Family Survey, Italy; 1992 Family Survey, Sweden.

In general, the results show large changes or even reversals in the effects of educational attainment on both marriage and cohabitation for all four countries. The patterns are clearest and sharpest for Canada, and particularly for cohabitation. For Canada, the shift moves the pattern away from the sort of pattern that would indicate an independence effect to followers of Becker. Among the oldest cohort, the least educated were the most likely to marry and the least likely to cohabit; these effects had reversed (in the case of marriage) or at least attenuated (the case of cohabitation) among the youngest cohort.

Italian and Swedish women show the same pattern of change as in Canada vis-à-vis cohabitation, with all converging to the U.S. pattern. In Italy and Sweden, there was a strong positive effect of education on the likelihood of cohabiting among members of the oldest cohort (risk ratio of 3.4 for Italian women with a university degree and one of 2.2 for Sweden). With each younger cohort, the relative risks for the least educated have increased and those for the most educated have decreased in each country, so that in the final cohort, there was no discernible relationship between education and the likelihood of entering a first cohabiting union. This clearly suggests that the early innovators vis-à-vis cohabitation in these three countries were the more educated, but their rate of growth since then has been slower than that of the less educated. The same trend has been underway in the United States, where the least educated are the most likely to cohabit among the youngest cohort.

Clearly, the factors underlying union entry, both in terms of cohabitation (our focus here) and in terms of marriage, which we do not review, have been changing. Furthermore, these changes imply that Becker's theories—that it is more educated women who will avoid marriage and, if they form unions at all, will choose cohabitation—that are rapidly becoming inappropriate. Rapid change is stressful, not just for the social fabric, but also for the individuals living through it. My hope is that as new patterns become increasingly institutionalized, conflict will become less common.

STEPCHILDREN

The problem of stepchildren is perhaps even more acute than that of cohabitation. Not only have male-female relationships become much less stable and committed in most industrialized countries due to the rise in divorce and cohabitation, but parenthood has become a much less central and stable element in men's lives, a trend that is much less frequently noted. The connections between men and children have become complex. Their relationships with their biological children have become complex, because they are increasingly unlikely to live with them. However, they are increasingly likely to live with other children—the children of their current partner—creating new complex connections.

The stepchild problem, whether in conjunction with marriage or cohabitation, raises complex questions for men, because, despite rapid changes in gender roles, men's role as provider has not eroded (Bernard, 1981; Koball, 1997), although women, too, are increasingly expected to maintain a near continuous provider role (South, 1991). Complex parenthood also challenges the "provider" question directly, both for biological children who are often absent and for the stepchildren who are often present. The providing question for absent biological children is well known—the proverbial "deadbeat dad" syndrome. Less attention has been paid to the question of stepchildren. Although in most countries there is normally no legal obligation for a man to support a woman's children from another union unless there is formal adoption (Moffitt, Reville, & Winkler, 1995), most men realize that this is unrealistic, and that the children will be claimants on their income, at least while they remain together in the household. The proportion of men living with children of their partner (but who are not their own) is not small. In the United States, 12% of men aged 28 to 43 are living with at least some such children among those living with children at all.

The research I report on next is part of another comparative analysis, this one focusing on differences in fatherhood in the United States and Sweden (Bernhardt & Goldscheider, 1999). We use the same Swedish data as for the previous analysis, and the National Survey of Families and Households (Sweet, Bumpass, & Call, 1988), for the U.S. data (as the NSFG, the data set in the FFS project, did not survey men). For this project we have coined a new term for stepparenthood—*household parenthood*. It combines both married and cohabiting relationships. We ask, which men hold *family* roles, and *which* family roles?

Based on the centrality of men's provider role in both the United States and Sweden, our argument, broadly, is that in each country, men with more resources should be more likely to hold paternal roles, with stronger effects for biological children than for stepchildren. We also expect that the financial support Sweden provides for families with children complements and supports men's provider role, allowing men to remain in families even at fairly low levels of resources. In the United States, the system of public support for families has tended to drive men with the least resources out of families; the high financial burden of children is driving those with more out of families with children, as well.

Our analysis focuses on differences between the family statuses of men in the United States and Sweden, distinguishing partnership and parenthood types. This analysis uses multinomial logistic regression with a dependent variable based on a combination of parental and partnership statuses. Each began as a mutually exclusive three-category variable: partnership (married, cohabiting, no coresident partner) and parent (biological only, household, and no coresident children), but we combined the nine possible combinations into seven categories. Three involve married people: living with (a) biological children, (b) no children, and (c) at least one household child. For cohabitors, we can only distinguish between those (d) with some children and (e) no children, and similarly for those with no partner, we distinguish between those (f) with some children and (g) no children. This last category, men with no coresidential role as partner or parent, serves as the reference category in the regressions. Because our focus is on forming and maintaining coresidential family ties as union partners and parents, we refer to these men as "living outside a family," although, of course, they might be living with parents or other relatives.

Our results for income are shown Figure 3.1. Earning more income increases men's likelihood of holding each of these family roles in both countries, relative to living outside a family, indicated by the fact that all of the coefficients are positive. The effect of income is generally stronger for marriage and single parenthood (the top three and the lowest bars) than for cohabitation (the two bars below the married), although the difference is less in Sweden than in the United States. Among the married, the effect of income is also stronger for biological children than for household children (compare the highest and the third bars), with little difference in the gap between the two coefficients between the two countries (although, proportionately, the difference is greater in the United States). This suggests that in each country, the more institutionalized status—marriage and biological fatherhood—is more highly selected financially than is the less institutionalized status—cohabitation and household parenthood.

The effects of income are considerably greater for Swedish men than for U.S. men. A man earning $1,000 more than another otherwise similar man has increased his odds of living in some family status nearly twice as much in Sweden as in the United States. If we consider income in tens of thousands rather than thousands, a Swedish man earning the equivalent of an additional $10,000 in kroner has odds of living with a spouse and biological children that are 43% greater than his odds of having no committed residential ties. Earning $10,000 more in the United States, in contrast, only increases such a man's likelihood of being a married father by 22%. The difference in the effect of income in Sweden is even greater for the other family statuses.

The much larger coefficients on income in Sweden than the United States imply that attaining a regular income is a stronger signal for family membership for Swedish men than for U.S. men. American men in and out of families are much more economically heterogeneous than are those in Sweden, with a standard deviation approximately equal to the mean in the United States whereas in Sweden this ratio is about half the mean (data not presented). Hence, in the United States, men need less income to hold "provider" status, but there are many high-earning men outside of family roles.

Reviewing other findings briefly, we found that household fathers do not differ significantly from married biological fathers in any respect in Sweden, beyond being more likely to have children living elsewhere. In the United States, such fathers are much more selective of other characteristics likely to increase stress in their lives, particularly low education and childhood family breakup. This suggests that conflict in stepparent households is likely to be much greater in the United States, where the stresses are so much greater, than in Sweden.

FIG. 3.1
Effect of Income on Men's Family Status.

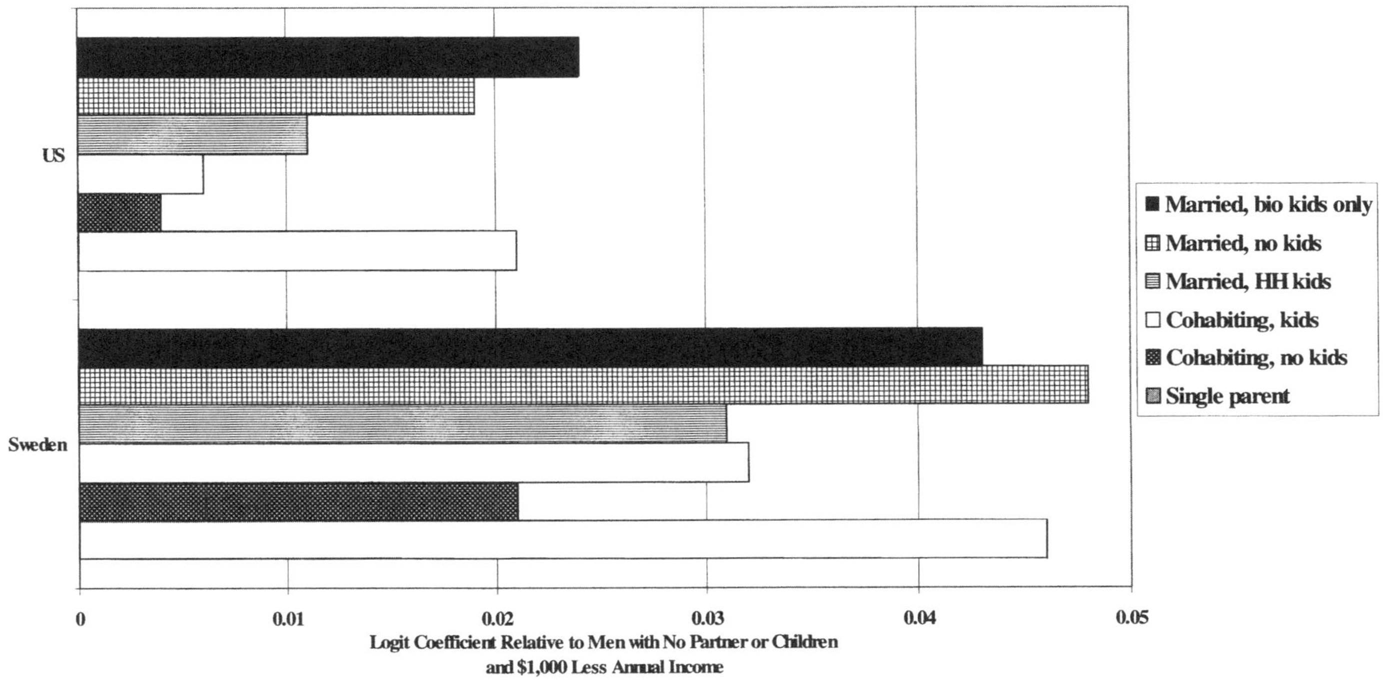
US
Sweden
0
0.01
0.02
0.03
0.04
0.05
Logit Coefficient Relative to Men with No Partner or Children
and $1,000 Less Annual Income
Married, bio kids only
Married, no kids
Married, HH kids
Cohabiting, kids
Cohabiting, no kids
Single parent

DISCUSSION

What do these differences in relationships with context, both over time for co-habitation and between countries for stepparenthood, reveal about couple conflict? In an atmosphere of low interpersonal conflict, perhaps little. But where the potential for conflict is great, the factors identified here—essentially financial stress on men seeking to hold a confused provider role (stepfatherhood) and on couples seeking to negotiate roles and relationships under rapidly changing rules (cohabitation and marriage)—seem likely to increase conflict.

As a demographer of living arrangements, I feel that it is likely that there have been real increases in violence, not just in the reporting of violence. There has been a decline in household size, removing the adult children, servants, and unmarried relatives, who often serve as enforcers of appropriate behavior. Furthermore, there has been the near vanishing of neighborly dropping in due to the effect of the telephone, resulting in an enormous increase in privacy. This makes it more of a problem to enter a physically vulnerable relationship, or to bring in one's vulnerable children. It is my hope that people entering new relationships will expect greater commitment than most cohabitations involve, and that commitment should extend to the children.

Physical vulnerability, however, is greatly enhanced by *financial* vulnerability. In the United States, with its near-total lack of public financial support for families, too many women say they cannot afford to leave an abusive relationship if they have children to support. Too many daughters say that their mothers did not want to have to leave, and so did not attend to their daughters' reports and fears. In Sweden, the social workers are less concerned about the potentially physically and sexually abusive male in families; rather, they have the opposite worry. Given that a single parent can support a family, as a result of family allowances and subsidized day care, social workers are concerned that low-earning men are dependent on women and children, rather than the reverse, as in the United States. Clearly, in the Swedish context, it is the men who are sometimes economically vulnerable while the children and their caregivers are much less so. In most cases, of course, both men and women in Swedish families with children are financially secure, relieving that substantial stressor in their lives.

REFERENCES

Becker, G. (1973). A theory of marriage: Part I. *Journal of Political Economy, 81*, 4.

Becker, G. (1974). A theory of marriage: Part II. *Journal of Political Economy, 82*, 2.

Becker, G. (1991). *A treatise on the family* (enlarged ed.). Cambridge, MA: Harvard University Press.

Bernard, J. (1981). The good provider role: Its rise and fall. *American Psychologist, 36*, 1-12.

Bernhardt, E., & Goldscheider, F. (1999). *Men, resources and family living: The determinants of union and parental status in the United States and Sweden.* Unpublished paper.

Booth, A., & Dabbs, J. (1993). Testosterone and men's marriages. *Social Forces, 72,* 463-477.

Cherlin, A. (1996). *Public and private families: An introduction.* New York: McGraw-Hill.

Goldscheider, F., & Turcotte, P. (1998). Evolution of factors influencing first union formation in Canada. *Canadian Studies in Population, 28,* 145-173.

Goldscheider, F., Turcotte, P. & Kopp, A. (1999, August). *The changing determinants of women's first union formation in industrialized countries: The United States, Canada, Italy, and Sweden.* Paper presented at the European Population Conference, The Hague.

Koball, H. (1997). *Gender roles and the transition to marriage.* Unpublished doctoral dissertation, Brown University, Providence, RI.

Moffitt, R., Reville, R., & Winkler, R. (1995, April). *Beyond single mothers: Cohabitation, marriage, and the U.S. welfare system.* Paper presented at the annual meetings of the Population Association of America, San Francisco.

Parsons, T. (1949). The social structure of the family. In R. Anshen, (ed.), *The family: Its function and destiny* (pp. 173-201). New York: Harper and Brothers.

Ross, H., & Sawhill, I. (1975). *Time of transition: The growth of families headed by women.* Washington, DC: Urban Institute Press.

South, S. (1991). Sociodemographic differentials in mate selection preferences. *Journal of Marriage and the Family, 53,* 928-940.

Sweet, J., Bumpass, L., & Call, V. (1988). *The design and content of the National Survey of Families and Households.* Working paper NSFH-1, Center for demography and Ecology. Madison, WI: University of Wisconsin.

Udry, R. (1994). The nature of gender. *Demography, 31,* 561-573.

United Nations. (1996). *Sexual behavior, reproductive health and fertility regulation in countries with economies in transition.* A project undertaken by the Population Activities Unit of the Economic Commission for Europe. Unpublished. 19 pp.

van de Kaa, D. J. (1987). Europe's second demographic transition. *Population Bulletin 42,* 1-57.

4

Searching for the Roots of Marital Conflict in Uxoricides[1] and Uxorious Husbands[2]

Rena L. Repetti
UCLA, Dept. of Psychology

In their provocative chapter on the evolutionary origins of conflict in couples, Wilson and Daly argued that there was an advantage to individuals who closely monitored for threats to their proprietary claims and who defended their claims. In particular, in our evolutionary history, there was a survival advantage conferred on males who were more aware of and sensitive to threats of sexual infidelity in a mate. Therefore, questions about the sexual fidelity of a female partner arouse violent inclinations that, at least in the past, functioned to control and protect the male's claims. That is, the use of coercive control and violence with a female partner was effective in reducing covert extra-pair mating, and thus improved the male's inclusive fitness. Certain characteristics of a partner, such as her youth or attractiveness, or characteristics of the relationship, such as its exit costs or its stability, act as cues regarding the likelihood of threats to male propriety claims. To a nonexpert like myself, this reasoning makes sense. Most family researchers would agree with the assumption that "the reason why marriage exists has first and most basically to be understood in terms of its reproductive function." Moreover, there is certainly clear evidence that threats to sexually based proprietary claims are anger arousing, instigate aggressive tendencies, and sometimes even lead to violent behavior (just as other threats that arouse anger can do). The fact that men's feelings of jealousy based on sexual proprietorship are a motivational factor in *some* cases of marital violence is indisputable. However, Wilson and Daly assumed that threats to proprietary claims are *the major* source of violence in marriage. Two types of evidence are presented in support of this claim: the increased risk of homicide in de facto marital unions relative to registered unions, and age patterns of risk.

My comments in this chapter have two goals. First, I challenge some of the inferences made by Wilson and Daly by suggesting plausible alternative explanations for the two main pieces of evidence that were presented. Second, I argue for a different approach, one that supplements the Wilson and Daly perspective by viewing marital conflict as the absence of cooperation. From this perspective, the evolutionary roots of conflict would lie at least as much in an understanding of cooperation as in an understanding of aggression.

---

[1] Uxoricides — wife killings.
[2] Uxorious — doting on or affectionately submissive toward one's wife.

COMPARISONS OF REGISTERED AND DE FACTO UNIONS

Wilson and Daly had the innovative idea to compare registered and de facto unions. They clearly outlined how de facto unions have more of the characteristics that should threaten husbands' proprietary claims (e.g., lower exit costs or the presence of dependent offspring from prior unions). Moreover, they showed that, consistent with their hypothesis, risk of homicide is much greater in the de facto unions. Of course, whenever two groups that exist in nature (as opposed to having been created in the laboratory) are compared, there's always the problem of identifying the key factor or factors that account for observed differences between the two groups. Evolutionary theory pointed Wilson and Daly to a particular set of characteristics of the two types of marital unions that would predict different homicide rates. However, testable alternative hypotheses are suggested by a consideration of factors associated with selection *out* of registered marriages, through divorce, factors that act as barriers to selection *into* registered marriages, and factors that contribute to selection *into* de facto unions.

As Wilson and Daly pointed out, de facto unions, compared to registered marriages, encompass a much more heterogeneous group of relationships in many different respects, and that certainly complicates comparisons of de facto and registered marriages. The de facto unions include everything from visiting unions, to "on again-off again" relationships, to long-term committed marriages. As Wilson and Daly showed, de facto unions are less likely to endure. That means that, on average, the population of de facto unions are of shorter duration than the population of registered marital unions.

Violence during the first few years of registered marriages is a strong predictor of divorce (Rogge & Bradbury, 1999). Therefore, the population of registered married couples, especially those married more than a few years, has already "evolved" to exclude much physical abuse and violence. The greater violence that is observed in de facto marital unions, relative to registered unions, must be explained to some degree by the fact that violent marriages are likely to end. The same process probably also acts to keep violent mates from marrying in the first place. That is, the couple ends the relationship before getting legally married, or they are less likely to reach a level of commitment needed to get legally married. Indeed, male violence is associated with relationship dissolution in both de facto and registered marriages in the United States (DeMaris, 2000). So, through a process of selection into the group of registered marriages and a process of selection out of the group of registered marriages, the average level of violence in registered marriages is maintained at a relatively low level.

Wilson and Daly also pointed out that there is more sexual activity in de facto marriages, and this is consistent with the "sperm competition hypothesis." However, increased sexual activity may be explained by other differences, such as length of the relationship, or the presence of children. On average, frequency of sex decreases over the life-span of a relationship (Liu, 2000), and the presence of children is also associated with a decrease in sexual activity in a marriage (Apt & Hurlbert, 1992). So, two other characteristics of the de facto unions in the samples —shorter average length and greater likelihood of being childless—would also predict increased sexual activity.

This analysis suggests that it is critical to know the length of the unions that are being compared. How does the amount of violence, risk of homicide, and frequency of sexual activity compare in de facto and registered unions of the same duration?[3] A finding of increased risk of homicide in de facto unions, compared to registered unions of the same length, would suggest the importance of other differences between the two types of unions. Exit costs may be one factor to consider but, as suggested later, there are others as well.

AGE PATTERNS IN RISK OF HOMICIDE

Daly and Wilson presented us with fascinating age patterns of risk of being murdered by one's husband (younger women are at greater risk in registered marriages and older women are at greatest risk in de facto marriages), which cannot be explained by income patterns.

Registered Marriages

Evolutionary psychologists point out that—other characteristics being equal— youth makes a woman a more desirable partner to others. A wife's youth therefore acts as a cue to her husband that he is at risk of losing her to another man which, in turn, threatens the husband's proprietary claims. According to Wilson and Daly, that is why younger wives in registered marriages are at an increased risk of being murdered by their husbands. There are at least three other possibilities for the correlation between a wife's age and marital violence. A wife's age correlates both with the age of her husband and with the duration of the marital union. We know that age in men is negatively correlated with risk of violent behavior and, as already noted, more enduring marriages are less likely to be violent (Rogge & Bradbury, 1999). Therefore, the observed increase in risk of violence to younger wives in registered marriages may have little to do with the wife's age and more to do with her husband's age and the length of the union.

It is also important to note that a wife's youth may also have a direct impact on her risk of being murdered by her husband, not because of threats to his proprietary claims, but because older women are less likely to contribute to the escala-

---

[3] The criteria for determining the length of a marital (or marital-type) union are not necessarily straightforward. For example, the date on which a couple was legally married would not mark the beginning of their union if, prior to the legal wedding, the partners were living together. In that case, the period during which the relationship qualified as a de facto marriage should be included in determining the union's total duration.

tion of angry or aggressive conflicts with their husbands. In other words, prior life experiences may provide an advantage in dealings with a violent mate. With greater experience and maturity, an older woman's responses to her husband's aggressive behavior may be more likely to de-escalate (rather than further inflame) the conflict, or she may have the foresight to escape from the situation before harm occurs. This hypothesis could be addressed by comparing the responses of younger and older women to their spouses' angry and aggressive behaviors.

De Facto Marriages

The age patterns for murder of de facto wives is different. It is the "middle-aged" wives in de facto unions who are at an increased risk of violence. Wilson and Daly associated this with the presence of stepchildren in the de facto unions of middle-aged women. The data they presented suggest that the presence of children from a former union increases the likelihood of homicide. The argument is that because stepchildren are a potent source of conflict about the allocation of joint resources, they threaten the solidarity of the marital union and, thereby, pose a threat to the proprietary claims of the husband. Of course, children are sources of conflict for all marriages (whether registered or de facto). We know, for example, that the birth of the first child is often associated with a decline in marital satisfaction (Belsky & Kelly, 1994). Stepchildren are an even greater source of stress and conflict. De facto unions may be more affected by the presence of children, both biological children and stepchildren, because these unions are less stable than registered unions, and less stable relationships may be more vulnerable to all stressors.

There is another possible explanation for the excess risk of homicide among middle-aged women in de facto marital unions that has nothing to do with the presence of children from a prior union. (By excess, I mean the elevated risk in this age group that is above and beyond the overall risk due to being in a de facto union.) Again, consider the average differences in the duration of the two types of relationships. The population of registered marriages involving women in the 35 to 54 age bracket includes a large percentage of long-lasting unions. These are marriages that have already passed the critical threshold for divorce due to violence in the first few years of the union. The women in the 35 to 54 age bracket who are in de facto marriages are in some mixture of new relationships and long-lasting unions. Many of these relationships have not yet passed the critical threshold for "divorce"—or breakup—due to violence in the first few years of the union. One way to test the hypothesis that middle-aged women in de facto marriages have an excess risk of being killed by their husbands because their marriages tend to be of shorter duration would be to compare homicide rates among middle-aged women in registered and de facto unions *of the same duration*.

The data presented by Wilson and Daly paint a different picture for women in the 15 to 34 age bracket. Although there is still an overwhelming increase in risk among those in the de facto unions, the difference in risk between the two types of marriage is not as great at this age as it is in the 35 to 54 age bracket. This may be because the characteristics of the two types of marriages and of the individuals in these two types of marriages are not as different among younger women as they are among older women. First, a large percentage of the population of registered marriages involving younger women are still of relatively short duration. Many have not yet passed the threshold for divorce due to violence. So, in terms of length of the relationship, registered and de facto unions involving younger women are more similar.

In addition, de facto marriages are more common among relatively young women, so there may not be as many selection factors acting at this age as there are at older ages. In fact, many of the de facto marriages among women in the 15 to 34 age group will be registered marriages by the time the women are middle-aged. By selection factors, I am referring to a set of "third variables" representing undesirable personality characteristics that accounts for an association between a tendency toward violent behavior and finding oneself in less stable relationships. The population of potential partners for new relationships among the middle-aged population (of men and women) probably contains a disproportionate number of potential mates with liabilities for violent behavior (e.g., poor emotion regulation, alcoholism, drug abuse, psychopathology). These are the people who never selected into a marriage or who were selected out of a marriage. So, any differences between the personality characteristics of partners in the two types of relationships may be exaggerated among middle-aged couples. Differences in the population of individuals who are in the two types of unions would not be as great among younger men and women.

In short, there are several reasons why, compared to middle-aged adults, young adults and their marriages in the de facto group may more closely resemble the individuals and marriages in the registered group. First, on average, the two types of marital union are of more similar duration among younger adults. Second, a greater frequency of de facto unions among younger adults means that fewer selection factors are at work producing differences between the two groups at this stage in the life cycle. Third, there are differences in the pool of potential mates for new unions in the two age groups (and de facto unions are more likely to be new unions).

SUMMARY

Wilson and Daly presented marital researchers with intriguing comparisons and hypotheses that should stimulate further thinking and study. Although I am not an expert in their field, I believe the evolutionary analysis they present would be strengthened by a consideration of the effects that selection processes may have on characteristics of marital unions and potential new mates. First, I have suggested a process that acts on the population of marriages (both registered and de facto) to exclude violent unions over time. Because, at any given point in time, the population of registered marriages includes a relatively large percentage of long-lasting unions, the average risk of homicide will be lower than it is in de facto marital unions, which are less enduring. This alternative explanation for increased risk of homicide in de facto unions can be ruled out by comparing registered and de facto unions of the same duration.

Second, just as a tendency toward violence is associated with selection out of marital unions, there may be other factors (also associated with violent behavior and a lack of impulse control) that act as barriers to selection into marital unions. Personality traits or other individual characteristics associated with proneness toward violence may make one less likely to enter into and remain in a long-lasting marital union. If there is such a selection process at work, then the pool of potential new mates (for either type of union) becomes less and less desirable as men and women age. This alternative explanation for increased risk of homicide in de facto unions and, especially, among middle-aged women in de facto unions, can be ruled out by comparing the characteristics of husbands in registered and de facto unions. Some of the risk factors worth considering are alcoholism and other forms of drug abuse, a history of violence or problems with the law, and psychopathology (Hamberger, Lohr, Bonge, & Tolin, 1996; Leonard & Quigley, 1999; Leonard & Senchak, 1996). It would seem important to control for factors like these in comparisons of the two types of marital unions.

In short, I am suggesting that there are selection processes acting on entry into and exit from marital unions, processes that have cumulative effects on the characteristics of registered and de facto unions at any given point in time (in particular, their level of violence). There would also be an expected effect on the pool of potential new mates such that, in successively older age groups, there is a lower proportion of potential new mates with the characteristics that are desirable for stable, nonviolent unions.

CONFLICT AS A BREAKDOWN IN COOPERATION

Although I am not an evolutionary psychologist, I take this opportunity to venture an argument for a different perspective on the biological roots of marital conflict, one that focuses not on aggression but, instead, on the evolutionary underpinnings of cooperation. I suggest this shift for several reasons. First, most marital conflict does not involve physical aggression. Second, what is known about the characteristics of marital conflict is not always consistent with what is known about spousal violence. For example, men are much more likely than are women to be the aggressors in violent marriages. However, the work of Andrew Christensen and others shows a very distinct pattern of demand-withdraw in marital conflicts, with wives more often assuming the demand role and husbands more often assuming the withdraw role (Christensen & Heavey, 1993). In my own research, I have found that men respond to daily stressors at work by withdrawing from marital interaction, not with greater irritability or anger (Repetti, 1989).

In order to understand the roots of physical aggression in marriage, it makes sense to study threats and other stimuli that are highly arousing, such as Wilson and Daly have done. But, to understand marital conflict per se, it is equally important to understand how marital partners take care of their needs, pursue their goals, and manage at the same time to cooperate with the needs and goals of other family members. In their focal chapter for this volume (chap. 5), Bradbury, Rogge, and Lawrence defined marital conflicts as "social interactions in which the spouses hold incompatible goals." If conflict can be viewed as a breakdown in cooperation or, at the very least, a situation in which the balance between cooperation and self-interest tilts toward self-interest, then the search for the evolutionary roots of marital conflict should include a consideration of the evolutionary roots of cooperation.

Of course, this approach to conflict envisions a very different scene from the image of a husband murdering his wife. Here I am picturing the smaller, more common daily conflicts in marriage, when the goals, needs, or desires being pursued by one member of the couple are not shared or are interfered with by the other member. For example, imagine the following conversation between a husband and wife whose different needs at the moment are in conflict. He complains, "I've let you know that I need a little support right now, but all you want to do is watch TV." She responds, "I'm tired and just want to watch the Yankees game, but you keep starting a conversation." Note that each member of this couple is operating from the assumption that the partner should accommodate his or her personal needs in some way. The source of conflict is the perception that the partner has not provided this expected level of support. Or, picture a mother and father with different childrearing priorities. She complains, "I think our kids should eat nutritious meals, and you take them out for fast food." He responds, "You insist on home-cooked dinners and we waste an hour cleaning up the kitchen every night." This couple works from the assumption that they share responsibility for the care of their children and their home. The source of conflict here is a failure to conform to the partner's values and priorities for child nutrition and housework. Conflicts of this sort are, no doubt, fueled and exacerbated by physiological and emotional arousal (e.g., an emotional state of anger), and they can escalate into aggressive and even violent interactions. What I am suggesting is that the process begins with a breakdown in the normal or expected level of cooperation in the marriage.

What I find remarkable about marriage is the form that it takes. Most marriages endure for more years than is required to rear a young child, and many last a lifetime. How extraordinary that *this* is how humans evolved to reproduce. Marriage requires extreme cooperation. What should be surprising to us is how little conflict and how much cooperation there is in marriage. An uxorious husband is one who dotes on or is affectionately submissive toward his wife. There are many more uxorious husbands than there are uxoricides. Cooperation in caring for relatively helpless offspring is central to any understanding of the reproductive function of marriage. The capacity to cooperate must have improved the survival and successful reproduction of the individuals who displayed that trait. In order to understand the evolutionary roots of marital conflict, we do need to study the roots that dig into the soil of aggression. That is where we can expect to find some of the underpinnings of how humans respond to threats in their marriage. But we also need to understand the roots of conflict that ultimately emerge from the soil of cooperation, in particular when it breaks down and why.

Wilson and Daly wrote a fascinating chapter filled with stimulating ideas that call our attention to the deepest origins of marital behavior. Their perspective raises important basic questions that should be pursued by family researchers.

ACKNOWLEDGMENTS

I'd like to thank the participants in the Couples in Conflict symposium at Pennsylvania State University (November 1-2, 1999), as well as John Gallalee, Shirley McCarthy, and Mark Grinblatt for very helpful comments on an earlier draft of this chapter. Preparation of this chapter was supported by a grant from the National Institute of Mental Health (R29-48593). Correspondence should be sent to Rena Repetti at UCLA—Dept. of Psychology, 405 Hilgard Avenue, Los Angeles, CA 90095-1563. Email: repetti@psych.ucla.edu.

REFERENCES

Apt, C. V., & Hurlbert, D. F. (1992). Motherhood and female sexuality beyond one year postpartum: A study of military wives. *Journal of Sex Education and Therapy, 18,* 104-114.

Belsky, J., & Kelly, J. (1994). *The transition to parenthood.* New York: Delacorte.

Christensen, A., & Heavey, C. L. (1993). Gender differences in marital conflict: The demand-withdraw interaction pattern. In S. Oskamp & M. Costanzo (Eds.), *Gender issues in contemporary society* (pp. 113-141). Newbury Park, CA: Sage.

DeMaris, A. (2000). Till discord do us part: The role of physical and verbal conflict in union disruption. *Journal of Marriage and the Family, 62,* 683-692.

Hamberger, L. K., Lohr, J. M., Bonge, D., & Tolin, D. F. (1996). A large sample empirical typology of male spouse abusers and its relationship to dimensions of abuse. *Violence and Victims, 11,* 277-292.

Leonard, K. E., & Quigley, B. M. (1999). Drinking and marital aggression in newlyweds: An event-based analysis of drinking and the occurrence of husband marital aggression. *Journal of Studies on Alcohol, 60,* 537-545.

Leonard, K. E., & Senchak, M. (1996). Prospective prediction of husband marital aggression within newlywed couples. *Journal of Abnormal Psychology, 105,* 369-380.

Liu, C. (2000). A theory of marital sexual life. *Journal of Marriage and the Family, 62,* 363-374.

Repetti, R. L. (1989). Effects of daily workload on subsequent behavior during marital interaction: The roles of social withdrawal and spouse support. *Journal of Personality and Social Psychology, 57*, 651-659.

Rogge, R. D., & Bradbury, T. N. (1999). Till violence does us part: The differing roles of communication and aggression in predicting adverse marital outcomes. *Journal of Consulting and Clinical Psychology, 67*, 340-351.

II

What Are the Interpersonal Roots of Couple Conflict? What Are the Consequences for Individuals and Couples?

5

Reconsidering the Role of Conflict in Marriage

Thomas Bradbury
Ronald Rogge
Erika Lawrence
University of California, Los Angeles

The quality and stability of marriage has important consequences for our society and for the physical and emotional well-being of spouses and their children. Understanding the factors that give rise to variability in marital functioning is therefore important, particularly because interventions for couples and families will be more effective to the extent they are based on sound empirical findings. In their quest to clarify the nature and course of marital functioning, researchers have focused heavily on communication and on the behaviors that spouses exchange, and more specifically on interpersonal conflict and the behaviors displayed in those situations in which spouses hold incompatible goals or differing opinions. But how important is conflict and the management of conflict in determining the course and outcome of marriage? Do the data indicate that conflict warrants a central and dominant role in our models of marriage and marital intervention? The purpose of this chapter is to address these questions, and more generally to take stock of the research literature on marital conflict and to identify gaps in the field. In doing so we first show briefly that conflict does enjoy special status as a concept of central importance in research on marriage. We then offer some reasons why we believe it is valuable to reevaluate the significance accorded to marital conflict in the field, and we suggest some ways in which our understanding of the interpersonal processes that give rise to differing marital outcomes can be refined and, more important, revised.

Before turning to these issues, we would like to outline the orientation we take in addressing the role of conflict in marriage, as it helps to qualify some of the ideas presented here. First, following Kurt Lewin (1948; see also Fincham, Bradbury, & Grych, 1990), marital conflicts are defined as those social interactions in which the spouses hold incompatible goals. These goals need not be conscious and articulated by the spouses, and the goals might be quite specific (e.g., disagreeing over whether you should be allowed to learn how to surf) or they might be quite general (e.g., disagreeing over the amount of independence one has in the relationship). Conflict arises when one spouse pursues a goal, or talks about pursuing that goal, and in so doing interferes with the goals the partner holds. The focus of much of the work in the field is on the nature of these incompatibilities, on understanding what couples do when discussing and trying to resolve their differing goals, and on how these variables covary with indexes of marital functioning.

Second, we assume not only that most forms of aggression would be subsumed by this definition of conflict, but also that it is meaningful to talk about physical and nonphysical forms of conflict as separate entities. In fact, marital interaction researchers have focused traditionally on problem-solving discussions without recognizing links between them and physical aggression, although there is evidence that this focus is beginning to change. For the most part we refer to verbal conflict in the absence of physical conflict, although later we note how these two forms of conflict may differentially predict marital quality and marital dissolution.

Third, the focus here is primarily on conflict between spouses within a marriage and on the implications of this conflict for the course and outcome of the marriage. This focus is adopted with the recognition that conflict has effects in addition to those on marital functioning, most notably on the physical and mental health of the spouses and any children involved, but for now those effects are outside the scope of this presentation.

Finally, we are strongly in favor of basic research on marriage and marital interaction that will shape and guide our interventions. This is in part because marital and family scholars have a great deal to offer policy makers as well as couples and families, but also because adopting practical application as one of our goals provides us with objective criteria (are we preventing more divorces? reaching more people with our interventions? easing the transition to parenthood?)- against which we can gauge our progress. Application-oriented research also encourages us to conduct controlled experiments to test theoretical claims about the importance of particular variables (see Bradbury, in press).

CONFLICT AS A CENTRAL FOCUS IN ANALYSES OF MARRIAGE

The claim that conflict is accorded special status in the literature on marriage is supported by three kinds of evidence. *Theories of marriage* focus heavily on how couples contend with their differences of opinion. For example, the widely influential social learning conception of marriage holds that "Distress results from couples' aversive and ineffectual responses to conflict. When conflicts arise, one or both partners may respond aversively by nagging, complaining, distancing, or becoming violent until the other gives in, creating a coercive cycle that each partner contributes to or maintains" (Koerner & Jacobson, 1994, p. 208). Similarly, Gottman's recent theorizing about the determinants of marital outcomes focuses heavily on the role of behavior during conflict (Gottman, 1994; Gottman, Swanson, & Murray, 1999). Christensen and Walczynski (1997) likewise asserted that "conflict is the most important proximal factor affecting satisfaction in the relationship and ultimately its course" (p. 250), although they did qualify this by noting that in the early stages of a relationship positive forces are more influential than conflict in determining whether a relationship will form and develop.

A great deal of *research on marriage* emphasizes what spouses do when they disagree with each other. Consider, for example, that a PsycINFO search with the keywords *love* and *marital* turns back 462 entries (*love* and *marriage* produce 687), whereas *conflict* and *marital* yield 2,654 entries (*conflict* and *marriage* yield 1,192). This is more than even *communication* and *marital* (1,782; *communication* and *marriage* yield 994). *Social support* and *marital* produce 1,247 entries; *social support* and *marriage* produce 444. Thus, although not all of these entries will be empirical papers, and although we cannot put too much stock in these figures without a more detailed content analysis of the papers, by and large it appears that conflict dominates the picture on marriage. Moreover, there has been very little observational research on marriage that examines interactions other than conflict, and it comes as little surprise that most reviews on marital interaction focus almost exclusively on conflict and problem-solving behavior (e.g., Bradbury & Karney, 1993; Weiss & Heyman, 1997). Most interactional tasks developed within the marital area in the last 20 years are designed, either implicitly or explicitly, to promote problem solving and conflict, and of course most coding systems are slanted toward capturing negative behaviors of various kinds. This is to be expected in view of the strong theoretical emphasis on conflict, of course, but it is also reasonable to expect discriminant data from tasks and coding systems that would demonstrate whether behaviors displayed during problem-solving discussions are unique to that situation or whether they arise in other marital exchanges. As we note later, few data of this kind are available.

Third, conflict resolution is a key target of intervention in *psychological interventions for marriage*. In behavioral marital therapy, for example, which is the most widely studied form of marital therapy developed to date, one important goal is to help couples address deficiencies in their conflict resolution skills (e.g., Jacobson & Holtzworth-Munroe, 1986). This orientation is unavoidable in most cases and is certainly difficult to criticize, because virtually by definition most couples seeking marital therapy are not successful in solving their problems. However, the most well-developed intervention even for couples planning marriage, the Prevention and Relationship Enhancement Program (PREP; e.g., Floyd, Markman, Kelly, Blumberg, & Stanley, 1995) developed by Markman and colleagues, is also predicated on the view that modifying how couples manage conflict and negativity in their relationship is the surest way to prevent their marriages from deteriorating. So even in a population where serious, overt conflict probably does not predominate, and where the goal is to prevent adverse marital outcomes well before they appear on the horizon, management of conflict is hypothesized to be an important focus for change.

In short, although there are important exceptions to the observations being made here—there are, for example, many conceptions of marriage, studies of marriage, and programs designed to help marriage in which conflict plays an ancillary role or is absent altogether—these seem to be exceptions that prove the more general rule that "conflict is king" when it comes to analyzing marriage and particularly marital communication. It is worth speculating about why this is so, and it seems plausible to infer that this emphasis comes about because interest in the observation of marital communication developed principally among clinical psychologists—Gerald Patterson, Robert Weiss, and John Gottman, for example —who were working directly with distressed couples and families seeking marital therapy, and because heated conflict and poor problem-solving was very salient in this population. (Harold Raush, who published an important book with colleagues Barry, Hertel, & Swain in 1974 entitled *Communication, Conflict, and Marriage* that arguably launched the observational study of marriage, studied newlyweds rather than established couples, yet he too focused heavily on conflict.) This has proven to be an exceptionally fruitful point of departure for studying what transpires between spouses in marriage. It has enabled the development and refinement of paradigms for studying marital communication and using diary methods, laboratory methods, and self-report measures, and it has revealed an enormous amount about the psychological interior of distressed marriages. Yet whereas there are unambiguous advantages to studying marital conflict, there are also clear benefits to being skeptical about how central this concept should be in our theories of marriage and marital dysfunction. Questioning the importance of conflict at this point might deepen the prevailing understanding of those aspects of marital interaction that predate marital dysfunction and might strengthen the interventions made available to couples. We turn next to consider some ideas and some data that we believe support this skepticism and that may open up new avenues for research and treatment.

SOME CRACKS IN THE FACADE: REASONS FOR REEVALUATING THE ROLE OF CONFLICT IN MARRIAGE

More difficult than merely making the claim that conflict is prominent in current thinking about marriage is making the argument that this is in some way misguided or inappropriate, or that it fails to capture well the phenomena of greatest importance. The basis for our argument—that a strong focus on conflict has led to an incomplete and inadequate portrayal of marital functioning, and perhaps more inadequate than is typically recognized—is outlined later. Before getting to that it is useful to digress briefly to address the question of what exactly are the phenomena of importance in the field of marital research. Of course, this is a difficult question to answer definitively because there are many such phenomena, but at the core there appears to be great interest in two: identifying in basic research the factors that cause variability in marital quality and marital dissolution, and identifying in treatment research the factors that can be modified so that adverse marital outcomes—marital dissatisfaction and marital dissolution—can be prevented or alleviated. (For the purposes of this analysis, the idea that marital dissolution can be a beneficial outcome in some cases is not addressed.)

Implications of Basic Research for Therapy versus Prevention

It would be reasonable to assume that solving the first part of this problem, why marriages fail, would be fundamentally important to solving the second part of this problem, preventing or treating marital failure. However, I think this assumption holds only in the case of prevention: Knowing why marriages generally fail should prove very informative in developing interventions that would prevent that from happening, or at least in identifying those couples who are at elevated risk for later difficulties and who should therefore be targeted with interventions. In the case of treatment for existing marital distress, on the other hand, there are many idiosyncratic responses to marital distress (e.g., anger, resignation, depression, hostility), and unhappy couples often wait a long time before seeking therapy. A lot happens after the early stages of marital deterioration, and for therapy to be effective it has to contend with both the original source of the distress and the distance and pain that it generated within the marriage. As a result, knowing why marriages succeed or fail may be related only peripherally to the interventions that are developed for treating marital distress; clinical outcome research and perhaps even intensive case studies are likely to be far more important than basic research on marital dysfunction for developing and refining therapies (see Bradbury, Johnson, Lawrence, & Rogge, 1998, for additional discussion of this point).

So where does this leave us? The preventive approach holds great intrinsic appeal, particularly because it has the potential to reach large numbers of couples (about three couples in four are married in a religious organization; see Stanley, Markman, St. Peters, & Leber, 1995) and because it can allow us to reach these couples early, before marital distress affects them and their children. Consequently, the focus here is primarily on the extent to which conflict and the management of conflict helps us to predict and explain the deterioration of initially satisfied marriages, and on the extent to which modification of conflict enables us to facilitate the development of durable, reasonably fulfilling marriages that would not otherwise have achieved this outcome.

Longitudinal Studies

Perhaps the most obvious place to look for evidence of an association between conflict and marital outcomes is the longitudinal literature, where some 15 to 20

---

[1] Many of these studies use observational data, which is a clear strength, but in interpreting these studies it is important to remember that this tends to reduce sample size and hence statistical power, and that this constrains our set of predictive variables to those collected typically within a 10- or 15-minute span of time. However, the available evidence does suggest that these behavioral samples are temporally stable — Kiecolt-Glaser (personal communication September 1999) reports a .74 correlation for couple negative behavior from the first to third years of marriage, for example — and representative of the kinds of discussions couples have (see Bradbury, 1994; Foster, Caplan, & Howe, 1997).

studies have been conducted to address this link.[1] At first glance, the findings from this literature appear to offer reasonably strong support for the notion that behavior during problem-solving discussions, and negative behavior in particular, plays some role in the generation of marital dissatisfaction. Referring to the meta-analysis published in 1995 by Karney and Bradbury, with particular emphasis on those aggregate variables that have been examined in five or more studies, we see that when predicting wives' subsequent satisfaction there is an aggregate effect size r of -.06 for husbands' negative behavior ($n = 8$ studies) and -.25 for wives' own negative behavior ($n = 6$ studies). When predicting husbands' subsequent satisfaction there is an r of -.20 for husbands' own negative behavior ($n = 5$ studies) and -.21 for wives' negative behavior. (Positive behavior has not been studied enough times for stable estimates here, and no behaviors have been studied enough in relation to marital stability to produce highly dependable findings, although across four studies there is an r value of -.17 linking couple negative behavior to marital dissolution.)

These findings are promising, but they also raise several important considerations. First, the effects are relatively modest in magnitude. If these coefficients are reasonably good estimates of the association between negative behavior and subsequent marital satisfaction, they suggest that the majority of the variability in satisfaction—more than 90% if you favor squaring correlation coefficients as a means of estimating explained variance, or 75% to 85% if you do not (see Ozer, 1985)—is due to other factors. Second, lurking within these effect sizes are some troubling inconsistencies in the literature. These inconsistencies can be viewed as suppressing the observed effect sizes noted earlier, but they can also be viewed as raising some serious questions about the true links between problem-solving behavior to changes in marital quality. In a controversial paper, Gottman and Krokoff (1989), for example, found that higher levels of wives' anger appeared to be beneficial for marriage over time (cf. Woody & Costanzo, 1990; also see Bradbury, Cohan, & Karney, 1998; Smith, Vivian, & O'Leary, 1991), leading them to propose that conflict engagement is desirable. Karney and Bradbury (1997) obtained a similar result using growth curve modeling for computing 8-wave (4-year) satisfaction trajectories for a sample newlyweds, and we suggested that early on in marriage, negativity can reflect commitment to the marriage whereas later it might represent discontent with the marriage. More recently, Gottman, Coan, Carrere, and Swanson (1998) reported that higher levels of anger shortly after marriage do not discriminate between couples who go on to have happy and unhappy marriages a few years later. Johnson (1999), on the other hand, found that observed anger reliably predicts the rate at which newlywed marriages deteriorate over 4 years—more anger was found to be detrimental. So even for a relatively narrow set of variables, we see null effects, inverse effects, and direct effects of negativity on change in satisfaction, and these discrepancies cannot be attributed easily to sample characteristics or statistical methods.

To take another example, Gill, Christensen, and Fincham (1999) reported, reasonably enough, that wives' marital quality declines over 12 months to the extent they display higher levels of negative behavior and lower levels of positive behavior. However, Gill et al. also found that husbands' positive behavior is detrimental to their own satisfaction and beneficial to their wives' satisfaction, and to complicate matters further these findings hold only using raw change scores for husbands' satisfaction and regressed change scores for wives' satisfaction. So even in studies in which some replicable findings emerge, other counterintuitive findings are also obtained, and as a result it is difficult to discern the signal in the literature amidst all the noise (see Fincham & Beach, 1999, for additional discussion). It is tempting to discount those findings that do not conform to theoretical expectations, whatever those expectations might be, but the unexpected findings are too common to overlook and discounting them might result in missing an opportunity to reevaluate in some more fundamental way the role of conflict in marriage.

In evaluating findings such as these, it also bears noting that they are usually obtained over relatively short spans of time in marriage—typically a year or two—which would seem to favor demonstrating the effects of behavior on later satisfaction more than would a study over a longer span of time. Also, in many cases samples include couples at all stages of the marital life cycle, from newlyweds to retirees, who are likely to vary widely in their level of satisfaction at the onset of data collection. Because of this variability in initial status, following these couples over time will confound the onset of discord with the continuing course of marital discord. The latter is not really under debate at this point, as we suspect there is consensus that arguments will make a troubled marriage worse. But studying the onset of distress and its continuing course simultaneously certainly clouds the question of why couples become distressed initially. Because we can expect that couples who are already distressed will display higher levels of negativity than couples who are not distressed, the presence of established, distressed couples in a sample probably exaggerates the true effects of conflict behavior on marital deterioration. This is because at least some of the observed effects of problem-solving behavior on marital outcome might be due to the effects of pre-existing distress on later distress as mediated by conflict behavior. This effect is rather different from the effects of conflict behavior, independent of concurrent satisfaction, on later distress, which is the association of greater theoretical and practical importance in this literature. On the other hand, (a) it is the more distressed couples and presumably the couples who are at risk for divorce who drop out of longitudinal studies, which may lead to underestimates of the effects of conflict on outcomes, and (b) there is more variability in change in satisfaction in younger couples than in more established couples (see Bradbury, Campbell, & Fincham, 1995, Study 2; Kurdek, 1998), which may increase the relative magnitude of the effects of problem-solving behavior in this subsample.

Finally, it remains an open question whether the effects reported to date are due to the observed behavioral codes, or whether associations arise at least in part because couples with more difficult or serious problems have more heated discussions. Perhaps the profile of problems that a couple is facing is as important as the way they discuss any one of them (see Weiss & Heyman, 1997, for a discussion of this point). This is a bit of a "chicken and egg" problem: Do couples have more heated discussions because they are contending with weightier problems, or are couples contending with weightier problems because the caliber of their interactional skills and tendencies does not allow them to make much headway with their differences of opinion? Answering this question will not be easy, but ruling out the contributing role of either the overall level of problems in the marriage or the severity of the specific problem-solving discussion being observed would seem to be important if we want to assert that it is the way couples address, manage, and resolve conflict, more than the content or severity of those problems, that gets them into trouble. This may seem like splitting hairs—is it the content of what couples talk about independent of process, the way they talk about their problems independent of content, or some interaction between the two that enables prediction of marital outcomes?—but the answer to this question really does constrain the strength of inferences we can make about the causal role of conflict in marriage, and it has important implications for how we approach the prevention of marital distress.

Prediction Analyses

Recent claims that marital outcomes can be predicted with high accuracy from problem-solving behavior—in excess of 90% in some cases—would appear to contradict the argument being developed here (for a review, see Rogge & Bradbury, 1999a). However, we believe that a close analysis of these studies raises some doubts about these claims. First, some of the studies collect their initial data from established couples, many of whom are already maritally distressed. Buehlman, Gottman, and Katz (1992), for example, who reported predictive accuracy of approximately 94%, studied couples who had a child aged 4 or 5 and who had satisfaction scores ranging from 27 to 147 on the Marital Adjustment Test (Locke & Wallace, 1959). As noted earlier, behavioral data from distressed couples is probably a manifestation of the distress, and this will tend to inflate the predictive power of the behavioral codes. The predictor variables may simply represent initial stages of the ultimate outcome rather than the underlying factors that cause the outcome.

Second, in several studies, extreme groups of happy and unhappy (or divorced) couples are sampled, and problem-solving behaviors are used as the outcomes that problem-solving behaviors predict. This will also inflate levels of prediction, as Williams and Jurich (1995) showed.

Third, most studies are relatively small, the proportions of divorced couples in the samples are relatively low, and the number of predictor variables is relatively large. As Betz (1987) noted, discriminant function analysis with a high ratio of predictors to subjects will capitalize on random fluctuations between groups, and it is relatively easy to increase predictive levels under these conditions.

Finally, and perhaps most important, to our knowledge a true predictive study has yet to be conducted in the marital area. That is, a specific set of decision rules developed on one or more samples has not been applied to an entirely new sample to determine whether those rules actually work, in the absence of any post-hoc modifications; instead, a new set of equations, sometimes overlapping with old equations when common variables are available, is developed with each new sample. This is necessary and desirable in the early stages of developing predictive models, but it is important to note in discussing these data that the prediction work that has been done to date begins when the outcomes are already known, and the independent variables are then examined so that they optimize classification of couples. Thus, although there is good reason to believe that marital outcomes will be predictable with a reasonably high level of accuracy in the not-too-distant future, the available studies do not yet confirm accurate prediction and, hence, their relevance to the role of conflict in marital outcomes is not yet apparent.

Treatment Studies

It would be ideal to be able to turn to an experimental study in which young, nondistressed couples were assigned randomly to groups in which problem-solving behavior was and was not manipulated, with regular follow-up data over the next several years on behavior and relationship satisfaction. As it turns out, we can come close to this ideal using data from a treatment outcome study conducted by Kurt Hahlweg and colleagues in Munich (Hahlweg, Markman, Thurmaier, Engl, & Eckert, 1998; Hahlweg, Thurmaier, Engl, Eckert, & Markman, 1998). They were not able to assign couples randomly to treatments, because in order to conduct the study under the auspices of the Catholic church in Germany it was necessary to allow couples to choose whether they wanted to receive the German version of PREP, which in this case was a 6-session, 15-hour program administered in a small-group format that focused on effective communication and problem-solving skills. Couples who did not choose PREP either received treatment as usual in the community or received no treatment; these groups did not differ from each other and formed the control group.

At a preassessment, the treated and control groups did not differ in their satisfaction scores (as assessed with the Marital Adjustment Test; Locke & Wallace, 1959) or in their observed problem-solving skills (as assessed with the Kategoriensystem fur Partnerschaftliche Interaktion or KPI; Hahlweg et al., 1984). Observational data collected at postassessment, and at 18, 36, and 60 months, indicate that husbands and wives in the treated group ($n = 55$) were far more positive and far less negative during problem-solving discussions than were the control couples ($n = 17$), with effect sizes that were consistently in the .40 to .50 range, and that did not dissipate over the 5-year study period. What is interesting about this study, and what makes it important in the present analysis, is that at the same time these large behavioral differences were obtained there was a corresponding group difference in relationship satisfaction only at 36 months, with the treated couples reporting greater satisfaction. So even though the treated couples were observed to be superior in their problem-solving abilities at all four points following intervention, they were more satisfied with their relationships at only one point during this period, and the effect size here was .20 for wives and .25 for husbands. Problem-solving behavior had been reliably changed, but change in satisfaction was not nearly as consistent or as strong.[2] These findings indicate that (a) behaviors other than those that promote effective problem-solving may be needed to bring about enduring changes in relationship satisfaction, and (b) the traditional repeated-measures MANOVA approach to assessing treatment outcome may not be sensitive enough for capturing change in relationship satisfaction. Indeed, growth curve modeling of these data does show that the rate of deterioration in relationship satisfaction in the treated group, at least for wives, is greater than that in the control group (Bradbury, Thurmaier, et al., 1998). More to the point, this study is highly significant because it shows that change in couples' problem-solving behavior can be generated—that couples can learn to behave more effectively when discussing a marital issue where they have a difference of opinion—but that doing so does not necessarily lead to large and durable changes in relationship satisfaction.

Conclusion

In short, there is good reason to argue that problem-solving behavior, either as it occurs naturally among couples or as it arises as a result of specialized training in educational programs, may not be as consequential as is commonly believed for the long-term well-being of marriage. We offer three related observations here before turning in the next section to two major implications of this possibility. First, it seems plausible that the salience of conflict in couples seeking marital therapy and the cross-sectional findings demonstrating consistent problem-solving deficits in distressed couples (compared to their nondistressed counterparts; e.g., Gottman, 1979) were mistakenly interpreted as showing that conflict was a central cause of marital dysfunction. The conflict displayed by distressed couples may be at least to some extent a consequence of their distress in addition, perhaps, to being a cause of it. Factors that differentiate happy and unhappy couples, on a between-couples basis, may be rather different from those factors that transform a happy couple into a unhappy one, and it may be that the descriptive findings should not be overextended when causal hypotheses are being advanced. Indeed, we find surprisingly few reliable correlations between observed behavior and marital sat-

---

[2] One couple (1.6%) in the treated group, and 4 couples (12.5%) in the control group, ended their marriage in divorce. This suggests that modification of marital problem-solving behavior may prevent divorce, but a larger number of divorces and true random assignment of couples to groups is necessary before this conclusion is warranted.

isfaction in newlywed samples, even when we have a substantial range of marital satisfaction scores (e.g., Karney & Bradbury, 1997), which suggests that the linkage between problem-solving behavior and satisfaction later in marriage is something that develops over time.

Second, the notion that conflict may play a more restricted role than is commonly believed is consistent with findings about the frequency of marital disagreements. In an equal-probability sample of 778 couples, McGonagle, Kessler, and Schilling (1992) found that about 80% of their sample reported marital disagreements once per month or less, with more than half of the respondents indicating that they disagreed less than once a month. These findings were consistent over 3 years and were largely corroborated by a subsample of couples completing daily diaries. This sample involved established couples (average duration was 17.1 years) and years married correlated inversely (albeit weakly, $r < .17$) with disagreement frequency, and hence may not be directly relevant to the onset of marital distress, but these data do suggest that marital research and theory may be emphasizing a class of events that is not all that frequent in most marriages. Again, the belief that conflict is pervasive may be a holdover from clinical observation of distressed couples, who are probably not representative of couples in general or even couples who are maritally distressed. Of course, it is not necessary for conflict to be frequent in order to be influential in marriage, but these data do raise the question of whether something this infrequent warrants strong emphasis as a cause of marital difficulties and whether other, more common aspects of marital communication might be worthy of consideration.

Finally, it behooves us to remember that most couples probably do not base their decision of whether to marry on the quality of their problem-solving abilities and how they manage their conflicts. Many couples will not have had sufficient opportunity to confront major difficulties prior to marriage. If they have, they may not progress toward marriage at all, or they may downplay these difficulties and focus on their compatibility as their relationship evolves and as they make decisions about whether or not to marry. The spouses in our studies seem to proceed toward marriage because they enjoy being with each other, because they have similar interests, because their families and social networks support their relationship, and, perhaps most important, because they feel that they can talk to and be understood by their partner. Spouses do mention conflict as a factor that affects their likelihood of marrying, but this tends to be relatively rare compared to other reasons (see Surra & Hughes, 1997). If positive relationship features such as listening, self-disclosure, understanding, support, sexuality, and compatibility are more important in the early development of marriage than are negative relationship features, such as conflict and problem resolution, then perhaps it is the erosion of these positive features that leads to discontent with the marriage, at least for some couples. (As we argue later, marital dissatisfaction and dissolution may have different antecedents over the first several years of marriage, with dissatisfaction being linked more closely with the quality of interpersonal communication.) This may lead to increases in conflict, or to preexisting conflict having a greater impact on the relationship; as the qualities of the relationship that initially attracted spouses to it begin to diminish, perhaps negative characteristics can "take root" more easily and contribute to marital deterioration. The more general point is that we begin to think differently about conflict and problem solving when we adopt more of a developmental perspective on marriage and when we consider those aspects of serious dating relationships that lead people to want to formalize them into marriage.

CONFLICT IN CONTEXT: AIMS FOR FUTURE RESEARCH

The main point of the previous section is not that conflict and how it is managed are negligible in producing variability in marital outcomes, but instead that it may be less important than our theories, research, and interventions tend to suggest. The evidence that leads to this conclusion—the cracks in the façade—are perhaps best understood as clues that suggest one of two strategies for future research in this area. First, it is possible that conflict is indeed important in marriage but existing research has not yet been conducted in a manner that can demonstrate this consistently. The strategy here would be to *refine* our approach to studying conflict so that its specific role is clarified. Second, we could assume that enough evidence has accumulated from reasonably sound studies to indicate that it is timely to expand the focus in research on determinants of marital outcomes beyond conflict. The strategy here would be to *revise* our approach to studying marriage in the interests of identifying variables and processes that strengthen our predictive power and that improve our interventions. We believe that the second strategy will be more fruitful in the long run, but we begin with a brief overview of ways that research on conflict might be enhanced.

Refining Our Understanding of Conflict in Marriage

A few changes that should improve research on marital conflict have already been noted, particularly in longitudinal research, including the use of samples of couples that are relatively homogenous in marital duration and marital quality (such as newlyweds), analyzing the severity of the problems couples encounter and discuss along with any problem-solving behaviors that they display, and studying these variables in relation to longitudinal trajectories of marital satisfaction. Several other directions for research are also evident.

Situational Triggers. First, little is known about the situations and circumstances that trigger marital conflict in the natural environment. Asking couples to monitor their disagreements and conflicts on a daily basis could prove informative (cf. Halford, Gravestock, Lowe, & Scheldt, 1992), and we may well find that the typical observational procedure—of asking spouses to identify jointly an area of disagreement and then working toward a mutually satisfying resolution—does not resemble the topography of conflicts as they arise and resolve in their day-to-day lives. In particular, self-monitoring studies will probably show that one partner or the other (but not both) will bring up some complaint about the other partner's behavior, whereas in the laboratory we assume that both people will want to talk about the same problem at the same time and will be more or less equally motivated to do so. Our unsystematic impression is that some wives, more than husbands, approach the laboratory setting as an opportunity to air their grievances, and husbands are often put on the defensive as a result. This may mean that we are getting a biased view of conflict with standard observational procedures. Studying conflict onset in the home will help to overcome this problem, as would separate laboratory tasks in which one partner is allowed to raise a problem he or she sees in the relationship (see Christensen & Shenk, 1991, for an example of this approach). Laboratory procedures are also not particularly useful in detecting how couples withdraw and disengage during or after their disagreements; again, appropriately designed diary studies could shed light on this (for examples of self-monitoring studies with married couples, see Huston & Vangelisti, 1991; Repetti, 1989; Thompson & Bolger, 1999).

Does Problem-Solving Solve Problems? A second direction for future research on conflict would be to take seriously the notion that effective problem-solving is beneficial to marriage, by examining the natural history and progression of important marital disagreements over time and their impact on the marriage. Thus, it is possible that the link between observed conflict behavior and marital outcomes is not stronger because the intervening steps are not well articulated. A key question here would be whether the quality of interactional process actually predicts problem resolution, which then foreshadows marital change, or whether interactional process serves to create a more encompassing affective climate within the marriage (e.g., "I feel understood and appreciated" vs. "I should not be treated this way") that in turn leads spouses to emphasize or deemphasize specific problems and, over time, promotes certain long-term outcomes. The assumption in the literature tends to be that the latter mechanism operates, although this is rarely tested directly. To clarify how problem-solving behavior might come to affect marital outcomes, data are needed that address not simply the trajectory of global marital satisfaction, but also temporal changes in the status of specific marital disagreements (cf. Storaasli & Markman, 1990).

Sequence and Patterning. Finally, it may be premature to discount the role of conflict and problem solving in marriage until better methods for quantifying sequence and patterning in observed interaction are developed and applied. Theorists from diverse orientations assume that interaction cannot be well understood without capturing the interdependence and patterning of the full range of behaviors that spouses display. However, the most widely used procedures, such as lag-sequential analysis and log-linear analysis, typically allow us to glimpse only a few codes at a time, over relatively few lags, and often require dropping couples who do not have sufficient numbers of specific codes. These methods also assume that the second behavior analyzed in a typical lag 1 or "tit for tat" sequence is actually a response to the preceding behavior, when in fact it may be unrelated to that behavior or refer to events that happened much earlier in the interaction. Moreover, with these methods relatively rare but highly influential behaviors—behaviors that change the tone and direction of the interaction—cannot be readily identified. (See Johnson & Bradbury, 1999, for a study in which topographical analysis of interactions showed that newlywed couples in which one spouse failed to respond to a specific emotional expression by the partner appeared to be at elevated risk for marital deterioration over 12 months.) These concerns, along with the assumption that base rates of codes are probably reasonably efficient in ordering couples on the basis of their interactional process, and the lack of standardized software for statistical analysis of sequences, are probably responsible for the general retreat from sequential analysis of marital interaction data over the past several years. Yet returning to the basic question of how behavioral interdependence can be extracted and quantified may yield stronger evidence for an association between conflict and marital outcomes.

Revising our Understanding of Conflict in Marriage

If we adopt the view that conflict and marital problem-solving behavior can, at best, account for a relatively small proportion of the variability in eventual marital outcomes, then the question of what other factors should be considered—either on their own or, more plausibly, in conjunction with problem-solving behavior—must be confronted. Even if higher estimates of the association between conflict and marital outcomes emerge, there will be a need to understand them in relation to other interactional processes and other factors that impinge on marriage. The fact that many reliable, albeit somewhat weak and inconsistent, links between problem-solving behaviors and marital outcome have been obtained suggests that the strength of these links is being moderated by factors as yet unidentified.

Social Support. In line with this argument, we have already alluded to the notion that conflict may become consequential for marital outcomes particularly after positive interactional aspects of the relationship have decayed or when these positive features are already weak. Positive behavior in marriage has been largely overlooked, probably because early studies showed that positive behaviors during problem-solving discussions did little to discriminate happy and unhappy couples. However, findings by Huston and Chorost (1994) indicate that the longitudinal association between negative behavior (as assessed not in observed problem-solving discussions but in a daily telephone checkup with spouses) is moderated by spouses' expressions of affection, and there has long been speculation that positive behaviors outside of conflict, most notably in the domain of social support, are important contributors to satisfaction in marriage (e.g., Barker & Lemle, 1984; Coyne

& DeLongis, 1986). Focusing here has intuitive appeal, in part because the majority of young couples in our samples are now in dual-career marriages, which places a premium on how spouses help each other handle problems that arise outside of marriage, and in part because the opportunities for a spouse to respond (or fail to respond) empathically to the daily stresses and strains encountered his or her partner would seem to be ubiquitous.

There has been an upsurge of interest in social support in marriage (e.g., Bodenmann, 1997; Carels & Baucom, 1999; Katz, Beach, Smith, & Myers, 1997) and particularly in studying social support using observational methods (e.g., Cutrona, 1996; Saitzyk, Floyd, & Kroll, 1997). In our own work we find that marital outcomes over 24 months are predicted by the positive and negative behaviors spouses display, as newlyweds, when each spouse is instructed to discuss (in two separate interactions) something that they would like to change about themselves (Pasch & Bradbury, 1998). (Recent stressful events were considered as a prompt for these discussions, but pilot testing revealed that spouses differed considerably in the events they encountered). The tenor of these interactions is rather different from that of problem-solving discussions, yet couples experiencing marital distress after 2 years of marriage were observed initially to display higher levels of negative behavior and lower levels of positive behavior in this task relative to couples going on to have either satisfying or highly satisfying marriages. (These results tend to be stronger for wives, but they are in the expected direction for husbands. They also tend to be stronger for the behaviors of the partner in the role of offering support than the person receiving it.) Moreover, there was evidence that (a) wives' positive and negative support behaviors predicted marital outcomes even after controlling for husbands' and wives' negative affect in a standard problem-solving discussion, which displayed an association with marital outcomes that was quite similar to that obtained with the social support codes, and (b) wives' negative affect in the problem-solving discussion interacted with wives' negative helper behavior and husbands' negative helpee behavior to predict marital outcomes. Consistent with speculation that conflict may be more consequential when positive behavioral features of the relationship are compromised, these interactions demonstrated that the association between wives' negative affect during marital conflict and marital outcomes was stronger when there were higher levels of negativity by husbands and wives during discussion of a personal issue that the husband wanted to change.

What are the implications of these data for understanding conflict and the course of marriage? In contrast to the large literature on marital interaction, which assumes that it is primarily the management of conflict that determines how marriages change and deteriorate, these data indicate that the behaviors spouses display in a rather different context—one focusing on the support and understanding that one spouse can offer to the partner, and on personal concerns that arise explicitly outside the domain of marital problems—can also prove informative about marital development. In fact, negative behaviors displayed in the problem-solving task and those displayed in the social support task (which correlated in the .30 to .40 range) were predictive of marital deterioration in much the same way. This may mean that the information yielded by marital problem-solving discussions is not unique to that context, and that evidence of maladaptive communication may emerge regardless of which particular vantage point one takes in studying marital interaction. Marital disruption might arise not solely from mismanagement of conflict but from some more basic and pervasive communicative failure, perhaps in the ability to understand, appreciate, and respond appropriately to the partner's point of view. The notion that the marriages of some couples may be at risk for failure because they tend to transform affectively significant interpersonal encounters into adversarial exchanges suggests that we should strive to understand the full range of maladaptive interpersonal exchanges in marriage, not solely those that arise when marital problems are being discussed.

Spousal Characteristics. A surprising assumption in models of marriage that emphasize interpersonal behavior as a key cause of marital outcomes is that spousal characteristics are relatively uninformative. In commenting on the large longitudinal study by Kelly and Conley (1987), which demonstrated that marital incompatibility over 45 years was associated with acquaintance-rated neuroticism and impulsivity during courtship, Gottman (1994, p. 87) observed: "What is the advice that results from the prediction that neurotic people have unstable marriages? Is it, 'Don't marry a neurotic'? Or is it, 'First cure your neurosis and then get married?' It seems that research based on an individual psychopathology model, particularly one that is global or not specific, has little to say about the possible mechanisms that lead to marital dissolution."

An alternative perspective, one prompted in part by meta-analytic evidence that effect sizes relating neuroticism to marital quality and marital dissolution are on par with those for negative behavior (on the order of -.15 over six studies on marital quality and -.20 over six studies on marital dissolution; see Karney & Bradbury, 1995), is that individual characteristics such as neuroticism contribute to the general level of satisfaction in a marriage whereas negative behavior in marital interaction contributes to changes in satisfaction. Two studies, examining newlywed couples over 4 years (Karney & Bradbury, 1997) and parents of first-born sons from when they were 10 to 60 months of age (Belsky & Hsieh, 1998), support this conception well. Thus, in one sense, Gottman (1994) appears to be correct in stating that neuroticism does not contribute directly to a mechanism of marital deterioration, yet a personality style marked by negativity and anxiety may set the level or starting point at which a behavioral mechanism operates. Although Karney and Bradbury (1997) did not find a significant interaction between neuroticism and problem-solving behavior in the prediction of marital outcomes, perhaps owing to a relatively small sample size, an implication of this view is that conflict is more influential in marriage when spouses are prone to experiencing negative emotions.

Other studies also suggest that consideration of individual characteristics will strengthen our understanding of marriage and alter how we think about conflict. Intergenerational effects linking parental divorce to offspring divorce are well established (e.g., Bumpass, Martin, & Sweet, 1991), and Amato (1996) presented data to indicate that problematic interpersonal behaviors in the offspring's marriage (e.g., domineering, angry, jealous, critical behaviors) mediate this link, more so than socioeconomic variables and attitudes about divorce. Together with Sanders, Halford, and Behrens' (1999) study showing that observed problem-solving behavior in couples planning marriage is significantly worse when the wife comes from a divorced family, there is mounting evidence to suggest that marital conflict is, in part, a vehicle by which individual risk factors that are present prior to marriage become manifest in eventual marital dysfunction. Of course, individual risk probably extends beyond parental divorce to include such factors as personal history of psychopathology (which, in the case of affective disorders, lowers age at marriage and raises the likelihood of marital dissatisfaction; see Gotlib, Lewinsohn, & Seeley, 1998) and attachment history (which is related to rejecting behaviors in marital problem-solving discussions; see Kobak & Hazan, 1991). It seems plausible that these individual risk factors operate on marital outcomes through other behavioral mechanisms as well.

The more general point here is that heavy emphasis on conflict as the generative mechanism in marital dysfunction may lead us to overlook how conflict (and other interpersonal behaviors) might be part of a more encompassing mechanism, a mechanism that appears to include the personal risk factors or enduring vulnerabilities that spouses bring to marriage. Recognizing this possibility suggests that efforts to prevent adverse marital outcomes could be enhanced by delineating fully the individual characteristics that increase risk for marital problems, possibly developing interventions specifically for at-risk couples, and targeting interventions to this population. Along these lines, we recently found that the predictors of marital instability over the first 5 years of marriage appear to differ from the predictors of marital quality, such that marital dissolution is tied more closely to individual risk factors whereas marital quality is a function of observed problem-solving behavior (Rogge, Bradbury, Hahlweg, Engl, & Thurmaier, 1999). Hostile personality traits and negative affectivity in particular are implicated in the prediction of marital dissolution, which replicates and refines prior data showing that physical aggression in marriage foreshadowed marital dissolution in newlyweds whereas observed anger and contempt predicted marital quality in the couples that remained intact over 4 years (Rogge & Bradbury, 1999b). This suggests that different approaches may be needed for the prevention of marital distress and divorce, and that research on individual characteristics can supplement research on marital interaction to inform prevention efforts.

Ecological Niches. The impression one gets in reading the literature on marital interaction is that the central struggle in marriage is between the competing needs and goals of the two spouses, and that if couples can manage this well they increase their chances of a satisfying relationship. There is perhaps a certain truth to this, but it may be at least as productive to see this struggle partly as an outgrowth of the life events, family constellation, socioeconomic standing, and stressful circumstances that define a couples' ecological niche. Stated more strongly, it may be at least as important to examine the struggle that exists between the couple (or the family more generally) and the environment they inhabit as it is to examine the interpersonal struggles that are the focus of much of our work. Some of the variability in marital distress might be the result of couples not having enough resources of whatever kind—personal, interpersonal, financial—to manage or improve the environment in which they find themselves. To be sure, spouses and couples are not innocent victims of the world to which they are exposed (see Davila, Bradbury, Cohan, & Tochluk, 1997), and it is important to not overlook the active role that people play in determining the ecological niches they occupy. Nevertheless, a shift in the way we think about marriage—from conceiving spouses not as natural adversaries who must be taught to manage their differing needs and preferences but as a team, with assets and liabilities, that must adapt to a complex set of tasks and situations in order to sustain their marriage and family—may lead us to improve models of how marriages fail and to enhance the interventions that can be devised to modify marital outcomes.

Such a shift is supported by a solid body of research. For example, using a diary procedure with air traffic controllers and their wives, Repetti (1989) showed that wives' social support can decrease husbands' anger in the home following workdays marked by high levels of air traffic volume and poor visibility. Although it is possible that some third variable accounts for this correlation, it is difficult to argue that it is the marital behavior that drives the environmental variables with data such as these. In an observational study of white- and blue-collar workers, Krokoff, Gottman, and Roy (1988) found that level of negativity is associated with occupational status. Cohan and Bradbury (1997), in a study of newlyweds, showed that husbands reporting more life events displayed more anger and less sadness in a problem-solving discussion, whereas wives reporting more life events were less positive and more negative in their verbal behaviors. And, finally, in a longitudinal study conducted over 3 years with a predominantly rural sample, Conger, Rueter, and Elder (1999) found that economic pressure predicts observed marital conflict, which in turn predicts marital distress.

Thus, although there are important exceptions to this theme (e.g., McGonagle et al., 1992, found no association between number of life events and frequency of marital disagreements), evidence from diverse sources indicates that the behaviors spouses display in marital interaction, and particularly when attempting to resolve marital difficulties, are tied reliably to aspects of their ecological niche. This indicates that analysis of conflict behavior without reference to these contextual variables provides an incomplete understanding of that behavior, and we might speculate that the associations observed in these studies probably extend to other forms of marital behavior as well, such as social support. Although preventive interventions that focus strongly on changing interpersonal behaviors are quite efficient in that they can attend to common elements across many marriages (i.e., disagreements and how they are discussed) rather than features that will tend to be unique (e.g., specific life events and stressors), it may be that there is a core set of effective strategies that can be devised to help couples protect the interior of their marriage from the stressors that impinge on them. Perhaps even informing couples that external stressors can affect the way they deal with their marital problems will encourage them to attribute their difficulties to factors outside their marriage, and to respond less with criticism or anger and more with compassion and understanding when confronting marital disagreements. Some couples may make these attributions naturally, and this may be moderating the effects of problem-solving behavior on marital outcomes.

CONCLUSION

The idea that how couples manage marital conflict causes their marital outcomes, and the corollary that modification of conflict management skills can prevent marital distress and dissolution, is elegant in its simplicity and broad in its impact on the field. However, the data reviewed in this chapter suggest that these assumptions may oversimplify the determinants of marital dysfunction and, as a result, may limit unduly the interventions devised for helping couples.

We observed that behavioral data collected outside the domain of marital problem solving, involving the manner in which spouses respond when the partner talks about an important personal concern, yields findings similar to those obtained with conflict behavior. This indicates that negativity foreshadowing the onset of marital deterioration can arise even in the absence of overt marital conflict, and hence that it may be a deficit more basic than poor management of conflict (e.g., a failure to connect emotionally with the partner, or to modify one's own behavior in the face of the partner's needs and requests) that sets a marriage on a difficult path.

However, in the same way that a strong focus on conflict probably limits the scope of research and practice, so too are statements about why marriages succeed and fail likely to be limited by a strong focus on interaction of any kind. In support of this point we noted that the characteristics and histories of individual spouses—including, for example, history of parental divorce and neurotic personality style—appear to increase the likelihood of maladaptive behavior in marriage and marital dysfunction, and perhaps even the ease with which they can be treated with preventive interventions. Further justification for expanding our basic research and interventions beyond those focusing primarily on interaction comes from research showing that the behaviors spouses exchange appear to be linked to their life events and circumstances.

Conflict may well be an important part of the mechanism by which happy marriages become distressed, and it may be centrally involved in the deterioration of marriages that are already failing. But conflict itself may not be a unique marker for poor marital communication, and communication appears to be rooted in the enduring traits and experiences that spouses would bring to any marriage and in the ecological niche in which their marriage exists. The main point of this chapter is to argue that models of marriage will yield better explanations, and models of intervention will yield better outcomes, to the extent that conflict is seen as one link in a longer chain of variables by which marriages that are initially rewarding become a source of pain and despair.

ACKNOWLEDGMENTS

Preparation of this chapter was supported by grants from the John Templeton Foundation and the National Institutes of Health.

REFERENCES

Amato, P. R. (1996). Explaining the intergenerational transmission of divorce. *Journal of Marriage and the Family, 58,* 628-640.

Barker, C., & Lemle, R. (1984). The helping process in couples. *American Journal of Community Psychology, 12,* 321-336.

Belsky, J., & Hsieh, K.-H. (1998). Patterns of marital change during the early childhood years: Parent personality, coparenting, and division-of-labor correlates. *Journal of Family Psychology, 12,* 511-528.

Betz, N. E. (1987). Use of discriminant analysis in counseling psychology research. *Journal of Counseling Psychology, 34,* 393-403.

Bodenmann, G. (1997). Dyadic coping: A systemic-transactional view of stress and coping among couples: Theory and empirical findings. *European Review of Applied Psychology, 47,* 137-141.

Bradbury, T. N. (1994). Unintended effects of marital research on marital relationships. *Journal of Family Psychology, 8,* 187-201.

Bradbury, T. N. (in press). Research on relationships as a prelude to action. *Journal of Social and Personal Relationships.*

Bradbury, T. N., Campbell, S. M., & Fincham, F. D. (1995). Longitudinal and behavioral analysis of masculinity and femininity in marriage. *Journal of Personality and Social Psychology, 68,* 328-341.

Bradbury, T. N., Cohan, C. L., & Karney, B. R. (1998). Optimizing longitudinal research for understanding and preventing marital dysfunction. In T. N. Bradbury (Ed.), *The developmental course of marital dysfunction* (pp. 279-311). New York: Cambridge University Press.

Bradbury, T. N., Johnson, M. D., Lawrence, E. E., & Rogge, R. D. (1998). Using basic research to craft effective interventions for marital dysfunction. In D. K. Routh & R. J. De Rubeis (Eds.), *The science of clinical psychology: Accomplishments and future directions* (pp. 265-278). Washington, DC: American Psychological Association.

Bradbury, T. N., & Karney, B. R. (1993). Longitudinal study of marital interaction and dysfunction: Review and analysis. *Clinical Psychology Review, 13,* 15-27.

Bradbury, T. N., Thurmaier, F., Engl, J., Karney, B. R., Hahlweg, K., & Markman, H. (1998, July). *Effects of a premarital intervention on 5-year longitudinal change in marital interaction and satisfaction.* World Congress of Behavioral and Cognitive Therapies, Acapulco, Mexico.

Buehlman, K. T., Gottman, J. M., & Katz, L. F. (1992). How a couple views their past predicts their future: Predicting divorce from an oral history interview. *Journal of Family Psychology, 5,* 295-318.

Bumpass, L. L., Martin, T. C., & Sweet, J. A. (1991). The impact of family background and early marital factors on marital disruption. *Journal of Family Issues, 12,* 22-42.

Carels, R. A., & Baucom, D. H. (1999). Support in marriage: Factors associated with on-line perceptions of support helpfulness. *Journal of Family Psychology, 13,* 131-144.

Christensen, A., & Shenk, J. L. (1991). Communication, conflict, and psychological distance in nondistressed, clinic, and divorcing couples. *Journal of Consulting and Clinical Psychology, 59,* 458-463.

Christensen, A., & Walczynski, P. T. (1997). Conflict and satisfaction in couples. In R. J. Sternberg & M. Hojjat (Eds.), *Satisfaction in close relationships* (pp. 249-274). New York: Guilford.

Cohan, C. L., & Bradbury, T. N. (1997). Negative life events, marital interaction, and the longitudinal course of newlywed marriage. *Journal of Personality and Social Psychology, 73,* 114-128.

Conger, R. D., Rueter, M. A., & Elder, G. H., Jr. (1999). Couple resilience to economic pressure. *Journal of Personality and Social Psychology, 76,* 54-71.

Coyne, J. C., & DeLongis, A. (1986). Going beyond social support: The role of social relationships in adaptation. *Journal of Consulting and Clinical Psychology, 54,* 454-460.

Cutrona, C. (1996). *Social support in couples.* Thousand Oaks, CA: Sage.

Davila, J., Bradbury, T. N., Cohan, C. L., & Tochluk, S. (1997). Marital functioning and depressive symptoms: Evidence for a stress generation model. *Journal of Personality and Social Psychology, 73,* 849-861.

Fincham, F. D., & Beach, S. R. H. (1999). Conflict in marriage: Implications for working with couples. *Annual Review of Psychology, 50,* 47-77.

Fincham, F. D., Bradbury, T. N., & Grych, J. H. (1990). Conflict in close relationships: The role of intrapersonal phenomena. In S. Graham & V. S. Folkes (Eds.), *Attribution theory: Applications to achievement, mental health, and interpersonal conflict* (pp. 161-184). Hillsdale, NJ: Lawrence Erlbaum Associates.

Floyd, F. J., Markman, H. J., Kelly, S., Blumberg, S. L., & Stanley, S. M. (1995). Preventive intervention and relationship enhancement. In N. S. Jacobson & A. S. Gurman (Eds.), *Clinical handbook of couple therapy* (pp. 212-226). New York: Guilford.

Foster, D. A., Caplan, R. D., & Howe, G. W. (1997). Representativeness of observed couple interaction: Couples can tell, and it does make a difference. *Psychological Assessment, 9,* 285-294.

Gill, D. S., Christensen, A., & Fincham, F. D. (1999). Predicting marital satisfaction from behavior: Do all roads really lead to Rome? *Personal Relationships, 6,* 369-387.

Gotlib, I. H., Lewinsohn, P. M., & Seeley, J. R. (1998). Consequences of depression during adolescence: Marital status and marital functioning in early adulthood. *Journal of Abnormal Psychology, 107,* 686-690.

Gottman, J. M. (1979). *Marital interaction: Experimental investigations.* New York: Academic.

Gottman, J. M. (1994). *What predicts divorce?* Hillsdale, NJ: Lawrence Erlbaum Associates.

Gottman, J. M., Coan, J., Carrere, S., & Swanson, C. (1998). Predicting marital happiness and stability from newlywed interactions. *Journal of Marriage and the Family, 60,* 5-22.

Gottman, J. M., & Krokoff, L. J. (1989). Marital interaction and satisfaction: A longitudinal view. *Journal of Consulting and Clinical Psychology, 57,* 42-52.

Gottman, J. M., Swanson, C., & Murray, J. (1999). The mathematics of marital conflict: Dynamic mathematical nonlinear modeling of newlywed marital interaction. *Journal of Family Psychology, 13,* 3-19.

Hahlweg, K., Markman, H. J., Thurmaier, F., Engl, J., & Eckert, V. (1998). Prevention of marital distress: Results of a German prospective longitudinal study. *Journal of Family Psychology, 12,* 543-556.

Hahlweg, K., Reisner, L., Kohli, G., Vollmer, M., Schindler, L., & Revenstorf, D. (1984). Development and validity of a new system to analyze interpersonal communication: The KPI. In K. Hahlweg & N. S. Jacobson (Eds.), *Marital interaction: Analysis and modification* (pp. 182-198). New York: Guilford.

Hahlweg, K., Thurmaier, F., Engl, J., Eckert, V., & Markman, H. J. (1998). Prevention of marital distress in Germany. In K. Hahlweg, D. H. Baucom, R. Bastine, & H. J. Markman (Eds.), *Prediction and prevention of marital distress and divorce* (pp. 191-216). Stuttgart: Kohlhammer.

Halford, W. K., Gravestock, F. M., Lowe, R., & Scheldt, S. (1992). Toward a behavioral ecology of stressful marital interactions. *Behavioral Assessment, 14,* 199-217.

Huston, T. L., & Chorost, A. F. (1994). Behavioral buffers on the effect of negativity on marital satisfaction: A longitudinal study. *Personal Relationships, 1,* 223-239.

Huston, T. L., & Vangelisti, A. L. (1991). Socioemotional behavior and satisfaction in marital relationships: A longitudinal study. *Journal of Personality and Social Psychology, 61,* 721-733.

Jacobson, N. S., & Holtzworth-Munroe, A. (1986). Marital therapy: A social learning-cognitive perspective. In N. S. Jacobson & A. S. Gurman (Eds.), *Clinical handbook of marital therapy* (pp. 29-70). New York: Guilford.

Johnson, M. D. (1999). *Behavioral antecedents of marital dysfunction.* Unpublished dissertation, University of California, Los Angeles.

Johnson, M. D., & Bradbury, T. N. (1999). Marital satisfaction and topographical assessment of marital interaction: A longitudinal analysis of newlywed couples. *Personal Relationships, 6,* 19-40.

Karney, B. R., & Bradbury, T. N. (1995). The longitudinal course of marital quality and stability: A review of theory, method, and research. *Psychological Bulletin, 118,* 3-34.

Karney, B. R., & Bradbury, T. N. (1997). Neuroticism, marital interaction, and the trajectory of marital satisfaction. *Journal of Personality and Social Psychology, 72,* 1075-1092.

Katz, J., Beach, S. R. H., Smith, D. A., & Myers, L. B. (1997). Personality and the marital context: The case for interactive conceptualizations of needs for spousal support. In G. R. Pierce & B. Lakey (Eds.), *Sourcebook of social support and personality* (pp. 257-278). New York: Plenum.

Kelly, E. L., & Conley, J. J. (1987). Personality and compatibility: A prospective analysis of marital stability and marital satisfaction. *Journal of Personality and Social Psychology, 52,* 27-40.

Kobak, R. R., & Hazan, C. (1991). Attachment in marriage: Effects of security and accuracy in working models. *Journal of Personality and Social Psychology, 60,* 861-869.

Koerner, K., & Jacobson, N. S. (1994). Emotion and behavioral couple therapy. In S. M. Johnson & L. S. Greenberg (Eds.), *The heart of the matter: Perspectives on emotion in marital therapy* (pp. 207-226). New York: Brunner/Mazel.

Krokoff, L. J., Gottman, J. M., & Roy, A. K. (1988). Blue-collar and white-collar marital interaction and communication orientation. *Journal of Social and Personal Relationships, 5,* 201-221.

Kurdek, L. A. (1998). The nature and predictors of the trajectory of change in marital quality over the first 4 years of marriage for first-married husbands and wives. *Journal of Family Psychology, 12,* 494-510.

Lewin, K. (1948). *Resolving social conflicts: Selected papers on group dynamics.* New York: Harper & Row.

Locke, H. J., & Wallace, K. M. (1959). Short marital adjustment prediction tests: Their reliability and validity. *Marriage and Family Living, 21,* 251-255.

McGonagle, K. A., Kessler, R. C., & Schilling, E. A. (1992). The frequency and determinants of marital disagreements in a community sample. *Journal of Social and Personal Relationships, 9,* 507-524.

Ozer, D. J. (1985). Correlation and the coefficient of determination. *Psychological Bulletin, 97,* 307-315.

Pasch, L. A., & Bradbury, T. N. (1998). Social support, conflict, and the development of marital distress. *Journal of Consulting and Clinical Psychology, 66,* 219-230.

Raush, H. L., Barry, W. A., Hertel, R. K., & Swain, M. A. (1974). *Communication, conflict and marriage.* San Francisco: Jossey-Bass.

Repetti, R. (1989). Effects of daily workload on subsequent behavior during marital interaction: The roles of social withdrawal and spouse support. *Journal of Personality and Social Psychology, 57,* 651-659.

Rogge, R. D., & Bradbury, T. N. (1999a). Recent advances in the prediction of marital outcomes. In R. Berger & M. T. Hannah (Eds.), *Preventive approaches in couples therapy* (pp. 331-360). New York: Brunner/Mazel.

Rogge, R. D., & Bradbury, T. N. (1999b). Till violence does us part: The differing roles of communication and aggression in predicting adverse marital outcomes. *Journal of Consulting and Clinical Psychology, 67,* 340-351.

Rogge, R. D., Bradbury, T. N., Hahlweg, K., Engl, J., & Thurmaier, F. (1999). *Prediction of marital satisfaction and dissolution over five years: Refining the two-factor hypothesis.* Manuscript submitted for publication.

Saitzyk, A. R., Floyd, F. J., & Kroll, A. B. (1997). Sequential analysis of autonomy-interdependence and affiliation-disaffiliation in couples' social support interactions. *Personal Relationships, 4,* 341-360.

Sanders, M. R., Halford, W. K., & Behrens, B. C. (1999). Parental divorce and premarital couple communication. *Journal of Family Psychology, 13,* 60-74.

Smith, D. A., Vivian, D., & O'Leary, K. D. (1990). Longitudinal prediction of marital discord from premarital expressions of affect. *Journal of Consulting and Clinical Psychology, 58,* 790-798.

Stanley, S. M., Markman, H. J., St. Peters, M., & Leber, B. D. (1995). Strengthening marriages and preventing divorce: New directions in prevention research. *Family Relations, 44,* 392-401.

Storaasli, R. D., & Markman, H. J. (1990). Relationship problems in the early stages of marriage: A longitudinal investigation. *Journal of Family Psychology, 4,* 80-98.

Surra, C. A., & Hughes, D. K. (1997). Commitment processes in accounts of the development of premarital relationships. *Journal of Marriage and the Family, 59,* 5-21.

Thompson, A., & Bolger, N. (1999). Emotional transmission in couples under stress. *Journal of Marriage and the Family, 61,* 38-48.

Weiss, R. L., & Heyman, R. E. (1997). A clinical-research overview of couples interactions. In W. K. Halford & H. J. Markman (Eds.), *Clinical handbook of marriage and couples interventions* (pp. 13-41). New York: Wiley.

Williams, L., & Jurich, J. (1995). Predicting marital success after five years: Assessing the predictive validity of the FOCCUS. *Journal of Marital and Family Therapy, 21,* 141-153.

Woody, E. Z., & Costanzo, P. R. (1990). Does marital agony precede marital ecstasy? A comment on Gottman and Krokoff's "Marital interaction and satisfaction: A longitudinal view." *Journal of Consulting and Clinical Psychology, 58,* 499-501.

6

Expanding the Study of Dyadic Conflict: The Potential Role of Self-Evaluation Maintenance Processes

Steven R. H. Beach

University of Georgia

Evidence documenting the importance of marital conflict continues to accumulate. For example, marital conflict has profound implications for individual well being (Coyne & Downey, 1991; O'Leary & Smith, 1991), and the link with depression is increasingly well established (Beach, 2000). Similarly, associations have been noted for physical and psychological abuse of partners (e.g., O'Leary, Malone, & Tyree, 1994). Particularly impressive has been the growth in information about the potential impact of marital conflict on physical health and family health.

Although married individuals are healthier on average than the unmarried (House, Landisn, & Umberson, 1988), marital conflict is associated with poorer health (Burman & Margolin, 1992; Kiecolt-Glazer et al., 1988). Marital conflict has also been tied to specific illnesses such as cancer, cardiac disease, and chronic pain (see Schmaling & Sher, 1997). Marital interaction studies suggest possible mechanisms that may account for these links by showing that hostile behaviors during conflict relate to alterations in immunological (Kiecolt-Glazer et al., 1993, 1997), endocrine (Kielcolt-Glaser et al., 1997; Malarkey, Kielcott-Glaser, Pearl, & Glaser, 1994), and cardiovascular (Ewart, Taylor, Kraemer, & Agras, 1991) functioning. Although consequential for both husbands and wives, marital conflict has more pronounced health consequences for wives (Kiecolt-Glaser et al., 1993, 1996, 1997; Malarkey et al., 1994). Thus, marital conflict has been linked to several facets of health, and this remains a vital area of research.

Marital conflict is also associated with important family outcomes, including poorer parenting (see Erel & Burman, 1995), poorer child adjustment (see Grych & Fincham, 1990), problematic attachment to parents (e.g., Owen & Cox, 1997), increased likelihood of parent child conflict (e.g., Margolin, Christensen, & John, 1996), and conflict between siblings (e.g., Brody, Stoneman, & McCoy, 1994). When manipulated experimentally, marital conflict also increases subsequent parent son conflict (Jouriles & Farris, 1992). Aspects of marital conflict that have a particularly negative influence on children include more frequent, intense, physical, unresolved, child-related conflicts and conflicts attributed to the child's behavior (see Cummings, Goeke-Morey, Papp, chap. 9, this volume; Fincham & Osborne, 1993).

DISAPPOINTMENT AND DISENCHANTMENT WITH A RESTRICTED PARADIGM

Given these compelling and important sequelae, it is small wonder that the study of marital conflict has engaged the attention of a large number of researchers over the past 25 years (see Fincham & Beach, 1999, for a review). Prominent in this research effort have been behavioral marital therapy researchers who have focused on providing a careful description of marital conflict behavior in anticipation of finding the pivotal elements that lead to marital dissolution or marital distress. As Bradbury, Rogge, and Lawrence (chap. 5, this volume) noted, however, this once-bright ambition now appears somewhat tarnished. The assumptions that occasioned the enthusiasm of the field no longer seem tenable. Instead, it seems we are now in need of a substantial change in direction if we are to continue to make progress. After briefly considering the need for a broader conceptualization of marital conflict, I review the case for viewing self-processes as a potentially important addition to our conceptual armamentarium, and as an important way to move forward in our understanding of marital conflict resolution.

Where Did the Study of Marital Conflict Go Wrong?

Perhaps surprisingly, the field of behavioral marital therapy (BMT) has a strong history of being theory focused (see Beach & Fincham, 2000). Among other influences (e.g., Blau, 1964; Homans, 1961), early BMT researchers cited Thibaut and Kelley's (1959) "The Social Psychology of Groups," and awareness of Thibaut and Kelley's theoretical framework was ubiquitous. Nearly all early, influential behavioral marital texts cited Thibaut and Kelley's (1959) and/or Kelley's (1979) work (e.g., Gottman, Notarius, Gonso, & Marman, 1976; Jacobson & Margolin, 1979; Stuart, 1980).

However, in the mid 1970s behavioral researchers became disenchanted with social psychological theory as an avenue for better understanding marital distress. This disenchantment appears to have been in response to research findings designed to test key aspects of interdependence theory. In particular, performance on prisoner dilemma games failed to discriminate distressed and nondistressed couples (e.g., Speer, 1972), but observed interaction did (e.g., Birchler, Weiss, & Vincent, 1975). These studies seemed to call into question the utility of methods drawn from social psychology, and to highlight the need for new methods to study patterns of interaction. In particular, the developments seemed to call for greater attention to direct observation of the behavior that transpired between partners during interaction episodes.

The direct study of behavioral differences in interaction also fit well with the behavioral approach of "task analysis," in which groups were contrasted to identify salient differences in behavior that were associated with better and worse outcomes. Thus, the new observational methods fit well with the prevailing behavioral zeitgeist. Thus, by the mid- to late 1970s the theoretical underpinnings of BMT were under siege by prominent behavioral marital researchers. In the place of theory it was suggested that the field adopt, at least temporarily, a broad descriptive agenda. In particular, it was proposed that researchers focus on observing and describing the key differences between the interactions of distressed and nondistressed couples (for an elaboration of this discussion, see Beach & Fincham, in press).

THREE KEY ASSUMPTIONS

Several assumptions were made, either explicitly or tacitly, which made sensible this disavowal of theory and its replacement with an observational, descriptive agenda. First, an argument had to be made that, for all couples, *conflict is inevitable*. This assumption has been made explicit in many treatment and prevention programs for marital distress, and may predate the behavioral movement. As noted by Gottman et al. (1976), both distressed and nondistressed couples report similar types of problems, merely with different severity. Or, as Markman, Stanley, & Blumberg (1994, p. 1) noted more pointedly, "Unfortunately, conflict is inevitable - it can't be avoided." A direct implication of this position is that because conflict will occur in all relationships, the major difference between couples that do better and worse must be in how they resolve that conflict. As Markman et al. (1994, p. 13) pointed out, "One of the most powerful things you can do to protect your marriage is learn constructive ways to handle conflict, differences, and disagreement." Interestingly, even as he helped set the broad descriptive agenda of the field, Gottman et al. (1976, p. XI) noted that "it has by no means been demonstrated that behavior during conflict resolution situations is what really counts in creating a satisfying marriage." As Bradbury et al. (chap. 5, this volume) indicated, this observation would prove to be prescient.

Second, as an extension of the first assumption, another assumption was made that *verbal problem-solving situations are central*. That is, perhaps because problems in the verbal and nonverbal behavior of distressed couples were so apparent during the couple's verbal problem-solving interactions, the full attention of the field was directed to verbal problem-solving situations as the appropriate focus of observation. Despite considerable discussion of the potential importance of other domains of marital interaction such as support and companionship (e.g., Weiss, 1978), these other potential contributors to positive or negative feelings in the relationship were relegated to a secondary status in the unfolding observational paradigm. Implicit in the argument for a focus on observation of couples during problem solving was the assumption that the way to deal with potential conflicts was to talk about them. Alternatively stated, this assumption implied that for potential conflicts of interest to be resolved adequately they must be articulated and settled in a clear and forthright manner. As subsequent work by Rusbult (1993) suggested, the focus on talking things out probably reflects a premature closure of this important topic. As I argue later, there may be many efficacious responses to potential conflict, and talking about the source of conflict does not exhaust the possibilities.

Finally, the method selected for examining conflict behavior was the behavioral task analysis. In particular, in line with the standard practice of the time, "competent" marital behavior in the form of interactions between nondistressed spouses was contrasted with "incompetent" behavior in the form of interactions between distressed spouses. This approach was designed to identify potentially trainable components that could differentiate the high-functioning group from the low-functioning group. A successful task analysis would provide clues regarding the way the high-functioning group managed to successfully solve problems that the other group failed to solve. Although it was successful in producing notable successes in the behavioral area, this approach carries with it the assumption that *correlation implies causation.*[1] That is, because one starts with cross-sectional differences between distressed and nondistressed couples, the approach requires the assumption that differences between distressed and nondistressed couples will provide clues about the causes of distress.

THE ACCUMULATION OF CONTRARY EVIDENCE

As is indicated by Bradbury et al. (chap. 5, this volume) and elsewhere (Fincham & Beach, 1999), the three assumptions that guided the observational research agenda no longer seem as plausible as they once did. Overt disagreement is not very frequent in a community sample (McGonagle, Kessler, & Schiling, 1992), and much of it may be accounted for by relatively intractable disagreements over division of labor (Kluwer, Heesink, & Van De Vliert, 1997). Some problems are simply harder to resolve than others, and thus may be more predictive of marital dissolution (Amato & Rogers, 1997). And, despite 25 years of research on marital conflict and a relatively clear picture of its topography, the evidence that cross-sectional differences between distressed and nondistressed couples can serve as predictors of decline in marital satisfaction remains in doubt (Fincham & Beach, 1999). In particular, there have been a series of reported "reversal effects" in the longitudinal prediction literature (see Bradbury et al., chap. 5, this volume; Fincham & Beach, 1999; Karney & Bradbury, 1995), and these effects do not appear to be artifactual. Unfortunately, reversal effects also do not appear to be reliable across coding systems or analytic strategies (or even within coding systems). Given the collapse of the initial assumptions that guided behavioral research on marital conflict, the atheoretical search for longitudinal predictors of discord and marital dissolution has increasingly taken

---

[1] Although beyond the scope of this chapter, it is interesting to note that the error in this line of research may not have been in the adoption of classical task analysis as a guiding, heuristic framework. This approach has proven to be quite fruitful in a number of contexts. It seems more likely that the error was in the use of nondistressed couples as the "competent" comparison group. Nondistressed couples may be facing sufficiently different circumstances that such couples' behavior provides little guidance as to what constitutes a "good" response to highly distressing conflict situations.

the appearance of a fishing expedition. Accordingly, the chances that an atheoretical approach will result in a cumulative science of marital conflict seems increasingly slim.

DEFINING CONFLICT

Before proposing ways in which to enhance or repair the study of marital conflict, it is important to state as clearly as possible the construct we hope to understand. First, it should be noted that not all conflicts are overt. Conflict can go undetected by one of the partners and have minimal impact on them. Indeed, premaritally and early in marriage, self-reported conflict is unrelated to satisfaction (Bradbury, Cohan, & Karney, 1998; Kelly, Huston, & Cate, 1985), and partners may often make virtues out of faults (Holmes & Murray, 1996), rendering potential sources of conflict moot. This observation is critical because it highlights the inadequacy of behavior during forced problem solving as the sole criterion measure of conflict behavior.

Second, "perceived conflict of interest", "incompatible goals, wishes, expectations", and "perceived interference with goal directed behavior" provide the starting point for the analysis of conflict (see Bradbury et al, chap. 5, this volume). However, not all such potential conflicts of interest result in actual conflict. Rather, some are instead successfully transformed into opportunities for cooperative interaction (see Rusbult, Yovetich, & Verette, 1996). This observation is important in that it highlights the potential for partners to preempt conflict through a variety of strategies. Likewise, many conflicts do not involve overt disagreement and may be handled in ways that do not depend on verbal exchange (e.g., behaving solicitously; Rusbult, 1993). In the remainder of this chapter I hope to elaborate the point that verbal problem solving may typically take a back seat to other strategies for preempting potential conflict. In illustrating this point I focus on my own and colleagues' recent work on self-processes in a couple context. This work illustrates how feedback that might be viewed as potentially upsetting for one member of the dyad may lead to changes in the way partners define themselves. In turn, such self-definitional changes can be instrumental in constructing a less conflicted and more supportive "team" effort. My basic premise, therefore, is that the self-processes I outline provide a window on the type of nonverbal conflict resolution that can work for couples to help them feel more like a team and less like adversaries.

SELF-EVALUATION MAINTENANCE; A MECHANISM TO FACILITATE COOPERATION, FIT AND PAIR BONDING?

The self-evaluation maintenance model (SEM; Tesser, 1988) describes a mechanism that seems well designed to guide the development of a mental representation that could, in turn, help regulate competition, focus efforts to fit with a partner, and thus facilitate pair bonding. According to the SEM model (Tesser, 1988), when the self performs better than close others in a given area, that area tends to remain central or "relevant" to one's self-definition. Conversely, performing relatively more poorly than close others is often associated with decreases in self-relevance (Tesser, 1988; Tesser & Campbell, 1982; Tesser & Paulhus, 1983), making it more likely that the individual will bask in the reflected glory of the other's good performance (Cialdini & Richardson, 1980). This process would be particularly useful in regulating competition and increasing perceived fit with a close other if it provided an occasion for the self to cede leadership in the area and perhaps even to reinforce the good performance of a partner.

It is important to note, however, that an area has only been ceded to the partner if it is viewed as more important to the partner than the self. If the importance of the area is reduced for both for the self and the partner, the resulting mental representation provides no additional guidance as to who should take the lead in the area or who should be expected to do better in the area. Accordingly, for relevance adjustments to have value as a social adaptation, self-relevance should diverge from partner relevance when the self is outperformed (for an extended discussion see Beach & Tesser, in press).

In the remainder of the chapter I review several recent studies that examine the capacity of spouses to make adjustments in response to feedback, and do so relatively readily. I begin by examining the issue of adjustments of self and partner relevance in response to feedback about relative performance. Then, I examine evidence regarding the affective impact of performance feedback and provide evidence that close relationships may be protected by ongoing adjustments of the self-evaluation maintenance system. Next, I review data showing that constraints on self-evaluation maintenance adjustments may produce problematic interaction under some circumstances. Finally, I examine division of decision-making power, and show that protection of the self-evaluation needs of both partners is associated with greater marital satisfaction.

Changing the Self

Is there evidence that adjustments in relevance occur when individuals are given feedback about their performance in comparison to a romantic partner? In a series of three studies (Beach, Whitaker, O'Mahen, & Tesser, 1999) it was found that both male and female reactions to comparison threats were in line with theoretical predictions of the SEM model. In Experiment 1 (dating college couples) and Experiment 2 (married couples from the community), participants completed a task that ostensibly measured an important skill, and were given either positive or negative feedback about their performance relative to the partner. In response to the feedback that the self had been outperformed, dating partners (Experiment 1) increased relevance to the partner relative to the self: $F(1,43) = 8.1, p < .01$. In the replication with marital partners (Experiment 2), the same pattern was found: $F(1,$

39) $= 24.49, p < .0001$. In addition, follow-up analyses indicated that the tendency to show divergence between self and partner relevance ratings was significantly stronger ($p < .05$) among the married couples. Thus, it appears that married couples continue to be open to the process of adjustment, and certain aspects of the process seem to be more intense for married couples than for dating couples. In particular, the tendency to create divergent self-representations, and thus maximize the complementarity of the dyad, seems greater among married partners.

Attenuating Negative Affective Reactions

Could the greater adjustment of self-relevance also provide a mechanism rendering affective reactions to being outperformed less negative (or more positive)? If so, this would provide another clue that such adjustments are potentially important in understanding conflict in close relationships. In a series of four studies (Beach et al., 1998), the SEM model was used to predict self-reported affect in response to doing better or worse than a romantic partner. Both negative affective reactions to comparison (i.e., those predicted by the original SEM model) and negative affective reactions to situations in which the partner was confronted with negative comparison (i.e., those predicted by the extended SEM model) were obtained. In addition, comparisons with romantic partners resulted in a different pattern of self-reported affect than did comparisons with strangers.

In the second study of this series (Beach et al., 1998, Study 2), 224 members of marital dyads completed a measure of recalled affect for the marital situations based on the Positive and Negative Affective Schedule (PANAS; Watson & Clark, 1988). Subjects were asked to think about tasks and activities representing each of eight conditions highlighted by the extended SEM model. These conditions are defined by crossing high and low self-relevance with high and low partner-relevance with whether self outperforms partner or partner outperforms self. Positive affect terms were summed and negative affect terms were subtracted to form a total "pleasantness" score. The effect of the eight potential SEM configurations on pleasantness of mood was examined via a 2 x 2 x 2 repeated measures of analysis of variance (ANOVA). The interaction effect predicted by the SEM model was found to be significant. The significant self-relevance by performance interaction indicated the relatively greater pleasantness of being outperformed when the task was low in self-relevance, whereas opposite was true for tasks high in self-relevance.

Of importance for current purposes, in Studies 3 and 4 of the series, affective reactions to being outperformed by the partner or a stranger were contrasted. In both studies it was found that reactions to being outperformed were relatively more muted with partners than with strangers. Reaction to being outperformed by the partner was relatively more pleasant (or at least was less unpleasant) than reaction to being outperformed by the stranger, and this was particularly true for areas of high self-relevance. Accordingly, it appears that when partners are free to make the adjustments predicted by the SEM model it may help protect them against negative reactions to being outperformed by the partner, even in areas of expertise.

Do Constraints on Self-Evaluation Maintenance Adjustments Create Problems?

It appears that romantic partners are able to make adjustments in self-relevance, and that such adjustments are potentially helpful in avoiding negative reactions. Perhaps, then, providing performance feedback while precluding the possibility of adjustments might lead to changes in behavior during a problem solving discussion (O'Mahen, Beach, & Tesser, 2000). In an investigation of the potential effect of SEM processes on couple's attempts to resolve problems, 129 couples were given feedback designed to produce either positive reflection (R+) for one partner and positive comparison (C+) for the other, negative comparison (C-) for one partner and positive comparison (C+) for the other, or negative comparison for one partner (C-) and negative reflection for the other (R-). In all conditions, subjects selected topic areas from a list of 30 topics and then engaged in a "trivial pursuit" type task, ostensibly competing against the partner. All interactions were done via the computer and feedback regarding relative performance was provided via the computer. Following the computer interaction couples were asked to engage in a 10-minute problem-solving interaction. The interactions were subsequently content analyzed using the MICS-IV, a widely used system for coding marital interaction, and three indexes of negative problems solving behaviors were constructed.

The effect of condition was significant in the predicted direction, and as predicted there was a strong linear trend across the three conditions. Accordingly, these results indicate that SEM manipulations can produce negative changes in communication behavior.

Distribution of Power and the SEM Model

It appears that SEM processes may be important in understanding changes in self-definition and claims perception of self and partner, and may be important as well in understanding relatively short-term changes in affect or negative problem-solving behavior. However, it is also important to examine the possibility that these processes may be related to marital satisfaction. Beach and Tesser (1993) assessed 90 married couples with regard to 24 decision-making areas. For each of the 24 decision making areas each spouse was asked to indicate whether the couple agreed for the most part in this area of decision making, whether decisions in this area were made primarily by the self or by the partner, whether making decisions in this area was important or not to the self, and whether making decisions in this area was important or not to the partner.

Responses were analyzed in a 2 x 2 x 2 x 2 x 2 repeated-measures ANOVA, with marital satisfaction as a between-couples factor and four within-couple factors (decision-making power by self-importance of the area by partner-importance of the area by gender). As predicted on the basis of the SEM model, a significant three-way interaction of power by importance-to-the-self by satisfaction was found. This result suggests that partners are more satisfied if they see the self and the partner as having spheres of decision-making power that fit with their areas of expertise. Given the O'Mahen et al. (in press) results reported earlier, it may be that part of the association with satisfaction may result from their greater ease in making decisions.

CONCLUSIONS

The study of marital conflict has not lived up to initial expectations. This is not to say that there have been no interesting or important findings with regard to the consequences of marital conflict; several such consequences have been uncovered. Rather, marital conflict has not accounted for as much variance in important marital outcomes as expected. As suggested by Bradbury et al. (chap. 5, this volume) it is important that we take another look at the decisions that were made in the 1970s and self-consciously attempt to expand the study of marital conflict. One avenue deserving exploration is the role of marital support in the longitudinal prediction of couple outcomes. Likewise, in this chapter I argue that we should explore the ways couples may come to redefine themselves or change their perceptions in order to alleviate potential conflict before it has a chance to develop.

Taken together, the studies reviewed here suggest strong potential for research on self-processes to inform research on marital conflict and marital support. In line with the request by Bradbury et al. (chap. 5, this volume) that the field be broadened in significant ways, the studies highlighted here also suggest the importance of broadening the field. Indeed, from the perspective of the self-evaluation maintenance model and its impact on couple interactions and couple satisfaction, there is a natural continuity among social support, conflict, and preconflict adjustments. If so, this framework suggests the value of both increasing the range of our dependent variables and increasing our focus to include "potential conflicts" that never turned into conflicts as well as overt conflicts that were eventually resolved. A particular emphasis of the current series of studies is that better understanding of conflict resolution and prevention may require that we examine nonverbal, nonproblem-solving approaches to problem resolution. Indeed, such approaches may be more frequently used in marriage than are explicit problem discussions.

The long-term direction suggested by this chapter is that of framing the field in a broader way and, by doing so, to better highlight the connections between the interrelated processes of support and conflict. We may also be able to better highlight the connection between the external niches within which couples live and the internal set of niches they create for themselves within the relationship. At a minimum, the current series of studies suggests that partners will have different reactions to overt verbal conflict or verbal offers of support depending on each partner's definition of the area of conflict and how the conflict fits into their claims of expertise. This leads to a number of interesting new hypotheses about the structure of conflict and the ways couples may create better fit with a particular partner. Finding the constraints that may commonly prevent self-protective adjustments, or the factors that reduce the need for self-protective adjustments, could help identify an additional starting point for marital prevention and marital intervention programs. At the same time, we may find that automatic self-protective responses play an important role in both the genesis and maintenance of marital conflict and marital dissatisfaction. If so, better explicating the way such processes are elicited and resolved seems particularly important for better understanding the implications of conflict for various couple, family, and individual outcomes.

REFERENCES

Amato, P. R., & Rogers, S. J. (1997). A longitudinal study of marital problems and subsequent divorce. *Journal of Marriage and the Family, 59*, 612-624.

Beach, S. R. H. (2000). *Marital and family processes in depression.* Washington, DC: American Psychological Association.

Beach, S. R. H., & Fincham, F. D. (2000). Marital therapy and social psychology: Will we choose explicit partnership or cryptomnesia? In G. Fletcher & M. Clark (Eds.), *Blackwell handbook of social psychology: Volume 2, interpersonal processes* (pp. 558-586). Oxford, NC: Blackwell.

Beach, S. R. H., & Tesser, A. (1993). Decision making power and marital satisfaction: A self-evaluation maintenance perspective. *Journal of Social and Clinical Psychology, 12*, 471-494.

Beach, S. R. H., & Tesser, A. (in press). Self-evaluation maintenance and evolution: Some speculative notes. In J. Suls & L. Wheeler (Eds.), *Handbook of social comparison: Theory and research.* New York: Plenum.

Beach, S. R. H., Tesser, A., Fincham, F. D., Jones, D. J., Johnson, D., & Whitaker, D. J. (1998). Pleasure and pain in doing well together: An investigation of performance related affect in close relationships. *Journal of Personality and Social Psychology, 74*, 923-938.

Beach, S. R. H., Whitaker, D. J., O'Mahen, H., & Tesser, A. (1999). *When differences are adaptive: Does performance feedback prompt self-other divergence?* Unpublished manuscript.

Birchler, G. R., Weiss, R. L., & Vincent, J. P. (1975). Multimethod analysis of social reinforcement exchange between maritally distressed and nondistressed spouse and stranger dyads. *Journal of Personality and Social Psychology, 31*, 349-360.

Blau, P. M. (1964). *Exchange and power in social life.* New York: Wiley.

Bradbury, T. N., Cohan, C. L., & Karney, B. R. (1998). Optimizing longitudinal research for understanding and preventing marital dysfunction. In T. N. Bradbury (Ed.), *The developmental course of marital dysfunction* (pp. 279-311). New York: Cambridge University Press.

Brody, G. H., Stoneman Z., & McCoy, J. K. (1994). Forecasting sibling relationships in early adolescence from child temperaments and family processes in middle childhood. *Child Development, 65*, 771-784.

Burman, B., & Margolin, G. (1992). Analysis of the association between marital relationships and health problems: An interactional perspective. *Psychological Bulletin, 112*, 39-63.

Cialdini, R. B., & Richardson, K. D. (1980). Two indirect tactics of image management: Basking and blasting. *Journal of Personality and Social Psychology, 39*, 406-415.

Coyne, J. C., & Downey, G. (1991). Social factors and psychopathology: Stress, social support, and coping processes. *Annual Review of Psychology, 42*, 401-425.

Erel, O., & Burman, B. (1995). Interrelatedness of marital relations and parent child relations: A meta-analytic review. *Psychological Bulletin, 118,* 108-132.

Ewart, C. K., Taylor, C. B., Kraemer, H. C., & Agras, W. S. (1991). High blood pressure and marital discord: Not being nasty matters more than being nice. *Health Psychology, 103,* 155-163.

Fincham, F. D., & Beach, S. R. H. (1999). Marital conflict. *Annual Review of Psychology, 50,* 47-77.

Fincham, F. D., & Osborne, L. N. (1993). Marital conflict and children: Retrospect and prospect. *Clinical Psychology Review, 13,* 75-88.

Gottman, J. M., Notarius, C., Gonso, J., & Marman, H. (1976). *A couple's guide to communication.* Champaign, Il: Research.

Grych, J. H., & Fincham, F. D. (1990). Marital conflict and children's adjustment: A cognitive-contextual framework. *Psychological Bulletin, 108,* 267-290.

Holmes, J. G., & Murray, S. L. (1996). Conflict in close relationships. In E.T. Higgins & A. Kruglanski (Eds.), *Social psychology: Handbook of basic principles* (pp. 622-654). New York: Guilford.

Homans, G. C. (1961). *Social behavior: Its elementary forms.* New York: Harcourt, Brace & World.

House, J. S., Landis, K. R., & Umberson, D. (1988). Social relationships and health. *Science, 241,* 540-545.

Jacobson, N. S., & Margolin, G. (1979). *Marital therapy.* New York: Brunner/Mazel.

Jouriles, E. N., & Farris, A. M. (1992). Effects of marital conflict on subsequent parent son interactions. *Behavior Therapy, 23,* 355-374.

Karney, B. R., & Bradbury, T. N. (1995). The longitudinal course of marital quality and stability: A review of theory, method, and research. *Psychological Bulletin, 118,* 3-34.

Kelley, H. H. (1979). *Personal relationships.* Hillsdale, NJ: Lawrence Erlbaum Associates.

Kelly, E. L., Huston, T. L., & Cate, R. M. (1985). Premarital relationship correlates of the erosion of satisfaction in marriage. *Journal of Social and Personal Relationships, 2,* 167-178.

Kielcolt-Glaser, J. K., Glaser, R., Cacioppo, J. T., MacCullum, R. C., & Snydersmith, M. (1997). Marital conflict in older adults: Endocrine and immunological correlates. *Psychosomatic Medicine, 59,* 339-349.

Kiecolt-Glaser, J. K., Kennedy, S., Malkoff, S., Fisher, L., & Speicher, C. E. (1988). Marital discord and immunity in males. *Psychosomatic Medicine, 50,* 213-229.

Kiecolt-Glaser, J .K., Malarkey, W. B., Chee, M., Newton, T., & Cacioppo, J. T. (1993). Negative behavior during marital conflict is associated with immunological down-regulation. *Psychosomatic Medicine, 55,* 395-409.

Kiecolt-Glaser, J. K., Newton, T., Cacioppo, J. T., MacCallum, R. C., & Glaser, R. (1996). Marital conflict and endocrine function: Are men really more physiologically affected than women? *Journal of Consulting and Clinical Psychology, 64,* 324-332.

Kluwer, E. S., Heesink, J. A. M., & Van De Vliert, E. (1997). The marital dynamics of conflict over the division of labor. *Journal of Marriage and the Family, 59,* 635-653.

Malarkey, W. B., Kielcolt-Glaser, J. K., Pearl, D., & Glaser, R. (1994). Hostile behavior during conflict alters pituitary and adrenal hormones. *Psychosomatic Medicine, 56,* 41-51.

Margolin, G., Christensen, A., & John, R. S. (1996). The continuance and spillover of everyday tensions in distressed and nondistressed families. *Journal of Family Psychology, 10,* 304-321.

Markman, H., Stanley, S., & Blumberg, S. L. (1994). *Fighting for your marriage.* San Francisco: Jossey-Bass.

McGonagle, K .A., Kessler, R. C., & Schiling, E. A. (1992). The frequency and determinants of marital disagreements in a community sample. *Journal of Social and Personal Relationships, 9,* 507-524.

Murray, S. L., Holmes, J. G., & Griffen, D. W. (1996). The benefits of positive illusions: Idealization and the construction of satisfaction in close relationships. *Journal of Personality and Social Psychology, 71,* 1155-1180.

O'Leary, K. D., Malone, J., & Tyree, A. (1994). Physical aggression in early marriage: Pre-relationship and relationship effects. *Journal of Consulting and Clinical Psychology, 62,* 594-602.

O'Leary, K. D., & Smith, D. A. (1991). Marital interactions. *Annual Review of Psychology, 42,* 191-212.

O'Mahen, H. A., Beach, S. R. H., & Tesser, A. (2000). Relationship ecology and negative communications in romantic relationships: A self-evaluation maintenance perspective. *Personality and Social Psychology Bulletin, 26,* 1343-1352.

Owen, M. T., & Cox, M. J. (1997). Marital conflict and the development of infant-parent attachment relationships. *Journal of Family Psychology, 11,* 152-164.

Rusbult, C. E. (1993). Understanding responses to dissatisfaction in close relationships: The exit-voice-loyalty-neglect model. In S. Worchel & J. A. Simpson (Eds.), *Conflict between people and groups: Causes, processes, and resolutions* (pp. 30-59). Chicago: Nelson-Hall.

Rusbult, C. E., Verette, J., Whitney, G. A., Slovik, L. F., & Lipkus, I. (1991). Accommodation processes in close relationships: Theory and preliminary empirical evidence. *Journal of Personality and Social Psychology, 60,* 53-78.

Rusbult, C. E., Yovetich, N. A., & Verette, J. (1996). An interdependence analysis of accommodation processes. In G. J. O. Fletcher & J. Fitness (Eds.), *Knowledge structures in close relationships* (pp. 63-90). Mahweh, NJ: Lawrence Erlbaum Associates.

Schmaling, K. B., & Sher, T. G. (1997). Physical health and relationships. In W. K. Halford & H. J. Markman (Eds.), *Clinical handbook of marriage and couples intervention* (pp. 323-345). London: Wiley.

Speer, D. C. (1972). Marital dysfunctionality and two person non-zero-sum game behavior. *Journal of Personality and Social Psychology, 21,* 18-24.

Stuart, R. B. (1980). *Helping couples change: A social learning approach to marital therapy.* New York: Guilford.

Tesser, A. (1988). Toward a self-evaluation maintenance model of social behavior. In L. Berkowitz (Ed.), *Advances in experimental social psychology* (Vol. 21, pp. 181-227). New York: Academic.

Tesser, A., & Campbell, J. (1982). Self-evaluation maintenance and the perception of friends and strangers. *Journal of Personality, 50,* 261-279.

Tesser, A., & Paulhus, D. (1983). The definition of self: Private and public self-evaluation maintenance strategies. *Journal of Personality and Social Psychology, 44,* 672-682.

Thibaut, J., & Kelley, H. H. (1959). *The social psychology of groups.* New York: Wiley.

Watson, D., & Clark, L. A. (1988). Development and validation of a brief measure of positive and negative affect: The PANAS scales. *Journal of Personality and Social Psychology, 54,* 1063-1070.

Weiss, R. L. (1978). The conceptualization of marriage from a behavioral perspective. In T. J. Paolino & B. S. McCrady (Eds.), *Marriage and marital therapy* (pp. 165-239). New York: Brunner/ Mazel.

7

Conflict and Control: Symmetry and Asymmetry in Domestic Violence

Michael P. Johnson

The Pennsylvania State University

I love the Bradbury, Rogge, and Lawrence chapter in this volume (chap. 5) for its brazenness in arguing, at a conference on conflict, that conflict isn't all that important—and for its thoughtful working out of that thesis. Their approach, however, does take us away from the initial questions posed for this session of the symposium: What are the interpersonal roots of couple conflict, and what are its consequences for individuals and couples? I want to get back to those questions, and in order to do so I am going to present some of my own work. My major point is that neither of these questions can be answered without making distinctions among types of conflict.

I spent much of the session by Daly and Wilson (see chap. 1) musing about the dangers of treating violence (even wife-murder) as if it were a unitary phenomenon. I work primarily in the area of domestic violence, and my mission these days is to convince others who work in that area that the domestic violence literature is full of serious mistakes, mistakes that arise because most researchers do not make what I consider to be some absolutely necessary distinctions among types of violence (Johnson, 1995, 1998, 1999; Johnson & Ferraro, 2000). The most visible of these errors, and perhaps the one with the most serious implications in terms of public misunderstanding of the nature of domestic violence, is the mistaken idea that women are as violent as men in intimate relationships. They are not, and I hope that this chapter convinces you of that.

From the very first page of Bradbury, Rogge and Lawrence's chapter (chap. 5), I felt uneasy. Their ostensibly quite reasonable definition of marital conflict is "those social interactions in which the spouses hold incompatible goals." It sounds so symmetrical and almost benign—the interaction of two people with incompatible goals. But when I read it, it certainly didn't seem to fit with the data I had just been looking at from a woman who described her husband as beating and humiliating her so regularly that she could no longer keep track of how often it had happened. When asked how many times, all she could say was, "Oh, at least 500 times."

The conflicts that are described by women entering shelters or filing Protection from Abuse Orders do not have the symmetrical feel of "incompatible goals." Instead, they seem to represent the single-minded commitment of one person to completely dominate and control another (Dobash & Dobash, 1979; Kirkwood, 1993; Pence & Paymar, 1993). Admittedly, because these "others" do not wish to be dominated and controlled, we *could* characterize the situation as one of "incompatible goals," but something very important seems to be missing in that description, and I think the heart of the problem is to be found in the implied symmetry of the definition.

In the domestic violence literature, symmetry has been at the center of a decades-long, unusually acrimonious debate over the nature of marital violence. It all started when the first National Family Violence Survey (NFVS) became available in the late 1970s. Suzanne Steinmetz (Steinmetz, 1977-78) published an infamous paper on "husband-battering," in which she used the NFVS data to support her argument that there was a problem of husband-battering that was perhaps as serious as that of wife-battering. Although the NFVS data did in fact show almost perfect gender symmetry of partner violence, other scholars quickly responded with rebuttals, arguing that all other studies had found that domestic violence is almost entirely male, and attacking the validity of the NFVS data. But study after study has appeared in the intervening decades, right up to this year (2000), that ostensibly show gender symmetry in partner violence. The talk shows love it.

The *scholarly* debate involves the two major groups of sociologists who study relationship violence. Here is an oversimplification of their differences. One group is usually referred to as the "family violence researchers," because they have studied a variety of types of family violence in addition to partner violence. Murray Straus and Richard Gelles, who designed the National Family Violence Surveys, are the best-known members of this group. The major methodology of this tradition is the large-scale survey, assessing violence by means of a set of survey questions called the Conflict Tactics Scales. In general, it is this group that argues that men and women are equally violent in intimate relationships. The other major group is usually referred to as the "feminist researchers," and the best known of them are Rebecca and Russell Dobash. This group uses data collected primarily in qualitative research focusing on women who are clients of public agencies such as shelters, the courts, hospitals, and so on. They argue that partner violence is male and rooted in patriarchal traditions.

What is striking about this debate is that both the family violence researchers and the feminist researchers are able to cite multiple studies to support their positions. Of course, each side sees fatal flaws in the other group's research strategies. On the one hand, the feminists present a measurement critique of survey research, arguing that the Conflict Tactics Scales ignore everything about violence that is important, merely counting number of incidents instead of attending to motives and consequences. On the other hand, the family violence folks present a sampling critique of feminist research, arguing that shelter and court samples have obvious selection biases. As Murray Straus put it, they deal with "clinical samples," whereas the surveys deal with "general samples" (Straus, 1990).

Well, I think they're both right. I'll get to measurement later, but my primary argument hinges on the sampling issue, with a different take on bias, however, than the one argued by Straus and his colleagues. The biases of shelter samples may be more obvious than those of general surveys, but the samples in so-called random-sample surveys *are equally biased.* We do *not*, in fact, interview random samples; we interview those who do not refuse to be interviewed. And the refusal rate is not trivial—the 1985 National Family Violence Survey actually had a refusal rate of 40%, not the 16% usually reported (Johnson, 1995).

I argue, therefore, that the results of these two types of research differ, not because one is biased and the other is not, but because both are seriously biased, and each gets at only one of the two major types of partner violence. What might those two types be? Well, if you look at the few characteristics of the violence that are measured in both types of research, here's what you see in the literature. First, there is the gender difference that started the argument. Feminist researchers, using public agency samples, find male violence. Family violence researchers, using general survey samples, find gender-symmetric violence. Second, the per-couple frequency of violent incidents is dramatically higher in shelter samples than it is in general samples (on the order of 10 times higher). Third, shelter data show almost universal escalation of the violence; general survey research shows very little escalation and considerable deescalation. Finally, in shelter data it is unusual for the woman to fight back, whereas general survey data show considerable so-called "reciprocity" of violence.

On the basis of this literature review, I published a paper in 1995 in which I argued that these two sampling tactics provide access to decidedly different, virtually nonoverlapping populations of violent couples—that there are two quite different types of partner violence, one gender symmetric, the other decidedly, if not entirely, male (Johnson, 1995).

This is where we return to the initial question for this session, the one about the interpersonal roots of conflict. What are the interpersonal roots of these two types of violence? I have argued that the characteristics of the heavily male type of violence are consistent with a general motive to control one's partner, a motive that is rooted in patriarchal ideas about relationships between men and women. The violence is used often because the abuser perceives that it needs to be, in order to subdue his partner or to display his power and control. Similarly, it escalates as required, an escalation that is likely to be necessary in a culture in which women in most cases are not willing to concede all power and control to their husbands. Finally, such a general pattern of power and control is likely in the long run to subdue physical resistance. I labeled this type of partner violence "patriarchal terrorism."

The other type of violence, which is more gender symmetric, is consistent with a more specific, narrowly focused motive to get one's way in a particular conflict situation, within a relationship in which there is *not* a general pattern of power and control, but in which specific arguments sometimes escalate into violence. Because it does not involve a general motive to control, it is less frequent, it does not escalate over time (in fact, it is likely to deescalate), and the violence is more likely to be reciprocated. I labeled it "common couple violence."

The defining difference between these two types of violence is a difference of motives, identified by means of the interpersonal dynamics that those motives produce across the many interactions that comprise a relationship. The defining characteristic of patriarchal terrorism is a general motive to control that activates a range of power and control tactics in addition to the use of violence. One model of such a pattern is the "Power and Control Wheel" that is used to characterize domestic violence in the shelter movement in which I am active. The model was developed in the Duluth batterers-education project on the basis of reports from shelter clients regarding the nature of their relationships with their abusers (Pence & Paymar, 1993). The general point of the model is that the violence in this pattern is only one of many control tactics employed in the service of a motive to exert general control over one's partner. Thus, if we want to distinguish this type of violence from common couple violence, our surveys need to ask questions not just about violence, but about a variety of control tactics, and this is where the measurement issue returns.

All of this post hoc speculation is based only on the differences in the gender, frequency, escalation, and reciprocity of the *violence* uncovered by the two types of sampling strategies. The literature that I reviewed in 1995 presented no direct evidence regarding the general use of a variety of control tactics. To test these ideas, I needed data that asked questions regarding a variety of control tactics in addition to violence, were likely to include both patriarchal terrorism and common couple violence, and provided information regarding both spouses. I turned to the internet, and in response to my query to a feminist list, Irene Frieze replied that she had a late-1970s data set that might meet my needs, and she sent me the data.

Frieze's data come from interviews with married or formerly married women living in southwestern Pennsylvania in the late 1970s. The mixed sampling design seemed likely to include both types of violence, because it included on the one hand women from shelters and the courts, and on the other hand a matched sample of women who lived in the same neighborhoods (Frieze, 1983; Frieze & Browne, 1989; Frieze & McHugh, 1992). My hope was that the court and shelter samples would include patriarchal terrorism, and that the neighborhood sample would include some cases of common couple violence.

From the lengthy interview protocols, I identified items tapping seven non-violent control tactics: threats, economic control, use of privilege, using children, isolation, emotional abuse, and sexual control. Each of these measures was standardized, and they were entered into a cluster analysis (for methodological details, see Johnson, 1999). The results indicated a two-cluster solution as optimal. As you can see in Table 7.1, the pattern is quite simple, with one cluster exhibiting a high average on all seven of the control tactics, the other being relatively low on all seven.

Table 7.1
Control Tactics by Cluster
(reports on both men and women from wives, n = 274)

Control Tactics

	Threats	Economic Control	Use of Privilege	Using Children	Isolation	Emotional Abuse	Sexual Control
High control Mean (n=109)	3.95	1.61	2.73	1.41	3.82	1.48	1.48
(Z)	(1.19)	(.97)	(1.04)	(.96)	(.95)	(1.07)	(1.29)
Low control Mean (n=439)	1.96	1.19	1.79	1.09	2.77	1.09	1.03
(Z)	(-.29)	(-.26)	(-.26)	(-.27)	(-.24)	(-.28)	(-.32)
Eta	.59	.49	.52	.49	.48	.53	.65

Are there violent people in both clusters? Remember, the clusters are defined by patterns of *nonviolent* control tactics. By simply combining each individual's cluster membership with information regarding whether he or she had ever been violent in their marriage, we can distinguish three types of spouses: nonviolent spouses, those involved in noncontrolling violence, and those involved in controlling violence. You can see in Table 7.2 that the controlling violence is almost entirely male, whereas the noncontrolling violence is not.

Table 7.2
Type of Individual Violence by Gender
(data on 272 husbands and 271 wives, as reported by wives)

	Husbands	Wives	N
Nonviolent	42%	58%	212
Noncontrolling violence	38%	62%	224
Controlling violence	98%	2%	107

Now, how do we identify terrorism and common couple violence? They are dyadic phenomena that require attention to the behavior of both partners in the marriage. Table 7.3 presents data only on violent individuals; that is, those who had been violent in their relationship at least once. It places individual violence within its dyadic context, distinguishing among four types of violent behavior. The first row, "mutual violent control," refers to controlling violence in a relationship in which both spouses are violent and controlling. There were only five such couples in this data set. The second row, "terrorism" with the "patriarchal" in parentheses, refers to relationships in which only one of the spouses is violent and

Table 7.3
Individual Violent Behavior in a Dyadic Context
(violent individuals only, as reported by wives)

	Husbands	Wives	N
Mutual violent control	50%	50%	10
(Patriarchal) Terrorism	97%	3%	97
Violent resistance	4%	96%	77
Common couple violence	56%	44%	146

controlling, and the other is not. In this data set, that violent and controlling spouse is the husband in 94 of the 97 cases, cases in which the term *"patriarchal* terrorism" is appropriate. The third row refers to cases in which the focal spouse is violent but not controlling, and his or her partner *is* both violent and controlling. I call it "violent resistance," and it is almost entirely a female form of violence in this sample of heterosexual relationships. Of course, that is because in these marriages almost all of the terrorism is male, and in some cases the wives do reply with violence. Finally, we have "common couple violence," individual noncontrolling violence in a dyadic context in which neither of the spouses is violent and controlling.

The relationship between gender and these types of violence supports the hypothesis that "terrorism" is indeed an almost exclusively male phenomenon in heterosexual marital relationships, thus appropriately referred to as "patriarchal terrorism," whereas common couple violence is close to gender symmetric, at least by these crude criteria. (Data on the frequency and severity of male and female common couple violence—not shown—indicate that by other criteria men are more violent than women even within common couple violence.)

Now, let's take a quick look at the characteristics of terrorism and common couple violence, to see if they it fall in line with what I found in my 1995 literature review:

1. The gender differences are clear. Patriarchal terrorism is 97% male, common couple violence only 56%. Because there are only three female terrorists in these data, I am going present the last three pieces of data looking only at violent men. It was, of course, male violence that was evaluated in the literature review cited earlier.
2. The violence in patriarchal terrorism is quite frequent; the median number of incidents in these marriages is 58. It is much less frequent in common couple violence, with a median of 14 violent events.
3. Patriarchal terrorism is reported to escalate in 76% of the cases, common couple violence in only 28%.
4. In most violent incidents in patriarchal terrorism, wives do not physically resist; the median of the ratio of number of times the wife has been violent to the number of times the husband has been violent is .17. In common couple violence they are much more likely to resist, the median ratio being .40.

These data do not leave much doubt that patriarchal terrorism and common couple violence are not the same phenomenon.

Finally, let me nail down my sampling argument, that general survey samples allow conclusions only about common couple violence, whereas "shelter" studies give access only to patriarchal terrorism. Again, looking only at male violence, Table 7.4 shows that the general sample accesses almost nothing but common

Table 7.4
Who's Finding Whom?
(violent husbands only, as reported by wives)

	Survey Sample ($\underline{n}$ = 37)	Court Sample ($\underline{n}$ = 34)	Shelter Sample ($\underline{n}$ = 43)
Mutual violent control	0%	3%	0%
Patriarchal terrorism	11%	68%	79%
Violent resistance	0%	0%	2%
Common couple violence	89%	29%	19%

couple violence, only 11% of the violence being patriarchal terrorism. In stark contrast, the court and shelter samples that are typical of feminist research show violence that is predominantly patriarchal terrorism.

What kind of mistakes can this generate? The original Steinmetz article was an excellent example of the danger of thinking that a general sample provides information about what we conventionally mean by domestic violence (i.e., patriarchal terrorism). Steinmetz related anecdotes about true husband-battering, involving women who were terrorists in the sense described earlier. She then cited general survey data, which we now know represents only common couple violence, to make her case that such battering is as serious a problem as is wife-battering. In fact, the data she presented have nothing to do with husband-battering. Serious as husband-battering is in the particular case, as a general phenomenon it is dramatically less frequent than wife-battering.

Similarly, one can err by assuming that the patterns observed in shelter samples describe all partner violence. It is common for shelter workers to argue in our educational programs that violence always escalates, that if he hit you once he'll do it again and it will get worse. That pattern is, as shown previously, much more true of patriarchal terrorism than of common couple violence, and patriarchal terrorism is what we see in our shelter work. However, most couples who experience violence, including those in our audiences, are involved in common couple violence, and for those audience members we are providing an inaccurate picture of the likely course of their relationships.

Dramatic as these sampling biases are, Table 7.4 also shows that neither type of male violence is found *exclusively* in one type of sample, implying that it is possible to study the differences between these two types of violence in a variety of research settings. First, the 11% of male violence in the general sample that is patriarchal terrorism indicates that, with large enough samples, it may be possible to study both common couple violence and patriarchal terrorism with survey data. In order to do that, of course, we need to include questions that will allow us to distinguish one from the other. Second, because women do bring cases of common couple violence to both the courts (29%) and shelters (19%), researchers in those contexts will be able to study the effects of various intervention strategies on the two types of violence. Again, however, it won't happen unless we gather information that will allow us to make these distinctions.

Why bother? Well, I hope you are convinced by now that we have to make these distinctions if we want to understand partner violence. The evidence you have just seen regarding the dramatic differences between patriarchal terrorism and common couple violence in terms of gender, per-couple frequency of incidents, escalation, and reciprocity should serve as a warning that until further notice we have to assume that the answers to *all* of our important questions may be different for the two different forms of violence.

For example, "What are the interpersonal roots of couple conflict?" For common couple violence, we may need to look to issues of effective communication or anger management. The roots may be found in the interaction processes involved in the current relationship. For patriarchal terrorism, we probably need to look somewhere other than the current relationship, at the origins of the husband's desperate need to control his wife. A number of studies suggest that the origins of such needs may be different for different men (Holtzworth-Munroe & Stuart, 1994; Jacobson & Gottman, 1998).

Or what about our second question: "What are the consequences for individuals and couples?" On the one hand, general survey studies, which I have shown tap primarily common couple violence, often report a surprising *lack* of any relationship between violence and marital satisfaction or stability. On the other hand, shelter studies, which tap primarily patriarchal terrorism, suggest deep dissatisfaction, and almost inevitable dissolution. But, of course, the ultimate consequences depend in some cases on the effectiveness of interventions.

Which brings me to my final point, and to one of the important questions addressed in the Bradbury, Rogge, and Lawrence chapter: "What are likely to be the most effective intervention strategies?" For common couple violence, the prognosis may be fairly positive, and anger management approaches and couples therapy of various kinds might be reasonable strategies.

The prognosis for intervention in patriarchal terrorism, however, is not good. So far, batterers reform programs have a dismal record of success. Intervention in patriarchal terrorism has to focus instead on the woman's safety. Women almost always do leave such relationships, as soon as they can put together the information and the financial resources they need to escape to a reasonably safe life for themselves and their children. Of course, that is what the women's shelter movement is all about. So, my final pleas are that you make distinctions and support your local women's shelter.

REFERENCES

Dobash, R. E., & Dobash, R. P. (1979). *Violence against wives: A case against the patriarchy.* New York: Free Press.

Frieze, I. H. (1983). Investigating the causes and consequences of *marital rape. Signs, 8(3),* 532-553.

Frieze, I. H., & Browne, A. (1989). Violence in marriage. In L. Ohlin & M. Tonry (Eds.), *Family violence* (Vol. 11, pp. 163-218). Chicago: University of Chicago Press.

Frieze, I. H., & McHugh, M. C. (1992). Power and influence strategies in violent and nonviolent marriages. *Psychology of Women Quarterly, 16(4),* 449-465.

Holtzworth-Munroe, A., & Stuart, G. L. (1994). Typologies of male batterers: Three subtypes and the differences among them. *Psychological Bulletin, 116(3),* 476-497.

Jacobson, N., & Gottman, J. (1998). *When men batter women: New insights into ending abusive relationships.* New York: Simon & Schuster.

Johnson, M. P. (1995). Patriarchal terrorism and common couple violence: Two forms of violence against women. *Journal of Marriage and the Family, 57,* 283-294.

Johnson, M. P. (1998, June). *Commitment and entrapment.* Paper presented at the Ninth International Conference on Personal Relationships, Saratoga Springs, NY.

Johnson, M. P. (1999, November). *Identifying patriarchal terrorism and common couple violence.* Paper presented at the National Council on Family Relations, Irvine, CA.

Johnson, M. P., & Ferraro, K. J. (2000). Research on domestic violence in the 1990s: The discovery of difference. *Journal of Marriage and the Family, 62,* 948-963.

Kirkwood, C. (1993). *Leaving abusive partners: From the scars of survival to the wisdom for change.* Newbury Park, CA: Sage.

Pence, E., & Paymar, M. (1993). *Education groups for men who batter: The Duluth model.* New York: Springer.

Steinmetz, S. K. (1977-78). The battered husband syndrome. *Victimology, 2,* 499-509.

Straus, M. A. (1990). Injury and frequency of assault and the "representative sample fallacy" in measuring wife beating and child abuse. In R. J. Gelles & M. A. Straus (Eds.), *Physical violence in American families: Risk factors and adaptations to violence in 8,145 families* (pp. 75-91). New Brunswick, NJ: Transaction.

8

Broadening the Scope of Couples Research: Pragmatics and Prevention

James V. Cordova

University of Illinois at Urbana-Champaign

The theme of this volume is couples in conflict. That theme was chosen because couples' conflict appears to contribute to a variety of societal ills, including domestic violence (Holtzworth-Munroe, Smutzler, Bates, & Sandin, 1997), psychopathology (Paykel, Myers, Dienelt, Klerman, Linenthal, & Pepper, 1989), substance abuse (Halford & Osgarby, 1993), children's mental and physical health (Cherlin, Furstenberg, Chase-Lansdale, & Kiernan, 1991; Emery, 1988), and aspects of the physical health of partners (Newton, Kiecolt-Glaser, Glaser, & Malarkey, 1995; Schmaling & Sher, 1997). In chapter 5, Bradbury, Rogge, and Lawrence contributed to this discussion by persuasively arguing that an overly narrow focus on conflict to the exclusion of other variables related to couples' distress and dissolution has inadvertently limited the scope, precision, and utility of our knowledge about the causes of marital deterioration. In making this argument they emphasized one point and alluded to another, both of which I would like to address in more detail. First, and most heavily emphasized, is their point that a range of phenomena in addition to conflict are likely to contribute in meaningful ways to the health or deterioration of a marriage, and that we as marital researchers should begin actively including a much broader range of relationship phenomena in our studies. The second point alluded to by Bradbury et al. is that adopting practical application as a goal should be a fundamental aspect of our pursuit of knowledge in this context. My goal in this chapter is to argue that our straddling the fence between positivism and pragmatism should be more deeply considered, and that an increased emphasis on the pragmatic truth criterion may be essential if expanding the scope of study in marriage beyond conflict is to adequately translate into useful knowledge.

TOWARD BROADENING THE SCOPE OF COUPLES RESEARCH

Bradbury, Rogge, and Lawrence argued that the marital field's emphasis on conflict, although it has proven fruitful to date, may also be limiting progress. They asserted that marital conflict is a low base rate phenomenon and thus may play a more restricted role than more frequently occurring phenomena. They also maintained that the developmental link between good problem-solving skills and the long-term health of marriage has not yet proven to be a strong one, suggesting that although conflict might differentiate distressed from happy couples, it might not be the most important factor determining the developmental course from happy couple to distressed couple. Finally, they argued that that there is a good possibility that other variables besides conflict may prove to be of equal or greater importance in the prediction and influence of marital deterioration. In particular, they cited positive relationship variables such as self-disclosure, demonstrated understanding, active listening, social support, sex, and compatibility. They also raised the issue that specific individual characteristics may create enduring vulnerabilities to relationship deterioration. Those characteristics include neuroticism, conflict and divorce in families of origin, psychopathology, and attachment history. Finally, they noted that extrafamilial stressors like economic hardship, work stress, and what they called struggles within a family's ecological niche may also contribute substantially to the satisfaction and stability of couples' relationships. These arguments are compelling and offer the promise of broadening the scope of couples research as well as increasing our precision in terms of predicting couples' developmental course.

I am persuaded by Bradbury et al's., argument, and agree that there are compelling reasons for us to begin actively broadening the scope of our research beyond a narrow focus on conflict and problem solving. In addition, however, and speaking more to the second point just cited, I emphasize more strongly the role of pragmatic considerations in the context of this broadening.

PRAGMATICS

Truth criteria (Pepper, 1942) refer to those principles by which we judge the belief-worthiness of data. Within the philosopher Rorty's (1982) formulation, they might be better conceived as the fundamental assumptions we make about the purpose or *function* that data are intended to serve. Both Pepper and Rorty were consistent in noting that the ultimate function of data differ depending on one's adopted philosophical "worldview" (Pepper's term). Rorty distinguished among Platonists, Positivists, and Pragmatists. Platonists do not really concern us in this context. However, Positivists and Pragmatists do, because I suspect that we as social scientists, and as relationship researchers in particular, have begun to drift between these two perspectives. In an attempt to briefly clarify this suspicion, I give a thumbnail description of each school.

For the Positivist, the assumption is that data function to bring us closer to the Truth with a capital T. In other words, one might say that the function of the scientific endeavor is to bring us closer and closer to *the* reality, which exists pristine and independent of the act of inquiry. Or even more simply, we gather data in an attempt to reveal to ourselves the way things really are. The belief-worthiness or quality of data are judged by the degree to which they can be argued to correspond with Reality or the Truth. Both Rorty and Pepper referred to this as the *correspondence theory of Truth*. Statements are true because they correspond to the way things are (Rorty, 1982). From this perspective, a description of a reliable association between two variables provides us with a glimpse of the Truth and is therefore of value. The Truth, by correspondence criteria, pursues a picture of an assumed reality, but does not necessarily require that the information be useful toward any particular goal.

On the other hand, for the Pragmatist, the assumption is that the function of data gathering is to precipitate effective action. To paraphrase Rorty paraphrasing Dewey, data for the pragmatist are seen as tools rather than pictures. In other words, we gather data to increase our effectiveness in the world rather than to take a picture of Reality. To put it even more simply, we gather data because doing so has proven to be one of the most useful of all human endeavors, ever. The quality of data from a pragmatic perspective are judged by the degree to which they are more or less useful within the context of a specified goal. According to William James, calling a statement "true" is a kind of compliment paid to sentences that have shown themselves to be useful within a particular context. From this perspective a demonstration of association is valuable only if it allows us to behave or cope more effectively. In this context, perhaps the most useful type of association is one in which the independent variable is *manipultable* and the effect on the dependent variable is *lawful*. Put differently, pragmatics hypothesizes that demonstrating that some action reliably results in a predictable consequent is likely to be the most useful type of data. Such a demonstration of utility does not, however, make any claim to correspond to some reality external to the demonstrated association.

My proposal is that we, as basic researchers in the marital area, begin to give more deliberate and serious consideration to the pragmatic truth criterion. My argument is that this is not simply an academic exercise, but that it may have dramatic implications for the questions that we choose to ask, the variables we choose to include in our studies, and the ultimate utility of our work in the alleviation of marital suffering. Specifically, I propose that we give serious consideration to the goals that we are adopting in our research and the degree to which we are committed to the pursuit of Truth or utility. My inclination is that if expanding the scope of basic couples research beyond conflict is to be fruitful, we as researchers will have to remain conscious of pragmatic truth criteria. As a beginning to the conversation, I argue that pragmatics should at least be a consideration, if not necessarily a requirement of basic couple functioning research.

PREVENTING MARITAL DETERIORATION:
BREADTH IS GOOD, PRAGMATICS ARE ESSENTIAL

In chapter 5, Bradbury et al. noted that the efforts of basic scientists in the field of couples research are most likely to be useful in efforts aimed at *preventing* relationship deterioration and the associated negative sequelae. I argue that both prevention and treatment programs can benefit from the efforts of basic scientists if pragmatic criteria are regularly considered early in the planning stage of basic research. In fact, I assert that an adequate therapeutic assessment of couple functioning is impossible without broad and pragmatic basic couples research. This has been made most clear to me during work developing the Marriage Checkup, a secondary/indicated prevention program for couples at risk for marital deterioration (Cordova, Warren, & Gee, in press). In this section I briefly outline the Marriage Checkup program to serve as an example demonstrating the essential role that broad and pragmatically informed basic couples research can play in prevention efforts.

Traditionally, interventions for couple distress have been at the tertiary level; providing treatment for couples distressed enough to actively seek therapy. Unfortunately, such interventions reach only a minority of couples that could benefit from treatment. Most distressed couples seek no treatment at all and, of those that do, most seek help from medical doctors and clergy (Doherty, Lester, & Leigh, 1986; Veroff, Douvan, & Kulka, 1981). In addition, there is reason to believe that for many couples, a tertiary intervention is simply too little too late (Jacobson & Follette, 1985; Jacobson, Schmaling, & Holtzworth-Munroe, 1987). On the other end of the spectrum, primary prevention programs have been developed and tested and appear quite promising (Markman, Floyd, Stanley, & Storaasli, 1988; Markman, Renick, Floyd, Stanley, & Clements, 1993). However, these programs are also limited in their utility because they target premarital and newlywed couples and do not address the needs of already-established couples. Between the extremes of tertiary and primary interventions are those couples in the early stages of relationship distress who may only have one or two significant problems that have not yet irreversibly damaged their relationship. These "at-risk" couples are the natural clientele of a secondary preventive program. However, no such program currently exists. In response to the need for the development of a secondary preventive, we have developed a program we call the Marriage Checkup (MC).

The MC is an informational marital health service consisting of two components—a thorough relationship assessment and a professionally delivered feedback report. The design is based on the principles of motivational interviewing (Miller & Rollnick, 1991), and the goals are to address immediate problems and prevent future relationship deterioration. Early treatment development research has provided promising evidence that the MC is effective at attracting both satisfied couples seeking guidance and reassurance, and couples that can be objectively identified as at risk for marital deterioration (Cordova, Warren, & Gee, in press).

ASSESSMENT OF COUPLE FUNCTIONING: USING DATA PRAGMATICALLY I

One of the basic premises of the MC is that couples must be provided with objective, accurate, predictive, and useful information pertaining to the health and stability of their relationships. The goal is to provide couples with information that they can use on their own to improve the quality and stability of their relationships, presenting that information in a way that maximizes its potential to motivate change. My contention is that such an assessment is most useful when what is being assessed has been empirically determined to be predictive of, or at least reliably associated with, marital deterioration. This is important for two reasons. First, it is assumed that variables that have a demonstrated relationship to marital deterioration are likely to be the most effective indicators of risk and the most effective targets of change. Second, motivational interviewing strategies require that people be provided with objective information supported by empirical research because the presentation of unbiased information is expected to be least likely to precipitate client defensiveness and most likely to increase motivation to change.

For example, the theory of change assumes that there is a difference in effectiveness between telling a couple that in the therapist's opinion their demand-withdraw style is bad for their marriage, and telling the couple that assessment results reveal a high degree of demand-withdraw behavior and that research studies have found demand-withdraw patterns to be associated with future marital deterioration. Theoretically, if partners are ambivalent about recognizing a problem and taking action to address it, then the first presentation is easier to discount and more likely to engender defensiveness. On the other hand, the second presentation, by providing a nonjudgmental description of the assessment results and research findings, is both less confrontational and more likely to be persuasive. Note, however, that the second presentation is only possible because the work of basic marital researchers provided evidence of the necessary association (e.g., Heavey, Christensen, & Malamuth, 1995). In addition, note that demand-withdraw behavior is, at least theoretically, a manipulable relationship characteristic. In other words, we identify a potential problem that the couple can do something about. If, on the other hand, the identified variable were not manipulable, like ethnicity or socioeconomic status, then providing that information to the couple does not suggest an appropriate course of action. In short, an intervention like the MC wholly depends on the information provided by basic researchers in order to be implemented effectively, but that information is only of use if it implies effective action.

In fact, the MC attempts to assess primarily those variables that have some basis in the empirical literature. Those variables include such demonstrated predictors of marital health and deterioration as global marital satisfaction (e.g., Karney & Bradbury, 1995), psychological and physical aggression (e.g.,

Holtzworth-Munroe et al., 1997), intimacy (e.g., Prager, 1995), sexual satisfaction (e.g., Karney & Bradbury, 1995), communication patterns (e.g., demand-withdraw; Christensen & Heavey, 1990), areas of desired change (Margolin, Talovic, & Weinstein, 1993), depressive symptoms (e.g., Beach, Whisman, & O'Leary, 1994), alcohol use (e.g., O'Farrell & Rotunda, 1997), and economic hardship (Conger, Rueter, & Elder, 1999). In addition, because the marital *interaction* literature has also identified potential predictors of satisfaction and stability, the MC includes a communication assessment using the standard problem solving paradigm for both a wife problem and a husband problem separately. Assessed from these interactions are behaviors that the literature has suggested are either healthy or corrosive. These include demand-withdraw patterns (e.g., Heavey et al., 1995), Gottman's four horsemen (Gottman, 1994), negative reciprocity (Cordova, Jacobson, Gottman, Rushe, & Cox, 1993), wives' softened start-up and husbands' acceptance of influence (Gottman, Coan, Carrere, & Swanson, 1998), and levels of positivity in relation to levels of negativity (Gottman, 1994; Huston & Chorost, 1994). Likewise, because Buehlman, Gottman, and Katz (1992) found that responses to questions about a couple's relationship history are statistically predictive of dissolution, the MC also includes the oral history interview (OHI) and assesses for such variables as "we-ness" and "husband fondness."

FEEDBACK ABOUT COUPLE FUNCTIONING: USING DATA PRAGMATICALLY II

All of the information gathered is compiled and used to construct a feedback report. It begins with basic identifying information and then recaps the couple's early history from first meeting through early marriage. This section is intended to begin the feedback session with what are almost always positive memories and an emphasis on the qualities of each partner that the other has found attractive and valuable. This section is informed by the work of Buehlman et al. (1992) and hypothesizes that a positive presentation of a couple's relationship history may not simply be a product, but may actually produce a positive relationship effect.

The report then provides a detailed description of the couple's strengths. These strengths vary from couple to couple, but might include highlighting areas of relationship satisfaction, emphasizing their commitment to marriage and children, emphasizing affection and compatibility, and highlighting those qualities or communication skills that have been shown to predict relationship stability. The function of this section of the report is to reorient couples toward their positive qualities. This is important for several reasons. First, couples often fail to appreciate the strengths they already possess and thus perceive their relationships more negatively than may necessarily be warranted. Second, a reorientation toward the positive qualities of the relationship begins to set the stage for positive sentiment override, which may help offset some of the day-to-day annoyances within the relationship. Third, the identified strengths form the basis from which the couple can work on their own to address or seek help for any identified problems. Finally, this section is provided before discussing the couples' problems in order to increase their hopefulness about their relationship before addressing their difficulties. Notice that this "strengths" section *requires* that literature tell us something useful about what is predictive of relationship stability and satisfaction. For example, we frequently use findings about positive relationship qualities (e.g., self-disclosure and social support, husband fondness, accepting influence) and even the absence of negative predictors (e.g., contempt and stonewalling). In short, the only way to offer an informed opinion about what relationship characteristics can be considered strengths is to have a broad basic predictive and pragmatically applicable marital literature to draw on.

The next section of the feedback report presents the raw scores from the relevant questionnaires along with objective interpretations of those scores. These are presented in an interviewing style designed to increase partners' motivation to attend to potentially problematic areas. A detailed description of these procedures would exceed the current page limitations but, in short, partners are asked for their responses to each set of scores and any responses that indicate an increased motivation to attend to and work on that area of the relationship are encouraged and specified. For example, partners scoring in the low range on the "conventionalization" scale of the revised Marital Satisfaction Inventory (Negy & Snyder, 1997; Snyder, 1997) might be informed that scores in that range tend to indicate that the partners might be under emphasizing the positive qualities of the relationship. The partners would then be asked for their reaction to that interpretation. Any response that indicated some increased awareness of that difficulty and willingness to work on it would be reflected and amplified. The goal would be to increase the likelihood that the partners would work to be aware of their tendency to under emphasize the positive qualities of their relationship and to moderate that tendency in the future. Data supporting the potential utility of this approach are primarily derived from the substance abuse literature (e.g., Miller & Rollnick, 1991).

The last section of the feedback report details any specific problem areas identified by the assessment, and provides a menu of suggested strategies for addressing those problems. Each of the sections of the feedback report, including review of the assessment results and the suggested strategies for addressing identified problems, draws heavily on the marital research literature. For example, the discussion of problem areas frequently focuses on providing partners with information to help normalize common problems such as early declines in marital satisfaction (e.g., Markman et al., 1993), declines in relationship satisfaction associated with the transition to parenthood (Belsky, 1990), and commonly encountered sexual problems (e.g., Spence, 1997). In addition, the available typologies research can be used to normalize couples' conflict styles, particularly with couples that can be described as volatile or conflict avoidant (Gottman, 1994; also see Fitzpatrick, 1988).

PRAGMATIC BASIC COUPLES RESEARCH

The point of describing the MC is to demonstrate that prevention programs are likely to rely heavily on the findings of basic couples research that identify both risk factors for relationship deterioration, as well as factors that protect against such deterioration. The work of basic researchers is likely to be most useful if it is both broad and pragmatically informed. Although it is necessary to assess and address conflict as part of prevention and treatment programs, focusing exclusively on conflict limits the breadth and potential effectiveness of these intervention. Other factors *do* play an important role in relationship functioning, and our clients can only benefit from our increasing knowledge of these factors. For example, because of the potential benefits to the couple, it is important to have information about relationship strengths as well as factors that are protective during predictable challenges like the transition to parenthood. It is also important to be able to provide useful information about other aspects of the relationship that might be affecting satisfaction and stability, including outside stress, psychopathology, and substance abuse.

My argument is that the MC and other prevention and treatment programs are able to make the most use of variables that imply useful action because either they are directly manipulable or at least they are lawfully related to other manipulable variables. As Bradbury et al. noted in chapter 5, although neuroticism has been consistently identified as predictive of relationship deterioration, it is difficult to determine how to make use of that information in a clinical intervention. My suspicion is that our pursuit of this type of knowledge has been primarily informed by our positivist leanings toward truth by correspondence criteria. In the context of the MC, however, it hardly seems useful to tell couples that one partner has scored highly on a neuroticism scale and that research has found this to be associated with relationship deterioration. What the couple is supposed to do with that information is not immediately obvious. On the other hand, if these basic studies had considered pragmatic truth criteria, then they might have also included variables more easily available for manipulation and assessed the relationship between those variables and neuroticism in the prediction of dysfunction. For example, if *awareness* of one's own neurotic tendencies were included as a variable, researchers could analyze whether such awareness moderates the relationship between neuroticism and marital distress. If awareness of neurotic tendencies did moderate the relationship between neuroticism and marital distress, then prevention and treatment scientists are provided with a finding that implies potentially effective action. Without such manipulable correlates, such information is at least, and unfortunately, of no use and may even be counter-therapeutic (because it implies an incurably corrosive condition). The same could be said of demographic or "niche" variables.

Although our inclinations toward a correspondence theory of truth are reasonable and likely to remain central to our science as we navigate the waters between positivism and pragmatism, my limited proposal is that a more active nod toward pragmatism during the design phase of our studies will be maximally beneficial to a progressive research program that has a positive impact on the quality of people's lives. Note that I am not arguing that basic scientists must wholly subvert their more positivist interests to pragmatic demands. However, I am asserting that we should consciously consider what the ultimate goals of our science are within this domain. To what degree do they involve taking a snapshot of reality and describing it as it would have itself described? And to what degree do they involve embracing the more mundane goal of discovering what works to improve people's lives?

REFERENCES

Beach, S. R., Whisman, M. A., & O'Leary, K. D. (1994). Marital therapy for depression: Theoretical foundation, current status, and future directions. *Behavior Therapy, 25,* 345-371.

Belsky, J. (1990). Children and marriage. In F. Fincham & T. Bradbury (Eds.), *The psychology of marriage* (pp. 87-117). New York: Guilford.

Buehlman, K., Gottman, J. M., & Katz, L. (1992). How a couple views their past predicts their future: Predicting divorce from an oral history interview. *Journal of Family Psychology, 5,* 295-318.

Cherlin, A. J., Furstenberg, F. F., Chase-Lansdale, P. L., Kiernan, K. E. (1991). Longitudinal studies of effects of divorce on children in Great Britain and the United States. *Science, 25,* 1386-1389.

Christensen, A., & Heavey, A. (1990). Gender and social structure in the demand/withdraw pattern of marital conflict. *Journal of Personality and Social Psychology, 59,* 73-81.

Conger, R. D., Rueter, M. A., & Elder, G. H. Jr. (1999). Couple resilience to economic pressure. *Journal of Personality and Social Psychology, 76,* 54-71.

Cordova, J. V., Jacobson, N. S., Gottman, J. M., Rushe, R., & Cox, G. (1993). Negative reciprocity and communication in couples with a violent husband. *Journal of Abnormal Psychology, 102,* 559-564.

Cordova, J. V., Warren, L. Z., & Gee, C. G. (in press). Motivational interviewing with couples: An intervention for at-risk couples. *Journal of Marital and Family Therapy.*

Doherty, W. J., Lester, M. E., & Leigh, G. K. (1986). Marriage encounter weekends: Couples who win and couples who lose. *Journal of Marital & Family Therapy, 12,* 49-61.

Emery, R. E. (1988). *Marriage, divorce, and children's adjustment.* Newbury Park, CA: Sage.

Fitzpatrick, M. A. (1988). *Between husband and wife: Communication in marriage.* Beverly Hills; CA: Sage.

Gottman, J. M. (1994). *What predicts divorce: The relationship between marital processes and marital outcomes.* Hillsdale; NJ: Lawrence Erlbaum Associates.

Gottman, J. M., Coan, J., Carrere, S., & Swanson, C. (1998). Predicting marital happiness and stability from newlywed interactions. *Journal of Marriage & the Family, 60,* 5-22.

Halford, W. K., & Osgarby, S. (1993). Alcohol abuse in clients presenting with marital problems. *Journal of Family Psychology, 6,* 1-11.

Heavey, C. L., Christensen, A., & Malamuth, N. M. (1995). The longitudinal impact of demand and withdrawal during marital conflict. *Journal of Consulting & Clinical Psychology 63,* 797-801.

Holtzworth-Munroe, A., Smutzler, N., Bates, L., & Sandin, E. (1997). Husband violence: Basic facts and clinical implications. In W. K. Halford & H. J. Markman (Eds.), *Clinical handbook of marriage and couples intervention* (pp. 129-151). New York: Wiley.

Huston, T. L., & Chorost, A. F. (1994). Behavioral buffers on the effect of negativity on marital satisfaction: A longitudinal study. *Personal Relationships, 1,* 223-239.

Jacobson, N. S., & Follette, W. C. (1985). Clinical significance of improvement resulting from two behavioral marital therapy components. *Behavior Therapy, 16,* 249-262.

Jacobson, N. S., Schmaling, K. B., & Holtzworth-Munroe, A. (1987). Component analysis of behavioral marital therapy: Two-year follow-up and prediction of relapse. *Journal of Marital and Family Therapy, 13,* 187-195.

Karney, B. R., & Bradbury, T. N. (1995). The longitudinal course of marital quality and stability: A review of theory, method, and research. *Psychological Bulletin, 118,* 3-34.

Margolin, G., Talovic, S., & Weinstein, C. D. (1993). Areas of change questionnaire: A practical approach to marital assessment. *Journal of Consulting and Clinical Psychology, 51,* 944-955.

Markman, H. J., Floyd, F., Stanley, S. M., & Storaasli, R. (1988). The prevention of marital distress: A longitudinal investigation. *Journal of Consulting and Clinical Psychology, 56,* 210-217.

Markman, H. J., Renick, M. J., Floyd, F. J., Stanley, S. M., & Clements, M. (1993). Preventing marital distress through communication and conflict management training: A 4- and 5-year follow-up. *Journal of Consulting and Clinical Psychology, 61,* 70-77.

Miller, W. R., & Rollnick, S. (1991). *Motivational interviewing: Preparing people to change addictive behavior.* New York: Guilford.

Negy, C., & Snyder, D.K. (1997). Ethnicity and acculturation: Assessing Mexican American couples' relationships using the Marital Satisfaction Inventory-Revised. *Psychological Assessment, 9,* 414-421.

Newton, T. L., Kiecolt-Glaser, J. K., Glaser, R., & Malarkey, W. B. (1995). Conflict and withdrawal during marital interaction: The roles of hostility and defensiveness. *Personality & Social Psychology Bulletin, 21,* 512-524.

O'Farrell, T. J., & Rotunda, R. J. (1997). In W. K. Halford & H. J. Markman (Eds.), *Clinical handbook of marriage and couples intervention* (pp. 555-583). New York: Wiley.

Paykel, E. S., Myers, J. K., Dienelt, M. M., Klerman, G. L., Linenthal, J. J., & Pepper, M. P. (1989). Life events and depression: A controlled study. *Archives of General Psychiatry, 20,* 753-760.

Pepper, S. C. (1942). *World hypotheses: A study in evidence.* Berkeley: University of California Press.

Prager, K. (1995). *The psychology of intimacy.* New York: Guilford.

Rorty, R. (1982). *Consequences of pragmatism.* Minneapolis: University of Minnesota Press.

Schmaling, K. B., & Scher, T. G. (1997). Physical health and relationships. In W. K. Halford & H. J. Markman (Eds.), *Clinical handbook of marriage and couples intervention* (pp. 323-336). New York: Wiley.

Snyder, D. K. (1997). *Marital Satisfaction Inventory-Revised.* Los Angeles: Western Psychological Services.

Spence, S. H. (1997). Sex and relationships. In W. K. Halford & H. J. Markman (Eds.), *Clinical handbook of marriage and couples intervention* (pp. 73-101). New York: Wiley.

Veroff, J., Douvan, E., & Kulka, R. A. (1981). *The inner American: A self-portrait from 1957 to 1976.* New York: Basic Books.

III

What Effects Does Couple Conflict Have on Children? How Do Individual Differences in Children Moderate These Effects?

9

Couple Conflict, Children, and Families: It's Not Just You and Me, Babe

E. Mark Cummings
Marcie C. Goeke-Morey
Lauren M. Papp
University of Notre Dame

How adults handle conflicts is a matter of significance to all members of the family. The issue is not simply whether or not conflicts occur. Conflict, broadly defined as disagreement or tension between couples, is inevitable in relationships. Moreover, the concern is not just the frequency of conflicts, because some couples may engage in lively, relatively frequent disagreements as productive, even perhaps enjoyed, means of solving everyday problems. Children may also learn valuable lessons concerning how to handle their own conflicts from observing adults' conflicts (Beach, 1995). On the other hand, despite these facts reflecting the "normalcy" of couple conflict, and recognizing that other, positive aspects of relationships are also important to family outcomes (Bradbury, Rogge, & Lawrence, chap. 5, this volume), the manner in which conflicts are handled is a significant matter for the psychological health and well-being of all members of the family (Beach & Nelson, 1990; Bradbury, 1998; Cummings, 1998; Emery, 1982; Grych & Fincham, 1990; Whisman, 2001).

Thus, an obvious, but nonetheless critical, issue is to develop advanced understanding of the distinctions between constructive and destructive couple conflicts, from the perspectives of both the adults and the children. Clearly, significant progress has been made on this front both in the study of couple conflict, and in the examination of the effects of couple conflict on children. However, despite some efforts at integrating these directions (Booth & Amato, 1994; Cummings & Davies, 1994; Fincham, 1998), research focusing on couple conflict, and the implications of these conflicts for the children, respectively, have continued to develop as largely distinct and independent fields of study.

INTEGRATING MARITAL AND CHILD DEVELOPMENT RESEARCH ON COUPLE CONFLICT

Consequently, one important contribution of this conference and associated volume is to stimulate exchange and awareness with regard to the convergence of interests for child and marital researchers in the study of couple conflict. For the child researcher it is important to recognize that parenting is not just a matter of the parent–child relationship, defined in isolation from other aspects of family functioning. The parent's role as a function of marital status and functioning merits consideration as an element of parenting, whether the marital relationship is intact, the couple is divorced, or the parent never married (Cummings, Goeke–Morey, & Graham, in press).

The marital (or other couple) system affects children both through the implications that children draw for their own functioning as a result of exposure to conflict (e.g., the processes set in motion in the children by the emotional security implications of conflict; Davies & Cummings, 1998) and by altering parenting practices in interaction with the children (Erel & Burman, 1995; Harold & Conger, 1997). Moreover, from a therapeutic perspective, recent research suggests that educating parents about better handling conflict may improve both the quality of marital *and* parent–child relationships, as well as have positive effects in terms of children's adjustment (Cowan & Cowan, 1999; Shifflett & Cummings, 1999). It is thus crucial for child researchers to draw on the knowledge gained from the study of marital relationships, but relatively few child development studies are informed by advanced theory and methods emerging from the study of couple conflicts (Fincham, 1998).

Similarly, for marital researchers, "its not just you and me, babe" when children are involved. The family is a system, and all members of the system, not just individuals and dyads, affect and are affected by significant family processes such as couple conflict. Thus, although children are influenced, they also influence couple conflict. Indicative of this relation, marriages are typically most discordant during the childrearing years, with marital conflict increasing after the birth of a first child (Belsky & Rovine, 1990). For example, children may become involved in attempting to ameliorate marital conflict, particularly in the context of high conflict or divorced marriages (Buchanan, Maccoby, & Dornbusch, 1991). Such mediation or other direct behavioral involvements or reactions to parental conflicts (e.g., heightened aggressivity following exposure to conflicts; Cummings, 1987), and parents' awareness of the children's cognitions, behaviors, and feelings, with regard to couple conflict, may affect the nature and course of interadult disputes. Child–rearing and other child–related topics or themes may frequently be a source of couple conflict. Thus, the child may be an unacknowledged, but significant, factor in couple conflict when one or both partners have children.

Moreover, ultimately, the determination of the distinction between constructive versus destructive conflict *within the family* will depend on *both* children's and couples' reactions to couple behaviors. Similarities in the nature of destructive and constructive conflict from the perspective of both children and adults have been reported (e.g., Cummings & Davies, 1994; Gottman, 1994), but there has been little direct study of the topic. For example, the developmental level of the child may limit full understanding of the intended meaning of couple conflict from the adults' perspective. Couple conflict in the context of other forms of relationships than marital ones may influence child outcomes. For example, the impact on children of a single parent's conflicts with multiple, and different, partners over the period of childhood may be a significant parenting influence (McLanahan & Sandefur, 1994). However, in the virtual absence of systematic research on these questions, the focus of the present discussion is on marital conflict and child development. Thus, child and marital researchers appear to have much to gain by drawing on the knowledge (theoretical, methodological, empirical) of each other's research traditions.

Hence, the value of more integrative themes in the study of the effects of couple conflict merits much more consideration than it has been given to date. However, another function of this chapter is to set the stage for a consideration of relations between couple conflict and child development. As a means of providing a foundation for this discussion, the bulk of the remainder of this chapter is concerned with providing a representation of that literature. Given space limitations, the treatment of each individual theme is necessarily brief. The questions are: (a) What do we know about the effects of marital conflict on the child, (b) what is the distinction between constructive and destructive conflict, (c) what is a framework for how children are affected by marital conflict, and (d) how can we think about effects over time from a process-oriented perspective? This discussion includes consideration of findings and new directions for addressing methodological and empirical gaps in the study of these questions (Cummings, Goeke–Morey, & Dukewich, in press) that are ongoing in our laboratory.

WHAT DO WE KNOW ABOUT THE EFFECTS OF MARITAL CONFLICT ON THE CHILDREN?

Clinical Implications

Marital conflict and violence does not stand as an isolated influence on the child, but is associated with multiple forms of dysfunction within the family that have potentially negative implications for children's adjustment, including divorce (Amato & Keith, 1991), maternal depression (Cummings & Davies, 1994b; Downey & Coyne, 1990), alcoholism (El-Sheikh & Cummings, 1997; West & Prinz, 1987), and sexual and physical abuse (Appel & Holden, 1998; Browne & Finkelhor, 1986; Jouriles, Barling, & O'Leary, 1987). For example, marital conflict is a factor in the effects of divorce on children before, during, and after the divorce occurs, including the sequelae of custody arrangements (Emery, 1988; 1994). Moreover, marital conflict and depression in adults are highly associated (Whisman, 2001), and, interestingly, marital conflict associated with depression has been more closely linked to some forms of adjustment problems in children than parental depression per se (Cummings & Davies, 1994b). Some have characterized exposure to high levels of marital conflict and violence as a form of emotional abuse (Jaffe, Wolfe, & Wilson, 1990). There is no doubt that marital conflict is a significant source of adversity in its own right (Grych & Fincham, 1990). Thus, although traditionally child development researchers have focused on parent–child relationships as influences on child development, it is becoming very evident that broader family systems, including relations between the child and marital system, need to be taken into account to more fully explain individual differences in children's pathways of development.

Children's Adjustment Problems. Conflict–ridden marital relations have been consistently linked with children's adjustment problems. Support for the association between marital conflict and child adjustment has been consistently reported for many years (Baruch & Wilcox, 1944; Gassner & Murray, 1969; Jouriles, Bourg, & Farris, 1991; Porter & O'Leary, 1980; Rutter, 1970; Towle, 1931) and is also reported cross–culturally (Lindahl & Malik, 1999; note also that extensive reviews are provided by Cummings & Davies, 1994; Grych & Fincham, 1990). It has long been shown that children from maritally discordant homes exhibit externalizing problems such as aggression and conduct issues. Moreover, as more sensitive measures of the impact on children's emotional functioning have been utilized (e.g., especially children's self–report of their own responses), increasingly children from high–conflict homes have been shown to evidence more internalizing problems such as anxiety, depression, and withdrawal. Children from high–conflict homes are also more likely to display lower social competence with peers, as well as academic problems such as poor grades and problems in intellectual achievement.

However, early research simply established relations between general marital adjustment and adjustment problems in children. The findings did not necessarily implicate marital conflict per se as the causal agent or clarify the nature of the processes involved. Other aspects of dysfunctional marriages also might contribute to adjustment problems in children; for example, a couple's unhappiness with each other or the absence of intimate communication between them (Jouriles, Bourg, & Farris, 1991). Recent work, however, identifies marital conflict as a particularly important aspect of marital functioning for children's development. For example, marital conflict has been shown to be typical of distressed marriages. Second, marital conflict has been found to be a better predictor of a wide range of children's problems than has general marital distress. Finally, marital conflict is more closely associated with children's problems than other individual aspects of distressed marriages (Cummings & Davies, 1994a).

Relations between marital conflict and children's adjustment problems are often reported in nonclinical samples, but are even more robust predictors of childhood disorders in clinical samples, particularly when there is marital violence (Jouriles, Bourg, & Farris, 1991). While mild to moderate relations between marital conflict and child adjustment are found when community samples are studied, moderate to strong relations are reported when at–risk samples (e.g., violent marriages) are examined (Fincham & Osborne, 1993; Wolfe, Jaffe, Wilson, & Zak,

1985). Thus, different pictures emerge with regard to the extent of relations between marital conflict and child adjustment as a function of the relative normality of family environments, implicating the broader family environment as significant to the effects associated with high marital conflict. Accordingly, the magnitude of relations between marital conflict and child adjustment is moderated by the overall adaptiveness and level of resource that characterize the family environment. In part, this may reflect the additive or multiplicative effects of multiple family stressors on children's adjustment; that is, risk for problems is increased as the number of forms of dysfunction within the family increases (Rutter, 1981).

Another likely factor is that forms of marital conflict are more negative and have more destructive implications for family relations in clinical samples. However, few studies have taken this issue head–on, and direct tests of these propositions are called for. Considerable weakness in traditional measurement strategies for assessing marital conflict also likely attenuates the size of correlations between marital conflict and children's adjustment problems (Cummings, Goeke–Morey, & Dukewich, in press). That is, most research on marital conflict and child development has relied on a small set of relatively global measures of marital conflict behaviors from the parent's perspective (see Grych, Seid, & Fincham, 1992, for an exception that provides assessment from the child's perspective). As we see later in this chapter, current and ongoing research from our laboratory is designed, in part, to address this gap, advancing new and multi method assessments of marital conflict based on laboratory and home–based measures, as well as questionnaire assessments.

Children's Social Competencies. Positive marital relations form a powerful foundation for healthy family functioning. The importance of the support and positive foundation for optimal parenting and family functioning that is provided by healthy, happy, intact marriages merits emphasis; the highly positive contribution of strong marriages is too often overlooked. Thus, marital satisfaction is linked with secure parent–child attachment and with positive father–child as well as mother–child relationships (Cummings & O'Reilly, 1997). Recent research suggests that secure interspousal relations compensate when marital partners have had insecure attachments to their own parents in childhood, and, as a consequence, foster the development of secure attachments with their own children (see Colin, 1996). Additionally, there are numerous correlates of intact marital relations (e.g., more optimal parenting practices) that also serve to foster the healthy socioemotional development of children. On the other hand, there has been relatively little systematic study of the positive effects of relatively constructive ways of handling conflict, so this issue is something of a gap in the literature.

Exposure to Marital Conflict. The effects on children of exposure to marital conflict have been repeatedly documented, especially in my own laboratory (see Table 9.1; Cummings & Davies, 1994a), but also in various other laboratories (e.g.,

Grych, 1998; Laumakis, Margolin, & John, 1998). Thus, we only briefly survey these data here.

Table 9.1
Studies of Links between Interadult Anger
and Children's Emotional Arousal

Study	Sample	Comparison	Response
	Studies of behavioral emotional responding		
Cummings, Zahn-Waxler, & Radke-Yarrow (1981)	24 children between 10 and 20 months of age; behavior in the home reported over a period of 9 months	Naturally occurring anger > naturally occurring affection	Distress, no attention and response
Cummings, Iannotti, & Zahn-Waxler (1985)	90 2-year-old children	Adults anger > adults positive emotions	Distress
Cummings (1987)	85 5-year-old children	Adults anger > adults positive emotions	Negative emotions, positive emotions preoccupation
El-Sheikh, Cummings, & Goetsch (1989)	34 4- to 5-year old children	Adults anger > adults positive emotions	Freezing, facial distress, postural distress, verbal concern, anger, smiling, preoccupation
Klaczynski & Cummings (1989)	40 first- to third-grade boys	Adults anger > adults positive emotions	Facial distress, postural distress, freezing
	Studies of self-reported emotions		
Cummings, Vogel, Cummings, & El-Sheikh (1989)	121 4- to 9-year-old children	Hostile, verbal, and nonverbal anger all > friendly interactions	Negative emotional responses (anger, fear, sadness)
Ballard & Cummings (1990)	35 6- to 10-year-old children	Verbal, indirect nonverbal, destructive, and aggressive anger all > friendly interactions	Anger, distress
Cummings, Ballard, El-Sheikh, & Lake (1991)	98 5- and 19-year-olds	Unresolved anger > partially resolved anger > friendly interactions	Anger, sadness, fear
Cummings, Ballard, & El-Sheikh (1991)	60 9- and 19-year-olds	Hostile, verbal, and nonverbal anger all > friendly interactions	Negative emotional responses (anger, fear, sadness)

Early Effects. Children's distress in reaction to marital conflict has been reported for children as young as 6 months of age (Shred, McDonnell, Church, & Rowan, 1991). Multiple emotional and behavioral reactions to marital conflict, including efforts to intervene and aggressive responding, are readily observed in 1–to 2–year-olds (Cummings, Zahn–Waxler, & Radke–Yarrow, 1981). In contrast to other forms of stress (e.g., separation), marital conflict remains a significant stressor for children throughout childhood, and, in fact, such responses are also reported in young adult children living away from home (Hall & Cummings, 1997). On the other hand, children's level of understanding and other aspects of responding may well change with age (Jenkins & Buccioni, 2000; Shifflet & Cummings, 1996).

Anatomy of Effects Due to Exposure. Children evidence the stressful effects of exposure to marital conflict in terms of multiple forms of responding. The major classes of responses that have been documented in the literature are outlined in Table 9.2. For example, emotional reactivity has been demonstrated in terms of multiple indicators of distress, physiological arousal (e.g., blood pressure), and behavioral dysregulation (intense displays of aggressivity; Cummings, Iannotti, & Zahn–Waxler, 1985). These patterns of reactions, which can be observed in children of all ages and throughout childhood, are well documented (Cummings & Davies, 1994a). However, children's efforts to regulate marital conflict or exposure to marital conflict by intervening or mediating in conflict becomes more pronounced beginning at school age (Cummings & Davies, 1994a; see also Buchanan, Maccoby & Dornbusch, 1991). Moreover, increased efforts at mediation and intervention are linked with more negative marital conflict histories, but it is not clear whether avoidance is associated with such histories (Cummings, 1998). Children's representations of the meaning of marital conflict also vary as a function of marital conflict histories in ways that might be expected, (i.e., more negative representations and expectations are linked with more negative marital

Table 9.2
Anatomy of the Effects of Marital Conflict on Children

Emotional Reactivity
• Facial: Distress, anger
• Motor: Inhibition, freezing, play slows or stops
• Self-report: Anger, sadness, fear
• Physiological: Heart rate, blood pressure, skin conductance, vagal tone
• Interpersonal: Aggression, support of siblings or peers
Regulation of Marital Conflict or Exposure to Marital Conflict
• Intervention, mediation, helping, being good
• Avoidance or withdrawal
Representations of Marital Relations
• Interpretation of the meaning or potential consequences for children s own well-being
• Interpretations of the meaning or potential consequences for others (e.g., the parents, siblings, family)

conflict histories; Davies & Cummings, 1998; Grych, 1998; Grych & Fincham, 1993). However, the study of the last major category of reactions (i.e., relations between marital conflict histories and children's representations of self, family, and the world) is in a relatively early stage of investigation. Because representations and other cognitions may be especially important as reflections of the impact of children's experiences with marital conflict on their long-term functioning, this gap is an especially significant one for a developmental understanding of effects.

Changes in Family Functioning, Especially Parenting

Recent research documents the finding that exposure to marital conflict affects children *both* directly due to exposure and indirectly by changing parenting practices (e.g., Harold & Conger, 1997; Harold, Fincham, Osborne, & Conger, 1997; Margolin, Christensen, & John, 1996; O'Brien, Bahadur, Gee, Balto, & Erber, 1997). In fact, a rather substantial literature has emerged to support relations between marital conflict and negative changes in parenting (Erel & Burman, 1995). Thus, parenting problems have been shown to be another pathway of the effects of marital conflict on children (Davies & Cummings, 1994). The spillover hypothesis provides one possible explanation. According to it, distress and hostility accompanying marital conflict are carried over into parenting practices, leading to changes in parental emotional availability (e.g., rejection, hostility, unresponsiveness) or control (e.g., lax monitoring, inconsistent or harsh discipline; Jouriles & Farris, 1992; Kitzmann, 2000; Mahoney, Boggio, & Jouriles, 1996; Margolin et al., 1996).

Marital Relations and Parenting Practices. Marital relations are predictive of the quality of parenting. That is, the consistency of parenting, the extent to which parenting is hostile or appropriate, the emotional availability of parents, and other parenting dimensions may be affected by the quality of marital relations. Emotional dimensions and qualities of parenting practices are particularly influenced by the quality of marital relations (Davies & Cummings, 1994).

Marital Relations and the Attachments Between Children and Parents

Marital relations are also predictive of the quality of the emotional bond or attachment that forms between parents and children; that is, the emotional security of the attachment between parents and children (Davies & Cummings, 1994). The effects may be due to reduced emotional availability and sensitive responsiveness, thereby leading to insecure attachment relations between parent and child over time. Alternatively, there may be a direct impact of exposure to marital conflict and violence on children by altering the child's sense of the safety and protection that can be provided by a violent or aggressive parent (Owen & Cox, 1997).

Sibling Relationships. Marital conflict is also linked with increased aggressivity and other problems between the siblings in families (Brody, Stonemann, & Burke, 1987; Stocker & Youngblade, 1999). This topic is less well investigated than the thoroughly demonstrated relations between marital conflict and diminished parenting practices but, nonetheless, appears to be a consistent finding. Interestingly, siblings may also support each other emotionally during exposure to parental conflict (Cummings & Smith, 1993). The attentiveness of siblings toward the well–being of the other is particularly marked in families in which one sibling has a disability (Nixon & Cummings, 1999).

WHAT IS THE DISTINCTION BETWEEN CONSTRUCTIVE AND DESTRUCTIVE CONFLICT? IT'S NOT WHETHER BUT HOW THE PARENTS FIGHT

The notion that "problem" marriages increase the likelihood of "problem" children is certainly not new. However, recent work suggests that the way parents handle their differences or conflicts is related to children's risk for psychopathology. As a consequence, research is increasingly concerned with discriminating between constructive and destructive interparental conflict styles from the perspective of the children, on the assumption that understanding such a distinction holds a key to predicting positive and negative outcomes for children due to the quality of interparental relations (Davies & Cummings, 1998). Adult–oriented research on marital quality and trajectories of marital relations over time has shown the importance of differentiating between constructive and destructive marital conflict styles, both for the purposes of scientific explanation and as a foundation for more effective therapeutic interventions (Gottman, 1994; Notarius & Markman, 1993). Next we provide a brief overview of the current status of knowledge in this area, based on a recent review of the evidence by Cummings, Davies, and Campbell (2000).

Destructive Conflict

Physical Aggression or Violence. There is considerable evidence that physical violence in marital disputes is highly distressing to children observing such behaviors, and increases children's risk for adjustment problems. The pattern of results indicates that physical violence is among the most disturbing forms of marital interaction for children, and is the most clearly linked with their adjustment problems. However, other forms of aggression are also disturbing to children, and are as related to children's adjustment problems as is interparental violence. Jouriles, Norwood, McDonald, Vincent, and Mahoney (1996) found that other forms of marital aggression (e.g., insulted or swore at the partner; threw, smashed, or kicked something; threatened to hit or throw something at the partner) and marital violence were each correlated with children's adjustment problems in a marital therapy sample and a women's shelter sample, respectively. Furthermore, the other forms of marital aggression assessed still related to children's adjustment problems, even after controlling for the frequency of marital violence. *Threats to the Intactness of the Family.* Some types of conflicts may contain messages that children find as disturbing as marital violence. Laumakis, Margolin, and John (1998) reported that conflicts involving threats to leave and those involving physical aggression elicited similar, high levels of negative reactions from children. Moreover, conflicts involving threats to leave and physical aggression elicited more negative emotional reactions and predictions of negative outcomes than did conflicts with name calling, negative voice, or conflicts with positive affect.

Nonverbal Conflict or the Silent Treatment. Nonverbal forms of conflict expression are not adequately assessed by any of the questionnaire instruments used to record rates of different forms of marital conflict in the home. However, children's reactions to analogue presentations of nonverbal conflict or "the silent treatment" indicate that they are significantly distressed by these behaviors and, in some studies, reactions to such behaviors are indistinguishable from reactions to overt verbal conflicts (Cummings & Davies, 1994a).

Intense Conflicts. It makes sense that more intense conflicts would be more disturbing than would less intense conflicts. There is support (Grych & Fincham, 1993) for the view that more intense conflicts elicit more negative reactions than do less intense conflicts, but effects may vary to some extent as a function of children's family history. Nixon and Cummings (1999) found that children from homes experiencing greater stress and distress due to the presence of a disabled sibling had a lower threshold for intensity of responding emotionally and behaviorally to conflict than did children from homes without a disabled sibling.

Conflicts about Child–related Themes. It makes sense intuitively that child-related themes of conflict would be more disturbing than other themes. There is also support for the notion that conflicts about child-related themes elicit more self-blame from children than do conflicts about other issues (Grych & Fincham, 1993). However, the literature overall is inconclusive on this point (Grych, 1998). Grych speculated that more important than whether the themes involve the children may be whether the themes have relatively serious negative implications for the family, regardless of the presence or absence of child content.

Withdrawal. In addition to overt conflict behavior, the withdrawal of parents from conflict may signal marital distress to children. The findings in this regard support the notion that children do not simply react to the expressiveness of conflict behavior. Katz and Gottman (1997) reported that husband withdrawal, indexed by observationally based codes of husband anger and stonewalling, predicted children's increased risk for adjustment problems. Cox, Paley, and Payne (1997) found that marital withdrawal was more predictive of negative child outcomes than was overt marital conflict. Again, the point is that these behaviors, although perhaps relatively subtle, can be reflective of significant marital distress, and it would appear from recent work that children are sensitive to the negative meaning of these communications.

Constructive Conflict

By contrast to these forms of conflict expression, which appear to increase children's risk for problems, other ways of handling conflict have been found to have little negative effect and may possibly function as protective or compensatory events in the context of family functioning.

Mutually Respectful, Emotionally Modulated Conflicts. Easterbrooks, Cummings, and Emde (1994) reported that toddlers evidenced little distress in reaction to conflictual discussions between parents in a sample of parents who almost always expressed conflicts in mutually respectful and emotionally well–modulated tones. On the other hand, parental anger expression, which was relatively uncommon, was associated with negative emotional reactions by children even in this study.

Conflict Resolution. A long series of analogue studies has demonstrated that children's distress, and other negative reactions, are dramatically reduced when conflicts are resolved (Cummings & Davies, 1994). Moreover, a recent field study based on a new questionnaire that assessed conflict resolution reported that marital conflict resolution was more consistently associated with child adjustment (i.e., reduced adjustment problems) than even negative elements of conflict (e.g., frequency, severity; Kerig, 1996).

Progress Toward Resolution and Other Information About Resolution . Analogue studies also indicate that children benefit from any progress toward resolution; that is, distress reactions are reduced even when parents (actors) do not fully resolve conflicts. Furthermore, children's distress reactions are also reduced even when adults have resolved conflicts behind closed doors, only indicating resolution by changed (to positive) affect after emerging from another room entered in the midst of conflict (see Cummings & Davies, 1994a). Children also benefit from hearing brief explanations indicating that conflicts have been resolved (Cummings, Simpson, & Wilson, 1993), or even that conflicts have *not* yet been resolved, but that parents expect that they will be eventually (Cummings & Wilson, 1999).

However, a gap in the research on destructive versus constructive conflict from the children's perspective is that the criteria for making this determination are multiple, varied, and somewhat hazy. Ideally, such determinations should be theoretically guided with regard to the issues about marital conflict that are most significant to the children and based on an assessment of children's own critical reactions to marital conflict behaviors. Goeke-Morey and Cummings (2000) provided a conceptually driven means for assessing children's evaluations of the relative constructiveness versus destructiveness of marital conflict from the children's perspective. We return to this issue later.

WHAT IS A FRAMEWORK FOR HOW THE CHILD IS AFFECTED BY MARITAL CONFLICT?

Sufficiently Inclusive Research Designs

The complexity of relations between marital conflict and children's outcomes necessitates sufficiently inclusive research designs so that major familial influences are considered, including possible mediators and moderators of child outcomes (Cummings, Goeke–Morey, & Dukewich, in press). Piecemeal consideration of the factors affecting children's adjustment and development is doomed to provide only partial answers to questions about the effects of marital conflict on the children. A framework that reflects the complexity of family processes and factors associated with the effects of marital conflict on children is presented in Figure 9.1. Consistent with the previous discussion, a distinction is made between constructive and destructive marital relations. Marital relations are portrayed as having direct effects on children's psychological functioning, but also indirect effects mediated by effects on parenting.

Mediators. One must account for "how" and "why" marital conflict affects children. It doesn't just happen—there is something in that black box. In our theorizing, psychological functioning (i.e., emotional, social, behavioral, cognitive, physiological reactions) is hypothesized as mediating children's adjustment, with the specific processes set in motion in the child by marital conflict processes either increasing vulnerability or increasing competence. Mediators are the "generative mechanism" by which an independent variable influences outcomes. In this instance, identifying mediators would mean explaining precisely how and why marital conflict leads to lack of social competencies or adjustment problems in children.

Moderators. On the other hand, effects are unlikely to be the same for all individuals and in all familial and extrafamilial contexts. Thus, there is the matter of "when" and "for whom" relations between variables are obtained. That is, moderators may alter the relations found between variables. Moderators specify the strength and/or direction of relations between an independent variable and an out-

FIG. 9.1
A Dynamic Process Model of the Pathways of Development over Time.

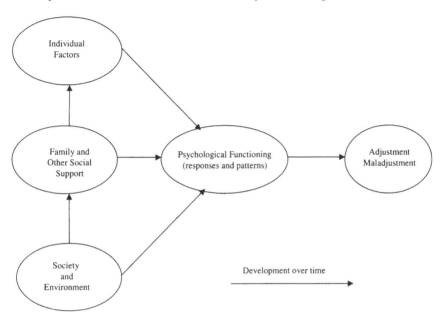

come. If moderators are identified, it means that the nature and degree of risk is not uniform across different conditions and people. Moderator variables may include family context (e.g., parental adjustment, family emotional climate, socioeconomic status, and other family factors) and child characteristics (e.g., gender, personality, or temperament), but also may include a variety of other factors (see Holmbeck, 1997, for a discussion of the distinction between mediators and moderators).

Development Over Time and Pathways of Development. The impact of marital conflict on children does not occur immediately, but rather over the course of many years. Thus, one must consider time and the effects of marital conflict over time; that is, a dynamic process model of transactions between intra– and extra–organismic factors in developmental contexts must be examined and explained (Cummings, Davies, & Campbell, 2000). Moreover, children's development is not static or fixed, but is best conceptualized in terms of pathways of development (see later discussion). Finally, developmental period, that is, children's age or stage of development, may also factor in their responding. The role of these developmental factors is signified by the notation of "development over time" in the figure.

The framework in Figure 9.1 thus places emphasis on studying specific contexts of exposure to marital conflict and the effects of marital conflict on the family. Individual differences between children in their reactions to marital conflict, including their histories of exposure to marital conflict and the multidimensional nature of coping processes are also central, as is the impact of marital conflict on changes in the family system's overall level of functioning. The intent of the framework is to capture a holistic perspective on marital relations, family functioning, and child development.

HOW CAN WE THINK ABOUT EFFECTS OVER TIME FROM A PROCESS-ORIENTED PERSPECTIVE?

The matter of how to conceptualize development over time is not an easy or simple one. Those who are not developmentalists may have been mercifully spared the need to think such thoughts. However, the issue must be addressed. Next, we offer some of our current perspectives, as they pertain to marital conflict and child development.

A Process–oriented Perspective on Mediators

Children's reactions to marital conflict are not just a matter of the current marital conflict stimuli to which they are exposed, but are also a function of past histories of exposure to marital conflict. A challenge for research is to account for how and why histories of marital conflict are related to children's adjustment problems over time. The goal of a process–oriented perspective is to account for these effects in terms of fine–grained analyses of specific effects on children's daily functioning in specific family contexts, including contexts of marital conflict.
Stress and Coping. An especially precise level of analysis of mediators is to assess reactions in terms of everyday stress and coping processes (Cummings, Zahn-Waxler, & Radke-Yarrow, 1981), tracking cumulative change over time at a microanalytic, multiresponse level of analysis. From a process–oriented perspective, an important issue is to account for how short–term fluctuations and changes in marital relations and children's reactions translate over time into relatively stable patterns of adjustment or maladjustment in children (Cummings & Cummings, 1988). The effects of family experiences on children may frequently reflect the occurrence of small, frequently subtle, changes in interpersonal and social behaviors in response to the occurrence of daily stressors or positive experiences (e.g., social support, happy moments; Cummings, 1998; Repetti, McGrath, & Ishikawa, 1999; Repetti & Wood, 1997). A reasonable hypothesis is that changes in children's coping responses, processes, and styles in the short term mediate long–term outcomes in children associated with marital conflict (see Figure 9.1; Davis, Hops, Alpert, & Sheeber, 1998).

Notably, parental diaries of marital conflict and child reactions in the home may provide data that are especially appropriate for understanding children's coping processes, responses, and styles at this level of analysis (Garcia–O'Hearn, Margolin, & John, 1997). By contrast, statistical or measurement approaches that assess mediators in terms of global self–reported assessments of psychological variables, particularly when based on a single self–reported assessment, may not adequately reflect the dynamic and transactional nature of the psychological processes that underlie children's development. Thus, they may provide only an approximate characterization of the nature of mediating processes, and incorrectly imply that children's response processes are static rather than dynamic. Of course, the most informative level of analysis is ultimately an empirical issue, and it may be that patterns, styles, or other higher–order levels of analysis, especially when based on multimethod and multiresponse assessments, are most reflective of the nature of children's psychological organization and functioning (e.g., Davies & Cummings, 1994).

Marital Conflict Histories and Children's Stress and Coping Responses: Sensitization. Of course, a process-oriented perspective requires a specific description of changes in children's daily response patterns over time that can be seen as potentially leading to adjustment problems. In that regard, considerable evidence has accumulated to indicate that children become more reactive to marital conflict in terms of numerous dimensions of responding as a function of greater histories of marital conflict (i.e., the sensitization hypothesis). These results underscore that it's not just the immediate conflict that matters, but that past histories of exposure to conflict also affect children's reactions. That is, sensitization occurs with repeated exposure to conflict. The prediction of this hypothesis is that, in response to the same current conflict, in relation to children from low–conflict homes, children exposed to high levels of conflict in the past evidence greater reactivity (e.g., more distress; more anger and aggression; more involvement in attempting to regulate the parents' conflict, such as efforts at mediation).

The sensitization notion suggests how changes occur in children's coping responses, processes, and styles as a function of marital conflict histories. Moreover, one can construct how such changes may over time lead to increased risk for adjustment problems (Cummings, Davies, & Campbell, 2000). Cummings and Davies (1994) provided a review of some of the evidence supporting this hypothesis at the time that volume went to press, and support for the proposition continues to accumulate, with few findings that contradict the model emerging (e.g., Davies & Cummings, 1998; Davis et al., 1998; El-Sheikh, 1997; Garcia–O'Hearn et. al, 1997; Gordis, Margolin, & John, 1997; Grych, 1998; Harold, Fincham, Osborne, & Conger, 1997; Ingoldsby, Shaw, Owens, & Winslow, 1999; Katz & Gottman, 1995a, 1995b; Laumakis, Margolin, & John, 1998; Margolin, Christensen, & John, 1996; Nixon & Cummings, 1999; O'Brien & Chin, 1998; O'Brien, Margolin, & John, 1995).

A new direction to further test the notion that histories of negative marital conflict behavior increase sensitization to conflict is to experimentally manipulate videotaped exposure to histories of constructive versus destructive conflict. The results of studies following this direction suggest that histories of exposure to *negative* conflict behaviors (intense verbal anger expression, lack of conflict resolution) sensitize children to conflict, but that histories of exposure to *positive* conflict scenarios (calm discussion, resolved conflict) do *not* result in sensitization to conflict (Davies, Myers, Cummings, & Heindel, 1999; El–Sheikh & Cummings, 1995; El–Sheikh, Cummings, & Reiter, 1996). Of course, reactions to conflict histories based on relatively brief exposures to analogue conflicts are likely to be less pronounced than are effects due to actual exposures to marital conflict in the home (e.g., Cummings et al., 1981). However, the demonstration of sensitization in a controlled experimental context does serve to diminish concerns about possible "third variable" interpretations. The findings of these experimental studies thus serve to support further the results of field studies comparing responses to conflict as a function of actual marital conflict histories in the home.

A THEORY ABOUT MEDIATING PROCESSES: THE EMOTIONAL SAFETY HYPOTHESIS

(Understanding at a Theoretical Level Why and How Children Are Affected)

Although evidence for sensitization has been reported for some time, until recently there was little progress toward articulating specific theories that might account for sensitization and other evidence pertinent to the nature of mediating processes. The notion of sensitization, in itself, is data descriptive but does not posit a conceptualization of the psychological nature of mediating processes.

At this point, two major theories have been proposed: (a) Davies and Cummings' (1994) emotional security hypothesis, and (b) Grych and Fincham's (1990) cognitive–contextual framework. These two models are generally complementary and make many similar points. For example, both models emphasize that children do not just react to the fact of conflict but more importantly to its meaning for them. The emotional security hypothesis specifies a *particular* meaning against which children appraise the implications of marital and family conflict for themselves and their families, suggests how that meaning is personal, and indicates why children respond emotionally (Davies & Cummings, 1994). Emotional security describes the goal of children's functioning in the face of marital conflict. Consistent with Bowlby's (1969) notion of control systems as applied to children's appraisals of threat and security, children's emotional and cognitive reactions to their appraisal of the emotional security implications of marital conflict are hypothesized to organize, motivate, and direct their responding around a set goal of desired emotional security. For example, if children perceive marital conflict to be a threat to emotional security, based on past history and the current nature of marital conflict behavior, they are expected to be highly reactive to marital conflict in the service of taking steps to again achieve the set goal of emotional security (i.e., reactivity that would be described as "sensitization"). On the other hand, if children do not appraise a threat to emotional security, they are expected to have little motivation to react, because the set goal of emotional security would already be achieved.

Specific Mediating Processes. Various specific regulatory systems are subsumed under the rubric of emotional security as an operating process (Cummings & Davies, 1996). These specific components are separate, but also interdependent, in the service of emotional security:

1. *Emotional reactivity*—This component consists of children's emotional reactivity and arousal, and their capacity to reduce, enhance, and/or maintain their emotionality in the face of conflict. For example, children's emotional organization of anger may be affected by exposure to higher amounts of anger based martial conflict (Jenkins, 2000). In terms of physiological responding, children from more socially "secure" families have more adaptive responses to family stresses (Flinn & England, 1995). The emotional security hypothesis adopts a functionalist perspective on the role of emotions and emotionality in children's appraisals and responding to stressful events (e.g., Campos et al., 1989); that is, as noted earlier, emotions are assumed to play a key role in organizing, directing, and motivating responding. Accordingly, emotional reactivity is expected to be the most fundamental and sensitive of the indicators of children felt emotional security in the face of marital conflict, particularly in response to immediate contexts of marital conflict.

2. *Internal representation of family relations*—Representations most relevant to children's emotional security consist of their interpretation of the meaning and potential consequences of marital conflict for their own well–being. These representations are proffered to be relatively accurate depictions of family life (Bowlby, 1973); thus, it follows that children who witness histories of negative conflict should be prone to developing insecure representations of family relations. Representations are expected to play a key role in the long-term sequelae of marital conflict for children's functioning. That is, once children form representational models of the parents' marital relations, these are expected to remain relatively stable and persistent over time.

3. *Regulation of exposure to family affect*—Emotional security also serves a motivational function by guiding children to regulate their exposure to stressful parental emotion. The issues with regard to an assessment of emotional

security include the repertoire of children's regulatory activities and behaviors (e.g., forms and styles of mediation behaviors), their threshold for
onset, and their appropriateness in specific contexts. Research has shown
that children from high–conflict homes more often use intervention in an
attempt to alleviate conflict (Buchanan et al., 1991; Cummings & Davies,
1994a). Regulatory strategies are expected to be particularly sensitive to
developmental level and age; that is, coping capacities are expected to
change substantially with age. Moreover, regulatory strategies are also expected to be quite sensitive to context. Thus, one would not expect children
to be nearly so likely to intervene in disputes between adult strangers as in
the disputes between their parents.

Notably, these regulatory processes are measurable and are consistent with
the patterns of responding reported in the literature on children's responding to
marital conflict (see Table 9.2). Moreover, each of these response domains has
been shown to be reactive to marital conflict histories and reflect specific response dimensions that evidence sensitization with repeated exposure to marital
conflict. In sum, whether one accepts or does not accept the merit of a higher-
order construct of emotional security, the specific cognitive, behavioral, and emotional regulatory systems that are hypothesized to service emotional security have
considerable basis in the empirical literature.

Some Supportive Evidence for the Theory. Some of the evidence in support of the
theory merits consideration. Whereas some of the evidence is no more than sug-
gestive, other evidence emerges from direct tests of theoretical propositions.

The Great Impact of Conflict Resolution. This notion of emotional security can
explain why negative reactions to conflict are dramatically ameliorated by conflict resolution, and why children are so sensitive to any evidence about possible
resolution, even when resolutions may be much briefer than conflict episodes.
That is, children are concerned about the meaning of conflicts for themselves and
their families, not just the occurrence of conflict. Conflict resolution greatly changes
the familial implications of otherwise anxiety–arousing social situations. Specifically, conflict resolution changes the emotional security implications of conflict.

Why Sensitization? The emotional reactivity construct can account for why children evidence sensitization, rather than habituation, when they have histories of
exposure to high marital conflict in the home, especially violence. It makes sense
that children from such homes would become more aroused, because these events
are more threatening, realistically, for them. That is, when there is high marital
conflict there is more likelihood that conflicts will proliferate to include the children, that a parent will be injured, and that the occurrence of conflicts will have
more negative short– and long–term implications for the child and family. Even

though these children are more distressed, it makes sense for them to also be more likely to try to intervene in conflicts, given the implications (Emery, 1989). In other words, conflicts pose a greater threat to these children's sense of emotional security. More generally, risk–taking behavior (e.g., intervention in interparental hostility) has been related to decreased confidence in the predictability of family events (Hill, Thomson–Ross, & Low, 1997), which is likely to be associated with high marital conflict.

A Test of Propositions. The most convincing support for the emotional security hypotheses is a recent study indicating that multimethod assessments of emotional security mediated relations between qualitative aspects of marital conflict and qualitative differences in child outcomes (Davies & Cummings, 1998). In this concurrent test, support was found for a theoretical pathway whereby negative marital conflict led to children's adjustment problems as mediated by reduced emotional security about marital relations. By contrast, greater emotional security mediated a pathway between constructive marital conflict properties (e.g., marital conflict resolution) and reduced adjustment problems (Davies, 1995). Of the components of emotional security, children's regulation of negative emotionality in reaction to marital conflict mediated pathways to both internalizing and externalizing (e.g., aggressiveness) disorders, and the children's representations of the quality of marital relations also mediated relations between marital conflict and children's internalizing problems (e.g., anxiety, depression). However, a limitation of this test with regard to inferences about causality is that it is based on a cross-sectional research design. Of course, tests in terms of prospective, longitudinal research designs are necessary to provide more convincing examination of the viability of the theory.

A Theoretical Basis for Defining Constructive, Destructive, and Productive Conflict. As noted earlier, although the distinction between constructive and destructive conflict holds considerable interest for both child and adult researchers concerned with the effects of couple conflict, there has not been a theoretical basis for how marital conflict behaviors should be classified in this regard. Thus, to some extent, such determinations must be regarded as uncertain or tentative. Goeke–Morey (1999) proposed that for the children, at least, their emotional security in reaction to exposure to marital conflict behaviors can serve as a theoretically informed basis for making this determination. In particular, consistent with the emotional security hypothesis, she proposed that the valence of children's emotional reactions in response to exposure to marital conflict provides a basis for making this determination. Thus, marital conflict behaviors that elicit significantly more negative than positive emotional reactions from children are classified as "destructive," whereas marital conflict behaviors that elicit significantly more positive than negative emotional reactions are classified as "constructive." The former might be seen as reducing a child's level of felt security, whereas the latter can be interpreted as actually increasing the child's level of felt security. Application of this classification system to children's responses also yielded a third category of marital conflict behavior; that is, those behaviors that resulted in no significant difference between negative and positive emotional responding. Notably, such behaviors tended to elicit very low levels of either positive or negative emotional responses. Goeke–Morey (1999) classified these behaviors as "productive"; that is, they tended to reflect a useful consideration of marital issues between the parents but did not impact on children's felt security.

To test these criteria for evaluating the relative constructiveness versus destructiveness of marital conflict behaviors from the children's perspective, 51 4– through 11– year–old children were presented with a series of 38 video clips reflecting a variety of commonly occurring marital conflict behaviors, including behaviors that tended to occur during or at the end of conflicts. A methodological innovation was that clips were kept short (5 to 10 seconds) and were very precisely defined. These procedures allowed testing of children's responses to a wide range of marital conflict behaviors and enhanced precision in evaluating the impact of specific marital conflict behaviors on the children. Children were asked to imagine that the actors were their parents and the setting was represented as if it were their own home. Past research has indicated the meaningfulness of children's responding in the context of this analogue procedure; that is, responding has been related to past histories of marital conflict in the home and children's current adjustment in ways that support the predictive validity of response patterns. To assess emotional security, children were asked how they would feel, and how much they would feel that way, after each video clip, using an interview schedule that simplifies the response context and has been demonstrated to elicit reliable responding about emotions even among very young children (e.g., 4– to 5– year–olds; Cummings, Vogel, Cummings, & El-Sheikh, 1989). Notably, all behaviors were represented as occurring in the context of a conflict; that is, a conflict stem was presented verbally by the experimenter and then a video clip was shown and described as indicating the behavior that the adults exhibited just following the conflict stem.

By the criteria described, the following emerged as "destructive" conflict behaviors for behaviors occurring *during* conflicts: physical aggression toward persons, physical aggression toward objects, threat, verbal anger, nonverbal anger, and withdraw. "Constructive" conflict behaviors were humor (mothers only) and affection. Productive conflict behaviors included humor (fathers only), calm discussion, problem-solving, and support. (See Table 9.3 for means and F-values for the comparisons of negative and positive emotional responses.) Notably, by these criteria "productive" conflict behaviors were considerably more prevalent than were constructive conflict behaviors, and there were few differences as a function of the gender of the parent initiating the conflict.

As noted earlier, the impact on emotional security of the behaviors occurring at the end of conflicts was also assessed. The following emerged as destructive

Table 9.3
**Means and F-Values for Differences in Children's Negative and
Positive Emotional Reactions to Behaviors Used During Marital Conflict**

Conflict Behavior	Negative	Positive	F
Father			
Physical aggression (object)	22.93	1.29	59.84**
Physical aggression (person)	19.17	1.78	46.81**
Threat	16.94	2.65	28.63**
Verbal anger	17.06	1.72	34.88**
Withdraw/avoid	11.33	3.92	7.36*
Nonverbal anger	11.28	2.28	15.49**
Calm discussion	5.65	4.58	.24
Problem-solving	3.17	7.06	3.74
Support	5.20	8.57	1.49
Humor	6.13	10.69	2.95
Affection	3.83	11.67	9.66*
Mother			
Physical aggression (object)	19.06	2.35	37.17**
Physical aggression (person)	19.08	1.14	59.24**
Threat	15.71	1.88	32.63**
Verbal anger	16.65	1.99	31.45**
Withdraw/avoid	15.84	1.54	34.90**
Nonverbal anger	13.60	2.31	23.45**
Calm discussion	4.50	4.51	.00
Problem-solving	3.03	5.53	1.68
Support	7.13	5.01	.59
Humor	2.04	12.78	21.39**
Affection	1.43	19.56	90.17**

Note. df = (1, 50)   ** p < .001, *p < .025
0 = not at all , 8 = a little, 15 = some, 22 = a lot, 30 = a whole lot

ways to end conflicts from the children's perspective: cold shoulder, verbal unresolved, and agreed to disagree (fathers only). Constructive ways to end conflicts were apology, compromise, changed topic (fathers only), and agreed to discuss later (fathers only). Productive ways to end conflicts included: gave-in, changed the topic (mothers only), agreed to disagree (mothers only), agreed to discuss later (mothers only). (See Table 9.4 for means and F-values for the comparisons of negative and positive emotional responses.) In this instance, the gender of the parent mattered more for the children's appraisal of the emotional security implications of the conflicts. In particular, fathers finding a way to leave the topic without clearly labeling the outcome (changed the topic, agreed to discuss later) was seen as a quite positive sign, whereas when mothers ended matters in this fashion it was only seen as a productive, not highly positive, outcome. Perhaps children are more confident that if dad changes the topic then the discussion is really over,

Table 9.4
Means and F-Values for Differences in Children's
Negative and Positive Emotional Reactions to Behaviors
Used at the End of Marital Conflict

Conflict Behavior	Negative	Positive	F
Father			
Verbal unresolved	15.25	2.06	18.38**
Cold shoulder 13.61	1.85	25.99**	
Give-in	6.07	7.52	.03
Agree to disagree	8.12	2.19	7.16*
Agree to discuss later	2.68	9.27	7.98*
Change topic	.81	12.49	31.85**
Apologize	2.58	12.25	15.44**
Compromise	1.09	15.25	45.57**
Mother			
Verbal unresolved	14.39	3.52	16.03**
Cold shoulder 10.10	3.92	5.22*	
Give-in	6.31	6.77	.03
Agree to disagree	3.75	6.98	1.80
Agree to discuss later	3.49	7.89	3.80
Change topic	5.45	7.00	.43
Apologize	2.81	11.97	15.26**
Compromise	.78	12.08	32.57**

Note. df = (1, 50) ** p < .001, *p≤.025
0 = not at all, 8 = a little, 15 = some, 22 = a lot, 30 = a whole lot

at least temporarily, whereas when mom changes the topic the issues will linger and the discussion will resurface. Likewise, when dad agrees to return to the topic later then children may be more confident that the conflict is essentially over, whereas when mom does so it is expected that she will return to the issues at a later time.

On the other hand, agreeing to disagree was seen as quite negative when fathers did it, but as productive when mothers took that direction. In this instance, children may feel that fathers' dismissing the prospect of a resolution indicates that they will continue to be angry about the situation in the future, whereas mothers adopting such a strategy is seen as a holding action and that mothers will likely revisit the prospect of achieving a resolution later. In short, children appear to make categorical interpretations of fathers' partial resolution strategies (i.e., as either constructive or destructive), whereas mothers' partial resolution strategies are interpreted as productive but not conclusive with regard to the meaning of the conflict for the parents. Thus, from the children's perspective, the same strategies for leaving conflict situations were interpreted quite differently for fathers and mothers, suggesting that children perceive that parents mean different things when engaging in exactly the same behaviors.

These results are generally supportive of distinctions made on the basis of the various, nontheoretically driven criteria for assessing the constructiveness versus destructiveness of marital conflict behaviors from the children's perspective. Moreover, the present methodology allowed for the assessment of children's reactions to several new categories of behaviors during and at the end of conflicts, thereby extending the range of investigation of the phenomena. For the most part, the behaviors that have typically been viewed as relatively destructive from the children's perspective were again found to have negative effects; that is, they appeared to reduce the child's sense of security. The greatest advance was in the conceptualization of nondestructive behaviors. Perhaps the most important conceptual implication was that some marital conflict behaviors are not either constructive nor destructive, but rather are more properly seen as productive from the child's perspective. That is, many ways in which parents behave in conflict situations do not affect children's emotional security one way or the other. In particular, calm discussion, problem solving, support, and various ways of ending conflicts without explicitly resolving them, particularly when done so by the mother, are perhaps better described as "ok" from the child's perspective, but not exactly reassuring.

In another element of the broader research direction of this study, parents were trained to provide diary reports of the occurrence of these same conflict behaviors in everyday marital conflict situations, as well as rate other aspects of marital conflict behavior. Parents also scored children's responding (see Table 9.5 for an outline of procedures; see also Cummings, Goeke–Morey, & Dukewich, in press, for a detailed description of this new methodological direction for diary reporting). Pertinent to gaps identified by Bradbury et al. in this literature (chap.

Table 9.5
Outline of New Diary Methodology

Parental Diaries - New Procedures
Parents thoroughly trained as observers
Clearly defined terminology, limited language load
Parents tested pre- and post-reporting for reliability
Both fathers and mothers complete diaries; relatively easy to complete
Record marital conflict and children's reactions for 6 days over a two-week period
Broader, more inclusive definition of marital conflict
Constructive and destructive categories included

5, this volume), advantages of this methodology for both child and adult research-ers include (a) investigation of marital conflict behaviors in the natural environ-ment; (b) obtaining a history of conflict behavior over a meaningful span of time, rather than only a snapshot; (c) obtaining data on withdrawal and avoidance of conflict in settings other than the laboratory, which may underestimate the role of these behaviors; (d) increasing the possibility of quantifying rare but pivotal mari-tal conflict events, given that marital conflict behavior is obtained over a substan-tial period of time; and (e) obtaining data on nonconflict as well as conflict behav-iors, albeit in the context of conflict (e.g., humor; social support).

We only have space to present a snapshot of some of the data pertinent to the present discussion. A particularly interesting initial finding, given the present dis-cussion, is that parents typically engage in what would be termed by the Goeke–Morey (1999) criteria as "productive" conflict behaviors, rather than either "con-structive" or "destructive" conflict behaviors (see Table 9.6). Moreover, and con-sistent with the Goeke–Morey (1999) report of responding to analogue presenta-tions of marital conflict, children typically respond to these productive conflict behaviors in an emotionally neutral fashion; that is, evidencing neither emotion-ally positive or negative reactions. Notably, our criteria for what we classified as conflict behavior was broad, including any disagreement or tension between the parents. However, the interesting; and revealing point is that most of the everyday marital conflict discussions were productive rather than either dramatically posi-tive or negative in their direction, at least from the perspective of the children. Of course, these analyses are preliminary and much further analysis remains.

Ongoing research in our laboratory continues to expand and further develop the conceptual, methodological, and theoretical directions discussed in this chap-ter. Our newest project is a three–wave longitudinal design, following 300 mari-tally intact families with children ranging in age from 8– to16– years–old (at the outset), for 3 consecutive years. In an attempt to better understand patterns of functioning in typically underrepresented families, an emphasis of this project is on recruiting a large sample of minority families with varying socioeconomic sta-tus. This design will provide a prospective, longitudinal test of causal models about how, why, and when marital conflict affects children's development. With

Table 9.6
Descriptive Statistics of Parental Diary Reports of Disagreements and Conflict Behaviors and Children's Behavioral Reactions for 6 Days Over a 2-Week Period

Diary Reports	Mean	Min	Max
Total Conflicts			
Number of conflicts			
Male report	3.97	0	21
Female report	4.78	1	20
Couples' behaviors during conflict			
Destructive	8.32	1	33
Productive	9.13	0	49
Constructive	1.58	0	13
Couples' behaviors at the end of conflict			
Destructive	1.68	0	10
Productive	4.97	0	29
Constructive	5.10	0	19
Conflicts in front of child			
Number of conflicts			
Male report	1.71	0	10
Female report	2.22	0	9
Children's behaviors during conflict (female report)			
Mediating	1.48	0	7
Externalizing	.12	0	1
Internalizing	.12	0	1
Unaffected/OK	3.58	0	15
Children's behaviors at the end of conflict (female report)			
Mediating	1.03	0	7
Externalizing	.36	0	4
Internalizing	.03	0	1
Unaffected/OK	3.09	0	17

the multimethod design employed (questionnaire, behavioral, analogue, and diary record), we attempt to capitalize on the strengths of each method while avoiding the weaknesses and pitfalls of any simple method. The design is intended to allow for a more complex and complete picture of marital and child functioning in the natural environment of the home than in past research (Cummings et al, 1981). In particular, guided by theory (the emotional security hypothesis), we hope to advance understanding of constructive, destructive, and productive marital conflict from the children's perspective.

CONCLUSIONS

The manner by which adults handle their conflicts is important for the security and well–being of all members of the family. With increasingly fine–tuned conceptualization, methodology, and theory, we are learning much more at the causal level of analysis about the nature of constructive and destructive conflict from both the children's and the adults' perspectives. This dual consideration is crucial for understanding the processes by which couple conflict influences all members of the family system. Although couple and child researchers continue to advance the knowledge of our respective fields, it is important to recognize the natural convergence of our interests. A promising goal for the future is to strive to integrate our respective fields of study toward more fully appreciating and understanding the complexity of the relations between couple conflict and the family.

ACKNOWLEDGMENTS

Preparation of this chapter was supported in part by a grant from the National Institute of Child Health and Human Development (HD 36261) to the first author.

REFERENCES

Amato, P. R., & Keith, B. (1991). Consequences of parental divorce for children's well-being: A meta-analysis. *Psychological Bulletin, 110,* 26-46.

Appel, A. E., & Holden, G. W. (1998). The co-occurrence of spouse and physical child abuse: A review and appraisal. *Journal of Family Psychology, 12,* 578-599.

Baruch, D. W., & Wilcox, J. A. (1944). A study of sex differences in preschool children's adjustment coexistent with interparental tensions. *Journal of Genetic Psychology, 64,* 281-303.

Beach, B. (1995). *The relation between marital conflict and child adjustment: An examination of parental and child repertoires.* Unpublished manuscript.

Beach, S. R. H., & Nelson, G. M. (1990). Pursuing research on major psychopathology from a contextual perspective: The example of depression and marital discord. In G. H. Brody & I. E. Siogel (Eds.), *Methods of family research: Biographies of research projects: Vol. 2. Clinical populations* (pp. 227-259). Hillsdale, NJ: Lawrence Erlbaum Associates.

Belsky, J., & Rovine, M. (1990). Patterns of marital change across the transition to parenthood. *Journal of Marriage and the Family, 52*, 5-19.

Booth, A., & Amato, P. R. (1994). Parental marital quality, parental divorce, and relations with parents. *Journal of Marriage and the Family, 56*, 21-34.

Bowlby, J. (1969). *Attachment and loss: Vol. 1. Attachment.* New York: Basic Books.

Bowlby, J. (1973). *Attachment and loss: Vol. 2. Separation.* New York: Basic Books.

Bradbury, T. N. (Ed.) (1998). *The developmental course of marital dysfunction.* Cambridge, UK: Cambridge University Press.

Brody, G. H., Stoneman, Z., & Burke, M. (1987). Family system and individual child correlates of sibling behavior. *American Journal of Orthopsychiatry, 57*, 561-569.

Browne, A., & Finkelhor, D. (1986). Impact of sexual abuse: A review of the research. *Psychological Bulletin, 99*, 66-77.

Buchanan, C. M., Maccoby, E. E., & Dornbusch, S. M. (1991). Caught between parents: Adolescents' experience in divorced homes. *Child Development, 62*, 1008-1029.

Campos, J. J., Campos, R. G., & Barrett, K. C. (1989). Emergent themes in the study of emotional development and emotion regulation. *Developmental Psychology, 25*, 394-402.

Colin, V. L. (1996). *Human attachment.* New York: McGraw-Hill.

Cowan, P. A., & Cowan, C. P. (1999, August). *What an intervention design reveals about how parents affect their children's academic achievement and social competence.* Paper presented at the conference "Parenting and the Child's World: Multiple Influences on Intellectual and Social-Emotional Development," Bethesda, MD.

Cox, M. J., Paley, B., & Payne, C. C. (1997, April). *Marital and parent-child relationships.* Paper presented at the biennial meeting of the Society for Research in Child Development, Washington, DC.

Cummings, E. M. (1987). Coping with background anger in early childhood. *Child Development, 58*, 976-984.

Cummings, E. M. (1998). Children exposed to marital conflict and violence: Conceptual and theoretical directions. In G. W. Holden, R. Geffner, & E. N. Jouriles (Eds.) *Children exposed to martial violence: Theory, research, and applied issues* (pp. 257-288). Washington, DC: American Psychological Association.

Cummings, E. M., Ballard, M., & El–Sheikh, M. (1991). Responses of children and adolescents to interadult anger as a function of gender, age, and mode of expression. *Merrill–Palmer Quarterly, 37*, 543-560.

Cummings, E. M., Ballard, M., El–Sheikh, M., & Lake, M. (1991). Resolution and children's responses to interadult anger. *Developmental Psychology, 27*, 462-470.

Cummings, E. M., & Cummings, J. L. (1988). A process–oriented approach to children's coping and adults' angry behavior. *Developmental Psychology, 27*, 462-470.

Cummings, E. M., & Davies, P. T. (1994a). *Children and marital conflict: The impact of family dispute and resolution.* New York: Guilford Press.

Cummings, E. M., & Davies, P. T. (1994b). Maternal depression and child development (Annual Research Review). *Journal of Child Psychology and Psychiatry, 35*, 73-112.

Cummings, E. M., & Davies, P. T. (1996). Emotional security as a regulatory process in normal development and the development of psychopathology. *Development and Psychopathology, 8*, 123-139.

Cummings, E. M., Davies, P. T., & Campbell, S. B. (2000). *Principles, research and practice directions of developmental psychopathology: Applications for the study of childhood disorders and families.* New York: Guilford.

Cummings, E. M., Goeke–Morey, M. C., & Dukewich, T. L. (in press). The study of relations between marital conflict and child adjustment: Challenges and new directions for methodology. In F. D. Fincham & J. H. Grych (Eds.) *Child development and interparental Conflict.* Cambridge, UK: Cambridge University Press.

Cummings, E. M., Goeke–Morey, M. C., & Graham, M. A. (in press). Interparental relations as a dimension of parenting. In M. M. Bristol-Power, J. G. Borkowski, & S. L. Landesman (Eds.), *Parenting and the child's world: Multiple influences on intellectual and socio-emotional development.* Mahweh, NJ: Lawrence Erlbaum Associates.

Cummings, E. M., Iannotti, R. J., & Zahn–Waxler, C. (1985). The influence of conflict between adults on the emotions and aggression of young children. *Developmental Psychology, 21,* 495-507.

Cummings, E. M., & O'Reilly, A. W. (1997). Fathers in family context: Effects of marital quality on child adjustment. In M. E. Lamb (Ed.), *The role of the father in child development* (3rd ed., pp. 49-65). New York: Wiley.

Cummings, E. M.. Simpson, K. S., & Wilson, A. (1993). Children's response to interadult anger as a function of information about resolution. *Developmental Psychology, 29,* 978-985.

Cummings, E. M., & Smith, D. (1993). The impact of anger between adults on siblings' emotions and social behavior. *Journal of Child Psychology and Psychiatry, 34,* 1425-1433.

Cummings, E. M., Vogel, D., Cummings, J. S., & El–Sheikh, M. (1989). Children's responses to different forms of expression of anger between adults. *Child Development, 60,* 1392-1404.

Cummings, E. M., & Wilson, A. (1999). Contexts of marital conflict and children's emotional security: Exploring the distinction between constructive and destructive conflict from the children's perspective. In M. J. Cox & J. Brooks–Gunn (Eds.), *Conflict and cohesion in families: Causes and consequences* (pp. 105-129). Mahweh, NJ: Lawrence Erlbaum Associates.

Cummings, E. M., Zahn-Waxler, C., & Radke–Yarrow, M. (1981). Young children's responses to expressions of anger and affection by others in the family. *Child Development, 52,* 1274-1282.

Davies, P. T. (1995). *Children's emotional security as a mediator in the link between marital conflict and child adjustment.* Unpublished doctoral dissertation, West Virginia University, Morgantown.

Davies, P. T., & Cummings, E. M. (1994). Marital conflict and child adjustment: An emotional security hypothesis. *Psychological Bulletin, 116,* 387-411.

Davies, P. T., & Cummings, E. M. (1998). Exploring children's emotional security as a mediator of the link between marital relations and child adjustment. *Child Development, 69,* 124-139.

Davies, P. T., Myers, R. L., Cummings, E. M., & Heindel, S. (1999).Adult conflict history and children's subsequent responses to conflict: An experimental test. *Journal of Family Psychology, 13,* 610-628.

Davis, B. T., Hops, H., Alpert, A., & Sheeber, L. (1998). Child responses to parental conflict and their effect on adjustment: A study of triadic relations. *Journal of Family Psychology, 12,* 163-177.

Downey, G., & Coyne, J. C. (1990). Children of depressed parents: An integrative review. *Psychological Bulletin, 108,* 50-76.

Easterbrooks, M. A., Cummings, E. M., & Emde, R. N. (1994). Young children's responses to constructive marital disputes. *Journal of Family Psychology, 8,* 160-169.

El–Sheikh, M. (1997). Children's response to adult-adult and mother-child arguments: The role of parental marital conflict and distress. *Journal of Family Psychology, 11,* 165-175.

El–Sheikh, M., & Cummings, E. M. (1995). Children's responses to angry adult behavior as a function of experimentally manipulated exposure to resolved and unresolved conflict. *Social Development, 4,* 75-91.

El–Sheikh, M., & Cummings, E. M. (1997). Marital conflict, emotional regulation, and the adjustment of children of alcoholics. In K. C. Barrett (Ed.), *The communication of emotion: Current research from diverse perspectives. New directions for child development,* (No. 77, pp. 25-44). San Francisco: Jossey-Bass.

El–Sheikh, M., Cummings, E. M., & Reiter, S. (1996). Preschoolers' responses to ongoing interadult conflict: The role of prior exposure to resolved versus unresolved arguments. *Journal of Abnormal Child Psychology, 24,* 665-679.

Emery, R. E. (1982). Interparental conflict and the children of discord and divorce. *Psychological Bulletin, 92,* 310-330.

Emery, R. E. (1989). Family violence. *American Psychologist, 44,* 321-328.

Emery, R. E. (1994). *Renegotiating family relationships.* New York: Guilford.

Emery, R. E. (1999). *Marriage, divorce, and children's adjustment* (2nd ed.). Thousand Oaks: Sage.

Erel, O., & Burman, B. (1995). Interrelatedness of marital relations and parent-child relations: A meta-analytic review. *Psychological Bulletin, 118,* 108-132.

Fincham, F. D. (1998). Child development and marital relations. *Child Development, 69,* 543-574.

Fincham, F. D., & Osborne, L. N. (1993). Marital conflict and children: Retrospect and prospect. *Clinical Child Psychology, 13,* 75-88.

Flinn, M. V., & England, B. G. (1995). Childhood stress and family environment. *Current Anthropology, 36,* 854-866.

Garcia–O'Hearn, H., Margolin, G., & John, R. S. (1997). Mothers' and fathers' reports of children's reactions to naturalistic marital conflict. *Journal of the American Academy of Child and Adolescent Psychiatry, 36,* 1366-1373.

Gassner, S., & Murray E. J. (1969). Dominance and conflict in the interaction between parents of normal and neurotic children. *Journal of Abnormal Psychology, 74,* 33-41.

Goeke–Morey, M. C. (1999). *Children and marital conflict: Exploring the distinction between constructive and destructive marital conflict.* Unpublished doctoral dissertation, University of Notre Dame, Notre Dame, IN.

Gordis, E. B., Margolin, G., & John, R. S. (1997). Marital aggression, observed parental hostility, and child behavior during triadic family interaction. *Journal of Family Psychology, 11,* 76-89.

Gottman, J. (1994). *Why marriages succeed or fail.* New York: Simon & Schuster.

Grych, J. H. (1998). Children's appraisals of interparental conflict: Situational and contextual influences. *Journal of Family Psychology, 12,* 437-453.

Grych, J. H., & Fincham, F. D. (1990). Marital conflict and children's adjustment: A cognitive-contextual framework. *Psychological Bulletin, 108,* 267-290.

Grych, J. H., & Fincham, F. D. (1993). Children's appraisals of marital conflict: Initial investigations of the cognitive-contextual framework. *Child Development, 64,* 215-230.

Grych, J. H., Seid, M., & Fincham, F. D. (1992). Assessing marital conflict from the child's perspective. *Child Development, 63,* 558-572.

Hall, E., & Cummings, E. M. (1997). The effects of marital and parent-child conflicts on other family members: Grandmothers and grown children. *Family Relations, 46,* 135-144.

Harold, G. T., & Conger, R. D. (1997). Marital conflict and adolescent distress: The role of adolescent awareness. *Child Development, 68,* 330-350.

Harold, G. T., Fincham, F. D., Osborne, L. N., & Conger, R. D. (1997). Mom and dad are at it again: Adolescent perceptions of marital conflict and adolescent psychological distress. *Developmental Psychology, 33,* 333-350.

Hill, E. M., Thomson–Ross, L., & Low, B. S. (1997). The role of future unpredictability in human risk–taking. *Human Nature, 8,* 287-325.

Holmbeck, G. N. (1997). Toward terminology, conceptual, and statistical clarity in the study of mediators and moderators: Examples from the child clinical and pediatric psychology literatures. *Journal of Consulting and Clinical Psychology, 65,* 599-610.

Ingoldsby, E. M., Shaw, D. S., Owens, E. B., & Winslow, E. B. (in press). A longitudinal study of interparental conflict, emotional and behavioral reactivity, and preschoolers' adjustment problems among low-income families. *Journal of Abnormal Child Psychology, 27,* 343-355.

Jaffe, P., Wolfe, D. A., & Wilson, S. K. (1990). *Children of battered women.* Newbury Park, CA: Sage.

Jenkins, J. M. (2000). Marital conflict and children's emotions: The development of an anger organization. *Journal of Marriage and the Family, 62,* 723-736.

Jenkins, J. M., & Buccioni, J. M. (2000). Children's understanding of marital conflict and the marital relationship. *Journal of Child Psychology and Psychiatry and Allied Disciplines, 41,* 161-168.

Jouriles, E. N., Barling, J., & O'Leary, K. D. (1987). Predicting child behavior problems in maritally violent families. *Journal of Abnormal Child Psychology, 15,* 497-509.

Jouriles, E. N., Bourg, W. J., & Farris, A. M. (1991). Martial adjustment and child conduct problems: A comparison of the correlation across subsamples. *Journal of Consulting and Clinical Psychology, 59,* 354-357.

Jouriles, E. N., & Farris, A. M. (1992). Effects of family research designs: A model of interdependence. *Communications Research, 17,* 462-482.

Katz, L. F., & Gottman, J. (1995a). Vagal tone predicts children from marital conflict. *Development and Psychopathology, 7,* 83-92.

Katz, L. F., & Gottman, J. (1995b, April). *Marital conflict and child adjustment: Father's parenting as a mediator of children's negative peer play.* Paper presented at the Meeting of the Society for Research in Child Development, Indianapolis, IN.

Katz, L. F., & Gottman, J. (1997). *Positive parenting and regulatory physiology as buffers from marital conflict and dissolution.* Paper presented at the biennial meeting of the Society for Research in Child Development, Washington, DC.

Kerig, P. K. (1996). Assessing the links between interparental conflict and child adjustment: The conflict as and problem-solving scales. *Journal of Family Psychology, 10,* 454-473.

Kitzmann, K. M. (2000). Effects of marital conflict on subsequent triadic family interactions and parenting. *Developmental Psychology, 36,* 3-13.

Klaczynski, P. A., & Cummings, E. M. (1989). Responding to anger in aggressive and nonaggressive boys. *Journal of Child Psychology and Psychiatry, 30,* 309-314.

Laumakis, M. A., Margolin, G., & John, R. S. (1998). The emotional, cognitive, and coping responses of preadolescent children to different dimensions of preadolescent children to different dimensions of conflict. In G. W. Holden, R. Geffner, & E. N. Jouriles (Eds.) *Children exposed to marital violence: Theory, research, and applied issues* (pp. 257-288). Washington, DC: American Psychological Association.

Lindahl, K. M., & Malik, N. M. (1999). Martial conflict, family processes, and boys' externalizing behavior in Hispanic American and European American families. *Journal of Clinical Child Psychology, 28,* 12-24.

Mahoney, A., Boggio, R., & Jouriles, E. (1996). Effects of verbal marital conflict on subsequent mother-son interactions in a child clinical sample. *Journal of Clinical Child Psychology, 25,* 262-271.

Margolin, G., Christensen, A., & John, R. S. (1996). The continuance and spillover of everyday tensions in distressed and nondistressed families. *Journal of Family Psychology, 10,* 304-321.

McLanahan, S., & Sandefur, G. (1994). *Growing up with a single parent: What hurts, what helps.* Cambridge, MA: Harvard University Press.

Nixon, C. L., & Cummings, E. M. (1999). Sibling disability and children's reactivity to conflicts involving family members. *Journal of Family Psychology, 13,* 274-285.

Notarius, C., & Markman, H. (1993). *We can work it out: Making sense of marital conflict.* New York: Putnam.

O'Brien, M., Bahadur, M., Gee, C., Balto, K., & Erber, S. (1997). Child exposure to marital conflict and child coping responses as predictors of child adjustment. *Cognitive Therapy and Research, 21,* 39-59.

O'Brien, M., & Chin, C. (1998). The relationship between children's reported exposure to interparental conflict and memory biases in the recognition of aggressive and constructive conflict words. *Personality and Social Psychology Bulletin, 24,* 647-656.

O'Brien, M., Margolin, G., & John, R. S. (1995). Relation among marital conflict, child coping, and child adjustment. *Journal of Clinical Child Psychology, 24,* 346-361.

Owen, M. T., & Cox, M. J. (1997). Marital conflict and the development of infant-parent attachment relationships. *Journal of Family Psychology, 11,* 152-164.

Porter, B., & O'Leary, K. D. (1980). Martial discord and childhood behavior problems *Journal of Abnormal Child Psychology, 8,* 287-295.

Repetti, R. L., McGrath, E., & Ishikawa, S. (1999). Daily stress and coping in childhood and adolescence. In A. J. Goreczny & M. Hersen (Eds.), *Handbook of pediatric and adolescent health psychology* (pp. 3-32): Boston: Allyn & Bacon.

Repetti, R. L., & Wood, J. (1997). Families accommodating to chronic stress: Unintended and unnoticed processes. In B. Gottlieb (Ed.), *Coping with chronic stress* (pp. 191-220). New York: Plenum.

Rutter, M. (1970). Sex differences in response to family stress. In E. J. Anthony & C. Koupernik (Eds.), *The child in his family* (pp. 165-196). New York: Wiley.

Rutter, M. (1981). Stress, coping, and development: Some issues and some questions. *Journal of Child Psychology and Psychiatry, 22,* 323-356.

Shifflett, K., & Cummings, E. M. (1999). A program for educating parents about the effects of divorce and conflict on children. *Family Relations, 48,* 79-98.

Shred, R., McDonnell, P. M., Church, G., & Rowan, J. (1991, April). *Infants' cognitive and emotional responses to adults' angry behavior.* Paper presented at the biennial meeting of the Society for Research in Child Development, Seattle, WA.

Simpson, K., & Cummings, E. M. (1996). Mixed message resolution and children's responses to interadult conflict. *Child Development, 67,* 437-448.

Stocker, C. M., & Youngblade, L. (1999). Marital conflict and parental hostility: Links with children's sibling and peer relationships. *Journal of Family Psychology, 13,* 598-609.

Towle, C. (1931). The evaluation and management of marital status in foster homes. *American Journal of Orthopsychiatry, 1,* 271-284.

West, M. O., & Prinz, R. J. (1987). Parental alcoholism and childhood psychopathology. *Psychological Bulletin, 102,* 204-218.

Whisman, M. A. (2001). The association between depression and marital dissatisfaction. In S. R. H. Beach (Ed.), *Marital and family processes in depression.* Washington, DC: American Psychological Association.

Wolfe, D. A., Jaffe, P., Wilson, S. K., & Zak, L. (1985). Children of battered women: The relation of child behavior to family violence and maternal stress. *Journal of Consulting and Clinical Psychology, 53,* 657-665.

10

The Impact of Interparental Conflict on Adolescent Children: Considerations of Family Systems and Family Structure

Christy M. Buchanan
Robyn Waizenhofer
Wake Forest University

Cummings, Goeke-Morey, and Papp's review and critique of what we know about children's responses to conflict (chap. 9) raises many interesting and important issues. We focus our comments primarily on two of these issues. The first is the need to have a systems perspective when considering the impact of conflict on children. The second is the importance of examining the impact of interparental conflict in different contexts. The context we consider is family structure, in particular whether the conflict takes place in a divorced or intact marriage.

FAMILY SYSTEMS AND THE ROLE OF PARENT-CHILD RELATIONSHIPS IN MEDIATING CONFLICT AND CHILDREN'S ADJUSTMENT

In emphasizing a family systems perspective on conflict, Cummings et al. pointed to the need to recognize that the marital relationship will certainly affect children. They also called attention to the fact that children affect the marital relationship-an important fact that is less commonly considered in interpretations of the research on marital conflict. Furthermore, Cummings et al. noted that one mechanism by which marital conflict is believed to affect children is through conflict's interference with optimal parenting and parent-child relationships. Thus, the link between interparental conflict and children's adjustment is explained at least in part by the increased parental rejection, hostility, and lax control that occurs when parents are caught up in conflict with one another.

We emphasize here the need to bring a family systems perspective together with the notion of parent-child relationships as a mediator of interparental conflict and children's adjustment. Most of the research examining parent-child relationships as a mediator of interparental conflict and adjustment has taken a "dyadic" perspective. In other words, it examines the relationships between a child and each parent individually (e.g., one parent's responsiveness to the child or the con-

149

trol exercised by one parent toward the child), and looks at predictors or consequences of characteristics of each separate dyad. Yet, the family systems literature
suggests that it may also be important to consider triadic patterns of relationships
or patterns that reflect the relationship the child holds with both parents simultaneously (e.g., Emery, Joyce, & Fincham, 1987; Minuchin, 1974). As one example,
a very close relationship with the mother may have a different meaning in the
context of a close relationship with the father than it does in the context of a
hostile or a distant relationship with the father.

Defining Terms

Before proceeding further with hypotheses about interparental conflict and triadic
patterns of parent-child relationships, it is necessary to consider the terms that
have been used in the literature to describe different triadic patterns. In the clinical and developmental literatures, various labels have been used to describe al-
tered patterns of parent-child relationships that develop in situations of interparental
conflict, including (but not limited to) triangulation, loyalty conflicts, alignment,
coalitions, scapegoating, and detouring. A review of literature using family systems terms such as these reveals a great deal of inconsistency in how they are
used, particularly in the developmental and empirical literature. For example, triangulation has been defined-either explicitly or through how it is measured-as
trying to maintain a balanced relationship with both parents (Minuchin, Rosman,
& Baker, 1978), or vacillating between them (Robin & Foster, 1989). Triangulation has also been described more broadly as a situation when a third party is
drawn into the conflict between two other parties (Protinsky & Ecker, 1990;
Protinsky & Gilkey, 1996), or, similarly, a situation where a child experiences
some combination of pressure to side, torn loyalties, or alliances (Healy, Stewart,
& Copeland, 1993; Westerman, 1987). In some cases, triangulation is equated
with pressure to take sides in a conflict (Grych, Seid, & Fincham, 1992; Lopez,
Campbell, & Watkins, 1989; Woodward & West, 1979), and in some cases it is
suggested to be an outcome of such pressure (Emery et al., 1987). Yet other sources
equate triangulation specifically with scapegoating (Bowen, 1971; Edwards &
Foster, 1995), cross-generational alliances (Kerig, 1995), role reversal (Jacobvitz
& Bush, 1996), or playing parents off against each other (Healy et al., 1993).

After reviewing these various ways of using and defining family systems terms,
we decided on a set of definitions to use for our own research (see Fig. 10.1;
Buchanan & Waizenhofer, 1998). We assigned to the term triangulation the most
general meaning available, which was the use of a third party (e.g., the child) in
some way to diffuse tension created by conflict in a pair (e.g., the parents). Whether
triangulation in this sense is avoidable in situations of interparental conflict is an
empirical question. But, by definition, family systems theory predicts that the risk
of triangulation is increased when parents are in conflict.

FIG. 10.1
Hierarchy of Family Systems Concepts.

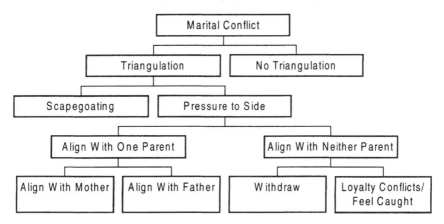

There are, then, different mechanisms for using a third party to diffuse the tension, or for triangulating. One mechanism is scapegoating (or detouring). In scapegoating, the parental conflict is not openly acknowledged; instead, the parents focus on the child as a source of problems (e.g., illness, behavior problems). Attention is thus drawn away from the conflict or tension between parents (Broderick, 1993; Emery et al., 1987). In fact, such couples most likely appear happy and satisfied with their relationship on commonly used survey measures of conflict (Kerig, 1995).

Another mechanism of triangulation, which involves open acknowledgment of the parental conflict, is the application of explicit or implicit pressure to side with one or the other party. Pressure to side may then result in one of several types of patterns (Emery et al., 1987; Minuchin et al., 1978). Alignment may occur if a child gives in to the pressure to side, taking the side of one parent, and also experiencing active anger or strong disengagement (as opposed to apathy) toward the other parent. The anger or disengagement toward the nonallied parent is likely a more defining feature of this relationship than the feelings of closeness toward the allied parent (Haley, 1971; Wallerstein & Kelly, 1980). In fact, the child may experience contradictory feelings toward the allied parent (Minuchin, 1974).

A child can also presumably resist pressure to side. Thus, withdrawal may occur when children respond to the pressure to side by withdrawing emotionally from both parents (Emery et al., 1987). It seems possible that the affective relationship with parents in this instance can be either disengaged or conflictual, but the defining feature is the emotional distance from both parents.

When children resist pressure to take sides by trying to maintain a balanced, close relationship with both parents, they become "caught between parents," or experience loyalty conflicts. Although some scholars equate this situation with triangulation (Healy et al., 1993; Minuchin et al., 1978; Robin & Foster, 1989), we call it "feeling caught" or "loyalty conflicts" in order to distinguish it from the broader phenomenon of third-party engagement.

Testing the Model

All of these patterns ought to have repercussions for children's emotional and behavioral adjustment. In our own work, the focus has been on adolescent children, so our predictions are tailored to this age group. For example, one would predict that attempting to maintain loyalties to two opposing parents would be especially emotionally distressing and linked to depressed mood or anxiety, whereas the detachment from parents characteristic of withdrawal ought to be linked to more peer orientation and deviance (Barnes & Farrell, 1992; Ryan & Lynch, 1989). There is some evidence that alliances are linked with deviant behavior (Mann, Borduin, Henggeler, & Blaske, 1990) and anger, but also with reduced levels of anxiety (Johnston & Campbell, 1988; Lampel, 1996).

Research that the first author conducted in the late 1980s with Eleanor Maccoby and Sandy Dornbusch in fact indicated that loyalty conflicts, or feeling caught between parents, mediated between adolescent-perceived conflict (4 1/2 years after divorce) and both depression and deviance, although the link between feeling caught and adjustment was stronger for depression (Buchanan, Maccoby, & Dornbusch, 1991, 1996). This research addressed only the one pattern of torn loyalties. In more recent research with adolescents in their last 2 years of high school (N = 201) that examined other patterns besides feeling caught, and that distinguished between interparental conflict and pressure to take sides, indicates the following[1]:

1. Conflict between parents predicts felt pressure to side as well as each of the triadic patterns except aligning with the father (see Table 10.1). The patterns are also not mutually exclusive, indicated in part by their intercorrelations. The possibility that parent-child relationship patterns fluctuate over time has been noted by family systems theorists (e.g., Minuchin et al., 1978), and underscores the tremendous complexity in the links between conflict and children's adjustment that Cummings et al. stressed. Felt pressure to side also predicts all of the triadic patterns (see Table 10.1), although in our data it does not mediate the relation between interparental conflict and the triadic patterns. Although this may reflect errors in conceptualization of the role of pressure to side, it may also reflect inadequate measurement. Given that this is the first empirical attempt to distinguish between interparental conflict and a child's felt pressure to take sides in the conflict as predictors of parent-child relationship patterns, further research is warranted.

---

[1]*See also* Buchanan and Louca (1999), who reported on only a subset of the final sample of adolescents that was ultimately recruited for the study, but included more detailed information on study procedures and measures.

Table 10.1
Links Among Interparental Conflict, Pressure to Side, and Triadic Patterns Among High School Students (N = 201)

	1	2	3	4	5	6
Conflict	1.00					
Pressure to side	.57**	1.00				
Align with the mother	.28**	.29**	1.00			
Align with the father	.11	.28**	.17*	1.00		
Withdrawal	.32**	.22**	.05	.15*	1.00	
Loyalty conflicts	.55**	.79**	.23**	.24**	.31**	1.00

*p < .05, **p < .01

2. Conflict, pressure to side, and each of the triadic patterns except for aligning with the father predicted depression, but not deviance, which is predicted only by alignment with the father and withdrawal (see Table 10.2). Consistent with Cummings et al.'s point that relations between conflict and adjustment tend to be small in nonclinical samples, the present relations are quite modest, although significant. The link between conflict and only depression as a measure of adjustment demonstrates another point that Cummings et al. stressed-the importance of the link between interparental conflict and internalizing problems. As they noted, this link is often revealed when children are the reporters of their emotional state, as they were in this instance.

3. Patterns of parent-child relationship do mediate between conflict or pressure to side and depression. When patterns were tested individually as mediators, the link between conflict and depression and between pressure to side and depression was mediated by all of the triadic patterns except aligning with the father. When alignment with the mother, withdrawal, and loyalty conflicts were tested simultaneously as mediators, loyalty conflicts dropped out as an important predictor of depression, although alignment with the mother and withdrawal maintained their mediating role (see Table 10.3 and Figs. 10.2 and 10.3).

In summary, in our initial research testing a family systems model of the role of triadic relationship patterns as mediators of the link between interparental conflict and adolescents' adjustment in a nonclinical setting, some-but not all-of the hypotheses of the model received support. The research has been exploratory and has several limitations, including a cross-sectional design, reliance on adolescent self-reports, and somewhat crude survey measures of concepts that were originally developed in a clinical setting. However, further research using this approach is merited in order to more fully understand how children in the family system get used in conflict, and how this affects their relationships with both parents. Fur-

Table 10.2
Links between Interparental Conflict, Pressure to Side, Triadic Patterns, and Adjustment Among High School Students ($N=201$)

	Depression
Conflict	.16*
Pressure to Side	.15*
Align with Mother	.26*
Align with Father	.01
Withdrawal	.32**
Loyalty Conflicts	.21**

$* p < .05, ** p < .01$

thermore, it would be useful to look at emotional, behavioral, and cognitive reactions to felt pressure to side and to the different triadic patterns. Our research has focused on adolescents' cognitive representations of family relations. The research has not actually linked those representations with affective or behavioral reactions in the face of conflict. Thus, for example, Cummings et al. talked about the potential importance of children's behavioral intervention in family conflicts. It seems logical that children who feel torn between parents would be more likely to intervene in marital conflicts, but this has not, in fact, been documented. Children who are aligned may be equally likely to intervene, but perhaps with different aims.

Table 10.3

**Results of Regression Analyses Testing the Mediating Role
of Triadic Patterns in the Link Between Interparental
Conflict/Pressure to Side and Depression**

Dependent Variable	N	Model	Independent Variables	β	R^2	R^2 Change (last step)
Depression	200	1	Gender of child	-.18*	.06	
			Interparental conflict	.16*		
		2	Gender of child	-.15*	.19	$F = 10.37$**
			Interparental conflict	-.04		
			Align with the mother	.22**		
			Withdraw	.30**		
			Loyalty conflicts	.07		
Depression	200	1	Gender of child	-.17*	.05	
			Pressure to side	.13+		
		2	Gender of child	-.15*	.19	$F = 11.15$**
			Pressure to side	-.07		
			Align with the mother	.22**		
			Withdraw	.30**		
			Loyalty conflicts	.10		

Note: Two regressions are reported testing mediational hypotheses for both interparental conflict-depression and pressure to side-depression. First, depression is predicted with conflict or pressure to side, with gender of child entered as a control. Second, depression is predicted with the original two variables plus the three triadic patterns.

$* p < .05, ** p < .01, + p < .10$

THE ROLE OF FAMILY STRUCTURE

Several of the points raised by Cummings et al. are relevant to the question of whether the impact of conflict varies by family structure. As Cummings et al. noted in chapter 9, "The magnitude of the relations between marital conflict and child adjustment is moderated by the overall adaptiveness, and level of resource, that characterizes the family environment." Furthermore, multiplicity of stresses raises the risk that problems will emanate from exposure to marital conflict. Different family structures (e.g., divorced vs. nondivorced; mother vs. father vs. joint custody; cohabiting vs. married or remarried) may well be expected to differ in their level of risk factors, adaptiveness, and resources. Additionally, family structure may affect children's cognitive appraisals of the implications of conflict for self and family (Forehand, Wierson, McCombs, Brody, & Fauber, 1989) as well as the emotional security ramifications of the conflict. Children of divorce have typically experienced more conflict-and more poorly resolved conflict-in their past than have children in nondivorced homes (Buchanan & Heiges, in press). Thus, they may be more highly sensitized to conflict that does occur (Cummings & Davies, 1994).

Most studies that have compared the impact of interparental conflict on children in divorced versus nondivorced homes indicate that this aspect of family structure does not moderate the association between conflict and aspects of the parent-child relationship or children's adjustment (Buchanan & Heiges, in press). Exceptions include two studies showing a stronger link between interparental conflict and negative parent-adolescent relationships in recently divorced homes (Fauber, Forehand, Thomas, & Wierson, 1990; Forehand, Wierson, Thomas, & Fauber, 1991) and a stronger link between conflict and disenchantment toward marriage among young adults from nondivorced homes (Kozuch & Cooney, 1995). In our own research looking at triadic patterns of relationships, the relationships between conflict or pressure to side and the triadic patterns were very similar for adolescents in divorced and nondivorced homes, with one exception-and in this case the impact of conflict was moderated by both family structure and gender (see Fig. 10.4). Among girls, alignment with the mother in response to conflict or pressure to side was more likely if they were in nondivorced than in divorced homes. Among boys, alignment with mothers was more likely in divorced than nondivorced homes. This three-way interaction of family structure, gender, and interparental conflict was not predicted, but may reflect that it is easier to enlist boys in an alliance against their fathers when that father has left the family. Girls may feel safe taking a mother's side and expressing anger toward their fathers as long as the father is in the family, but may become especially concerned about losing ties with their fathers, and thus more hesitant to align against him, when the father is not physically present. One hesitates to speculate too much on the reasons for this interaction, however, until further research replicates the finding.

In general, however, the existing research on divorced versus intact family structure as a moderator of conflict and adjustment does not address the complexity that may exist. We need to examine whether moderation occurs more at certain times than others (e.g., in the immediate aftermath of divorce; many years after divorce) or on certain types of "outcomes" (e.g., parent-child relationships, attitudes toward marriage).

It is also possible that the mechanism of impact differs by family structure. For example, children of intact marriages may be affected more by frequent exposure to conflict, whereas children of divorce-although exposed to less frequent conflict-may be affected by the negative modes of resolution (Camara & Resnick, 1989; Forehand & McCombs, 1989; Forehand & Thomas, 1992) or by the high proportion of child-related conflicts (Ahrons, 1981; Cummings & Davies, 1994; Maccoby & Mnookin, 1992) that tend to occur between divorced couples. Cummings et al. stressed the need to look more closely at the different components of conflict, and this need is certainly present in the research on family structure. The triadic patterns of relationships I have discussed may also be differentially likely in different family structures (Buchanan & Heiges, in press).

Research also exists that addresses differences in the link between conflict and adjustment by other aspects of family structure (e.g., custody arrangement, amount of visitation with noncustodial parent). Space limitations preclude a thorough examination of these data, but in general they indicate that conflict probably has a more negative impact in joint custody (Buchanan et al., 1991, 1996) and possibly in high visitation arrangements as well. The data on this point are not unequivocal, however, and suggest that the manner in which conflict is handled and the degree to which custody or visitation arrangements allow or reflect a good relationship with the visited parent must be considered in tandem with the structural arrangement (Buchanan, 1997). Furthermore, there is some evidence that hostility expressed by a custodial father has a more negative impact on children than hostility expressed by a custodial mother (Buchanan, Maccoby, & Dornbusch, 1992, 1996). Perhaps a father's anger is more threatening than a mother's, or perhaps such hostility is more likely to affect a father's parenting than it is a mother's parenting. As Cummings et al.'s newest research suggests, the same behaviors may have different meanings to children depending on whether they emanate from a mother or a father. Our data concur in pointing to the need for a better understanding of the ways in which mothers and fathers express their anger toward one another, and the ways in which children interpret anger on the part of each parent.

SUMMARY

In summary, to further our understanding of the impact of interparental conflict on children, we need to look more closely at the impact of conflict on various dimensions of the parent-child relationship, including triadic patterns. In addition, we need to illuminate the experience and meaning of interparental conflict in different family forms.

REFERENCES

Ahrons, C. R. (1981). The continuing coparental relationship between divorced spouses. *American Journal of Orthopsychiatry, 51,* 416-428.

Barnes, G. M., & Farrell, M. P. (1992). Parental support and control as predictors of adolescent drinking, delinquency, and related problem behaviors. *Journal of Marriage and the Family, 54,* 763-776.

Bowen, M. (1971). The use of family theory in clinical practice. In J. Haley (Ed.), *Changing families.* New York: Grune & Stratton.

Broderick, C. B. (1993). *Understanding family process: Basics of family systems theory.* Newbury Park, CA: Sage.

Buchanan, C. M. (1997). Issues of visitation and custody. In G. Bear, K. Minke, & A. Thomas (Eds.), *Children's needs II: Development, problems, and alternatives* (pp. 605-613). Bethesda, MD: National Association of School Psychologists.

Buchanan, C. M., & Heiges, K. L. (in press). Effects of post-divorce conflict on children. In F. Fincham & J. Grych (Eds.), *Child development and interparental conflict.* Cambridge, MA: Harvard University Press.

Buchanan, C. M., & Louca, M. B. (1999, April). *The association between marital conflict and parent-child relationships: Differences by age and family structure.* Paper presented at the biennial meeting of the Society for Research in Child Development, Albuquerque, NM.

Buchanan, C. M., Maccoby, E. E., & Dornbusch, S. M. (1991). Caught between parents: Adolescents' experience in divorced homes. *Child Development, 62,* 1008-1029.

Buchanan, C. M., Maccoby, E. E., & Dornbusch, S. M. (1992). Adolescents and their families after divorce: Three residential arrangements compared. *Journal of Research on Adolescence, 2,* 261-291.

Buchanan, C. M., Maccoby, E. E., & Dornbusch, S. M. (1996). *Adolescents after divorce.* Cambridge, MA: Harvard University Press.

Buchanan, C. M., & Waizenhofer, R. N. (1998, February). *Patterns of triadic relationships after divorce among late adolescents.* Paper presented at the biennial meeting of the Society for Research on Adolescence, San Diego, CA.

Camara, K. A., & Resnick, G. (1989). Styles of conflict resolution and cooperation between divorced parents: Effects on child behavior and adjustment. *American Journal of Orthopsychiatry, 59,* 560-575.

Cummings, E. M., & Davies, P. (1994). *Children and marital conflict: The impact of family dispute and resolution.* New York: Guilford.

Edwards, D. L., & Foster, M. A. (1995). Uniting the family and school systems: A process of empowering the school counselor. *School Counselor, 42,* 277-291.

Emery, R. E., Joyce, S. A., & Fincham, F. D. (1987). The assessment of marital and child problems. In K. D. O'Leary (Ed.), *Assessment of marital discord* (pp. 223-262). Hillsdale, NJ: Lawrence Erlbaum Associates.

Fauber, R., Forehand, R., Thomas, A. M., & Wierson, M. (1990). A mediational model of the impact of marital conflict on adolescent adjustment in intact and divorced families: The role of disrupted parenting. *Child Development, 61,* 1112-1123.

Forehand, R., & McCombs, A. (1989). The nature of interparental conflict of married and divorced parents: Implications for young adolescents. *Journal of Abnormal Child Psychology, 17,* 235-249.

Forehand, R., & Thomas, A. M. (1992). Conflict in the home environment of adolescents from divorced families: A longitudinal analysis. *Journal of Family Violence, 7,* 73-84.

Forehand, R., Wierson, M., McCombs, A., Brody, G., & Fauber, R. (1989). Interparental conflict and adolescent problem behavior: An examination of mechanisms. *Behaviour Research and Therapy, 27,* 365-371.

Forehand, R., Wierson, M., Thomas, A. M., & Fauber, R. (1991). A short-term longitudinal examination of young adolescent functioning following divorce: The role of family factors. *Journal of Abnormal Child Psychology, 19,* 97-111.

Grych, J. E., Seid, M., & Fincham, F. D. (1992). Assessing marital conflict from the child's perspective: The children's perception of interparental conflict scale. *Child Development, 63,* 558-572.

Haley, J. (1971). Toward a theory of pathological systems. In G. Zuk & I. Boszormenyi-Nagy (Eds.), *Family theory and disturbed families* (pp. 11-27). Palo Alto, CA: Science & Behavior Books.

Healy, J. M., Stewart, A. J., & Copeland, A. P. (1993). The role of self-blame in children's adjustment to parental separation. *Personality and Social Psychology Bulletin, 19,* 279-289.

Jacobvitz, D. B., & Bush, N. F. (1996). Reconstructions of family relationships: Parent-child alliances, personal distress, and self-esteem. *Developmental Psychology, 32,* 732-743.

Johnston, J. R., & Campbell, L. E. G. (1988). *Impasses of divorce: The dynamics and resolution of family conflict.* New York: Free Press.

Kerig, P. K. (1995). Triangles in the family circle: Effects of family structure on marriage, parenting, and child adjustment. *Journal of Family Psychology, 9,* 28-43.

Kozuch, P., & Cooney, T. M. (1995). Young adults' marital and family attitudes: The role of recent parental divorce, and family and parental conflict. *Journal of Divorce and Remarriage, 23,* 45-62.

Lampel, A. K. (1996). Children's alignment with parents in highly conflicted custody cases. *Family and Conciliation Courts Review, 34,* 229-239.

Lopez, F. G., Campbell, V. L., & Watkins, C. E. (1989). Effects of marital conflict and family coalition patterns on college student adjustment. *Journal of College Student Development, 30,* 46-52.

Maccoby, E. E., & Mnookin, R. H. (1992). *Dividing the child: Social and legal dilemmas of custody.* Cambridge, MA: Harvard University Press.

Mann, B. J., Borduin, C. M., Henggeler, S. W., & Blaske, D. M. (1990). An investigation of systemic conceptualizations of parent-child coalitions and symptom change. *Journal of Consulting and Clinical Psychology, 58,* 336-344.

Minuchin, S. (1974). *Families and family therapy.* Cambridge, MA: Harvard University Press.

Minuchin, S., Rosman, B. L., & Baker, L. (1978). *Psychosomatic families: Anorexia nervosa in context.* Cambridge, MA: Harvard University Press.

Protinsky, H., & Ecker, S. (1990). Intergenerational family relationships as perceived by adult children of alcoholics. *Family Therapy, 27,* 217-222.

Protinsky, H., & Gilkey, J. K. (1996). An empirical investigation of the construct of personality authority in late adolescent women and their level of college adjustment. *Adolescence, 31,* 291-295.

Robin, A. L., & Foster, S. L. (1989). *Negotiating parent-adolescent conflict: A behavioral-family systems approach.* New York: Guilford.

Ryan, R. M., & Lynch, J. H. (1989). Emotional autonomy versus detachment: Revisiting the vicissitudes of adolescence and young adulthood. *Child Development, 60,* 340-356.

Wallerstein, J. S., & Kelly, J. B. (1980). *Surviving the breakup: How children and parents cope with divorce.* New York: Basic Books.

Westerman, M. A. (1987). "Triangulation," marital discord and child behaviour problems. *Journal of Social and Personal Relationships, 4,* 87-106.

Woodward, J. B., & West, L. W. (1979). A model for observing and classifying triangulation phenomenon in groups. *International Journal of Group Psychotherapy, 29,* 149-162.

11

Understanding Child and Adolescent Response to Caregiver Conflict: Some Observations on Context, Process, and Method

Rand D. Conger
Iowa State University

The chapter by Cummings, Goeke-Morey, and Papp (chap. 9, this volume) reflects a program of research that can serve as a model in the social and behavioral sciences for careful, systematic research on an important developmental issue. For almost 20 years, Dr. Cummings and several different collaborators have sought to determine the degree to which various dimensions of conflict between caregivers affect the emotional, behavioral, and cognitive adjustment of children. Especially compelling, they have relied on a variety of research strategies, ranging from laboratory experiments to in-person interviews, to evaluate how children respond to conflict and the processes through which their responses might be generated. Also important, they have employed several different measurement techniques, including the actual observation of behavioral responses, to assess the theoretical constructs of interest. Their investigations have demonstrated the significance of caregiver conflict in children's lives, and have prompted increasing theoretical and empirical activity related to this important domain of family research.

In their chapter for this volume, Cummings and his colleagues organized their observations around four key questions: What do we know about the effects of marital conflict on the child? What is the distinction between constructive and destructive conflict? What is a framework for how children are affected by marital conflict? How can we think about effects over time from a process-oriented perspective?

To remain consistent with their presentation, I address these same questions in the following comments, and use examples from my own research to illustrate the points I wish to make. In considering these questions, my perspective clearly reflects my training as a sociologist. For example, my work on couple conflict has been concerned not only with internal family processes but also with conditions within the community (e.g., economic recession) that affect these processes. Consistent with the perspective provided by Cummings, Goeke-Morey and Papp (chap. 9, this volume) in their process model of child development, we believe that an important dimension of the next steps in this area of research will be an examination of the broader social contexts that affect both caregiver conflict and child development.

WHAT DO WE KNOW ABOUT THE EFFECTS OF MARITAL CONFLICT ON THE CHILD?

In chapter 9, Cummings et al. reviewed a large body of literature demonstrating that marital conflict negatively affects child adjustment. They also suggested the important corollary that positive relations between parents should foster the competent development of children and adolescents. As they noted, the latter issue remains largely ignored by researchers, and should be investigated in future comprehensive studies of family process and child development. In terms of marital relations and adjustment problems, previous research demonstrates that marital conflict in particular, and not the quality of marriage in general, appears to have the primary influence on developmental difficulties. Moreover, Cummings et al. noted that these differential influences may have either a direct or indirect effect on child adjustment.

The thesis that different dimensions of the marital relationship may differentially affect child adjustment problems has been supported in recent research with data from the Iowa Youth and Families Project (IYFP), which we conducted from 1989 through 1992. This study of over 400 rural Iowa families included two parents, a target child in the seventh grade in 1989, and a sibling within 4 years of age of the target child. The original study continues as the Family Transitions Project, which is investigating the early adult development of the IYFP youth and a comparable cohort of rural young people raised in single-parent families during adolescence. In recent analyses with the IYFP sample, we have demonstrated the importance of investigating different domains of marital functioning and marital conflict, and also the importance of considering differential effects by child gender.

For the 1989 family assessment, we constructed three measures of marital functioning: (a) marital distress (MD) was comprised of parents' reports of dissatisfaction with their relationship and thoughts of divorce; (b) observed conflict between parents (OB) was based on observer ratings of parent anger and hostility toward one another during a marital discussion task and a problem-solving task videotaped in the participants' homes; and (c) conflicts over childrearing (CCR) were assessed through parent, target, and sibling reports of parents' disagreements about how to raise children in the family. As a first step in the analyses, these marital measures were used to predict the target adolescent's externalizing problems (delinquency and substance use) 2 years later in 1991. Thus, the time ordering of the variables reduced the likelihood that child problems were producing difficulties in the marriage. Consistent with expectations, the results in Table 11.1 show that observed, general conflict in marriage and specific conflicts over childrearing, but not general marital distress, increase risk for later externalizing problems for both boys and girls. For example, for Model 1 for the combined sample of boys and girls, the standardized regression coefficient for conflicts over childrearing predicting externalizing behaviors was .19 ($p < .05$).

Table 11.1
Standardized Regression Coefficients for Externalizing Problems
Regressed on Marital Variables (N = 366)

Marital Variables	Combined Sample		Gender Subsamples	
	Model 1	Model 2	Boys	Girls
Main effects				
MD	–.05	–.06	–.05	–.06
OB	.10*	.24*	–.03	.26*
CCR	.19*	.05	.32*	.05
Gender	.26*	.52*		
Interaction effects				
MD x G	—	.01		
OB x G	—	–.55*		
CCR x G	—	.32*		
R^2	.115	.141	.084	.067

* $p < .05$

The findings in Table 11.1 also indicate, however, that boys were most affected by conflicts over childrearing whereas girls were most distressed by generalized conflicts between parents. It seems that boys are placed at greater risk when parents' disagreements relate directly to them whereas girls are sensitive to the emotional tone of the marriage more generally. These findings are consistent with earlier reports from this project, which demonstrated that girls tend to be more directly influenced by the moods of their parents whereas male adolescents are most responsive to parental behaviors directly related to the lives of these boys (Conger et al., 1992, 1993).

Consistent with the thesis regarding indirect effects of marital conflict on child adjustment, we also found that observed parent negative affect (anger, hostility, derogation) toward the child partially mediated the effects of marital conflict on externalizing behaviors. For example, the standardized regression coefficients in Fig. 11.1 show that observed conflict between parents in 1989 predicted mothers' negative affect toward the target children in 1990 (e.g., b* = .29 from observed conflict to mothers' negative affect toward girls). Negative affect, in turn, was significantly related to externalizing behaviors in 1991 for both boys and girls. Also consistent with Cummings et al., however, was the finding that observed conflict continued to have a direct association with later behavior problems for girls, and conflict over childrearing had the same connection for boys. Clearly, other mediators are required to explain this continued direct effect, as becomes apparent in relation to the subsequent questions posed by Cummings et al.

FIG. 11.1
Marital Conflict, Maternal Behavior, and Adolescent Externalizing Problems. Standardized path coefficients, boys' results in parentheses.
* p < .05; AGFI = .95 for boys' model, .99 for the girls' model.

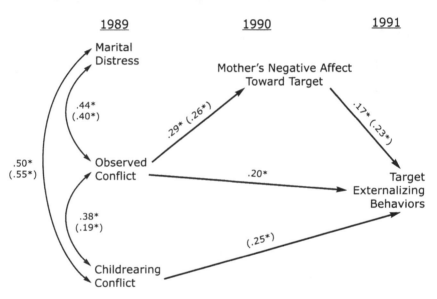

WHAT IS THE DISTINCTION BETWEEN CONSTRUCTIVE AND DESTRUCTIVE CONFLICT?

In response to this question, Cummings and his colleagues carefully evaluated differences in the nature of conflict between caregivers. They hypothesized that certain types of destructive conflict will have an adverse influence on children's development, whereas constructive conflict by caregivers may actually promote child competence. From Cummings et al.'s analysis, there appear to be two important distinctions between these two types of conflict. First, conflicts may differ in terms of the emotional context in which they occur. Cummings et al. noted that destructive conflict typically reflects negative affect such as anger, aggression, and hostile withdrawal from interaction. Constructive conflict, on the other hand, occurs within a context of mutual respect and positive emotional affect. Preliminary analyses reported in the chapter indicate that children are most adversely influenced by conflict that is negative rather than positive in emotional tone. These distinctions regarding affect, however, require caution in both theoretical and methodological approaches to research in this area.

For example, in my research we have tended to equate conflict with negative affect. This strategy would be inappropriate following the Cummings et al. conceptualization. Indeed, it may be that work in this area should identify disagreement between caregivers as the appropriate construct, and this disagreement may be either positive or negative in emotional tone. In any case, to pursue the notion of constructive and destructive conflict as proposed by Cummings and his colleagues requires a very clear use of terminology that distinguishes between the concepts of conflict and emotional expression.

The degree to which caregivers resolve a disagreement represents the second distinction between constructive and destructive conflict. According to Cumming et al., and consistent with analyses they provided in a later section of chapter 9, children will be least negatively influenced by conflicts that promise resolution, and even positively affected by parents who effectively resolve their differences. This problem-solving dimension of conflict resolution has enormous potential for distinguishing among possible developmental outcomes for children and adolescents. In fact, effective problem solving by parents should reduce the amount of conflict to which children are exposed, and should spill over into interactions with children, much as the negative affect expressed during caregiver conflicts has been demonstrated to generalize to parent/child exchanges (Harold & Conger, 1997). A recent report from the Iowa Youth and Families Project suggests the importance of effective problem-resolution strategies in marital conflicts.

Accumulating evidence suggests that conflicts in marriage lead to increasing marital distress or dissatisfaction that, in turn, intensifies conflict or disengagement in the relationship (Gottman, 1993; Matthews, Conger, & Wickrama, 1996). The ultimate threat to children involves not only exposure to conflict but also risk for ultimate dissolution of the marital relationship. Fig 11.2 illustrates findings from the IYFP demonstrating that marital conflict in 1990, as rated by trained observers, only predicts marital distress in 1991, as reported by spouses, when couples demonstrate poor problem-solving skills (Conger, Rueter, & Elder, 1999). Couples who engaged in effective problem-resolution strategies during a video-taped problem-solving task largely avoided increasing distress in their marriage as a function of earlier disagreements. As indicated by observer ratings, effective couples were able both to identify solutions to problems that were mutually beneficial and to move from solution identification to problem resolution. Presumably, these problem-solving strategies break the cycle of marital conflict and distress, thus exposing children to less conflict and more effective problem-solving skills over time. Consistent with these findings, we agree with the argument by Cummings and his colleagues (chap. 9, this volume) that future research should investigate the nature and intergenerational transmission of these constructive behaviors.

FIG. 11.2
The Interaction of Effective Problem Solving and Marital Conflict in Predicting Marital Distress. Adapted from Conger et al. (1999).

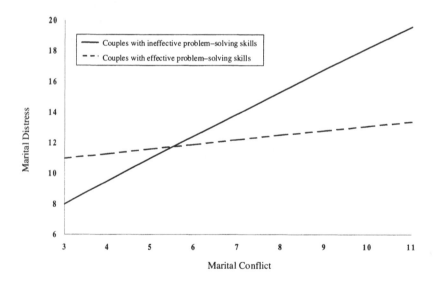

WHAT IS A FRAMEWORK FOR HOW THE CHILD IS AFFECTED BY MARITAL CONFLICT?

In this section of their chapter, Cummings and his colleagues proposed a general model for studying child and adolescent response to marital conflict. They noted that broader contextual issues, such as community environment, should be taken into account in future research. They proposed that specific mediating and moderating conditions must be considered at the family, community, and individual levels to adequately understand the impact of conflict on the child. For example, the analyses discussed earlier and provided in Table 11.1 and Fig. 11.1 suggest that gender may moderate the impact of conflict, as suggested in their chapter.

Our research has been most consistent with the broader conceptual model proposed by Cummings and his colleagues. We have been primarily concerned with how family economic conditions affect the behaviors and emotions of parents, including the degree of conflict they experience in their relationship. Consistent with the spill over hypothesis, our Family Stress Model of economic hardship proposes that these conflicts will disrupt parenting practices, thus increasing risk for child adjustment problems and declines in competent functioning (e.g., Conger et al., 1992, 1993). In the latest extension of this research, we are studying almost 900 African-American children between 10 and 11 years of age and their families.

The Family and Community Health Study includes families from both Iowa and Georgia. Among the participants are 422 children who live in two-caregiver households. Children were recruited from the community, and they were studied in whichever type of home arrangement they brought with them. Children living with two caregivers included those with two biological parents (39%), stepparents or romantic partners living together with only one partner biologically related to the target child (33%), or two caregivers that shared some other type of nonromantic relationship, such as mother and grandmother (28%). Our hypothesis was that conflicts between caregivers in general, and not just between those who are married or romantically involved, would have an influence on child development similar to that found for married couples.

The investigation uses the same combination of observational and self-report methodology as employed in the IYFP. Results of initial analyses are consistent with expectations. First, there were no differences in the findings related to the type of caregiver relationship; therefore, the sample was merged and the results for the combined set of families with two caregivers are provided in Fig. 11.3. Because there were no gender differences in child effects, the findings also are combined for boys and girls. As suggested by our earlier research and consistent with the Cummings, Goeke-Morey, and Papp conceptual model, conflict between caregivers was positively related to a set of adverse family circumstances, including economic hardships and the resultant depressed moods of both caregivers. The conflict measure consisted of reports by both caregivers that their relationship was high on conflict and on withdrawal or low warmth. Conflict predicted disruptions in nurturant and involved parenting (b* = -.42), as evaluated by trained observers and family members, which promoted positive child adjustment (b* = .66) in the form of school success, persistence in difficult and demanding tasks, and a positive mood about self and life in general as reported by the target child.

FIG. 11.3
Empirical Evaluation of the Family Stress Model; maximum likelihood estimation, standardized coefficients, N = 422, Comparative Fit Index = .99; all coefficients statistically significant at p < .05.

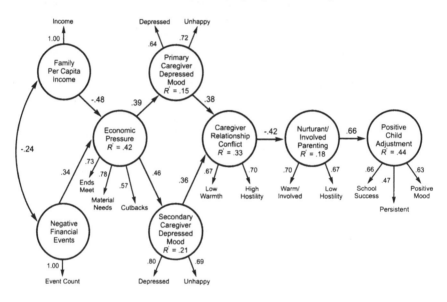

The overall message of these findings is that family stressors and parent emotional problems intensify conflicts between caregivers. When caregiver conflict is high, parents become less nurturant or involved and more hostile with their children. These decrements in parenting are associated with less child competence. Taken together, the findings are quite supportive of the general process model for child development proposed by Cummings and his colleagues.

HOW CAN WE THINK ABOUT EFFECTS OVER TIME FROM A PROCESS-ORIENTED PERSPECTIVE?

In discussing this final question in chapter 9, Cummings and his co-authors provided a variety of theoretical and methodological suggestions concerning the advancement of research on marital conflict and child development. Especially noteworthy, they emphasized the need to study the processes through which children successfully or ineffectively cope with caregiver conflict. Their approach led them to the consideration of recently developed microanalytic techniques (i.e., daily diaries) for assessing caregiver conflicts and child response on a daily basis. Cumming et al. reasonably argued that this form of data gathering will help illuminate the gradual sensitization of children to their parents' conflicts, and also provide information regarding the differential effects of constructive and destructive conflict behaviors. Also important, they proposed that the specific coping responses employed by children will have a major impact on their general adjustment over time. Indeed, Cummings et al. suggested that children's interpretation of conflict will provide the primary mediator through which conflict has an effect on long-term development. They discussed a published theoretical test of their hypotheses (Davies & Cummings, 1998) as well as preliminary findings from more recent work that support the basic tenants of their theoretical and empirical approach.

In research I have conducted with my colleague, Dr. Gordon Harold, we have generated findings consistent with this time-ordered, process-oriented perspective (Harold & Conger, 1997). Again turning to the IYFP sample, Fig. 11.4 provides results from a model evaluating the influence of marital conflict on adolescent internalizing symptoms over a 3-year time period. Because there were no adolescent gender differences in the findings, boys and girls are combined in the analyses. There are several important features to the analyses provided in Fig. 11.4, all of which support the perspective on studies of marital conflict offered by Cummings and his collaborators. First, marital conflict relates to change in internalizing symptoms over time both through disruptions in parenting (i.e., increased hostility toward the target adolescent) and through adolescent cognitive representations or awareness of that conflict. These two avenues of influence represent the direct and indirect pathways discussed throughout chapter 9.

Second, the self-reported behavior of the adolescent influences his or her perceptions of parental behaviors (e.g., $b^* = .119$ between adolescent self-reported internalizing symptoms in 1989 and their perception of marital conflict frequency in 1990). This finding reinforces the need for the use of diverse measurement strategies and appropriate controls in analyzing resultant data, as suggested by Cumming et al. Third, the results demonstrate that not only does marital conflict spill over into hostility toward the child, adolescent awareness of marital conflict also spills over into their interpretation of parental hostile behavior toward them, independent of observable parent behaviors, as reflected in the standardized regression coefficient of .284 from adolescent awareness of conflict frequency to adolescent perception of parental hostility. Consistent with the sensitization hypothesis, adolescents appear to be wary of parents' actions and, perhaps, interpret their parents' behaviors as hostile as a function of their conflict toward one another, independent of their hostile behaviors toward the adolescent. Finally, the results in Fig. 11.4 clearly indicate that risk of internalizing problems increases

FIG. 11.4

Maximum Likelihood Estimation of the Conceptual Model for Internalizing Symptoms for the Combined Sample of Boys and Girls. *p < .10;
**p < .05; ***p < .01 From Harold & Conger, 1997.

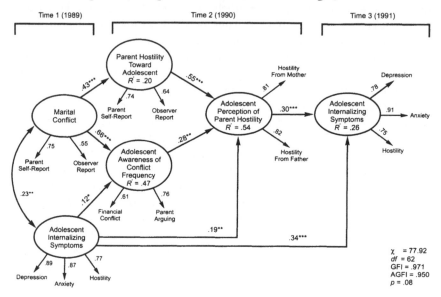

over time as a function of this set of behavioral and interpretational mechanisms.
These findings indicate the value of the process-oriented perspective proposed by
Cummings Goeke-Morey, and Papp for studies of caregiver conflict and child
adjustment.

CONCLUSIONS

It is a privilege to have the opportunity to review the work and insights of Dr.
Cummings and his co-authors. As noted at the beginning of these comments, their
work provides an important model for programmatic research on a significant
developmental issue. Additionally, Dr. Cummings' work has led the way in the
development of research and theory on child and adolescent response to conflicts
between caregivers. In this closing note, however, I want to focus on some important methodological insights from the Cummings, Goeke-Morey, and Papp chapter that apply not only to this specific field of research, but also to the study of life
course issues in general.

Three decades ago, a Norwegian social researcher by the name of Galtung
(1969) observed that psychology is sometimes described as a science that says a

great deal about very little, and that sociology is sometimes described as a science that says very little about very much. He was referring to the fact that psychologists often use sophisticated and extensive measures of human emotions, thoughts, and behaviors with small or nonrepresentative samples, whereas sociologists often use limited measures with very large and diverse population-based samples that allow the evaluation of broader social contextual issues in research on human behavior. In his work, Cummings has moved from detailed measurement in laboratory studies with small samples to the assessment of marital conflict and child adjustment in community populations. In his extension to the community, he has retained much of the quality of measurement that he developed in the laboratory.

From my perspective, his research has begun to join the best research practices of our respective disciplines by taking systematically constructed measures from laboratory settings to the community. In a limited way, we have sought to achieve this same integration in our research with majority and minority families. I believe that this joining of the sociological and psychological perspectives on research with families and children will provide major advances in our understanding of family processes and child adjustment in general, and caregiver conflict and child development in particular.

ACKNOWLEDGMENTS

During the past several years, support for this research has come from multiple sources, including the National Institute of Mental Health (Grants MH00567, MH43270, MH48165, and MH51361), the National Institute on Drug Abuse (Grant DA05347), the Bureau of Maternal and Child Health Grant (MCJ-109572), the MacArthur Foundation Research Network on Successful Adolescent Development Among Youth in High-Risk Settings, and the Iowa Agriculture and Home Economics Experiment Station (Project No. 3320).

REFERENCES

Conger, R. D., Conger, K. J., Elder, G. H., Jr., Lorenz, F. O., Simons, R. L., & Whitbeck, L. B. (1992). A family process model of economic hardship and adjustment of early adolescent boys. *Child Development, 63,* 526-541.
Conger, R. D., Conger, K. J., Elder, G. H., Jr., Lorenz, F. O., Simons, R. L., & Whitbeck, L. B. (1993). Family economic stress and adjustment of early adolescent girls. *Developmental Psychology, 29,* 206-219.
Conger, R. D., Rueter, M. A., & Elder, G. H., Jr. (1999). Couple resilience to economic pressure. *Journal of Personality and Social Psychology, 76,* 54-71.
Davies, P. T., & Cummings, E. M. (1998). Exploring children's emotional security as a mediator of the link between marital relations and child adjustment. *Child Development, 69,* 124-139.

Galtung, J. (1969). *Theory and methods of social research*. New York: Columbia University Press.

Gottman, J. M. (1993). A theory of marital dissolution and stability. *Journal of Family Psychology, 7,* 57-75.

Harold, G. T., & Conger, R. D. (1997). Marital conflict and adolescent distress: The role of adolescent awareness. *Child Development, 68,* 333-350.

Matthews, L., Conger, R. D., & Wickrama, K. A. S. (1996). Work-family conflict and marital quality: Mediating processes. *Social Psychology Quarterly, 59,* 62-79.

12

Increasing Precision in the Study of Interparental Conflict and Child Adjustment

John H. Grych
Marquette University

Research examining the impact of interparental conflict on children has evolved from describing the parameters of this association to proposing and testing mechanisms by which exposure to conflict may lead to adverse outcomes in children. Although it is clear that exposure to high levels of interparental conflict is related to greater adjustment problems, many questions remain regarding how and under what conditions conflict between couples affects their children. Both conflict and child adjustment are complex, multifaceted constructs, and our understanding of which aspects of conflict may be detrimental to children and which aspects of child functioning are affected by conflict is limited. This is due in part to a lack of specificity in assessing these constructs and the processes hypothesized to account for their association (also see Holmbeck, 1997). This chapter considers how increasing precision in the conceptualization and measurement of conflict, adjustment, and the pathways proposed to link them can produce a clearer picture of the ways in which discord in the couple relationship may affect children's development.

INCREASING PRECISION IN THE ASSESSMENT OF INTERPARENTAL CONFLICT

Conflict between couples can involve a wide array of behaviors and a range of emotions. As Cummings, Goeke-Morey, and Papp (chap. 9, this volume) argued, all manifestations of conflict are not likely to be equally harmful for children and in fact, exposure to certain kinds of conflict may even be beneficial (also see Cummings & Davies, 1994; Grych & Fincham, 1990). Understanding the impact of conflict on children, then, requires clear specification of the kinds of interactions that occur when parents disagree. However, most studies examining relations between conflict and adjustment have obtained fairly global assessments of interparental conflict. Typically, conflict is measured with questionnaires that tap the frequency of particular behaviors (e.g., hitting, yelling, compromising), which are then grouped into more general categories reflecting particular classes of behaviors (e.g., verbal aggression) or simply an estimate of how often parents disagree.

This approach has been useful for establishing a link between couple conflict and adjustment problems, but aggregating across diverse behaviors also has some limitations. First, it affords little insight into which aspects of conflict are linked to child functioning. Analogue studies indicate that children are quite sensitive to variations in the expression and resolution of conflict (for reviews, see Cummings & Davies, 1994; Cummings et al., chap. 9, this volume), but the most commonly used marital conflict questionnaires yield only global measures of conflict frequency or aggression. Although several questionnaires have been developed that make finer distinctions among types of conflict behavior (e.g., Christensen & Sullaway, 1984; Grych, Seid, & Fincham, 1992; Kerig, 1996), they are not widely used, perhaps because they tend to be longer than global measures. However, even questionnaires designed to measure more specific dimensions of conflict may not be as sensitive as intended because some aspects of conflict tend to covary. For example, couples who become physically aggressive when conflict occurs also are likely to be poorer at resolving discord, and to have more conflicts as a result. Consequently, measures purporting to assess particular types of conflict behavior may be tapping a cluster of related behaviors, making inferences about the specified behavior unclear and potentially misleading.

Second, focusing solely on behavior ignores the role of affect, which may be critical for determining the impact of conflict on children. Whereas certain behaviors, such as physical aggression, will be threatening to children regardless of parents' affect, the meaning of many less extreme behaviors is likely to depend on the affect that accompanies them. Shifflett-Simpson and Cummings (1996) found that children attended to both affect and behavior when observing simulated interparental conflict, and marital research suggests that the quality of emotional expression is an important predictor of marital satisfaction and dissolution (e.g, Gottman, 1993). Consequently, systematic study of children's responses to emotions such as contempt and hostility may shed light on what aspects of conflict are detrimental to children's functioning.

In chapter 9, Cummings, Goeke-Morey, and Papp described a more microanalytic approach to assessing conflict that focuses on specific conflict behaviors, and to a lesser extent, affective expression. They offered a categorical scheme that defines behaviors as destructive, constructive, or productive according to their implications for the child's emotional security. Particular behaviors were classified by assessing children's affective response to very brief videotaped vignettes portraying each behavior (Goeke-Morey, 1999). Behaviors that elicited predominantly negative affect were labeled "destructive" because they were viewed as posing a threat to children's emotional security, those that led to positive affect were classified as "constructive" and seen as enhancing children's sense of security, and behaviors eliciting relatively little or balanced affective responses were termed "productive."

This approach is promising because it offers a conceptually derived, empirically based scheme for organizing specific conflict behaviors and investigating their impact on children. However, because the meaning and impact of any behavior is shaped by the affective and behavioral context of the ongoing interaction, children's reactions to isolated behaviors may not provide a reliable index of how those behaviors would be perceived during an actual conflict. Analogue studies have shown that constructive resolution can significantly decrease the distress reported by children observing verbally aggressive conflicts (e.g., Cummings, Ballard, El-Sheikh, & Lake, 1991), and thus a particular behavior may be perceived differently depending on the emotions and behavior that precede and follow it. In addition, although children's perspectives of conflict are important theoretically (see Grych & Cardoza-Fernandes, 2001), individual differences in children's sensitivity to conflict may result in variability in the definition of particular behaviors as constructive or destructive. Thus, although this approach is a strong step toward achieving more precision in assessing conflict, examining how other aspects of an interaction (e.g., emotional expression, resolution) affect children's responses to particular behaviors is likely to provide a more comprehensive understanding of children's perceptions of conflict.

The potential for other aspects of an ongoing interaction to shape the impact of particular conflict behaviors complicates efforts to fine-tune the assessment of couple conflict. Because certain behaviors and emotions covary, it may be most effective to assess particular patterns of interaction rather than specific behaviors. For example, the extent to which parents exhibit hostility or contempt, aggressive behavior, and poor conflict resolution may capture a meaningful cluster of behavior. Questionnaires that obtain more fine-grained assessment of conflictual interactions would be useful for determining which behaviors tend to "hang together," and the analogue approach described by Cummings et al. in chapter 9 could be utilized to examine how systematically varying aspects of these clusters may affect children's perceptions of the interaction. Together, these methods offer the potential to more precisely assess what kinds of interactions children witness, and thus to better understand which aspects of conflict are linked to child adjustment. Similarly, complementary developments in the assessment of child adjustment are needed to determine which aspects of children's functioning are related to conflict.

INCREASING PRECISION IN THE ASSESSMENT OF CHILD OUTCOMES

The majority of studies examining links between conflict and child functioning have used indexes of adjustment problems as outcome measures. It clearly is important to document that children living in highly discordant homes are at elevated risk for maladjustment, but a sole focus on adjustment problems results in limited understanding of how conflict may affect other aspects of children's development (e.g., peer relations, mental representations of family relationships).

For example, in order to test the hypothesis that exposure to certain types of conflict may be beneficial for children, it is necessary to examine theoretically relevant outcomes such as their social competence or conflict resolution skill, rather than to simply document lower levels of pathology. Thus, greater precision in understanding the effects of conflict will be possible when adjustment is conceptualized and measured more broadly.

A second limitation of existing studies examining the association between conflict and adjustment is that they reveal little about individual differences in children's functioning. The principle of multifinality states that the same experience can lead to different developmental outcomes in different children (see Cicchetti & Cohen, 1995); however, testing relations between conflict and adjustment across children may obscure the presence of subgroups of children displaying distinctly different patterns of adjustment. In contrast, person-oriented analyses (e.g., Bergman & Magnusson, 1997) have the potential to further our understanding of the outcomes associated with interparental conflict by utilizing the child, rather than a particular variable, as the focus of analysis.

This approach was illustrated by a recent study of children exposed to severe interparental aggression. Grych, Jouriles, Swank, McDonald, and Norwood (2000) used cluster analysis to examine the possibility that different patterns of adjustment may be found in this population. They assessed 228 8- to 14-year-old children living in shelters for battered women on three key indexes of adjustment: children's reports of internalizing problems (Children's Depression Inventory [CDI]—Kovacs, 1981; Revised Children's Manifest Anxiety Scale [RCMAS]—Reynolds & Richmond, 1978), maternal reports of externalizing problems (Child Behavior Checklist [CBCL]—Achenbach, 1991), and children's reports of self-esteem (Coopersmith Self-Esteem Inventory [CSI]—Coopersmith, 1981). The cluster analysis, which was cross-validated on independent halves of the sample, revealed five different patterns of scores on the adjustment measures. These patterns are displayed in Fig. 12.1.

The largest group (31% of the sample) consisted of children who exhibited relatively low levels of internalizing and externalizing problems and relatively high self-esteem. None of these children or their mothers reported clinically significant levels of behavior problems. A second group (19% of the sample) demonstrated elevated levels of both internalizing and externalizing problems, with externalizing symptoms predominating; 86% of these children scored above the clinical cutoff score on the CBCL and showed elevated CDI scores, although only 9% of the children exceeded the cutoff for clinically significant symptomatology. The third group (21%) was characterized by high levels of externalizing problems (89% in the clinical range) but low levels of internalizing problems and relatively high self-esteem. The fourth group (18%) showed elevated levels of internalizing problems, although relatively few children were in the clinical range (5%), and little sign of externalizing problems. Finally, the smallest group (11%) had the highest levels of internalizing problems (65% of these children scored above the

FIG. 12.1

Cluster Analysis of Adjustment Scores in a Sample of Children of Battered Women. *From* **Grych, Jouriles, Swank, McDonald, & Norwood (2000). Reprinted with permission.**

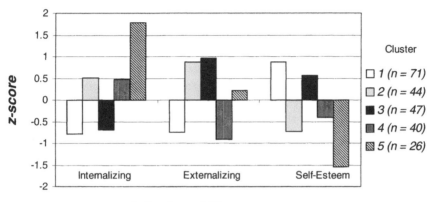

Adjustment Measures

clinical cutoff on the CDI) and a significant percentage of children demonstrating externalizing problems (42% in the clinical range on the CBCL). Thus, this person-centered approach indicated that, although children from violent homes *as a group* evidence elevated levels of both internalizing and externalizing problems, there are identifiable subgroups of children exhibiting different patterns of adjustment.

The next step is to understand why children exposed to the same kind of stressor manifest such diverse outcomes. As an initial foray into investigating this question, Grych and his colleagues (2000) examined whether the groups of children identified in the cluster analyses differed on several individual and family variables. They found that the groups could not be distinguished on the basis of any demographic variables, including gender, but did differ in the amount and type of aggression children reported witnessing and their appraisals of parental conflict.

Briefly, children's ratings of interparental and parent-child aggression appeared to fit a dose-effect model of the effects of family violence on children, at least for fathers' behavior. Children exhibiting the greatest maladjustment (elevated levels of both internalizing and externalizing problems) reported the most exposure to fathers' violence toward mothers and fathers' aggression toward the children themselves. The lowest levels of each type of violence were found in children who exhibited no adjustment problems. It is important to note that these apparently well-adjusted children still were exposed to enough violence that their mothers sought shelter, which underscores the need to study resilience in this population as well as maladjustment. Finally, children's perceptions and appraisals of interparental conflict also differed across the adjustment clusters. In the cognitive-contextual framework (Grych & Fincham, 1990), appraisals are given a central role in shaping the impact of interparental conflict on children, but they rarely have been investigated in children exposed to interparental violence (Jouriles, Spiller, Stephens, McDonald, & Swank, 2000). The findings showed that, although the pattern of results differed somewhat for different types of appraisals, in general more negative appraisals were associated with elevated levels of maladjustment, and internalizing problems in particular.

This study suggests that person-oriented analyses can complement variable-oriented approaches by examining variability in the outcomes associated with interparental conflict. It also provides another way to investigate hypothesized pathways between conflict and adjustment. Like the assessment of these constructs, research on processes proposed to explain how conflict may affect children has been somewhat limited (an issue addressed in the final section of this chapter).

INCREASING PRECISION IN RESEARCH ON INTERVENING PROCESSES

There has been considerable progress in recent years in the development of conceptual models describing mechanisms by which exposure to conflict may adversely affect children. Both indirect (i.e., mediated by parenting) and direct (unmediated) processes have received empirical support, but there have been few attempts to integrate these types of pathways into an integrative model (see Cummings et al., chap. 9, this volume). Moreover, Holmbeck (1997) argued that many investigations designed to test particular models have been unclear about the specific nature of processes proposed to link conflict and adjustment. In particular, terms like *mediator* and *moderator* have been used inconsistently and at times incorrectly, resulting in confusion about how conflict is hypothesized to affect children.

In addition, there is a need to develop more precise predictions regarding links between conflict and specific child outcomes. Most studies have tested associations between conflict and maladjustment without distinguishing among different kinds of adjustment problems that might arise. It is unlikely, however, that the same processes would explain very different developmental sequelae (e.g., internalizing vs. externalizing problems). For example, modeling is frequently proposed to be a process by which directly witnessing conflict could lead to child maladjustment, but this mechanism provides a much more plausible account of the development of externalizing than internalizing problems.

Grych, Fincham, Jouriles, and McDonald (in press) recently proposed a specific pathway between children's appraisals of conflict and internalizing problems. Building on the cognitive-contextual framework, they argued that children's appraisals of threat and self-blame mediate the association between their exposure to interparental conflict and the development of problems such as depression, anxiety, and low self-esteem. As a mediator, appraisal is conceptualized as a psychological process that explains how witnessing conflict could cause internalizing problems. Grych and colleagues (in press) hypothesized that children who feel highly threatened and unable to cope with conflict, or see themselves as responsible for causing or failing to stop interparental conflict, are at risk for developing persistent feelings of sadness, anxiety, and helplessness. Children's appraisal of particular conflicts is proposed to be influenced by both the nature of the conflict that occurs and contextual factors, such as children's prior exposure to conflict (also see Grych & Fincham, 1990). Experimental evidence from analogue studies shows that children witnessing increasingly hostile conflict and conflict in which the topic concerns the child experience greater threat and self-blame (Grych, 1998; Grych & Fincham, 1993), and that their prior exposure to conflict also predicts certain appraisals, such as threat and coping efficacy (Grych, 1998). Several studies also have documented associations between these appraisals and internalizing problems (e.g., Cummings, Davies, & Simpson, 1994; Grych, Seid, & Fincham, 1992; Kerig, 1998b). The key test for mediation is whether appraisals account for the association between conflict and adjustment when these associations are tested simultaneously.

Grych and colleagues (in press) tested this proposed mediational pathway in two large samples of children, one drawn from the community (n = 319; ages 10 to 14) and another from battered women's shelters (n = 145; ages 10 to 12). Children's exposure to conflict was assessed with the Conflict Properties scale of the Children's Perception of Interparental Conflict Scale (CPIC; Grych, Seid, & Fincham, 1992), which assesses conflict frequency, intensity (aggression, tendency to escalate), and resolution. Reports of internalizing problems were obtained from children and their teachers in the community sample and from children and their mothers in the shelter sample; externalizing problems were also assessed through both child and teacher reports in the community sample and by maternal reports alone in the shelter sample. Mediation was tested with multivariate multiple regression, which simultaneously regresses child and teacher/parent reports of each type of adjustment on children's appraisals and perceptions of conflict. Results of these analyses were largely consistent across the two samples. Both perceived threat and self-blame were found to independently mediate the association between children's exposure to conflict and internalizing problems for boys in both samples and girls in the shelter sample. For girls in the community sample, only threat was a significant mediator. No significant mediational results were found for externalizing problems. Similar results were found in other recent studies that tested links among conflict, appraisals, and adjustment (Dadds, Atkinson, Turner, Blums, & Lendich, 1999; Kerig, 1998b), alough one study failed to find a mediating effect for appraisals (Kerig, 1998a). All of these studies have been cross-sectional and consequently cannot demonstrate that appraisals actually cause maladjustment, but the results provide support for a specific link among threat, self-blame appraisals, and internalizing problems.

CONCLUSION

Research on the association between marital and child problems has become increasingly sophisticated as empirical evidence has accumulated showing that marital conflict is a better predictor of child adjustment than are either marital quality or marital status. Continuing to improve the precision with which conflict and adjustment are conceptualized and measured is likely to lead to more thorough understanding of how interactions between parents affect their children. It is possible that further specification of these constructs may shift the focus of the field from conflict per se to the expression of particular behaviors or emotions that undermine or facilitate children's adjustment; it may be that the occurrence of aggression or expression of contempt between spouses is harmful to children whether or not they take place in the context of conflict. Although it is clear that conflict is distressing to children and that exposure to high levels of conflict is a risk factor for the development of child maladjustment (see Cummings & Davies, 1994), there are many questions yet to answer regarding which aspects of conflict affect which aspects of children's functioning (also see Fincham, 1998).

REFERENCES

Achenbach, T. M. (1991). *Integrative guide for the 1991 CBCL/4-18, YSR, and TRF profiles.* Burlington, VT: University of Vermont Department of Psychiatry.

Bergman, L. R., & Magnusson, D. (1997). A person-oriented approach in research on developmental psychopathology. *Development and Psychopathology, 9,* 291-320.

Christensen, A., & Sullaway, M. (1984). *Communication Patterns Questionnaire.* Unpublished questionnaire, University of California, Los Angeles.

Cicchetti, D., & Cohen, D. J. (1995). Perspectives on developmental psychopathology. In D. Cicchetti & D. J. Cohen (Eds.), *Developmental psychopathology, vol. 1: Theory and methods* (pp. 3-22). New York: Wiley

Coopersmith, S. (1981). *Self-esteem inventory.* Palo Alto, CA: Consulting Psychology Press, Inc.

Cummings, E. M., Ballard, M., El-Sheikh, M., & Lake, M. (1991). Resolution and children's responses to interadult anger. *Developmental Psychology, 27,* 462-470.

Cummings, E. M., & Davies, P. T. (1994). *Children and marital conflict.* New York: Guilford.

Cummings, E. M., Davies, P. T., & Simpson, K. S. (1994). Marital conflict, gender, and children's appraisals and coping efficacy as mediators of child adjustment. *Journal of Family Psychology, 8,* 141-149.

Dadds, M. R., Atkinson, E., Turner, C., Blums, G. J., & Lendich, B. (1999). Family conflict and child adjustment: Evidence for a cognitive-contextual model of intergenerational transmission. *Journal of Family Psychology, 13,* 194-208.

Fincham, F. D. (1998). Child development and marital relations. *Child Development, 69,* 271-279.

Goeke-Morey, M. C. (1999). *Children and marital conflict: Exploring the distinction between constructive and destructive marital conflict behaviors.* Unpublished doctoral dissertation, University of Notre Dame, Notre Dame, IN.

Gottman, J. M. (1993). A theory of marital dissolution and stability. *Journal of Family Psychology, 7,* 57-75.

Grych, J. H. (1998). Children's appraisals of interparental conflict: Situational and contextual influences. *Journal of Family Psychology, 12,* 437-453.

Grych, J. H., & Cardoza-Fernandes, S. (2001). Understanding the impact of conflict on children: The role of social cognitive processes. In J. Grych & F. Fincham (Eds.), *Interparental conflict and child development* (pp. 157-187). Cambridge: Cambridge University Press.

Grych, J. H., & Fincham, F. D. (1990). Marital conflict and children's adjustment: A cognitive-contextual framework. *Psychological Bulletin, 108,* 267-290.

Grych, J. H., Fincham, F. D., Jouriles, E. N., & McDonald, R. (in press). Interparental conflict and child adjustment: Testing the mediational role of appraisals in the cognitive-contextual framework. *Child Development.*

Grych, J. H., Jouriles, E. N., Swank, P. R., McDonald R., & Norwood, W. D. (2000). Patterns of adjustment among children of battered women. *Journal of Consulting and Clinical Psychology. 68,* 84-94.

Grych, J. H., Seid, M., & Fincham, F. D. (1992). Assessing marital conflict from the child's perspective: The Children's Perception of Interparental Conflict Scale. *Child Development, 63,* 558-572.

Holmbeck, G. N. (1997). Toward terminological, conceptual, and statistical clarity in the study of mediators and moderators: Examples from the child-clinical and pediatric psychology literatures. *Journal of Consulting and Clinical Psychology, 65,* 599-610.

Jouriles, E. N., Spiller, L. C., Stephens, N., McDonald, R., & Swank, P. (2000). Variability in adjustment of children of battered women: The role of child appraisals of interparent conflict. *Cognitive Therapy and Research, 24,* 233-249.

Kerig, P. K. (1996). Assessing the links between interparental conflict and child adjustment: The Conflicts and Problem Solving Scales. *Journal of Family Psychology, 10,* 454-473.

Kerig, P. K. (1998a). Moderators and mediators of the effects of interparental conflict on children's adjustment. *Journal of Abnormal Child Psychology, 26,* 199-212.

Kerig, P. K. (1998b). Gender and appraisals as mediators of adjustment in children exposed to interparental violence. *Journal of Family Violence, 15,* 345-363.

Kovacs, M. (1981). Rating scales to assess depression in school-aged children. *Acta Paedopsychiatry, 46,* 305-315.

Reynolds, C. R., & Richmond, B. O. (1978). What I Think and Feel: A revised measure of children's anxiety. *Journal of Abnormal Child Psychology, 6,* 271-280.

Shifflett-Simpson, K., & Cummings, E. M. (1996). Mixed message resolution and children's responses to interadult conflict. *Child Development, 67,* 437-448.

IV

What Policies and Programs Influence Couple Conflict? What Works? What Doesn't Work? Where Do We Go From Here?

13

Helping Families Change:
From Clinical Interventions to Population-Based
Strategies

Matthew R. Sanders

The University of Queensland

The family provides the first, and most important, social, emotional, interpersonal, economic, and cultural context for human development and, as a result, family relationships have a profound influence on the well-being of children and parents. The parent-child relationship has a pervasive influence on the psychological, physical, social, and economic well-being of children. Disturbed interpersonal relationships within the family are generic risk factors and positive interpersonal relationships are protective factors that are related to a wide variety of mental health problems from infancy to old age (Sanders, 1995). Many significant mental health, social, and economic problems are linked to disturbances in family functioning and the breakdown of family relationships (Chamberlain & Patterson, 1995; Patterson, 1982; Sanders & Duncan, 1995). Epidemiological studies indicate that family risk factors such as poor parenting, family conflict, and marriage breakdown strongly influence children's development (e.g., Cummings & Davies, 1994; Dryfoos, 1990; Robins, 1991). Specifically, a lack of a warm positive relationship with parents; insecure attachment, harsh, inflexible, rigid, or inconsistent discipline practices; inadequate supervision of and involvement with children; marital conflict and breakdown; and parental psychopathology (particularly maternal depression) increase the risk that children develop major behavioral and emotional problems, including substance abuse, antisocial behavior and juvenile crime (e.g., Coie, 1996; Loeber & Farrington, 1998).

Although family relationships are important, the transition to parenthood for many couples bring new challenges. Parents generally receive little preparation beyond the experience of having been parented themselves; with most learn, on the job and through trial and error (Risley, Clark, & Cataldo, 1976; Sanders et al., 1999). The demands of parenthood are further complicated when parents are without partners; have low incomes; do not have access to extended family support networks (e.g., grandparents, trusted family friends) for advice on childrearing; or experience the stress of relationship conflict, separation, divorce, or repartnering (Lawton & Sanders, 1994; Sanders, Nicholson, & Floyd, 1997).

This chapter examines the contributions and limitations of current approaches to family intervention and the prevention and treatment of child psychopathology and family distress. The rationale for the development, implementation, and evaluation of a comprehensive multilevel, preventively oriented parenting and family support intervention as a population intervention is described, as well as the scientific basis of this approach.

DEFINITION OF FAMILY INTERVENTION

Family intervention is defined broadly as a therapeutic process, which helps modify psychological distress of individuals by targeting their interpersonal relationships within the family. Typically, family interventions aim to change aspects of family functioning that are related to the etiology, maintenance, relapse, or exacerbation of an individual's functioning. This may include attempts to alleviate behavioral or emotional problems of individual family members, relationships between family members (marital partners, parent-child relationships, sibling relationships), or relationships between the family and the broader community. The approach is broadly educative and emphasizes reciprocity among family members. Hence, this definition incorporates parenting interventions that aim to improve parent-child relationships, and marital interventions that target the marital dyad to be considered, along with more traditional family therapies. The term family intervention is preferred to family therapy, because it allows both prevention and treatment studies to be included.

THE CONTRIBUTION OF FAMILY INTERVENTION

Although there are many different approaches to family intervention, this chapter concentrates on the application of models of behavioral family intervention (BFI) based on social learning theory (Patterson, 1982). BFI has the strongest empirical support of any form of child psychotherapy or approaches to family intervention (Brestan & Eyberg, 1998; Kazdin & Wassell, 2000; Sanders, 1995, 1996). There have been several recent comprehensive reviews that have documented the efficacy of BFI as an approach to helping children and their families (Lochman, 1990; McMahon, 1999; Sanders, 1996, 1998; Taylor & Biglan, 1998). This literature is not revisited here in detail. There is clear evidence that BFI can benefit children with disruptive behavior disorders, particularly children with oppositional defiant disorders (ODD) and their parents (Forehand & Long, 1988; McMahon & Wells, 1998; Webster-Stratton, 1994). The empirical basis of BFI is strengthened by evidence that the approach can be successfully applied to many other clinical problems and disorders including attention deficit hyperactivity disorder (Barkley, Guevremont, Anastopoulos, & Fletcher, 1992), persistent feeding difficulties (Turner, Sanders, & Wall, 1994), pain syndromes (Sanders, Shepherd, Cleghorn, & Woolford, 1994), anxiety disorders (Barrett, Dadds, & Rapee, 1996), autism and developmental disabilities (Schreibman, Kaneko, & Koegel, 1991), achievement problems, and habit disorders, as well as everyday problems of normal children (see Sanders, 1996; Taylor & Biglan, 1998 for reviews of this literature). Meta analyses of treatment outcome studies often report large effect sizes (Serketich & Dumas, 1996), with good maintenance of treatment gains (Forehand & Long, 1988). Treatment effects have been shown to generalize to school settings (McNeil, Eyberg, Eisenstadt, Necomb, & Funderburk, 1991) and to various community settings outside the home (Sanders & Glynn, 1981). Parents participating in these programs are generally satisfied consumers (Webster-Stratton, 1989).

It is also becoming increasingly evident that the benefits of BFI are not restricted to children, with several studies now showing effects on other areas of family functioning, including reduced maternal depression and stress, increases in parental satisfaction and efficacy, and reduced marital conflict over parenting issues (e.g.,, Nicholson & Sanders, 1999; Sanders, Markie-Dadds, Tully, & Bor, 2000; Sanders & Shallcross, 2000).

BFIs have met a number of important scientific and clinical criteria that strengthen confidence in the intervention approach. These include the following:

1. Replicated findings: The primary treatment effects showing that decreases in parental negative disciplinary behavior and increases in parents' use of a variety of positive attending and other relationship-enhancing skills lead to improved child behavior have been replicated many times in different studies, involving different investigators, in several different countries, with a diverse variety of client populations (Sanders, 1999) .

2. Demonstrations of clinically meaningful outcomes for families: Clinically meaningful outcomes have been demonstrated by applying rigorous criteria for clinical improvement such as the clinical reliable change index (Jacobson & Truax, 1991) for child outcomes. These have shown that as many as 75% of children evidence clinical reliable change. Furthermore, there is little evidence that parenting interventions produce negative side effects, symptom substitution, or other adverse family outcomes.

3. The effectiveness of different delivery modalities: There is increasing evidence showing that a variety of delivery modalities can produce similar positive outcomes for children including individual, group, telephone-assisted and self-directed variants of parenting programs (e.g.,, Connell, Sanders, & Markie-Dadds, 1997; O'Dell, 1974; Sanders et al., 1999).

4. High levels of consumer acceptability: High levels of consumer satisfaction have been repeatedly demonstrated in different controlled evaluations of BFI and for specific parenting techniques advocated (see McMahon, 1999; Webster-Stratton, 1989).

5. Effectiveness with a range of family types: In the area where the strongest support for BFI is evident (namely for disruptive behavior problems in preadolescent children), interventions have been successfully used with two- parent families, single parents, and stepfamilies (Nicholson & Sanders, 1999).

In sum, these findings confirm that BFI is a powerful clinical resource for effecting change in family relationships for a wide range of behavioral and emotional problems in children.

LIMITATIONS OF CURRENT APPROACHES TO FAMILY INTERVENTION

Despite the clear evidence supporting the efficacy and effectiveness of BFI, there are a number of significant limitations with current approaches that must be addressed by researchers and practitioners if these interventions are to have any significant impact on family relationships at a community level.

A major concern for the family intervention field in general is that empirically supported interventions are underutilized by professionals and are not readily accessible to families who might benefit from them (Taylor & Biglan, 1998). Most children with behavioral problems receive no professional assistance from mental health professionals (Zubrick et al., 1995). For example, in a large sample of 4- to16- year-old children, only 2% of children with an identifiable mental health problem had received any specialist mental health assistance. Furthermore, there are low participation rates in parent education, particularly in families who are considered most at risk for the development of serious problems (Sanders, Markie-Dadds, & Turner, 1999). Nonevaluated parent education and family support programs continue to dominate the field, where programs are offered to the public with no known effects. In the absence of any meaningful form of accountability or quality control to ensure evidence-based family interventions are promoted, the public is exposed to a diverse range of untested and, in some instances, even potentially harmful interventions.

Empirically supported family intervention programs generally have limited reach. It is also of continuing concern that indigenous and ethnic minority groups have low representation in clinical outcome trials. These groups are among the most disadvantaged sectors of the community, and are more likely to drop out from intervention (Kazdin & Wassell, 2000). For example, even though indigenous Australian aboriginal children are at greatly increased risk for poorer health, premature mortality, school underachievement, involvement in juvenile crime, child abuse, and addictive behavior, to this author's knowledge there has not been a single controlled published evaluation of a parenting or family intervention program with that population (Sanders, 1995). Access problems are compounded by the relative inflexibility of delivery formats required by most interventions, particularly the requirement for face-to- face session attendance during re.gular working hours. For families with both parents working or families living in rural, remote, or otherwise isolated areas, meeting this attendance requirement can be an insurmountable problem.

Another criticism of family intervention as a risk-reduction approach is that it may simply be insufficient as an intervention on its own, particularly for complex problems such as conduct disorder, ADHD, and drug abuse where there are multiple interacting risk factors. Some researchers have argued from epidemiological evidence that longer more intensive multirisk factor interventions covering home, school, peer groups, and the children themselves are required to prevent conduct disorders (Kazdin, 1997; McMahon & Slough, 1996). However, it has still yet to be convincingly demonstrated through long-term outcome studies that such an approach will be more effective than targeting a more limited subset of risk and protective factors such as parenting skills, maternal depression or marital discord. One of the major problems for families with limited resources even receiving multiple interventions can add to the burden of care already experienced by the family (e.g., additional appointments, more professionals to deal with, extra costs), particularly if the child has special needs such as a chronic disability.

THE CHALLENGES AHEAD

There are many challenges facing the field of family intervention. Perhaps the most important is to reorient our focus from treatment outcome studies to the development and evaluation of a population perspective to family problems, including the effective dissemination of what is known to work in promoting effective parenting and positive family relationships. A comprehensive population-based strategy is required. This strategy needs to be designed to enhance parental competence, prevent dysfunctional parenting practices, promote better teamwork between partners, and thereby reduce an important set of family risk factors associated with behavioral and emotional problems in children. In order for such a population approach to be effective, several scientific and clinical criteria need to be met (Taylor, 1999):

• Knowledge of the prevalence and incidence of child outcomes being targeted: A number of studies in the United States, Canada, United Kingdom, New Zealand, Germany, and Australia have established the prevalence rates of behavioral and emotional problems in children, showing that about 18% of children experience behavioral or emotional problems (e.g., Zubrick et al., 1995). Parents themselves report a high level of concern about their child's behavior and adjustment. For example, in a recent epidemiological survey of Queensland parents, when asked "Do you consider your child to have a behavioral or emotional problem?" 28% said yes (Sanders et al., 1999), reflecting the high degree of parental concern about children.

• Knowledge of the prevalence and incidence of family risk factors: Some studies that have established the incidence and prevalence of child behavior problems have also examined parenting practices, disciplinary styles, and marital conflict. For example, Sanders et al., (1999), found that 70% of parents of children under the age of 12 years report they smack their children at least occasionally, 3% reported hitting their child with an object other than their hand, and 25% of parents reported significant disagreements with partners of parenting issues.

• Knowledge that changing specific family risk and protective factors leads to a reduction in the incidence and prevalence of the target problem: An effective population-level parenting strategy must make explicit the kinds of parenting practices that are considered harmful to children. The core constructs believed to underpin competent parenting need to be articulated so that targets for intervention can be specified. The validity of the model of family intervention would be greatly strengthened if improvements in child functioning were shown to be directly related to specific changes that decrease the dysfunctional and increase competent parenting variables specified by the model. For example, there is now considerable evidence to support the proposition that teaching parents positive parenting and consistent disciplinary skills results in significant improvements in the majority of oppositional and disruptive children, particularly young children, attesting to the importance of reducing coercive patterns of coercive parent-child interaction (Patterson, 1982).

Having Effective Family Interventions

A population perspective requires a range of effective family interventions to be available. The approach to family intervention must also be subjected to comprehensive and systematic evaluation with rigorous scientific controls using either intrasubject replication designs or traditional randomized controlled clinical trials with sufficient statistical power to detect meaningful differences between intervention and control conditions. An effective family intervention strategy should seek to demonstrate that short-term intervention gains maintain over time, are cost effective relative to no intervention alternative interventions or usual community care, and are associated with high levels of consumer satisfaction and community acceptance. It is not sufficient just to demonstrate that a strategy results in improvements in family interaction based exclusively on parental reports, although this is a necessary first step. The mechanisms purported to underlie the improvements in family interaction must also be demonstrated to change and be responsible for the observed improvements.

Family Interventions Must be Culturally Appropriate. An effective population strategy should be tailored in such a way that it is accessible, relevant, and respectful of the cultural values, beliefs, aspirations, traditions, and identified needs of different ethnic groups. Factors such as family structure, roles and responsibilities, predominant cultural beliefs and values, child-raising practices and developmental issues, and sexuality and gender roles may be culturally specific and need to be addressed. Although there is much to learn about how to achieve this objective in a multicultural context, it is likely that sensitively tailored parenting programs can be effective with a variety of cultural groups. It is important that the multicultural context within which assessment, intervention, and research programs operate is made clear in evaluations. There is an ethical imperative to ensure that interventions designed to provide skills to parents and children in the dominant culture are not at the expense of language and other competencies or values in the child's own culture.

Interventions Need to be Widely Available. A key assumption of a population-based approach is that parenting and other family intervention strategies should be widely accessible in the community. It is important that barriers to accessing parenting and other family intervention programs are reduced. Inflexible clinic hours may prevent working parents from participating in parenting programs. Families most in need of help with emotional and behavioral problems often do not have or seek access to support services. Families who are socially and economically disadvantaged are less likely to refer themselves for help. In addition, the family intervention services may be viewed as coercive and intrusive, rather than as helpful. Use of the internet, CD-rom-based applications, and media interventions all have the potential to increase the reach of interventions to hard-to-access groups; however, such approaches require systematic evaluation. Note, though, that Halford, Sanders, and Behrens(under review), in a recent evaluation of a relationship education program known as Self-PREP for couples early in marriage, showed that the prevention of relationship distress only occurred for high-risk couples (those with either a family of origin history of parental divorce or family violence) and not for low-risk couples, who were more distressed than a control group at a follow-up 4 years later.

WHAT IS THE TRIPLE P-POSITIVE PARENTING PROGRAM?

In an effort to address some of the limitations just discussed, the Triple P-Positive Parenting Program, a multi-level, preventively oriented parenting and family support strategy, has been developed by the author and his colleagues at the University of Queensland in Brisbane, Australia. The program aims to prevent severe behavioral, emotional and developmental problems in children by enhancing the knowledge, skills, confidence, and teamwork of parents. The program has five levels of intervention on a tiered continuum of increasing strength (see Table 13.1) for parents of preadolescent children from birth to age 12, although a version for parents of teenagers is also under development.

The rationale for this tiered multilevel strategy is that there are differing levels of dysfunction and behavioral disturbance in children, and parents have differing needs and desires regarding the type, intensity, and mode of assistance they require. The multilevel strategy is designed to maximize efficiency, contain costs, avoid waste and over servicing, and ensure that the program has wide reach in the community. Also, the multidisciplinary nature of the program involves the better utilization of the existing professional workforce in the task of promoting competent parenting.

The program targets four different developmental periods from infancy to preadolescence. Within each developmental period, the reach of the intervention can vary from being very broad (targeting an entire population) or quite narrow (targeting only high-risk children). This flexibility enables individual practitioners to determine the scope of the intervention given their own service priorities and funding. Alternatively, the program can be delivered as a government-funded service provided on a free-to-consumer basis.

Table 13.1
The Triple P Model of Parenting and Family Support

Level of Intervention	Target Population	Intervention Methods	Program Materials	Possible Target Behaviors
1. Universal Triple P	All parents interested in information about promoting their child's development.	Anticipatory well child care involving the provision of brief information on how to solve developmental and minor behavior problems. May involve self-directed resources, brief consultation, group presentations and mass media strategies.	*Positive Parenting* booklet *Positive Parenting* tip sheet series *Families* video series *Every Parent Triple P Program Guide*	Common every day behavior difficulties
2. Selective Triple P	Parents with a specific concern about their child's behavior or development.	Provision of specific advice for a discrete child problem behavior. May be self-directed or involve telephone or face-to-face clinician contact or group sessions.	Level 1 materials *Primary Care Triple P Practitioner's Manual* Developmental wall chart Consultation flip chart	Bedtime routine difficulties Temper tantrums Meal time behavior problems Toilet training
3. Primary Care Triple P	Parents with specific concerns about their child's behavior or development that require active skills training.	Brief therapy program (1 to 4 clinic sessions) combining advice, rehearsal and self-evaluation to teach parents to manage a discrete child problem behavior.	Level 1 and 2 materials	As for Level 2 Persistent eating problems Pain management
4. Standard Triple P	Parents of children with more severe behavior problems. Parents wanting intensive training in positive parenting skills.	Intensive program focussing on parent-child interaction and the application of parenting skills to a broad range of target behaviors. Includes generalisation enhancement strategies. May be self-directed or involve telephone or face-to-face clinician contact or group sessions.	Level 1 to 3 materials *Every Parent's Self-Help Workbook Standard Triple P Practitioner's Manual and Every Parent's Family Workbook Group Triple P Facilitator's Manual and Every Parent's Group Workbook*	General behavior management concerns Aggressive behavior Oppositional Defiant Disorder Conduct Disorder Learning difficulties
5. Enhanced Triple P	Parents of children with concurrent child behavior problems and family dysfunction	Intensive program with modules including home visits to enhance parenting skills, mood management strategies and stress coping skills, and partner support skills.	Levels 1 to 4 materials *Enhanced Triple P Practitioner's Manual and Every Parent's Supplementary Workbook*	Persistent conduct problems Concurrent child behavior problems and parent problems (such as relationship conflict, depression). Child maltreatment

Theoretical Basis of Triple P

Triple P is a form of behavioral family intervention based on social learning principles (e.g., Patterson, 1982). Triple P aims to enhance family protective factors and to reduce risk factors associated with severe behavioral and emotional problems in preadolescent children. Specifically, the program aims to enhance the knowledge, skills, confidence, self-sufficiency and resourcefulness of parents of preadolescent children; promote nurturing, safe, engaging, non-violent, and low-conflict environments for children; promote children's social, emotional, language, intellectual, and behavioral competencies through positive parenting practices.

The program content draws on:

1. Social learning models of parent-child interaction that highlight the reciprocal and bidirectional nature of parent-child interactions (e.g., Patterson, 1982). This model identifies learning mechanisms, that maintain coercive and dysfunctional patterns of family interaction, and predict future antisocial behavior in children (Patterson, Reid, & Dishion, 1992). As a consequence the program specifically teaches parents positive child management skills as an alternative to coercive parenting practices.

2. Research in child and family behavior therapy and applied behavior analysis that has developed many useful behavior change strategies, particularly research focusing on rearranging antecedents of problem behavior through designing more positive-engaging environments for children (Risley, Clark, & Cataldo, 1976; Sanders, 1992, 1996).

3. Developmental research on parenting in everyday contexts-the program targets children's competencies in naturally occurring everyday contexts, drawing heavily on work that traces the origins of social and intellectual competence to early parent-child relationships (e.g., Hart & Risley, 1995; White, 1990). Children's risk of developing severe behavioral and emotional problems is reduced by teaching parents to use naturally occurring daily interactions to teach children language, social skills, and developmental competencies and problem-solving skills in an emotionally supportive context. Particular emphasis is placed on using child-initiated interactions as a context for the use of incidental teaching (Hart & Risley, 1975). Children are at greater risk for adverse developmental outcomes, including behavioral problems, if they fail to acquire core language competencies and impulse control during early childhood (Hart & Risley, 1995).

4. Social information processing models that highlight the important role of parental cognitions such as attributions, expectancies and beliefs as factors that contribute to parental self-efficacy, decision making and behavioral intentions (e.g., Bandura, 1977, 1995). Parents' attributions are specifically targeted in the intervention by encouraging parents to identify alternative social interactional explanations for their child's behavior.

5. Research from the field of developmental psychopathology has identified specific risk and protective factors that are linked to adverse developmental outcomes in children (e.g., Emery, 1982; Grych & Fincham, 1990; Hart & Risley, 1995; Rutter, 1985). Specifically, the risk factors of poor parent management practices, marital family conflict, and parental distress are targeted risk factors. As parental discord is a specific risk factor for many forms of child and adolescent psychopathology (Grych & Fincham, 1990; Rutter, 1985; Sanders & Markie-Dadds, 1997), the program fosters collaboration and teamwork between carers in raising children. Improving couples communication is an important vehicle to reduce marital conflict over child rearing issues, and to reduce personal distress of parents and children in conflictual relationships (Sanders, Markie-Dadds, & Turner, 1998).

Triple P also targets distressing emotional reactions of parents including depression, anger, anxiety, and high levels of stress, especially with the parenting role (Sanders, Markie-Dadds, & Turner, 1999). Distress can be alleviated through parents developing better parenting skills, which reduces feelings of helplessness, depression, and stress. Enhanced levels of the intervention use cognitive-behavior therapy techniques of mood monitoring, challenging dysfunctional cognitions and attributions, and by teaching parent's specific coping skills for high-risk parenting situations.

6. A population health perspective to family intervention involves the explicit recognition of the role of the broader ecological context for human development (e.g., Biglan, 1995; Mrazek & Haggerty, 1994; National Institute of Mental Health, 1998). As pointed out by Biglan (1995), the reduction of antisocial behavior in children requires the community context for parenting to change. Triple P's media and promotional strate.gy as part of a larger system of intervention aims to change this broader ecological context of parenting. It does this via normalizing parenting experiences (particularly the process of participating in parent education), by breaking down parents sense of social isolation, increasing social and emotional support from others in the community, and validating and acknowledging publicly the importance and difficulties of parenting. It also involves actively seeking community involvement and support in the program by the engagement of key community stakeholders (e.g., community leaders, businesses, schools, and voluntary organizations).

Self-regulation and Parental Competence

The approach to promoting parental competence views the development of a parent's capacity for self-regulation as central skill. This involves teaching parents skills that enable them to become independent problem solvers. Karoly (1993) defined self regulation as follows:

[Self-regulation refers to those processes, internal and or transactional, that enable an individual to guide his/her goal directed activities over time and across changing circumstances (contexts). Regulation implies modulation of thought, affect, behavior, and attention via deliberate or automated use of specific mechanisms and supportive metaskills. The processes of self-regulation are initiated when routinized activity is impeded or when goal directedness is otherwise made salient (e.g., the appearance of a challenge, the failure of habitual patterns, etc. . . p.25.]

This definition emphasizes that self-regulatory processes are embedded in a social context that not only provides opportunities and limitations for individual self-directedness, but also implies a dynamic reciprocal interchange between the internal and external determinants of human motivation. From a therapeutic perspective, self-regulation is a process whereby individuals are taught skills to modify their own behavior. These skills include how to select developmentally appropriate goals, monitor a child's or the parent's own behavior, choose an appropriate method of intervention for a particular problem, implement the solution, self-monitor the implementation of solutions via checklists relating to the areas of concern; and identify strengths or limitations in individuals' performance and set future goals for action.

This self-regulatory framework is operationalized to include:

1. Self-sufficiency: Because a parenting program is time limited, parents need to become independent problem solvers so that they trust their own judgment and become less reliant on others in carrying out basic parenting responsibilities. Self-sufficient parents have the resilience, resourcefulness, knowledge, and skills to parent with confidence.

2. Parental self-efficacy: This refers to a parent's belief that he or she can overcome or solve a parenting or child management problem. Parents with high self-efficacy have more positive expectations about the possibility of change.

3. Self-management: The tools or skills that parents use to become more self-sufficient, include self- monitoring, self-determination of performance goals and standards, self-evaluation against some performance criterion, and self-selection of change strategies. Because all parents are responsible for the way they choose to raise their children, parents select which aspects of their own and their child's behavior they wish to work on, set goals for themselves, choose specific parenting and child management techniques they wish to implement, and self-evaluate their success with their chosen goals against self determined criteria. Triple P aims to help parents make informed decisions by sharing knowledge and skills derived from contemporary research into effective child rearing practices. An active skills training process is incorporated into Triple P to enable the skills to be modeled and practiced. Parents receive feedback regarding their implementation of skills learned in a supportive context, using a self-regulatory framework (see Sanders & Dadds, 1993).

4. Personal agency: Here the parent increasingly attribute changes or improvements in their situation to their own or their child's efforts rather than to chance, age, maturational factors, or other uncontrollable events (e.g., spouses' bad

parenting or genes). This outcome is achieved by prompting parents to identify causes or explanations for their child's or their own behavior.

Encouraging parents to become self-sufficient means that parents become more connected to social support networks (partners, extended family, friends, child-care supports). However, the broader ecological context within which a family lives cannot be ignored (poverty, dangerous neighbourhoods, community, ethnicity, culture). It is hypothesized that the more self-sufficient parents become, the more likely they are to seek appropriate support when they need it, advocate for children, become involved in their child's schooling, and protect children from harm (e.g., by managing conflict with partners, and creating a secure, low-conflict environment).

PRINCIPLES OF POSITIVE PARENTING

Five core positive parenting principles form the basis of the program. These principles address specific risk and protective factors known to predict positive developmental and mental health outcomes in children. These core principles translate into a range of specific parenting skills, which are outlined in Table 13.2.

Ensuring a Safe and Engaging Environment. Children of all ages need a safe, supervised, and therefore protective environment that provides opportunities for them to explore, experiment, and play. This principle is essential to promote healthy development and prevent accidents and injuries in the home (Peterson & Saldana, 1996; Wesch & Lutzker, 1991). It also is relevant to older children and adolescents who need adequate supervision and monitoring in an appropriate developmental context (Dishion & McMahon, 1998; Forehand, Miller, Dutra, & Watts-Chance, 1997). Triple P draws on the work of Risley and his colleagues, who articulated how the design of living environments can promote engagement and skill development of dependent persons from infancy to old age (Risley et al., 1976).

Creating a Positive Learning Environment. Although this involves educating parents in their role as their child's first teacher, the program specifically targets how parents can respond positively and constructively to child-initiated interactions (e.g., requests for help, information, advice, attention) through incidental teaching to assist children learn to solve problems for themselves. Incidental teaching involves parents being receptive to child-initiated interactions when children attempt to communicate with the parents. The procedure has been used extensively in the teaching of language, social skills, and social problem solving (e.g., Hart & Risley, 1975, 1995). A related technique known as "Ask, Say, Do" involves teaching parents to break complex skills down into discrete steps, and to teach children the skill sequentially (in a forward fashion) through the use of graded series of prompts from the least to the most intrusive.

Table 13.2
Core Parenting Skills

Observation skills	Parent-child relationship enhancement skills	Encouraging desirable behavior	Teaching new skills and behaviors	Managing misbehavior	Preventing problems in high-risk situations	Self-regulation skills	Mood management and coping skills	Partner support and communication skills
Monitoring children's behavior	Spending quality time	Giving descriptive praise	Setting developmentally appropriate goals	Establishing ground rules	Planning and advanced preparation	Setting practice tasks	Catching unhelpful thoughts	Improving personal communication habits
Monitoring own behavior	Talking with children	Giving non-verbal attention	Setting a good example	Using directed discussion	Discussing ground rules for specific situations	Self-evaluation of strengths and weaknesses	Relaxation and stress management	Giving and receiving constructive feedback
	Showing affection	Providing engaging activities	Using incidental teaching	Using planned ignoring	Selecting engaging activities	Setting personal goals for change	Developing personal coping statements	Having casual conversations
			Using Ask, Say, Do	Giving clear, calm instructions	Providing incentives		Challenging unhelpful thoughts	Supporting each other when problem behavior occurs
			Using behavior charts	Using logical consequences	Providing consequences		Developing coping plans for high-risk situations	Problem solving
				Using quiet time	Holding follow up discussions			Improving relationship happiness
				Using time-out				

Using Assertive Discipline. Specific child management strategies are taught that are alternatives to coercive and ineffective discipline practices (e.g., as shouting, threatening or using physical punishment). A range of behavior-change procedures that are alternatives to coercive discipline are demonstrated to parents, including selecting ground rules for specific situations; discussing rules with children; giving clear, calm, age-appropriate instructions and requests; logical consequences; quiet time (non-exclusionary time-out); time-out; and planned ignoring. Parents are taught to use these skills in the home as well as in community settings (e.g., getting ready to go out, having visitors, and going shopping) to promote the generalization of parenting skills to diverse parenting situations (see Sanders & Dadds, 1993, for more detail).

Having Realistic Expectations. This involves exploring with parents their expectations, assumptions, and beliefs about the causes of children's behavior, and choosing goals that are developmentally appropriate for the child and realistic for the parent. There is evidence that parents who are at risk of abusing their children are more likely to have unrealistic expectations of children's capabilities (Azar & Rohrbeck, 1986). Developmentally appropriate expectations are taught in the context of parents' specific expectations concerning difficult and prosocial behaviors rather than through the more traditional age-and-stages approach to teaching about child development.

Taking Care of Oneself as a Parent. Parenting is affected by a range of factors that impact on a parents' self-esteem and sense of well-being. All levels of Triple P specifically address this issue by encouraging parents to view parenting as part of a larger context of personal self-care, resourcefulness, and well-being, and by teaching parents practical parenting skills that both parents are able to implement. In more intensive levels of intervention (Level 5), couples are also taught effective marital communication skills and are encouraged to explore how their own emotional state affects their parenting and consequently their child's behavior. Parents develop specific coping strategies for managing difficult emotions including depression, anger, anxiety, and high levels of parenting stress at high-risk times for stress.

CORE FEATURES OF TRIPLE P

There are several other distinctive features of Triple P as a family intervention which are discussed below.

   • Principle of program sufficiency: This concept refers to the notion that parents differ in the strength of intervention they may require to enable them to independently manage a problem. Triple P aims to provide the minimally sufficient level of support that parents require to do their job. For example, parents seeking advice on a specific topic (e.g., tantrums) can receive clear, high-quality, behaviorally specific advice in the form of a parenting tip sheet on how to manage or prevent a specific problem. For such a parent, Levels 1 or 2 of Triple P would constitute a sufficient intervention.

• Flexible tailoring to identified risk and protective factors: The program enables parents to receive parenting support in the most cost-effective way possible. Within this context, a number of different programs of varying intensity have been developed. For example, Level 5 provides intervention for additional family risk factors, such as marital conflict, mood disturbance and high levels of stress.

• Varied delivery modalities: Several of the levels of intervention in Triple P can be delivered in a variety of formats, including individual face to face, group, telephone-assisted, or self-directed programs, or a combination. This flexibility enables parents to participate in ways that suit their individual circumstances, and allows participation from families in rural and remote areas who typically have less access to professional services.

• Wide potential reach: Triple P is designed to be implemented as an entire integrated system at a population level. However, the multilevel nature of the program enables various combinations of the intervention levels and modalities within levels to be used flexibly as universal, indicated, or selective prevention strategies, depending on local priorities, staffing, and budget constraints. Some communities using Triple P will use the entire multilevel system, whereas other may focus on getting the Level 4 group program implemented at a population level, while seeking funding support for the other levels of intervention.

• A multidisciplinary approach: Many different professional groups provide counsel and advice to parents. Triple P was developed as a professional resource that can be used by a range of helping professionals. These professionals include community nurses, family doctors, pediatricians, teachers, social workers, psychologists, psychiatrists, and police officers, to name a few. At a community level, rigid professional boundaries are discouraged and an emphasis put on providing training and support to a variety of professionals to become more effective in their parent consultation skills. Exclusive reliance on a single discipline, such as clinical psychology, will almost guarantee that there is no impact on family relationships at a population level.

DIFFERENT LEVELS OF INTERVENTION

LEVEL 1: Universal Triple P (Media and Promotional Strategy)

A universal prevention strategy targets an entire population (national, local community, neighborhood, or school) with a program aimed at preventing inadequate or dysfunctional parenting (Mrazek & Haggerty, 1994). Several authors have noted that the media has been underutilized by family intervention researchers (e.g.,

Biglan, 1992). Evidence from the public health field shows that media strategies can be effective in increasing community awareness of health issues, and have been instrumental in modifying potentially harmful behavior such as cigarette smoking, lack of exercise and poor diet (Biglan, 1995; Sorenson, Emmons, Hunt, & Johnson, 1998). Universal Triple P aims to use health promotion and social marketing strategies to promote the use of positive parenting practices in the community, increase the receptivity of parents toward participating in the program, increase favorable community attitudes towards the program and parenting in general, destigmatize and normalize the process of seeking help for children with behavior problems, increase the visibility and reach of the program, counter alarmist, sensationalized or parent blaming messages in the media.

A Triple P promotional campaign is coordinated locally by a Triple P coordinator. Program coordinators use a media resource kit, which currently consists of the following elements: 30-second television commercial promoting the program for broadcast as a community service announcement (CSA); 30-second radio commercial announcing the program; series of 40 and 60-second audio sound capsules on positive parenting; 52 newspaper columns on Triple P dealing with common parenting issues and topics of general interest to parents; self-directed information resources in the form of positive parenting tip sheets and a series of videos for parents, which depict how to apply behavior management advice to common behavior and developmental problems; printed advertising materials (posters, brochures, business cards, coffee mugs, positive parenting t-shirts, and refrigerator magnets); a series of press releases and sample letters to editors of local television, radio, newspapers and community leaders requesting their support and involvement with the program; and a program coordinator guide to use of the media kit.

To illustrate such an approach, a media campaign on parenting based around a television series ("Families") that was shown on a commercial television network in New Zealand is discussed later in this chapter. The centerpiece of this media campaign was 13 30-minute episodes of an infotainment-style television series, "Families". This program was shown at prime time 7:30 p.m. on a Wednesday evening on the TV 3 commercial television network from October through December 1995. The program was funded by New Zealand on Air and private business donations (Tindall Foundation).

The use of am infotainment-style television program was to ensure the widest reach possible for Triple P. Such programs are very popular in both Australia and New Zealand and, according to ratings data, frequently attract around 20 to 35% of the viewing audience (Neilson, 1997). The series used an entertaining format to provide practical information and advice to parents on how to tackle a wide variety of common behavioral and developmental problems in children (e.g., sleep problems, tantrums, whining, aggression) and other parenting issues. A 5-to 7-minute Triple P segment each week enabled parents to complete a 13- session Triple P program in their own home through the medium of television. A cross-promotional strategy using radio and the print media was also employed to prompt parents to watch the show and inform them of how to contact a Triple P infoline for more information about parenting. "Families" fact sheets, which were specifically designed parenting tip sheets, were also available through writing to a Triple P Center calling a Triple P information line, or through a retail chain.

A carefully planned media campaign has the potential to reach a broad cross-section of the population and to mobilize community support for the initiative. Hence, it is important to engage key stakeholders before the outreach commences to mobilize community support in advance. The primary target group for a Triple P- related campaign are the parents and carers of children who may benefit from advice on parenting. However, media messages are also seen or heard by professionals, politicians, and their advisers at various levels of government, voluntary organizations, as well as non-parent members of the public. These groups may be able to support other levels of the program through referring parents to the program, facilitating funding, or directly sending donations.

For some families, it is the only participation they will have in the program. Hence, designing the media campaign to ensure that messages are thematically consistent and culturally appropriate is critical to ensure that the messages are acceptable. This level of intervention may be particularly useful for parents who have sufficient personal resources (motivation, literacy skills, commitment, time and support) to implement suggested strategies with no additional support other than a parenting tip sheet on the topic. However, a media strategy is unlikely to be effective on its own if the parent has a child with a severe behavioral disorder or if the parent is depressed, maritally distressed, or suffering from major psychopathology. In these instances, a more intensive form of intervention may be needed.

LEVEL 2: Selective Triple P

Selective prevention programs refer to strategies that target specific subgroups of the general population that are believed to be at greater risk than others for developing a problem. The aim is to deter the onset of significant behavioral problems. The individual risk status of the parent is not specifically assessed in advance, but because such parents belong to a subgroup generally believed to be at risk they are targeted (e.g., all parents of toddlers). Level 2 is a selective intervention delivered through primary care services. These are services and programs that typically have wide reach, because a significant proportion of parents take their children to them and are therefore more readily accessible to parents than are traditional mental health services. They may include maternal and child health services, general practitioners and family doctors, day-care centers, kindergartens, and schools. These services are well positioned to provide brief preventively oriented parenting programs, because parents see primary care practitioners as credible sources of information about children who are not associated with the stigma often attached to specialist mental health services. For example, general medical practitioners are frequently asked by parents for advice regarding their children's behavior (Christopherson, 1982; Triggs & Perrin, 1989). Family doctors are the most likely source of professional assistance sought by parents of children with behavioral and emotional problems and are seen by parents as credible sources of advice for a wide range of health risk behaviors (Sanders & Markie-Dadds, 1997).

However, because primary care providers are typically not well trained in providing behavior management advice, adequate training is essential. The Triple P professional training program for general practitioners, child health nurses and other primary care providers is designed to improve early detection and management of child behavior problems, and to develop closer links with community-based mental health professionals and other specialist family services, including appropriate referral mechanisms. Selective Triple P is a brief usually 20-minute one-session consultation for parents with specific concerns about their child's behavior or development. A series of parenting tip sheets are used to provide basic information to parents on the prevention and management of common problems in each of four age groups (infants- Markie-Dadds, Turner, & Sanders, 1997; toddlers-Turner, Markie-Dadds, & Sanders, 1996; preschoolers- Turner, Sanders, & Markie-Dadds, 1996: Primary school-aged children-Sanders, Turner, & Markie-Dadds, 1996).

Four videotape programs complement the tip sheets for use in brief primary care consultations. All materials are written in plain English, and checked to ensure that the material is understandable at a Grade 6 reading level, is gender sensitive, and avoids technical language and colloquial expressions that might constitute barriers for parents from non-English-speaking backgrounds. Each tip sheet suggests effective, practical ways of preventing or solving common child management and developmental problems. Information is provided within a brief consultation format (up to 30 minutes), which clarifies the presenting problem, explains the materials, and tailors them to the family's needs. Families are invited to return for further help if they have any difficulties.

This level of intervention is designed for the management of discrete child problem behaviors that are not complicated by other major behavior management difficulties or family dysfunction. With Level 2 interventions, the emphasis is on the management of specific child behavior rather than developing a broad range of child management skills. Key indicators for a Level 2 intervention include the parent is seeking information, hence the motivational context is good; the problem behavior is relatively discrete; the problem behavior is of mild to moderate severity; the problem behavior is of a recent onset; the parents and/or child are not suffering from major psychopathology; the family situation is reasonably stable; and the family has successfully completed other levels of intervention and has returned for a booster session.

LEVEL 3: Primary Care Triple P

This is another selective more intensive prevention strategy targeting parents who have mild and relatively discrete concerns about their child's behavior or development (e.g., toilet training, tantrums, sleep disturbance). Level 3 is a four-session (20 minutes each) information-based strategy that incorporates active skills training and the selective use of parenting tip sheets covering common developmental and behavioral problems of preadolescent children. It also builds in generalization enhancement strategies for teaching parents how to apply knowledge and skills gained to non-targeted behaviors and other siblings.

The first session clarifies the history and nature of the presenting problem (through interview and direct observation), negotiates goals for the intervention, and sets up a baseline monitoring system for tracking the occurrence of problem behaviors. Session 2 reviews the initial problem to determine whether it is still current; discusses the results of the baseline monitoring, including the parent's perceptions of the child's behavior; shares conclusions with the parent about the nature of the problem (i.e., the diagnostic formulation) and its possible etiology; and negotiates a parenting plan (using a tip sheet or designing a planned activities routine). This plan may involve the introduction of specific positive parenting strategies through discussion, modeling or presentation of segments from the Every Parent's Survival Guide video. This session also involves identifying and countering any obstacles to implementation of the new routine by developing a personal coping plan with each parent. The parents then implement the program. Session 3 involves monitoring the family's progress and discussing any implementation problems. It may also involve introduction of additional parenting strategies. The aim is to refine the parents' implementation of the routine as required and provide encouragement for their efforts. Session 4 involves a progress review, troubleshooting for any difficulties the parent may be experiencing, positive feedback and encouragement, and termination of contact. If no positive results are achieved after several weeks, the family may be referred to a higher level of intervention.

As in Level 2, this level of intervention is appropriate for the management of discrete child problem behaviors that are not complicated by other major behavior management difficulties or family dysfunction. The key difference is that provision of advice and information alone is supported by active skills training for those parents who require it to implement the recommended parenting strategies. Children would not generally meet full diagnostic criteria for a clinical disorder-such as oppositional defiant disorder, conduct disorder, or ADHD—but there may be significant subclinical levels of problem behavior.

LEVEL 4: Standard Triple P / Group Triple P / Telephone assisted and Self-Directed Triple P (Intensive Parenting Skills Training)

This indicated preventive intervention targets high-risk individuals who are identified as having detectable problems, but who do not yet meet diagnostic criteria for a behavioral disorder. It should be noted that this level of intervention can target either individual children at risk or an entire population to identify individual children at risk. For example, a group version of the program may be offered universally in low-income areas, with the goal of identifying and engaging parents of children with severe disruptive and aggressive behavior. Parents are taught a variety of child management skills, including providing brief contingent attention following desirable behavior, how to arrange engaging activities in high-risk situations; and how to use clear, calm instruction, logical consequences for misbehavior, planned ignoring, quiet time (nonexclusionary time-out), and time-out. Parents are trained to apply these skills both at home and in the community. Specific strategies, such as planned activities training, are used to promote the generalization and maintenance of parenting skills across settings and over time (Sanders & Dadds, 1982). As in Level 3, this level of intervention combines the provision of information with active skills training and support. However, it teaches parents to apply parenting skills to a broad range of target behaviors in both home and community settings with the target child and siblings. There are several different delivery formats available at this level of intervention.

Standard Triple P

This 10-session program incorporates sessions on causes of children's behavior problems, strategies for encouraging children's development, and strategies for managing misbehavior. Active skills training methods include modeling, rehearsal, feedback, and homework tasks. Segments from Every Parent's Survival Guide (video) may be used to demonstrate positive parenting skills. Several generalization enhancement strategies are incorporated (e.g., training with sufficient exemplars, training loosely, varying the stimulus condition for training) to promote the transfer of parenting skills across settings, siblings, and time. Home visits or clinic observation sessions are also conducted in which parents self-select goals to practice, are observed interacting with their child and implementing parenting skills, and subsequently receive feedback from the practitioner. Further clinic sessions then cover how to identify high-risk parenting situations and develop planned activity routines. Finally, maintenance and relapse issues are covered. Sessions last up to 90 minutes each (with the exception of home visits, which should last 40 to 60 minutes each).

Group Triple P

Group Triple P is an eight-session program, ideally conducted in groups of 10 to 12 parents. It employs an active skills training process to help parents acquire new knowledge and skills. The program consists of four 2 hour group sessions, which provide opportunities for parents to learn through observation, discussion, practice, and feedback. Segments from Every Parent's Survival Guide (video) are used to demonstrate positive parenting skills. These skills are then practiced in small groups. Parents receive constructive feedback about their use of skills in an emotionally supportive context. Between sessions, parents complete homework tasks to consolidate their learning from the group sessions. Following the group sessions, four 15-to-30-minute followup telephone sessions provide additional support to parents as they put into practice what they have learned in the group sessions. Although delivery of the program in a group setting may mean that parents receive less individual attention, there are several benefits of group participation for parents, including support, friendship, and constructive feedback from other parents, as well as opportunities for parents to normalize their parenting experience through peer interactions.

Self-Directed Triple P

In this self-directed delivery mode, detailed information is provided in a parenting workbook, Every Parent's Self-Help Workbook (Markie-Dadds, Sanders, & Turmer, 1999) which outlines a 10-week self-help program for parents. Each weekly session contains a series of set readings and suggested homework tasks for parents to complete. This format was originally designed as an information-only control group for clinical trials. However, positive reports from families have shown this program to be a powerful intervention in its own right (Markie-Dadds & Sanders, 2000).

Some parents require and seek more support in managing their children than simply having access to information. Hence, the self-help program may be augmented by weekly 15-to-30-minute telephone consultations. This consultation model aims to provide brief, minimal support to parents as a means of keeping them focused and motivated while they work through the program, and assists in tailoring the program to the specific needs of the family. Rather than introducing new strategies, these consultations direct parents to those sections of the written materials that may be appropriate to their current situation.

Level 4 intervention is indicated if the child has multiple behavior problems in a variety of settings and there are clear deficits in parenting skills. If the parent wishes to have individual assistance and can commit to attending a 10-session program, the standard Triple P program is appropriate. Group Triple P is appropriate as a universal (available to all parents) or selective (available to targeted groups of parents) prevention parenting support strategy; however, it is particularly useful as an early intervention strategy for parents of children with current behavior problems. Self-Directed Triple P is ideal for families who live in areas where access to clinical services is poor (e.g., families in rural or remote areas). It is most likely to be successful with families who are motivated to work through the program on their own, and for whom literacy or language difficulties are not present. Possible obstacles to consider include major family adversity and the presence of psychopathology in the parents or child. In these cases, a Level 4 intervention may be begun, with careful monitoring of the family's progress. A Level 5 intervention may be required following Level 4, and in some cases Level 5 components may be introduced concurrently.

LEVEL 5: Enhanced Triple P (Family intervention)

This indicated level of intervention is for families with additional risk factors that have not changed as a result of participation in a lower level of intervention. It extends the focus of intervention to include marital communication, mood management and stress-coping skills for parents. Usually at this level of intervention children have quite severe behavior problems but these problems are complicated by additional family adversity factors.

Following participation in a Level 4 program, families requesting or deemed to be in need of further assistance are invited to participate in this individually tailored program (Enhanced Triple P). The first session is a review and feedback session in which parents' progress is reviewed, goals are elicited, and a treatment plan negotiated. Three enhanced individual therapy modules may then be offered to families individually or in combination: Home Visits, Coping Skills, and Partner Support. Each module is ideally conducted in a maximum of three sessions lasting up to 90 minutes each (with the exception of home visits, which should last 40 to 60 minutes each). Within each additional module, the components to be covered with each family are determined on the basis of clinical judgment and needs identified by the family (i.e., certain exercises may be omitted if parents have demonstrated competency in the target area). All sessions employ an active skills training process to help parents acquire new knowledge and skills. Parents are actively involved throughout the program with opportunities to learn through observation, discussion, practice, and feedback. Parents receive constructive feedback about their use of skills in an emotionally supportive context. Between sessions, parents complete homework tasks to consolidate their learning. Following completion of the individually tailored modules, a final session is conducted that aims to promote maintenance of treatment gains by enhancing parents' self-management skills and thus reduce parents' reliance on the clinician.

The first module, Home Visits, consists of up to three sessions conducted in the family's home. These sessions give parents opportunities to practice and receive personalized feedback on their application of the positive parenting strategies introduced in Level 4 Triple P. This process allows the parents and clinician to work together to identify and overcome obstacles and refine their implementation of these strategies. These sessions are largely self-directed, with parents setting their own goals, evaluating their own performance, and determining their own homework tasks. The second module, Coping Skills, is designed for parents experiencing personal adjustment difficulties that interfere with their parenting ability. These difficulties may include depression, anxiety, anger, or stress. The module consists of up to three sessions that help parents identify dysfunctional thinking patterns, and introduces parents to personal coping skills such as relaxation, coping statements based on stress inoculation training (Meichenbaum, 1974), challenging unhelpful thoughts (Beck, Rush, Shaw, & Emery, 1979), and developing coping plans.

The third module, Partner Support, (Dadds, Schwartz, & Sanders, 1987), is designed for two-parent families with relationship adjustment or communication difficulties. The module consists of up to three sessions, which introduce parents to a variety of skills to enhance their teamwork as parenting partners. The module helps partners improve their communication, increase consistency in their use of positive parenting strategies, and provide support for each other's parenting efforts. Parents may be taught positive ways of listening and speaking to one another, sharing information and keeping up to date about family matters, supporting each other when problems occur, and solving problems.

At the time of this writing, several additional Level 5 modules were being developed and trialed. These include specific modules for changing dysfunctional attributional retraining, improving home safety, modifying disturbances in attachment relationships, and employing strategies to reduce the burden of care on parents of children with disabilities. When complete these additional modules will comprise a comprehensive range of additional resources for practitioners to allow tailoring to the specific risk factors that require additional intervention.

This level of Triple P is designed as an indicated prevention strategy. It is designed for families who are experiencing ongoing child behavior difficulties after completing Level 4 Triple P, or who may have additional family adversity factors such as parental adjustment and partner support difficulties that are not resolved during Level 4 interventions.

EVALUATION

The evaluation of Triple P needs to be viewed in the broader context of research into the effects of BFI, as outlined earlier. Research into a system of behavioral family intervention that has eventually became known as Triple P began in 1977, with the first findings published in the early 1980s (e.g., Sanders & Glynn, 1981). Since that time the intervention methods used in Triple P have been subjected to a series of controlled evaluations using both intrasubject replication designs and traditional randomized control group designs (see Sanders & Dadds, 1993, for a review). Early studies (Sanders & Christensen, 1985; Sanders & Dadds, 1982; Sanders & Glynn, 1981) demonstrated that parents could be trained to implement behavior change and positive parenting strategies in the home, and many parents applied these strategies in out-of-home situations in the community and to other, nontargeted situations in the home. However, not all parents generalized their skills to high-risk situations after initial active skills training. These high-risk situations for lack of generalization are often characterized by competing demands and time constraints, or place parents under stress in a social evaluative context (e.g., shopping). For these parents, the addition of self-management skills such as planning ahead, goal setting, self-monitoring, selecting specific behavior change strategies in advance, and planning engaging activities to keep children busy was effective in teaching the parents to generalize their skills (Sanders & Dadds, 1982; Sanders & Glynn, 1981). Children receiving both the basic parenting skills training and planned activities training showed significantly lower levels of disruptive and oppositional behavior following intervention. After training parents showed increases in positive parent-child interaction and reduced levels of negativity. A later study showed that the same intervention methods were also effective with oppositional children who were mildly intellectually disabled (Sanders & Plant, 1989). This research established the core program as a 10-session individual parent training intervention. This intervention is known as a Standard Level 4 Triple P intervention.

Next we discuss some of the recent outcome trials in relation to different levels of the program.

Can Watching Television Change Parenting Practices? Two studies have recently evaluated the effects of the "Families" TV series on parent reports of child behavior and parenting practices. Sanders, Montgomery, and Brechman-Toussaint (in press) randomly assigned parents either to view videotapes of the weekly half-hour TV series, or to a control group that maintained their current TV viewing habits. Parents in the TV condition reported significantly lower levels of disruptive child behavior post-intervention than did controls, and maintained this improvement at 6 months follow-up. There was a high level of consumer satisfaction with the program, significant reduction in mothers' reports of dysfunctional parenting style, and increases in mothers' overall sense of parenting competence. These findings were extended in a systematic replication study that also included father completed measures (Sanders & Shallcross, 2000). The same effects on child behavior were reported by mothers, but interestingly there were significant reductions in both the frequency and intensity of parental conflicts over parenting issues, and lower levels of both maternal and paternal distress on measures of depression, anxiety, and stress. Also, mothers in the TV-viewing condition reported they were significantly more likely to use self-help materials for any future problems than did control mothers, but no less likely to use professionals if they needed help in the future.

How Effective are Written Self-directed Programs? Three projects have examined the effectiveness of a 10-session self-help version of the Level 4 Triple P for parents of preschool-aged children with oppositional behavior. In the first project, 64 parents with a child aged between 2 and 5 years were randomly assigned to either a self-help program or to a wait-list control group. All parents were concerned about their child's behavior. Parents in the self-help program received a copy of a parenting text (Every Parent) and a 10-session workbook (Every Parent's Workbook). At postintervention, parents in the self-help program used less coercive parenting practices than did parents in the wait-list group. Children in the self-directed condition were rated by their parents as having a significantly lower level of disruptive behavior than were children in the control group at postintervention. Improvements obtained in the self-directed group were maintained over a 6-month follow-up period.

In the second project, 24 families living in rural areas were randomly assigned to either an enhanced self-directed program or a wait-list control group. All families had a child aged between 2 and 5 years who was at high risk for the development of behavioral problems, on the basis of parental reports of significant disruptive behavior. Families in the enhanced self-directed condition received parenting materials (Every Parent and Every Parent's Workbook) plus weekly telephone consultations over a 10-week period. Following intervention, families in the enhanced self-directed condition showed significantly lower levels of disruptive child behavior, lower levels of coercive parent behavior, greater parenting competence, and reduced depression and stress when compared to families in the wait-list condition. At postintervention, 100% of children in the wait-list group and 33% of children in the intervention condition were in the clinical range for disruptive behavior. There was a high level of parent satisfaction with the intervention for mothers and fathers (Connell et al., 1997).

The third project (Markie-Dadds, Sanders, & Smith, 1997) compared families in three conditions: written information alone (standard self-directed), written information plus telephone counseling (enhanced self-directed) and wait-list control group. Forty-five families with a child aged between 2 and 5 years who was at risk for the development of behavioral problems participated in the program. Results indicate that the enhanced self-directed condition produced more positive outcomes for parents and children when compared with both the standard self-directed program and the wait-list group.

Cumulatively, these findings show that some parents with concerns about their child's behavior can overcome these difficulties through a structured self directed program. However, it remains to be determined what client or family characteristics predict good and poor outcomes with such programs.

Can Parenting Programs be Delivered Universally as a Population Intervention?
A large-scale population trial of a group version of Triple P in Perth in Western

Australia is in progress (Williams, Zubrick, Silburn, & Sanders, 1997). Preliminary results from this trial involving 800 families are promising. Families of 3-to 4-year-old children living in economically disadvantaged areas were enrolled in the program. Prior to enrollment in the program, 40% of children were in the clinically elevated range of parent-reported ECBI scores. This had reduced by approximately 50% at 1-year follow-up. There were also highly significant improvements in parents' use of dysfunctional discipline strategies, and mothers' ratings of depression and stress in Group Triple P.

Participation in the group program also resulted in significant reductions in marital conflict, parental stress, and depression, as well as significant improvements in marital satisfaction. The results from families who participated in Group Triple P were compared with a control group of 576 families who were similar in demographic characteristics. Families in the control group evidenced no significant change in child disruptive behavior postintervention or at 1-year follow-up. The majority of participants in the group program found the program interesting (97%), could learn and understand the information (76%), were able to use the suggested strategies (88%) and found the group sessions useful (88%).

How Effective is Individual Triple P? Several studies have shown that individually administered BFI is an effective intervention. For example, a large-scale randomized early intervention trial with high-risk 3-year-old children compared the efficacy of three levels of individual treatment (standard behavioral family intervention and enhanced behavioral family intervention) or a wait-list control (Sanders, Markie-Dadds, Tully, & Bor, 2000). Findings from this study suggest that Individual Triple P is effective in reducing child behavior problems and coercive parent behavior. Analyses of pre-to postassessment data showed that, at postassessment, mothers who participated in the two active therapist-assisted conditions reported significantly lower levels of child disruptive behavior than mothers in the wait-list condition. The reductions in oppositional and aggressive child behaviors were maintained 1 year following intervention. At pre-assessment, all children were in the clinical range for levels of aversive behavior. At post-assessment, and follow-up, only 40% of children in the therapy conditions were in the clinical range on measures of disruptive child behavior, whereas 75% of children in the wait-list control group fell within the clinical range at postassessment.

At postassessment, mothers in the therapy conditions reported higher levels of parenting competence and lower levels of physically aggressive behaviors toward their child compared to mothers in the wait-list condition. Mothers and fathers in the therapy conditions were less permissive with their child's misbehavior, used fewer verbal reprimands, and were less likely to rely on harsh discipline strategies when compared to mothers and fathers in the wait-list control group. Fathers in the enhanced condition also reported lower levels of physical aggression toward their child than did fathers in the waitlist condition.

Analyses of family observational data indicate that, at post-assessment, parents in the enhanced condition gave significantly more praise to their child than did parents in the wait-list condition. Analyses of parent problem-solving observational data showed that, at post-assessment, parents in the enhanced condition used more effective problem-solving techniques than did parents in the other two conditions, which in the longer-term follow-ups is predicted to improve maintenance effects. Mothers and fathers in both therapy conditions reported high levels of satisfaction with the program they received.

THE DISSEMINATION OF EVIDENCE-BASED FAMILY INTERVENTIONS

Clinical researchers who develop psychological interventions within controlled trials often lament how infrequently these interventions are employed by practitioners. There are many obstacles to the utilization of effective treatments. These include clinical researcher's lack of interest in the dissemination process, the perceived lack of reinforcement available where academic promotion and tenure depend on grants and publication rate, as well as significant obstacles to conducting controlled research into dissemination itself. Practitioners sometimes perceive clinical trials as having little generality to the clinical population they serve, because of the highly restrictive selection criteria used, elimination of comorbidity, the use of student therapists, and reliance on manualized treatments that necessarily place constraints on the extent of flexible tailoring that many practitioners value.

An Ecological Approach to Dissemination

There have been numerous concerns voiced about the gap between research and practice in the fields of both prevention and treatment (Biglan, Mzarek, & Carnine, 1999; Fixsen & Blase, 1993; Persons, 1997). The lack of professional adoption and use of empirically supported preventive interventions (and empirically supported psychosocial interventions in general) is a major concern (Prinz, 1998). Research is clearly needed to develop and evaluate methods of dissemination that promote the adoption and use of effective family-based preventive intervention programs.

An ecological approach to dissemination may be particularly useful. This approach essentially presumes that provider adoption and utilization of an intervention is greatly influenced by the organizational and interpersonal context in which the provider operates. Specifically, adoption may be influenced by the extent to which supervisors and administrators within the provider's local agency or organization provide supportive climate for the intervention in terms of internal advocacy, administrative support, and by facilitating providers' access to a supportive supervisory structure. Changing the consulting practices of service-delivery providers is a complex interaction among the nature of the intervention itself, the quality of the skills training for the provider, and the broader ecological context within which the provider delivers the intervention.

The approach used in the dissemination of Triple P targets three processes hypothesized to influence adoption (internal advocacy, administrative support, and supervisory structures). Professional change is more likely to occur when supervisors, managers, and professional colleagues support the adoption or change process (Backer, Liberman, & Kuehnel, 1986; Parcel, Perry, & Taylor, 1990; Webster-Stratton & Taylor, 1998); where peer supervision, feedback, and support are available (Henggeler, Melton, Brondino, Scherer, & Hanely, 1997; Parcel et al., 1990; Webster-Stratton & Taylor, 1998); and where computer technologies such as the Internet and e-mail services are used to support and provide consultative backup to professionals. In organizations where a culture of innovativeness is supported by management through the provision of resources and attention, greater success in establishing and implementing new projects is predicted.

Hence, the dissemination process must strategically form alliances with key administrative, line management staff, and other key stakeholders to ensure that the adoption process is supported by administrators and staff (Backer et al., 1986; Parcel et al., 1990; Webster-Stratton & Taylor, 1998). This process involves development of specific strategies for informing and educating administrators about the distinguishing features of the intervention, the potential benefits and responsibilities and costs of adoption. The dissemination intervention seeks to improve organizational support for the intervention by the engagement of key stakeholders, the identification of obstacles to effective use of the program by an organization, and the collaborative formulation of strategies for overcoming or minimizing the impact of the identified obstacles.

Internal Advocacy. Internal advocacy involves identifying at least one internal champion from an organization who can be engaged in interpersonal contact with key dissemination staff in order to foster internal support for the program (Webster-Stratton & Taylor, 1998). The process of innovation adoption usually begins with one or more agency members advocating the adoption of a new program (Rogers, 1995). Such an advocate is important in adopting agencies for innovations in general and innovative psychosocial preventive interventions in particular (Backer et al., 1986; Rogers, 1995). Advocates who become early adopters maintain a high level of opinion leadership compared with other types of adopters and, as such, have the potential to positively influence the adoption of an innovation within their organization and perhaps the adoption decisions made by other organizations (Rogers, 1995).

Administrative Support. There is an extensive literature showing that adoption of a new innovation is more likely to occur when leaders in an organization support the innovation (Backer et al., 1986; Parcel et al., 1990; Webster-Stratton & Taylor, 1998). In their review of program dissemination concepts, Fixsen and Blasé (1993) highlighted the importance of an 'integrated' system of dissemination, a key element of which is administrative support for the new innovation. Networking with key administrators and providing information about the program to these individuals is a common practice in the diffusion of innovation (Webster-Stratton & Taylor, 1998).

Supervisory Structures. Research has identified the importance of ongoing supervision and support to practitioners as a procedure in psychological practice (Holloway & Neufeldt, 1995), as a means of promoting greater utilization of the training undertaken by a practitioner (see review by Richmond, 1996), and as a means of maintaining program fidelity beyond initial training in a dissemination strategy (Henggeler et al., 1997; Parcel et al., 1990; Webster-Stratton & Taylor, 1998). Consultation with and the provision of additional assistance to the staff of an adopting agency have been postulated as being important in terms of successful program dissemination (Cowen, Hightower, Johnson, Sarno, & Weissberg, 1989; Parcel et al., 1990).

Effective supervision of agency staff involved in a program dissemination effort includes strategies of peer support and mentoring of practitioners who are new to the program (Webster-Stratton & Taylor, 1998). The task of ensuring that regular and appropriate supervision and support are provided to practitioners undertaking the new intervention is ultimately the responsibility of the administration of the adopting agency (Webster-Stratton & Taylor, 1998). The latter point underscores the importance of having an internal advocate in an administrative position within each adopting agency (noted earlier), one that can oversee the implementation process and advocate for practitioner support.

FUTURE DIRECTIONS

As there is increasing recognition of the important role of the family in influencing the lives of both children and adults, there are several ways in which this already important area can be further strengthened:

1. Increasing focus on healthy family functioning: Much of the outcome literature attesting to the efficacy of BFI has used measures of child negative or problem behavior (e.g., disruptive, compliant, or aggressive behavior) as the primary index of success. Although this emphasis is understandable given the priorities of funding agencies to treat or reduce distress or dysfunction, the relative absence of well-validated measures of prosocial or adaptive functioning has inadvertently contributed to perception of the approach as being negative rather than focusing on the healthy adaptive and positive effects of the interventions on children's sociability, empathy, and self-esteem. Also, there is a limited range of reliable well-validated measures of adaptive parental functioning, including key constructs such as parental self-efficacy and confidence, and competence in teaching children new skills.

2. Moving away from a skills deficit model: Although a skills deficit approach to identifying parental behaviors that are associated with poor child outcomes has enabled key parenting behaviors such as ne.gative reinforcement traps to be pinpointed, many families engaging in problematic parenting practices may show a number of strengths that are not well represented in characterizations of family functioning. A similar argument can be made for a shift from research on marital conflict to marital quality (e.g., Bradbury, Rogge & Lawrence, 2000).

3. Highlighting the "human" face of BFI: To counter perceptions that BFI is rigid, inflexible, and "cold," it is important that in both promoting professional training programs and the actual training programs themselves, efforts are made to underscore the true complexity, skillfulness, concern for therapeutic process, and flexibility of the approach. This means being more explicit about how issues such as client resistance, homework compliance problems, within-session parental conflict, and active skills training procedures such as behavioral rehearsal are used. High-quality, professionally produced videotapes are important tools to achieve these ends.

4. Increasing the use of technology: One important implication of the increasing use of technology-assisted therapies (particularly the Internet, interactive CDs, television, and self-help written and video materials) is that increasingly consumers will have direct independent access to psychological advice on a range of issues that in the past were only accessible through professional contact. Rather than professionals feeling threatened, if such self-help interventions fail, a whole new set of professional challenges emerge that will have to be addressed in training, such as how to diagnose error in implementing self-help programs, how to remotivate clients to retry a potentially effective program, and so on.

CONCLUSION

Family interventions are a powerful and underutilized resource. Increasingly, consumers need to be made aware of the advances in family intervention so that upward consumer leverage on professionals, services, and government-funded agencies requires increasing accountability, and that more extensive use is made of evidence-based interventions. Empirically supported parenting and family intervention strategies arguably should be the centrepiece of public health efforts to prevent family, relationship distress and mental health problems. Although it is undoubtedly true that healthy families lead to healthy, well-adjusted children, in order to achieve this ideal, family practitioners need to break away from a traditional delivery paradigm and adopt a far more contextual perspective in understanding and ameliorating parenting and other family difficulties in the community.

REFERENCES

Azar, S. T., & Rohrbeck, C. A. (1986). Child abuse and unrealistic expectations: Further validation of the Parent Opinion Questionnaire. *Journal of Consulting and Clinical Psychology, 54*(6), 867-868.

Backer, T. E., Liberman, R. P., & Kuehnel, T. G. (1986). Dissemination and adoption of innovative psychosocial interventions. *Journal of Consulting and Clinical Psychology, 54*(1), 111-118.

Bandura, A. (1977). Self-efficacy: Toward a unifying theory of behavioral change. *Psychological Review, 84*(2), 191-215.

Bandura, A. (1995). *Self-efficacy in changing societies.* New York: Cambridge University Press.

Barkley, R. A., Guevremont, D. C., Anastopoulos, A. D., & Fletcher, K. E. (1992). A comparison of three family therapy programs for treating family conflicts in adolescents with attention-deficit hyperactivity disorder. *Journal of Consulting and Clinical Psychology, 60*(3), 450-462.

Barrett, P. M., Dadds, M. R., & Rapee, R. M. (1996). Family treatment of childhood anxiety: A controlled trial. *Journal of Consulting and Clinical Psychology, 65,* 627-635.

Beck, A. T., Rush, A. J., Shaw, B. F., & Emery, G. (1979). *Cognitive therapy of depression.* New York: Guilford.

Biglan, A. (1992). Family practices and the larger social context. *New Zealand Journal of Psychology, 21*(1), 37-43.

Biglan, A. (1995). Translating what we know about the context of antisocial behavior into a lower prevalence of such behavior. *Journal of Applied Behavior Analysis, 28*(4), 479-492.

Biglan, A., Mrazek, P. J., & Carnine, D. (1999). Strategies for translating research into practice. Unpublished manuscript.

Bradbury, T., Rogge, R., & Lawrence, E. (2000). Reconsidering the role of conflict in marriage. In A. Booth, A. Crouter, & M. Clements (Eds.), *Couples in conflict.* Mahwah, NJ: Lawrence Erlbaum Associates.

Brestan, E.V., & Eyberg, S. M (1998). Effective psychosocial treatments of conduct-disordered children and adolescents: 29 years, 82 studies, 5, 272 kids. *Journal of Clinical Child Psychology, 27*(2), 180-189.

Chamberlain, P., & Patterson, G. R. (1995). Discipline and child compliance in parenting. In M. H. Bornstein (Ed.), *Handbook of parenting, Vol. 4: Applied and practical parenting* (pp. 205-225). Mahwah, NJ: Lawrence Erlbaum Associates.

Christopherson, E. R. (1982). Incorporating behavioral pediatrics into primary care. *Pediatric Clinics of North America, 29,* 261-295.

Coie, J. D. (1996). Prevention of violence and antisocial behavior. In R.D. Peters & R. J. McMahon (Eds.), *Preventing childhood disorders, substance abuse, and delinquency* (pp. 1-18). Thousand Oaks, CA: Sage.

Connell, S., Sanders, M. R., & Markie-Dadds, C. (1997). Self-directed behavioral family intervention for parents of oppositional children in rural and remote areas. *Behavior Modification, 21*(4), 379-408.

Cowen, E. L., Hightower, A. D., Johnson, D. B., Sarno, M., & Weissberg, R. P. (1989). State-level dissemination of a program for early detection and prevention of school maladjustment. *Professional Psychology: Research and Practice, 20*(5), 309-314.

Cummings, E. M., & Davies, P. (1994). *Children and marital conflict: The impact of family dispute and resolution.* New York: Guildford Press.

Dadds, M. R., Schwartz, S., & Sanders, M. R. (1987). Marital discord and treatment outcome in the treatment of childhood conduct disorders. *Journal of Consulting & Clinical Psychology, 55,* 396-403.

Dishion, T. J., & McMahon, R. J. (1998). Parental monitoring and the prevention of child and adolescent problem behavior: A conceptual and empirical formulation. *Clinical Child and Family Psychology, 1*(1), 61-75.

Dryfoos, J. G. (1990). *Adolescents at risk: Prevalence and prevention.* New York: Oxford University Press.

Emery, R. E. (1982). Interparental conflict and the children of discord and divorce. *Psychological Bulletin, 92*(2), 310-330.

Fixsen, D. L., & Blase, K. A. (1993). Creating new realities: Program development and dissemination. *Journal of Applied Behavior Analysis, 26*(4), 597-615.

Forehand, R. L., & Long, N. (1988). Outpatient treatment of the acting out child: Procedures, long term follow-up data, and clinical problems. *Advances in Behavior Research and Therapy, 10,* 129-177.

Forehand, R., Miller, K. S., Dutra, R., & Watts-Chance, M. W. (1997). Role of parenting in adolescent deviant behavior: Replication across and within two ethnic groups. *Journal of Consulting and Clinical Psychology, 65*(6), 1036-1041.

Grych, J. H., & Fincham, F. D. (1990). Marital conflict and children's adjustment: A cognitive-contextual framework. *Psychological Bulletin, 108*(2), 267-290.

Halford, W. K., Sanders, M. R., & Behrens, B. C. (2000). Repeating the errors of our parents? Family-of-origin spouse violence and observed conflict management in engaged couples. *Family Process, 39,* 219-235.

Hart, B., & Risley, T. R. (1975). Incidental teaching of language in the preschool. *Journal of Applied Behavior Analysis, 8*(4), 411-420.

Hart, B., & Risley, T. R. (1995). *Meaningful differences in the everyday experience of young American children.* Baltimore: Brookes.

Henggeler, S. W., Melton, G. B., Brondino, M. J., Scherer, D. G., & Hanely, J. H. (1997). Multisystemic therapy with violent and chronic juvenile offenders and their families: The role of treatment fidelity in successful dissemination. *Journal of Consulting and Clinical Psychology, 65,* 821-833.

Holloway, E. L., & Neufeldt, S. A. (1995). Supervision: Its contributions to treatment efficacy. *Journal of Consulting and Clinical Psychology, 63,* 207-213.

Jacobson, N. S., & Traux, P. (1991). Clinical significance: A statistical approach to defining meaningful change in psychopathology research. *Journal of Consulting and Clinical Psychology, 59,* 12-19.

Karoly, P. (1993). Mechanisms of self-re.gulation: A systems view. *Annual Review of Psychology, 44,* 23-52.

Kazdin, A. E. (1997). A model for developing effective treatments: Progression and interplay of theory, research, and practice. *Journal of Clinical Child Psychology, 26,* 114-129.

Kazdin, A. E., & Wassell, G. (2000). Therapeutic changes in children, parents, and families resulting from treatment of children with conduct problems. *Journal of the American Academcy of Child and Adolescent Psychiatry, 39,* 414-420.

Lawton, J. M., & Sanders, M. R. (1994). Designing effective behavioral family interventions for stepfamilies. *Clinical Psychology Review, 14,* 463-496.

Lochman, J. E. (1990). Modification of childhood aggression. In M. Hersen, R. M. Eisler, & P. M. Miller (Eds.), *Progress in behavior modification* (Vol. 25, pp. 47-85). New York: Academic.

Loeber, R., & Farrington, D. P. (1998). Never too early, never too late: Risk factors and successful interventions for serious and violent juvenile offenders. *Studies on Crime and Crime Prevention, 7*(1), 7-30.

Markie-Dadds, C., & Sanders, M. R. (2000). *Effectiveness of a self-directed program for parents of children at high and low risk of developing conduct disorder.* Unpublished manuscript, University of Queensland, St Lucia.

Markie-Dadds, C., Sanders, M. R., & Smith, J.I. (1997, July). *Self-directed behavioral family intervention for parents of oppositional children in rural and remote areas.* Paper presented at the 20th National Conference of the Australian Association for Cognitive and Behavior Therapy, Brisbane, Queensland.

Markie-Dadds, C., Sanders, M. R., & Turner, K. M. T. (1999). *Every parent's self-help workbook.* Brisbane, Australia: Families International Publishing.

Markie-Dadds, C., Turner, K. M. T., & Sanders, M. R. (1998). *Triple P tip sheet series for infants.* Brisbane, Australia: Families International Publishing.

Markie-Dadds, C., Turner, K. M. T., & Sanders, M. R. (1997). *Every parent's group workbook.* Brisbane: Families International Publishing.

McMahon, R. J. (1999). Parent Training. In S.W. Russ & T. Ollendick (Eds.) *Handbook of Psychotherapies with children and families* (pp. 153-180). NewYork: Plenum Press.

McMahon, R. J., & Slough, N. M. (1996). Family based intervention in the fast track program. In R. D. Peters & R. J. McMahon (Eds.), *Preventing childhood disorders, substance abuse, and delinquency* (pp. 90-110). Thousands Oaks: Sage.

McMahon, R. J., & Wells, K. C. (1998). Conduct problems. In E. J. Mash & R. A. Barkley (Eds.), *Treatment of childhood disorders* (pp. 111-207). New York: Guilford Press.

McNeil, C. B., Eyberg, S., Eisenstadt, T. H., Newcomb, K., & Funderburk, B. (1991). Parent child interaction therapy with behavior problem children: Generalization of treatment effects to the school setting. *Journal of Clinical Child Psychology, 20*(2), 140-151.

Meichenbaum, D. (1974). Self-instructional strate.gy training: A cognitive prothesis for the aged. *Human Development, 17*(4), 273-280.

Mrazek, P., & Haggerty, R. J. (1994). *Reducing the risks for mental disorders.* Washington: National Academy Press.

National Institute of Mental Health. (1998). *Priorities for prevention research at NIMH: A report by the national advisory mental health council workgroup on mental disorders prevention research* (NIH Publication No. 98-4321). Washington, DC: U.S. Government Printing Office.

Neilson, A.C. (1997). *People meter rating analysis.* Sydney, Australia: Author

Nicholson, J. M., & Sanders, M. R. (1999). Randomized control trial of behavioral family intervention for the treatment of child behavior problems in stepfamilies. *Journal of Marriage and Divorce 30*, 1-23.

O'Dell, S. (1974). Training parents in behavior modification: A review. *Psychological Bulletin 81*, 418-433.

Parcel, G. S. Perry, C. L., & Taylor, W. C. (1990). Beyond demonstration: Diffusion of health promotion innovations. In N. Bracht (Ed.), *Health promotion at the community level* (Vol. 15) (pp. 229-251). Newbury Park, CA: Sage.

Patterson, G. R. (1982). *Coersive family process.* Eugene, OR: Castalia.

Patterson, G. R., Reid, J. B. & Dishion, T. J. (1992). *Antisocial boys.* Eugene, OR: Castalia.

Persons, J. B. (1997). Dissemination of effective methods: Behavior therapy's next challenge. *Behavior Therapy, 28*, 465-471.

Peterson, L., & Saldana, L. (1996). Accelerating children's risk for injury: Mothers' decisions regarding common safety rules. *Journal of Behavioral Medicine, 19*, 317-331.

Prinz, R. J. (1998). Conduct disorders. In A. Bellack & M. Hersen (Eds.), *Comprehensive clinical psychology* (Vol. 5, pp. 527-538). London: Elsevier Science.

Richmond, R. L. (1996). Retracing the steps of Marco Polo: From clinical trials to diffusion of interventions with smokers. *Addictive Behaviors, 21*(6), 683-697.

Risley, T. R., Clark, H. B., & Cataldo, M. F. (1976). Behavioral technology for the normal middle class family. In E. J. Mash, L. A. Hamerlynck, & L. C. Handy (Eds.), *Behavior modification and families* (pp. 34-60). New York: Brunner/Mazel.

Robins, L. N. (1991). Conduct disorder. *Journal of Child Psychology and Psychiatry and Allied Disciplines, 32*(1), 193-212.

Rogers, E. M. (1995). *Diffusion of innovations* (4th ed). New York: Free Press.

Rutter, M. (1985). Family and school influences on behavioral development. *Journal of Child Psychology and Psychiatry, 26*, 349-368.

Sanders, M. R. (1992). Enhancing the impact of behavioral family intervention with children: Emerging perspectives. *Behavior Change, 9*(3), 115-119.

Sanders, M. R. (1995). *Healthy families health nation: Strategies for promoting mental health in Australia.* Brisbane: Australia Academic Press.

Sanders, M. R. (1996). New directions in behavioral family intervention with children. In T. H. Ollendick & R. J. Prinz (Eds.), *Advances in clinical child psychology, Vol. 18* (pp. 283-330). New York: Plenum.

Sanders, M. R. (1998). The empirical status of psychological interventions with families of children and adolescents. In L. L'Abate (Ed.). *Family psychopathology: The relational roots of dysfunctional behavior.* New York: Guildford.

Sanders, M. R. (1999). Triple P - Positive Parenting Program: Towards an empirically validated multilevel parenting and family support strategy for the prevention of behavior and emotional problems in children. *Clinical Child and Family Psychology Review, 2,* 71-90.

Sanders, M. R., & Christensen, A. P. (1985). A comparison of the effects of child management and planned activities training across five parenting environments. *Journal of Abnormal Child Psychology, 13,* 101-117.

Sanders, M. R., & Dadds, M. R. (1982). The effects of planned activities and child management training: An analysis of setting generality. *Behavior Therapy, 13,* 1-11.

Sanders, M. R., & Dadds, M. R. (1993). *Behavioral family intervention.* Boston: Allyn and Bacon, Inc.

Sanders, M. R., & Duncan, S. B. (1995). Empowering families: Policy, training, and research issues in promoting family mental health in Australia. *Behavior Change, 12,* 109-121.

Sanders, M. R., & Glynn, E. L. (1981). Training parents in behavioral self-management: An analysis of generalization and maintenance effects. *Journal of Applied Behavior Analysis, 14,* 223-237.

Sanders, M. R., & Markie-Dadds, C. (1997). Managing common child behavior problems. In M. R. Sanders, C. Mitchell, & G. J. A. Byrne (Eds.), *Medical consultation skills: Behavioral and interpersonal dimensions of health care* (pp. 356-402). Melbourne, Australia: Addison-Wesley-Longman.

Sanders, M. R., Markie-Dadds, C., Tully, L. A., & Bor, W. (2000). The Triple P - Positive Parenting Program: A comparison of enhanced, standard, and self-directed behavioral family intervention for parents of children with early onset conduct problems. *Journal of Consulting and Clinical Psychology, 68,* 1-17.

Sanders, M. R., Markie-Dadds, C., & Turner, K. M. T. (1998). *Practitioner's manual for Enhanced Triple P.* Brisbane, Queensland, Australia: Families International.

Sanders, M. R., Markie-Dadds, C., & Turner, K. M. T. (1999). *Practitioner's manual for Enhanced Triple P.* Brisbane, Australia: Families International Publishing.

Sanders, M. R., Montgomery, D. T., & Brechman-Toussaint, M. L. (in press). The mass media and the prevention of child behavior problems: The evaluation of a television series to promote better child and parenting outcomes. *Journal of Child Psychology and Psychiatry.*

Sanders, M. R., Nicholson, J. M., & Floyd, F. J. (1997). Couples' relationships and children. In W. K. Halford & H. J. Markman (Eds.), *Clinical handbook of marriage and couples interventions* (pp. 225-253). Chichester, UK: Wiley.

Sanders, M. R., & Plant, K. (1989). Generalization effects of behavioral parent training to high and low risk parenting environments. *Behavior Modification, 13,* 283-305.

Sanders, M. R., & Shallcross, E. (2000). *Effects of a television series on parenting and family survival skills on parent-child interactions.* Manuscript submitted for publication.

Sanders, M. R., Shepherd, R. W., Cleghorn, G., & Woolford, H. (1994). The treatment of recurrent abdominal pain in children. A controlled comparison of cognitive-behavioral family intervention and standard pediatric care. *Journal of Consulting and Clinical Psychology, 62,* 306-314.

Sanders, M. R., Tully, L. A., Baade, P., Lynch, M. E., Heywood, A., Pollard, G., & Youlden, D. (in press). *Living with children: A survey of parenting practices in Queensland.* Brisbane: School of Psychology, University of Queensland and Epidemiology Services, Queensland Health.

Sanders, M. R., Turner, K. M. T., & Markie-Dadds, C. (1996). *Triple P tip sheet series for primary schoolers.* Brisbane, Australia: Families International Publishing.

Schreibman, L., Kaneko, W. M., & Koegel, R. L. (1991). Positive affect of parents of autistic children: A comparison across two teaching techniques. *Behavior Therapy, 22*(4), 479-490.

Serketich, W. J., & Dumas, J. E. (1996). The effectiveness of behavioral parent training to modify antisocial behavior in children: A meta-analysis. *Behavior Therapy, 27,* 171-186

Sorensen, G., Emmons, K., Hunt, M., & Johnson, D. (1998). Implications of the results of community intervention trials. *Annual Review of Public Health, 19,* 379-416.

Taylor, C. B. (1999, September). *Population-based psychotherapy: Issues related to combining risk factor reduction and clinical treatment in defined populations.* Paper presented at the 29th Annual Congress of the European Association of Behavioral and Cognitive Therapies, Dresden, Germany.

Taylor, T. K., & Biglan, A. (1998). Behavioral family interventions for improving child-rearing: A review of the literature for clinicians and policy makers. *Clinical Child and Family Psychology, 1*(1), 41-60.

Triggs, E. G., & Perrin, E. C. (1989). Listening carefully: Improving communication about behavior and development: Recognizing parental concerns. *Clinical Pediatrics, 28*(4), 185-192.

Turner, K. M. T., Markie-Dadds, C., & Sanders, M. R. (1996). *Triple P tip sheet series for toddlers.* Brisbane, Australia: Families International Publishing.

Turner, K. M. T., Sanders, M. R., & Markie-Dadds, C. (1996). *Triple P tip sheet series for preschoolers.* Brisbane, Australia: Families International Publishing.

Turner, K. M. T., Sanders, M. R., & Wall, C. (1994). A comparison of behavioral parent training and standard education in the treatment of persistent feeding difficulties in children. *Behavior Change, 11,* 105-111.

Webster-Stratton, C. (1989). Systematic comparison of consumer satisfaction of three cost effective parent training programs for conduct problem children. *Behavior Therapy, 20,* 103-115.

Webster-Stratton, C. (1994). Advancing videotape parent training: A comparison study. *Journal of Consulting and Clinical Psychology, 62*(3), 583-593.

Webster-Stratton, C., & Taylor, T. K. (1998). Adopting and implementing empirically supported interventions: A recipe for success. In A. Buchanan & B. L. Hudson (Eds.), *Parenting, schooling and children's behavior: Interdisciplinary approaches* (pp. 127-160). Hampshire, UK: Ashgate.

Wesch, D., & Lutzker, J. R. (1991). A comprehensive 5-year evaluation of Project 12-Ways: An ecobehavioral program for treating and preventing child abuse and neglect. *Journal of Family Violence, 6*(1), 17-35.

White, B. L. (1990). *The first three years of life.* New York, NY: Prentice-Hall.

Williams, A., Zubrick, S., Silburn, S., & Sanders, M. R. (1997, May). *A population based intervention to prevent childhood conduct disorder: The Perth Positive Parenting Program demonstration project.* Paper presented at the 9th National Health Promotion Conference, Darwin, Northern Territory, Australia.

Zubrick, S. R., Silburn, S. R., Garton, A., Burton, P., Dalby, R., Carlton, J., Shepard, C., & Lawrence, D. (1995). *Western Australian child health survey: Developing health and well-being in the nineties.* Perth WA: Australian Bureau of Statistics and the Institute for Child Health Research.

14

The Challenge of Changing Couples

Richard J. Gelles
University of Pennsylvania

Matthew R. Sanders and his colleagues and collaborators should be congratulated and celebrated for accomplishing something rare. They have developed a behavioral family intervention (the Triple P-Positive Parenting Program), worked extremely hard to implement this program on a populationwide basis in Australia, and have carried out evaluations of the Triple P program that both meet the normal standards for scientific evaluations as well as find significant improvements produced by Triple P. The latter accomplishment is truly rare. As Sanders pointed out in the introduction to his chapter (chapter 13): "Non-evaluated parent education and family support programs continue to dominate the field, where programs are offered to the public with no known effects. . . . the public is exposed to a diverse range of untested and, in some instances, even potentially harmful interventions" (Sanders, chapter 13, this volume).

In my own field of specialization—child maltreatment and intimate violence—not only have nonevaluated family support programs dominated the field, but some programs, such as Intensive Family Preservation Services continue to dominate the field in spite of the fact that high-quality evaluations fail to support any of the hypotheses proposing positive outcomes for children and/or families (Gelles, 1996b, 2000; Heneghan, Horwitz, & Leventhal, 1996; National Research Council, 1998). Of late in the field of child maltreatment, there has been increasing use of a program developed in New Zealand, Family Group Conferencing, as a family support intervention in cases of child maltreatment. The adoption of this program expands even in the absence of any reasonable controlled evaluation of the programs (Bartholet, 1999).

My enthusiasm for the fact that the Triple P programs have been evaluated is matched by the impressive fact that the evaluations produced evidence to support the effectiveness of Triple P. Sanders and his colleagues are clearly the exception to "Rossi's iron rule" that the expected effect of a social program is zero (Moynihan, 1996). Sanders and his colleagues have found that the effect size for their behavioral family intervention is indeed greater than zero.

CONFLICT: A CONTINUUM OR TYPOLOGY?

There is reason to be somewhat cautious, however, when considering the good news offered by Sanders' work. Sanders and his colleagues endeavored to develop a population-based intervention that would consist of a family intervention that could treat or, better yet, prevent child psychopathology and family distress. There are a number of critical and important assumptions that underlie Sanders' work and the work addressed in the other "lead" chapters in this volume.

The focus of this volume in on couples in conflict. The "conflict" that has been discussed in the chapters ranges from disagreements and conflicts of interest, to conflicts severe enough to produce clinical indicators of child psychopathology (Sanders, chap. 13, this volume) to homicide (Daly & Wilson, chap. 1, this volume). Without overtly stating their assumptions, most authors have conceptualized conflict as a continuum ranging from minor to severe. One might view this as a linear continuum or a "normal distribution" in which "no conflict" and "severe" appear at the tails of the distribution, whereas most marital and parent-to-child conflict is in the middle of the distribution. A family's or group's placement along the continuum is presumed to be a function of the presence or absence of risk and protective factors. Thus, having a nonbiologically related male in the home or a "de facto marriage" is a risk for child maltreatment, and a registered or "legal union" is a protective factor. Behavioral family interventions such as Triple P are designed to either prevent a family from moving to a higher level of conflict or produce a movement from the severe side of the continuum to the more moderate and modest level of conflict.

The "continuum" model of conflict and the risk/protective equation have intuitive appeal and face validity. Sanders' research even adds empirical validity to the notion of the continuum. Nonetheless, there is a growing body of research (Gelles, 1991; Gottman et al., 1995; Holtsworth-Munroe & Stuart, 1994) that, at least with respect to violent conflict, identifies distinct types of offenders. The social, psychological, and physiological variables related to the onset and duration of violent conflict vary, not simply as a function of the risk/protective factor equation, but by type.

I have devoted other papers to this issue (Gelles, 1991, 1996a) and do not dwell on it here. My main point is that a risk/protective factor-based intervention whose aims are preventing or reducing conflict may work quite well for one type of conflict but be inapplicable or even harmful for other types of family and parental conflicts.

THE CORE CHALLENGE: BRINGING ABOUT CHANGE

A second important issue, raised both in Sanders' work with Triple P and the other discussions of couples conflict included in this volume, is how one brings about change. Change is a difficult task with regard to individuals—witness the struggle that the medical, public health, and health psychology communities have with smoking, sun exposure, diet, and exercise. Changing couples is even a greater challenge, and changing family systems is a daunting task.

Unfortunately, many clinicians and program designers underestimate the challenge of changing individual and family behavior. Building their clinical assumptions on the continuum model of risk and protective factors, a core assumption about change is that all one requires is a well-trained clinician and a sufficient abundance of resources, and change can be accomplished.

I have labeled this approach "The Knee-Jerk Model of Change." When confronted with a behavior that is noxious or harmful, the knee-jerk model of change, approaches the client or family in the following way:

"Did it?"

"Don't do it!"

The clinician can enhance the "Don't do it" with supportive resources or attempt to enforce the "Don't do it" with sanctions.

Some change requires a client and a family to initiate action rather than ceasing action. Here, the knee-jerk model approaches the problem with:

"Didn't do it?"

"Do it."

The "Do it" is facilitated by offering education or resources or is encouraged by pointing out or "dramatically enforcing" the negative personal and family consequences of the failure to take appropriate action.

The assessment of the knee-jerk model of change is typically binary. For the intervention to be successful, the outcome must either be a cessation of the noxious or harmful behavior, or the acquisition and enactment of appropriate behaviors (or, failing that, measured attitude change). Such an assessment paradigm misses or views as irrelevant the smaller degrees of cognitive or behavioral change.

WHY INTERVENTIONS HAVE SUCH MODEST IMPACT

As I noted at the outset of this chapter, the Triple P program is an exception to Rossi's iron rule that social interventions have no measurable impact. There are a number of reasons why most evaluations of interventions and treatment programs are generally unable to find evidence for program effectiveness. First and most pessimistically, it is possible that the programs and services, although well intended, are, in and of themselves, not effective. It is possible that the theories (mostly informal and untested) behind the programs and services may be inaccurate or inadequate, and the programs themselves, therefore may not be addressing the key mechanisms that cause the problem. Second, the programs or services may be effective, but they may not be implemented properly by the agencies and workers that are using the programs. For example, when the evaluation data for the Illinois Family First program were made public (Schuerman, Rzepnicki, & Littell, 1994), they failed to support the hypotheses that the program reduced out-of-home placement, costs, and/or improved family functioning. An initial reaction was that there was considerable variation in how intensive family preservation was being implemented at the different sites in Illinois. The overall implementation was also not true to the "Homebuilders" model of intensive family preservation. Thus, the lack of support for the effectiveness of the services was blamed on the programs not being properly implemented. Evaluations of home health visiting interventions do find significant effects, but they are often somewhat modest (Gomby, Culross, & Behrman, 1999; Olds et al., 1997). One limitation may be the implementation. Process evaluations have discovered that the full intervention was delivered only 55% of the time (Gomby et al., 1999). The problem of delivering the intervention also limited the effective impact of Triple P.

A third plausible explanation might be that the theory behind the program may be accurate and the program itself appropriate, but the "dose" may be too small. In terms of interventions designed to treat and prevent family violence, the National Academy of Sciences (National Research Council, 1998) concluded that the duration and intensity of the mental health and social support services needed to influence behaviors resulting from or contributing to family violence may be greater than initially estimated. With regard to social service interventions, the committee opined that: "The intensity of the parenting, mental health, and social support services required may be greater than initially estimated in order to address the fundamental sources of instability, conflict, stress, and violence that occur repeatedly over time in the family environment, especially in disadvantaged communities" (National Research Council, 1998, p. 118). Thus, it is likely that more services are necessary or the length of the interventions should be increased.

Finally, as I pointed out in the previous section, a limitation of family interventions is the crude way behavior change is conceptualized and measured. Many of those who design and implement interventions for couples in conflict assume that all (or at least most) parents, caretakers, and families are ready and able to change their behavior. One advantage that Sanders and his colleagues had in their evaluations is that their subjects were recruited by advertising for couples to participate in the study. Thus, they were able to examine couples who were probably highly motivated and ready for change.

The Process and Stages of Change

Research on behavior change clearly demonstrates that change is not a one-step, knee-jerk process (Prochaska & DiClemente, 1982, 1983, 1984; Prochaska, Norcross, & DiClemente, 1994). Rather, changing behavior is a dynamic process, and that one progresses through a number of stages, including relapse, in trying to modify one's behavior. There are also cognitive aspects to behavior change that can be measured.

One of the reasons why family interventions may have such modest success rates is that most interventions are "action" programs. These programs are often provided to individuals and families in what Prochaska and his colleagues called the *precontemplator* or *contemplation* stage of change (Prochaska & DiClemente, 1982, 1983, 1984). This is what others may refer to as denial or ambivalence about the need for change. For interventions to be more successful, there is a need to balance readiness for change with the immediate risk in a particular family (Gelles, 1996b).

THE IMPLICATIONS FOR INTERVENTIONS

The previous cautionary discussion about the limited impact of most behavioral family interventions does not necessarily lead to a pessimistic conclusion. First, Sanders' research clearly demonstrates that a theoretically based, carefully constructed, and well-implemented intervention can have a significant impact. Second, there are means of increasing the likelihood that more interventions will have the desired results. Most important, interventions need to be matched to individual's and families' readiness to change. As I noted earlier, Sanders evaluated his intervention on a population ready for an action intervention. Had Sanders' subjects been involuntarily assigned to the experiment, his results may have been more in line with Rossi's iron rule. Resistant or precontemplative families require interventions that focus on problem identification and consciousness raising more than those that are action based. In addition, for individuals and families who have achieved a level of improvement, it is important to provide relapse-prevention interventions that reduce temptations to fall back into old patterns of conflict, and enhance the processes that build confidence in maintaining new attitudes and behaviors.

In an ideal world, interventions would be funded and implemented based on evidence such as that provided by Sanders. Yet, as Sanders implied, most interventions and programs that aim at couples in conflict are premised on anecdotes and value positions, rather than reliable and valid data. In the United States, many programs gain favor as a result of effective marketing rather than data that meet the normal standards of scientific evidence.

However, family life educators, researchers, and practitioners should be cognizant of the policy reality that scientific evidence, anecdotes, and marketing play a less critical role on policymaking than do values. Values still control social policy. Interventions will be more likely to be supported, funded, and incorporated into social policy when they are consistent with the prevailing values of policymakers.

REFERENCES

Bartholet, E. (1999). *Nobody's children: Abuse and neglect, foster drift, and the adoption alternative.* Boston: Beacon Press.

Gelles, R. J. (1991). Physical violence, child abuse, and child homicide: A continuum of violence, or distinct behaviors? *Human Nature, 2,* 59-72.

Gelles, R. J. (1996a, December). *Research on violent offenders: Implications for understanding the nature of youth violence.* Paper presented at the International Study Group on Youth Violence and Control, Minerva Center for Youth Policy, University of Haifa, Israel.

Gelles, R. J. (1996b). *The book of David: How preserving families can cost children's lives.* New York: Basic Books.

Gelles, R. J. (2000). How evaluation research can help reform and improve the child welfare system. *Journal of Aggression, Maltreatment & Trauma, 4,* 7-28.

Gomby, D. S., Culross, P. H., & Behrman, R. E. (1999). Home visiting: Recent program evaluations— Analysis and recommendations. *The Future of Children, 9,* 4-26.

Gottman, J. M., Jacobson, N. S., Rushe, R. H., Shortt, J. W., Babcock, J,. La Taillade, J., & Waltz, J. (1995). The relationship between heart rate reactivity, emotionally aggressive behavior, and general violence in batterers. *Journal of Family Psychology, 9,* 227-248.

Holtsworth-Munroe, A., & Stuart, G. L. (1994). Typologies of male batterers: Three subtypes and differences among them. *Psychological Bulletin, 116,* 476-497.

Moynihan, D. P. (1996). *Miles to go: A personal history of social policy.* Cambridge, MA: Harvard University Press.

National Research Council. (1998). *Violence in families: Assessing prevention and treatment programs.* Washington, DC: National Academy Press.

Olds, D., Eckenrode, J., Henderson, C. R., Kitzman, H., Powers, J., Cole, R., Sidora, K., Morris, P., Pettit, L., & Luckey, D. (1997). Long-term effects of home visitation on maternal life course and child abuse and neglect: Fifteen-year follow-up of a randomized trial. *Journal of the American Medical Association, 278,* 637-648.

Prochaska, J. O., & DiClemente, C. C. (1982). Toward a more integrative model of change. *Psychotherapy: Theory, Research and Practice, 19,* 276-288.

Prochaska, J. O., & DiClemente, C .C. (1983). Stages and processes of self-change in smoking: Toward an integrative model of change. *Journal of Consulting and Clinical Psychology, 5,* 390-395.

Prochaska, J. O., & DiClemente, C .C. (1984). *The transtheoretical approach: Crossing traditional boundaries of change.* Homewood, IL: Dow Jones/Irwin.

Prochaska, J. O., Norcross, J. C., & DiClemente, C. C. (1994). *Changing for good.* New York: Morrow.

Schuerman, J., Rzepnicki, T. L., & Littell, J. H. (1994). *Putting families first: An experiment in family preservation.* New York: Aldine de Gruyter.

15

Policy Responses to Couple Conflict and Domestic Violence: A Framework for Discussion

Theodora Ooms
Center for Law and Social Policy
Washington, DC

Until about 3 decades ago, conflict between couples—even when it involved violence-was considered essentially a private matter, beyond the scope of government intervention. In this chapter I sketch the broad outlines of the landscape of the current policy response to different types of couple conflict, and to the separate but related issue of domestic violence. I then raise a few of the questions and issues that I believe need to be addressed in the future.

Couple conflict has several different meanings and outcomes. Dictionary definitions usually distinguish between conflict as a prolonged battle, struggle, or clash between at least two parties, and conflict as a controversy, difference, or disagreement.

In the latter sense of difference and disagreement, some degree of conflict is woven into the fabric of every relationship between two intimately involved individuals. Indeed, in many contemporary marriages, opportunities for conflict have increased because there are no longer any clear gender rules to follow and couples need to negotiate with each other constantly to decide who does what, when, and how. Furthermore, many couples today jointly make decisions that in earlier generations were typically made by one party.

However, it is not the existence of disagreement and conflict between couples but how they are expressed and resolved that brings couple conflict to the attention of public officials. Some couples handle differences and conflicts constructively, by either negotiating an agreement or agreeing to differ. In the course of the argument they may have expressed a lot of anger, but they will clear the air afterward by apologizing. With other couples, differences remain unresolved and act as continual irritants, the conflicts recycle and escalate, and eventually lead to an atmosphere of constant tension. In such cases a conflict is being used in the sense of prolonged struggle or a fight (battle) between two parties. This may cause one or other partner to periodically explode with hostile anger, or to increasingly withdraw from the relationship. Both responses are very destructive to the future of the relationship and may threaten the continuance of the marriage and lead to divorce. Public officials are becoming increasingly interested in finding ways to reduce the divorce rate.

Many high-conflict marriages, however, do not end in divorce, and many divorces are not the result of conflict. One recent longitudinal study found that in only one third of divorces with children were the couples in a high-conflict relationship (Amato & Booth, 1997).

Couple conflict can also include serious verbal abuse and intimidation, and acts of physical violence ranging from, pushing, slapping, and shoving to hitting with objects and weapons, which may result in physical injury and sometimes death. However, these kinds of violent couple interactions need to be carefully distinguished from domestic violence, because they require different kinds of interventions. Michael Johnson, in an article in 1995, explained why these are, in his view, two essentially quite different forms of couple violence (see also Johnson, chap.7, this volume; Johnson & Ferraro, 2000).

Johnson called the type of violence involved in domestic violence *patriarchal terrorism,* and it is "a product of patriarchal traditions of men's right to control 'their' women. . . that involves the systematic use of not only violence, but economic subordination, threats, isolation and other control tactics." In these cases, the woman is always the victim and never the perpetrator of the violence. The second form of couple violence Johnson called *common couple violence,* and is a product of less gendered and more interactive causal processes. "The dynamic is one in which conflict occasionally 'gets out of hand', leading usually to 'minor' forms of violence, and more rarely escalating into serious, sometimes even life-threatening, forms of violence" (Johnson, 1995, pp. 284-285). In these situations, as the family violence surveys show, women as well as men can be the perpetrators of acts of violence.

Johnson maintained that the failure to acknowledge that they are talking about basically different phenomena explains some of the rancorous debates between family violence researchers on the one hand and feminist researchers connected to the domestic violence community on the other (1995). (It also undoubtedly explains some of the confusions that arise among nonexperts and the media.) He noted that family violence researchers typically rely on survey research methodology, incorporating measures such as the well known conflict-tactics scale, whereas the feminists researchers typically conduct qualitative research with shelter populations and use criminal justice and court data.

Policy officials and advocates have paid most attention and allocated the most funds to the domestic violence type of couple violence. But there is beginning to be some interest among public officials and community leaders in supporting approaches that deal with couple conflict in general. These include couples and marriage education programs that teach engaged and married couples communication and conflict-resolution skills in order to strengthen their relationship, avoid destructive forms of conflict that may lead to divorce, and encourage less acrimonious coparenting after divorce. I group these policy and program responses into three broad categories:

Domestic violence programs and policies—these are currently receiving even more attention in the policy community as a result of the new requirements of welfare reform and tightening of child support enforcement.

Divorce mediation, and divorce and coparenting education—these are alternative, nonadversarial approaches to resolving disagreements and conflict between divorced and divorcing parents over child support, custody, visitation, and so forth.

Couples and marriage education, enrichment, and divorce prevention programs that aim to teach couples constructive ways of resolving their differences and conflicts.

Note that in this chapter I do not discuss couples counseling and marital therapy and whether they are included as covered services by medical insurance. They typically are not covered services.

These three programs' arenas exist somewhat separately from each other. They have different origins, funding sources, and underlying federal or state legislation; separate advocacy organizations, resource centers and clearinghouses; set apart membership, professional associations, and conferences; and so on. They draw on different research disciplines (or at least subdisciplines) and theoretical frameworks. In my cursory review of the literature prior to this symposium, I was struck by how little overlap there was among these arenas, and how little contact there is between the people working in each. I now take a closer look at each.

DOMESTIC VIOLENCE PROGRAMS

Violence against women is primarily partner violence. As reported in a recent national survey, 76% of the women (compared to 18% of the men) who were raped or otherwise physically assaulted (or both) since age 18 said the perpetrator was a current or former spouse, a cohabiting partner, or a date. According to survey estimates, approximately 1,500,000 women and 834,700 men are projected to be raped or physically assaulted by an intimate partner annually in the United States (as reported in Gladstone, 1999).

Spouse or partner abuse is defined somewhat differently in different studies, but measures—such as the often-used, Conflict Tactics Scale—typically include asking respondents to report on whether they have experienced any occasion in which one partner physically attacked the other, or, in the case of emotional abuse, used verbal intimidation or control to cause fear in the other partner. As noted earlier, *domestic violence* is a term used to identify intimate relationships when the male partner exercises control, domination, and intimidation over the woman in many spheres of her life, which typically includes but is not limited to physical abuse as measured in the surveys.

Although there were concerns expressed about wife beating by the Women's Christian Temperance Union and others decades earlier, it was the feminist revolution of the 1960s and 1970s that greatly increased public awareness of spouse/partner abuse and shifted public opinion to mobilize against it. Services for victims of domestic violence first began to appear in the mid-1970s and 1980s largely as a result of grassroots community action by and on behalf of battered women. Initially, the primary goals were to provide shelter to abused women (and their children) and help them become more independent. Current strategies also include helping those battered women who, for economic or other reasons, need to remain living with their partners consider a range of options for survival within the context of protecting their own and their children's safety. Advocates have also argued successfully for improved legal protection for women from the police and the courts, and states began to enact civil protection orders and other legal reforms.

Currently, there is a network of almost 1,800 domestic violence programs in the United States, and approximately 1,200 of these include shelter (Schecter & Edelson, 1999). These programs provide an array of services, including 24-hour crisis hotlines, housing assistance, food, clothing, shelter, and legal services. Funding for these low-budget, nonprofit organizations is typically from a variety of sources, including private foundations and state legislatures.

The first federal grants program, The Family Violence Prevention Act, was enacted in 1984, followed 10 years later in 1994 by the passage of the Violence Against Women Act (VAWA), which was part of the huge Omnibus Crime Act. This latter Act greatly increased funding to battered women's programs as well as programs for victims of rape, sexual assault, and stalking. Federal funding has been increasing each year, and in the 1999 appropriation it was nearly $440 million (Gladstone, 1999). The monies are administered by two federal agencies—the Department of Justice and the Department of Health and Human Services.

At the same time that the federal government began taking action, state legislatures enacted numerous laws to try to protect threatened and battered women (including restraining orders, warrantless arrests for misdemeanor assault, evictions order for the batterer, etc. By the mid-1980s, every state had a domestic violence coalition responsible for statewide training, technical assistance, and institutional reform. "As the devastating health and mental health consequences of violence against women were identified major organizations such as the American Medical Association mobilized public awareness campaigns and developed response protocols for their members. Now domestic violence is defined not only as a criminal justice issue, but also as a public health crisis" (Schecter & Edelson, 1999, p. 74).

There is growing awareness of the co-occurrence of domestic violence and child maltreatment (National Clearinghouse on Child Abuse and Neglect Information, 1999). Studies report that there is between a 30% to 60% overlap between violence against children and violence against women in the same families. In addition, even if they are not themselves victims of abuse, many children suffer from being witnesses to conflict and abuse between their parents, or between one parent and her or his partner. (*Family violence* is an umbrella term increasingly being used to include spouse/partner, child, and elder abuse.)

Historically, two distinct intervention systems—domestic violence (i.e. spouse abuse) and child abuse—were created, each with its own law enforcement and judicial mandates, institutions, and funding. However, there are a growing number of collaborations between these two sets of advocates and programs. In 1999, a report of the influential National Council of Juvenile and Family Court Judges recommended guidelines for policy and practice to obtain more effective collaboration between the two systems (Schecter & Edelson, 1999).

BATTERERS' PROGRAMS

Over this same period, batterers have been increasingly subject to arrest, prosecution, and punishment. Treatment programs for perpetrators of abuse have received much less attention and funding than have programs for the victims. The argument for providing treatment rather relying solely on punishment is that as many as a third of battered women who seek shelter return later to their abusers for a variety of reasons, many of them economic. And even if they do not return, the men are likely to abuse their next partner.

A few treatment programs for batterers emerged in the late 1970s, and currently a large number of batterers appearing in court are mandated to batterer treatment. This treatment most typically consists of small groups of men (5 to 15), is highly structured, focuses on teaching attitude and behavioral change, and lasts from 6 weeks to 8 months. Some programs offer individual or couples counseling, but these are often considered inappropriate and ineffective. A number of the group programs have been evaluated. Articles reviewing these studies conclude that participants who successfully complete the program show a high degree of success (between 53% and 85%), as measured in terms of stopping their physical abuse. However, these programs have a high dropout rate (Edelson, 1995; Tolman & Edelson, 1995). There are a few programs that try to treat the couple together, but they are controversial and are not recommended for the majority of cases of serious domestic violence.

WELFARE REFORM AND DOMESTIC VIOLENCE

Until recently, domestic violence advocates and organizations worked hard to make the point that domestic violence is a universal problem and occurs across race and class. However, there is a new acknowledgment of the high correlation of domestic violence with poverty, substance abuse, and mental illness, largely as a result of the passage of the 1996 Personal Responsibility and Work Opportunities Reform Act (PROWRA). The majority of women receiving welfare assistance have a man (intimate partner) in their lives. The domestic violence community and others became quite concerned that the increased work requirements and time limits and other requirements imposed on welfare recipients would lead to escalating rates of both spouse abuse and child abuse (see Brandwein, 1999).

Recent data from five major studies find that between 20% and 30% of welfare recipients are current victims of domestic violence (Raphael & Haennicke, 1999). In addition, welfare recipients who had ever been subject to abuse were much more likely to suffer higher rates of depression, substance abuse, and physical health problems. As well, several studies have found that, in some welfare families, physical abuse starts or is exacerbated when the welfare mother gets a job, because her partner can feel very threatened by her increasing autonomy (Raphael & Tolman, 1997).

These findings fueled concerns about the direct and indirect effects of welfare reform on battered women. Some battered women who comply with the requirements may experience increased abuse. Other battered women will not comply with the requirements out of fear or due to their multiple barriers to employment, and their noncompliance will lead to sanctions and cessation of assistance. On the other hand, advocates also point out that not all battered women present similar needs, and welfare reform can be a gateway to these women receiving effective services for the first time.

The Family Violence Option (FVO) was enacted in response to some of these concerns. It is an amendment to the federal welfare reform legislation, PRWORA, which allows states to waive the work requirement temporarily for women who are victims of domestic violence while they get help from domestic violence programs and shelter to protect their safety and the safety of their children. A recent report from the Taylor Institute of its survey of state implementation of the FVO reports that most states have chosen to adopt the FVO or adopted a similar state policy. The question is how well are women being informed of the availability of the temporary waiver, and how effective is a caseworker's assessment of domestic violence. The report recommends that the notice, assessment questions, and caseworker discussion are cognizant of the woman's privacy and relate to her ability to comply with law's requirements and access to services—for example, asking if there are any problems at home that would interfere with her working as compared with directly if the women has problems at home with her husband/ partner (Raphael & Haennicke, 1999).

CHILD SUPPORT ENFORCEMENT AND DOMESTIC VIOLENCE

For many years, prior to the passage of PRWORA, advocates had been concerned about the risks involved in enforcing a welfare client's cooperation with the child support system when she is a victim of domestic violence. Welfare recipients are required to cooperate and inform the child support workers of the name and whereabouts of their child's father, so that the child support workers are able to contact him and get him to pay child support. However, in cases where there has been abuse, the clients may be able to avoid doing so by claiming a "good cause" exemption in the law (Roberts, 1999). Some workers have seen this an unfortunate loophole, whereas others have been very ready to accede to the request. Yet, as several analysts have pointed out, the reality is more complex, because many abused women do not want the "good cause exemption" because they know they need the child support payments in order to survive and hence they want effective child support enforcement (Turetsky & Notar, 1999). This realization is leading courts, child support agencies, and domestic violence advocates to develop approaches that give the battered woman better information and more protection simultaneously as she cautiously pursues the process of cooperation with the system to get support (Menard & Turetsky, 1999; Roberts, 1999).

MEDIATION AND OTHER ALTERNATIVE APPROACHES TO DIVORCE CONFLICT

In response to the growing awareness that the adversarial divorce process itself often exacerbates couple conflict and is extremely costly, alternative approaches to settling these disputes have evolved. The best known of these is divorce mediation. The first experimental mediation programs were set up about 20 years ago in California. Since then the field has grown rapidly, although the growth rate has slowed in recent years.

Around eight states have statewide statutes mandating couples disputing custody to mediate. Local jurisdictions in another 30 or so states require mediation as well, and these often include large population centers such as Cook County (Chicago), Illinois. National training programs and standards of practice for divorce mediation have been established, membership associations exist for practitioners, and now thousands of individuals (mostly lawyers and social workers) have added mediation to the array of legal and mental health services offered to divorcing couples (Pearson, 1993). Mediation is now being used in many other situations of family and community conflict as well and various hybrids and quasi-mediated processes are evolving.

The hopes for mediation have been partially realized. It is no magic bullet, but studies have found that between 60% and 80% of mediated couples do reach agreement, and they do so in less time and at less cost to the parents. In general, the parents are highly satisfied with the process, and are more likely to comply and cooperate with the agreements. There is no empirical evidence that women are disadvantaged in mediated agreements. However, there is also no evidence that mediated settlements result in improved psychological outcomes for the children or the parents in the long run. In the view of a leading researcher in the field this is not surprising, given the limited nature of the intervention (Kelly, 1996). Mediation seems an especially useful service for the growing number of couples who seek *pro se* (i.e., do "it" yourself) divorces. The domestic violence community has been critical of the appropriateness of mediation for battered women due to the power imbalance between them and their spouses, and have raised the question of whether they should be automatically excluded from using this service. However, one scholar cited research that suggests there may be some types of couple violence in which mediation may be not only appropriate when particular safeguards are in place, but also more beneficial than the usual adversarial divorce process (Kelly, 1996).

COPARENTING EDUCATION

In addition to mediation, many courts now encourage or require that divorcing parents participate in divorce education or coparenting programs. Courts in more than 40 states have implemented parent education programs designed to help divorcing parents ease the trauma of the separation and divorce process for themselves and their children. Educational in approach, they are to be distinguished from counseling and mediation. As outlined in a recent report, they typically have three goals:

First, to provide parents with information about the effects of divorce and separation on children; second, to reduce divorce-related parental conflict by improving parents' ability to communicate with each other about their children; and third to provide parents with the skills and techniques that will enable them to parent more effectively and cooperatively after divorce and separation. Parent education progams also aim to minimize the long-term emotional, social, and academic problems experienced by children of divorce. (Davis, Levitan, & Singer, 1997, p. 9).

There is a growing trend to make these programs mandatory for divorcing parents. As of September 1994, almost 400 jurisdictions from 35 states had some type of formal mandate.

RESPONSIBLE FATHERHOOD PROGRAMS

Within the last 5 years, as part of a growing interest in fathers and promoting more involved fathering, a number of community-based programs have been set up that are targeted on low-income, noncustodial fathers primarily in the inner city, and aim to help these men fulfil the financial and psychological responsibilities of fatherhood (Bernard & Knitzer, 1999). Studies have shown that many low-income fathers do not fit the stereotype of the typical "deadbeat" divorced dad who refuses to pay support. In reality, these dads, typically never married to the child's mother, are in fact "dead-broke" and unable to pay support but remain intermittently connected to their families. These families have been dubbed "fragile families" (Mincy & Sorensen, 1998). Like their children's mothers, these fathers have no skills, very low levels of education, and little or no employment experience. In addition, they have frequently spent time in jail. They generally have no permanent abode and alternately live with their partner or with members of their own extended family.

The responsible fatherhood programs aim to get the fathers into jobs and become engaged with their children through the influence of peer-support group discussions and parent education. Father involvement requires the cooperation of the child's mother, but relations between the couple are often strained, if not actively hostile. As a result, some of the fatherhood programs have offered classes in anger management, mediation, and coparenting. The hope is that if these men are enabled to get and stay in jobs, and thus be able to pay support, this may help the entire family move out of poverty, stabilize relationships between the parents, and in a few cases may even lead to marriage. However, domestic violence advocates are somewhat wary, and recommend that responsible father programs need to carefully assess the parental relationships for the presence of domestic violence (Raphael & Tolman, 1997).

COUPLES AND MARRIAGE EDUCATION

The field of couples and marriage education has roots in the late 1960s and early 1970s and is now attracting widespread national attention, in part due to the research of marital researchers such as John Gottman at the University of Washington, Howard Markham and Scott Stanley at the University of Denver, and Bernard Guerney, formerly of Penn State University. There are now dozens of nationally known model curricula. As well, a Coalition for Marriage, Family and Couples Education (CMFCE) has been formed to serve as a clearinghouse and forum for exchange, and it attracts hundreds to its annual conference, *Smart Marriages* (see website *www.smartmarriages.com*).

Couples and marriage education takes place under both religious and secular auspices. The formats vary from evening courses to weekend-long seminars. But, in general, the couples meet in small-group workshops that include skills-building exercises and much interactive discussion. Some programs begin by giving a self-administered test to the couple—a premarital inventory. Several of the programs use married couples as mentors. There are curricula designed for high school students, engaged couples, the newly married, the remarried, marriages that need improvement, and those that are in crisis and on the verge of breakdown. Although there are important differences, most programs place a major emphasis on teaching communication skills, problem solving, and commitment, and many include anger management and financial management (see Family Impact Seminar, 1998). Although there are serious methodological difficulties in evaluating the success of these programs, some of the best designed and evaluated have shown promising results 5 years later.

OTHER POLICY DEVELOPMENTS RELATED TO COUPLES AND MARRIAGE

In response to the idea, partially supported by research, that the passage of no-fault divorce laws has contributed to the rise in divorce rates, the primary focus of advocates to date has been to reform divorce laws in order to make divorce more difficult to obtain. Louisiana in 1997 and Arizona in 1998 enacted covenant marriage laws, in which a couple can voluntarily choose a form of marriage that makes it somewhat more difficult to get a divorce. Many other states have introduced similar legislation. More recently, there has been growing interest in encouraging preventive interventions designed to strengthen marriage. Several state legislators have introduced bills to require or encourage premarital education before a couple can obtain a marriage license, but none have passed to date except in Florida.

Other kinds of prevention-oriented initiatives are being launched in several states and communities to strengthen marriage and reduce divorce (Ooms, 1998). At the heart of most of these efforts are programs designed to help improve couples' communication and reduce destructive conflict. The Florida Marriage Preparation and Preservation Act of 1998 provides a financial incentive for premarital education by offering a reduction in the marriage license fee to any couple who takes one of the approved courses. The law also requires 4 hours of relationships education to be taught to every high school student in the state. In 1998, the Governor of Utah established a high-level Commission on Marriage, and in early 1999, Governor Keating of Oklahoma launched a major marriage-strengthening initiative that is working with all the major sectors—religious, business, health, educators, government agencies, and the media—to find ways to help couples have more stable and satisfying relationships.

A related development in the religious sector is that, in over 100 communities, religious leaders from different denominations have gotten together and signed a Community Marriage Policy, a pledge that they will not marry anyone who has not participated in a serious premarital preparation course. In Michigan, the Greater Grand Rapids Community Marriage Policy agreement is much more comprehensive, and includes leaders from the public, nonprofit, religious, and business sectors in a communitywide effort to strengthen marriage and reduce the divorce rate. In addition, a few individual justices of the peace, or family court judges who perform civil ceremonies are also beginning to make a similar requirement of couples who ask them to perform a marriage ceremony.

These developments indicate a growing public interest in the topic of couples and marriage, and in the quality of the relationship between the couple. This presumably will create a greater demand for studies that will help us understand the different types of couple conflict and couple violence, their causes, and promising

remedial and preventive approaches to helping couples resolve conflict constructively and prevent domestic violence.

QUESTIONS FOR DISCUSSIONS AND FURTHER EXPLORATION

This brief descriptive overview of policy and program responses to couple conflict suggests a number of questions and issues that need to be addressed:

To what extent are these new policies and programs grounded in research?
How effectively is the scholarly community communicating its findings to the
policy/program community? Are scholars conducting policy/program-relevant
research—studying the questions to which public officials want the answers? What
bridges currently exist to facilitate or encourage interaction among the research,
program, and policy communities? What are the incentives or disincentives within
academia to conduct policy-relevant work?

·The boundaries among disciplines, perspectives, and programs in these three
different arenas are typically very rigid. To what extent are people conducting
research or working in the programs in one field or discipline aware of and working with people in the others? What is the overlap and what are some of the tensions that exist among them? What vehicles exist to cut across these boundaries
and encourage collaborative research and program development? For example, in
addition to promoting interchange among psychologists, sociologists, and demog-
raphers, forums are needed that bring them together with lawyers, economists,
public health officials, program administrators, and public officials whose combined perspectives and expertise are needed to understand the phenomenon of
couple conflict and domestic violence in their full complexity and develop appropriate interventions. To make communication and collaboration possible a critical
first step is to develop a common language—an agreement on definitions and
terms used to describe the range of couple behaviors of interest and concern.

• To what extent are program efforts to respond to serious conflict or violence
between the parental couple aware of and responsive to the needs of the children
who may be hurt directly or indirectly? To what extent are those focusing on
parental abuse of children aware of and able to deal with domestic abuse?

• Couple conflict in low-income populations frequently occurs among never-
married parents whether they cohabit or not. Divorce mediation, parenting education, and couples and marriage education are typically not easily available to these
couples. How should these curricula and approaches be adapted for their needs?
Who would sponsor and pay for them?

• The issue of training front-line staff to be able to screen for serious couple
conflict and domestic violence and learn how to respond appropriately is critical.
This training needs to be conducted across the human service community. Wel-

fare, maternal and child health, family support, early childhood, child abuse prevention, and a whole host of other publicly funded programs provide services to families with children at risk of domestic violence. A few welfare agencies have introduced to their staffs some protocols to screen for domestic violence, but otherwise there is very little training or support given to health professionals and other human services staff to help them assess the relationship between the parental couple in a holistic manner, including the positives and the negatives.

• We need to develop broader protocols that are culturally sensitive. We need to help front-line staff learn how to distinguish between a couple who may occasionally slap each other in the heat of an argument but whose relationship otherwise has many strengths (and who may appreciate referral to an educational program to learn better conflict resolution skills, an anger management program, or an alcohol treatment program), and those for whom there is a pattern of frequent, serious physical abuse and intimidation and fear (in which the victims may need immediate shelter and other services to keep them safe, and the perpetrator needs restraint and punishment).

In conclusion, over the past 3 decades public officials and program administrators have become much readier to develop interventions to respond to couple conflict and domestic violence. However, this field is in its infancy, and a great deal more work is needed. Scholars, practitioners, and advocates need to more carefully define the different types of couple conflict; identify the multiple causes and consequences for adults, children, and the community; and discuss which types of intervention are available and appropriate for the different types of situations. This information needs to be effectively and responsibly communicated to public officials and the public at large.

ACKNOWLEDGMENTS

I am very grateful to the following individuals for alerting me to important issues and guiding me to key publications: Jill Davies, Joan Entmacher, Paula Roberts, Peter Salem, Jana Singer, and Vicki Turetsky. However, the views expressed in this chapter are mine alone.

REFERENCES

Amato, P. E., & Booth, A. (1997). *A generation at risk: Growing up in an era of family upheaval.* Cambridge, MA: Harvard University Press.
Bernard, S. N., & Knitzer, J. (1999). *Map and track: State initiatives to encourage responsible fatherhood.* New York: Columbia University, National Center for Children in Poverty.
Brandwein, R. (Ed.). (1999). *Battered women, children and welfare reform: The ties that bind.* Thousand Oaks, CA: Sage.

Davis, A. L., Leviton, S. P., & Singer, J. B. (1997). *Mitigating the effects of divorce on children through family-focused court reform.* Baltimore, MD: Abell Foundation.

Edelson, J. L. (1995). *Do batterers' programs work?* Paper available on the website: www.mincava.umn.edu/papers/battrx.htm

Family Impact Seminar. (1998). *Strategies to strengthen marriage: What do we know? What do we need to know?* Washington, DC: Author. (Available from T. Ooms, 5111 Battery Lane, Bethesda, MD 20814, or at tooms@clasp.org)

Gladstone, L. W. (1999). *Violence Against Women Act: Federal funding and recent developments* (CRS Report for Congress. Order Code RS20195). Washington, DC: Congressional Research Service, Library of Congress.

Johnson, M. P. (1995). Patriarchal terrorism and common couple violence: Two forms of violence against women. *Journal of Marriage and the Family, 57,* 283-294.

Johnson, M. P., & Ferraro, K. J. (2000). Research on domestic violence in the 1990s: The discovery of difference. *Journal of Marriage and the Family, 62*(4).

Kelly, J. B. (1996). A decade of divorce mediation research: Some answers and questions. *Family and Conciliation Courts Review, 34*(3), 373-385.

Menard, A., & Turetsky, V. (1999). Child support enforcement and domestic violence. *Juvenile and Family Court Journal, 50*(2), 27-38.

Mincy, R. B., & Sorensen, E. J. (1998). Deadbeats and turnips in child support reform. *Journal of Policy Analysis and Management, 17*(1), 44-51.

National Clearinghouse on Child Abuse and Neglect Information. (undated.). *In harm's way: domestic violence and child maltreatment.* Washington, DC: Children's Bureau, U.S. Department of Health and Human Services. (Web site: www.calib.com/nccanch)

Ooms, T. (1998). *Toward more perfect unions: Putting marriage on the public agenda.* Washington, DC: Family Impact Seminar. (Available from T. Ooms, 5111 Battery Lane, Bethesda, MD 20814 or e-mail to tooms@clasp.org)

Pearson, J. A. (1993) *Family mediation.* A working paper for the National Symposium on Court-Connected Dispute Resolution Research.

Raphael, J., & Haennicke, S. (1999). *Keeping battered women safe through the welfare-to-work jounery: How are we doing?* Chicago: Taylor Institute.

Raphael, J., & Tolman, R. M. (1997). *Trapped by poverty, trapped by abuse: New evidence documenting the relationship between domestic violence and welfare.* Chicago: Taylor Institute.

Roberts, P. (1995). Pursuing child support for victims of domestic violence. In R. Brandwein (Ed.), *Battered women, children and welfare reform: The ties that bind* (pp. 59–78). Thousand Oaks, CA: Sage.

Schecter, S., & Edelson, J. L. (1999). *Effective intervention in domestic violence and child maltreatment cases: Guidelines for policy and practice. Recommendations from the National Council of Juvenile and Family Court Judges Family Violence Department.* Reno, NV: National Council of Juvenile and Family Court Judges.

Tolman, R.M., & Edelson, J. L. (1995). Intervention for men who batter: A review of research. In S. R. Stith & M. A. Straus (Eds.), *Understanding partner violence: Prevalence, causes, consequences and solutions* (pp. 262 – 273). Minneapolis, MN: National Council of Family Relations.

Turetsky, V., & Notar, S. (1999). *Models for safe child support enforcement.* Washington, DC: Center for Law and Social Policy.

16
Behavioral Family Intervention: Less "Behavior" and More "Family"

Robert E. Emery

Department of Psychology,
University of Virginia

Behavioral family intervention (BFI), as exemplified in the excellent chapter by Matthew Sanders (chap. 13, this volume), has been a groundbreaking treatment innovation. Sanders and other BFI originators rightly deserve praise for developing a systematic intervention that is grounded in theory. Even more, advocates of the approach deserve rich praise for moving beyond advocacy and systematically evaluating the outcomes of their therapeutic and preventative interventions. BFI is perhaps the most throughly researched intervention designed to benefit children and families and, like other cognitive behavior therapy researchers, BFI investigators have made a major contribution by promoting treatment outcome research even apart from the effectiveness of their favored intervention.

Sanders (chap. 13, this volume) also should be credited for carrying BFI well beyond the clinic, conducting evaluations of prevention trials, and expanding the focus of BFI. Although it shares a conceptual basis and many substantive features with behavioral family therapies, Sanders' Triple P-Positive Parenting Program deserves special note, because it has been translated into various public information programs (e.g., television programs, newspaper columns), has been made available in primary care settings (e.g., family physicians' offices), and has been modified for delivery in group education and group therapy formats. Clearly, effective treatment strategies need to be broadened in this manner if our interventions are to reach a broader audience and if the hope of prevention is going to be fulfilled. Sanders also should be recognized for his efforts to evaluate Triple P's effectiveness in these alternative delivery formats, because any benefits observed in the therapeutic context may not generalize to less intensive and more broadly aimed intervention. His data supporting the benefits of watching the "Families" television series (based on Triple P principles) are impressive in both method and the substance of the results. Finally, Sanders and Triple P should be credited with expanding the conceptual focus of behavioral family therapy beyond focusing solely on contingency management and incorporating program elements such as teaching parents to take advantage of early childhood educational opportunties, attending to parents' self-efficacy and attributions, recognizing some of the social contexts of parenting problems such as broader family conflict or individual parent psychopathology, and acknowledging the importance of the social ecology of family dysfunction.

These are major advances in behavioral family intervention in particular, and in child and family intervention more generally. Many advocates of family therapy discuss their creative techniques widely or suggest an expansion of their treatments into the realm of prevention. Matthew Sanders, however, is one of the very few family investigators who has actually made these next steps and, in so doing, maintained a commitment to empirical evaluation. In short, Sanders' actions speak louder than his words. Such a statement is, I believe, high praise when offered about a behavioral resesearcher.

My comments about BFI thus should be viewed as those of a friendly critic. My own clinical training was strongly grounded in behavior therapy, and my ongoing efforts in therapy and research show a strong, continuing commitment to clear constructs and empirical evaluation. As a researcher and as a family therapist, however, I do believe that it is time to expand the focus of behavioral family therapy in a manner that emphasizes "behavioral" less and "family" more. Specifically, I argue first that family interactions are more rich, both in terms of their biological origins and their social traditions, than is reflected in the conceptualizations found in behavioral family intervention; and, second, that we can broaden the scope of intervention even further if we truly view families in their ecological context.

MORE EMPHASIS ON FAMILY

Behavioral family intervention is a practical approach to human behavior. The intervention focuses less on the development of family interactions and more on how troubled family relationships can be changed or improved. The basic method of promoting change is through education. This approach reflects, I believe, an implicit developmental assumption that parents either do not know how to parent effectively or that they have been taught to be ineffective by accidental learning, especially by coercive interactions or negative reinforcement traps.

As I have elsewhere (Emery, 1992), I want to focus briefly on the construct of coercion, a concept that I find conceptually appealing and clinically relevant. Still, I want to use the rich coercion construct as a way of illustrating some shortcomings in social learning theories of family life. At its heart, coercion theory suggests that parents learn dysfunctional parenting accidentally, through negative reinforcement (Patterson, 1982). The classic coercive interaction goes something like this:

Child:	"I want an ice cream cone."
Parent:	"No. We'll be eating dinner soon."
Child:	"I WANT AN ICE CREAM CONE."
Parent:	"NO. I SAID IT'S ALMOST DINNER TIME."

Child: "I WANT AN ICE CREAM. I WANT AN ICE CREAM. I
                 WANT. . ."

Parent: "OK. Be quiet. Here it is. You better have room for dinner."

In this interaction, the child is positively reinforced for misbehaving, whereas the parent is negatively reinforced for giving in to the child's demands. Because both parties are rewarded, social learning theory indicates that the interaction will continue. Behavioral family therapists search for ways to break the coercive cycle; for example, by placing the child on an extinction schedule.

This leads to my first question about the coercion construct: Why is the following interaction not an episode of coercion but instead an example of (reasonably) good parenting?

Parent: "Time to make your bed."

Child: "No. I want to play."

Parent: "I SAID IT'S TIME TO MAKE YOUR BED."

Child: "NO. I WANT TO PLAY."

Parent: "DO YOU WANT TO MAKE YOUR BED OR GO TO TIME
                 OUT?"

Child: "OK. I'll make my bed, but I better get enough time to play."

In reinforcement terms, this second example is the same interaction as the first one. In the second case, however, the parent gets positively reinforced for making demands, whereas the child gets negatively reinforced for giving in to demands. So why is the first interaction coercion, whereas the second is acceptable parenting? The answer, I believe, is that imbedded in the coercion construct is an assumption about the appropriate distribution of power or authority in families—that is, parents should have more authority and children should have less.

This is an obvious and reasonable assumption, but I believe that, along with many other assumptions in BFI, assumptions about the appropriate parent–child power hierarchy should be made explicit. Why? For one, there seem to be some developmental qualifications on the assumption—that is, there may be periods of development when children benefit from testing limits, as a means of both increasing their own sense of efficacy and learning about rules beyond the immediate parent–child context. A few years ago, one of my four children was 14 years old and a second was 2 years old. Speaking as a parent, not as a psychologist, they both seemed to be in the middle of remarkably similar developmental phases. Both phases involved challenging parental limits, expanding the child's autonomy, and presumably gaining a sense of control in the process.

Sometimes my 2-year-old got her way after lying on the floor kicking and screaming. Sometimes my 14-year-old got her way after moping and complaining about my dictatorship. Both are examples of coercion and, to be honest, I did not have the physical or emotional energy to win every coercive interaction, nor did I wish to do so. It seemed to me as a parent (and there is developmental theory to support my intuition) that my daughters were learning something from our interactions beyond the immediate contingencies. Of course, there were some boundary issues in which I never yielded: My 2-year-old could not run into the street; my 14-year-old could not drive my car. Somewhere within those extremes, however, the boundaries of autonomy expanded for both of them, and I believe that, like other children, they benefited from winning some coercive interactions. They were learning to test me, to be independent, to make some decisions on their own, and although it did not seem so at the time, I hope they were learning to regulate their affect.

Another reason why I would urge behavioral family theorists to explicitly recognize the embedded issue of power hierarchies is that, although most of us can readily agree about the desired balance of power in parent–child relationships, the appropriate power dynamics of other relationships is far less clear. Our present concern is conflict among couples, not just between parents and children, and this brings us to widely debated questions about balancing power and control. Conflict management in couples' relationships would be less problematic if, as with parent–child relationships, social values or norms clearly prescribed the appropriate power dynamics for couples—that is, an increase in couples conflict is one cost of our increasingly pluralistic expectations for family roles, because individual couples now must negotiate their own rules for their own relationship rather than to simply follow expectations. Obviously, there are enormous benefits stemming from the greater individual choice in men's and women's family roles, and I am hardly advocating a rollback to the 1950s. Rather, I am simply pointing to the importance of implicit assumptions about the appropriate balance of power in relationships. Behavioral family therapists can encourage couples to negotiate without using coercive tactics, but BFI seemingly would be more complete and more relevant if the underlying power dynamics were explicitly recognized.

I have one more observation about coercion as an example of limited conceptualization in behavioral family intervention. In addition to normative developmental issues, we can and should ask why some children engage in coercive, demanding behavior more than others do. There are many reasons, but I want to raise just one that often is overlooked. Some children likely challenge their parents and other authority figures not because they want to win the interaction but because they want attention; that is, some children best succeed in getting their parents' negative attention with their misbehavior. If so, this suggests that extinction or other procedures designed to alter who wins the coercive interaction may be only a partial and perhaps an inappropriate solution to the troubled interaction. An adjunct or preferred option may be to increase parental attention at other times— that is, coercive interactions may not always be power struggles, as they are conceptualized in social learning theory, but instead may be intimacy struggles in which the child's ultimate goal is not to win but to get attention (Emery, 1992). More generally, I believe that social learning theorists need to expand the theory to incorporate the human need for love, for secure attachments in family relationships. After all, in our theories and in our lives, love is what distinguishes family relationships from most other close relationships.

Before turning to other issues, I want to note that these critiques and suggestions do not apply specifically to Sanders' approach to BFI. Indeed, as noted earlier, Sanders should be applauded for expanding the conceptual basis of his intervention programs. However, as a leading BFI researcher, Sanders is in a position to help to expand BFI theoretically as well as empirically.

WHY ISN'T BFI USED MORE FREQUENTLY?

Sanders and other behavior therapy researchers lament that many therapists and many families fail to use BFI despite evidence supporting the effectiveness of the intervention. Consistent with conceptualizations about the origins of troubled family interactions, this circumstance commonly is attributed to an educational failure. Families, and the professionals who work with families, just do not know what works, and when they are told what works, they don't listen.

Although Sanders clearly should be applauded for his active efforts in popularizing BFI among parents, professionals, and through the media, I suspect that the failure to disseminate knowledge adequately is not the central reason why BFI is not used more widely. Potential consumers and professionals seem eager to learn about scientific findings, especially if new treatments have the potential to benefit their physical or mental health. Most people know about the benefits of antibiotics or immunizations, for example, and most people use these treatments (although admittedly some "new agers" eschew these remedies). The public also has been quick to embrace psychoactive medications, perhaps, in part, because medications offer easy and cost-effective assistance, but also because many medications provide solid symptom relief. In short, it seems unlikely that a broader embrace of BFI only awaits better dissemination of the findings in this day of the mass media and the internet. Instead, I suggest that we consider two alternative explanations. First, perhaps BFI doesn't work as well as we would like, and second, perhaps many competing contingencies prevent parents from using strategies that might be more effective.

I cannot attempt to review the research literature on BFI in this short space, but I accept as a given that BFI is superior to no treatment. At the same time, I want to raise four questions about the extant research. First, to what extent has BFI proven to be superior to a credible placebo control or alternative treatment? I know of few studies that have included such comparison groups. Second, to what extent might the effectiveness of BFI be due to allegiance effects; that is, to the expectations of the investigators? Unlike medication trials, psychotherapy studies cannot be conducted in a double–blind design. The therapist knows what treatment he or she is offering, and the therapist usually holds an allegiance to one treatment (if more than one is offered). A recent meta–analysis indicated that 69% of the relative effectiveness of different forms of psychotherapy is attributable to allegiance effects (Luborsky et al., 1999). In short, could it be that a large part of the reason why BFI works is that the investigator believes it will work?

Third, BFI may not, in fact, work as well as alternative treatments or over the long term. Sanders (chap. 13, this volume) noted the effectiveness of BFI in treating ADHD, for example, but clinical trials comparing BFI and psychostimulants clearly indicate that medication (perhaps combined with therapy) is the more effective treatment in the short term (DuPaul, Barkley, & Connor, 1998). Defenders of BFI are quick to point to the limited long–term effectiveness of psychostimulants in treating ADHD, and it is true that there is no convincing demonstration of long-term benefit. But where is the evidence, not just the hope, that BFI will lead to greater effectiveness in treating ADHD in the long run? If the data are available, I am not aware of the research. Fourth and finally, perhaps there are some substantial benefits to BFI, but the ecology of family life prevents parents from implementing clear and consistent contingencies for their children's misbehavior. For example, parents in the middle of a difficult divorce may know that children need clear and consistent rules. However, parents may fail to be good parents because of their own guilt, preoccupation, or anger. I want to expand on this last point a bit, and use it to argue for even broader attempts to improve the ecology of family life.

IMPROVING THE SOCIAL ECOLOGY OF FAMILY LIFE

When I was in graduate school, behavioral family therapy was my preferred treatment, and in many cases, it still is. BFI is a sensible, empirically supported treatment, but it is a treatment that many people fail to follow. There are numerous reasons for the failure to follow recommendations, but a major one is that various other issues prevent parents from doing so. A parent may be too disturbed him- or herself, an ADHD child may be too demanding, or the family's life circumstances may be too overwhelming. It could be that these family stresses need to be addressed first if treatment is going to be effective, and it also seems that this approach increases the possibility of secondary prevention (Emery, Fincham, & Cummings, 1992).

Interparental conflict was the family problem that caught my attention at the time and has maintained my attention for over 20 years, because parental conflict is very common, often intense, and seemingly amenable to change. I became particularly interested in conflict between parents who were separated or divorced, because the disputes often seemed connected with either the substance of the law, legal procedures, or both. In 1980, I first heard the term "divorce mediation," a brand-new dispute-resolution procedure by which parents met with an independent third party in an attempt to negotiate parenting disputes and other aspects of the divorce settlement in a cooperative manner.

The idea of mediation held enormous appeal to me as a preventative intervention and as a way of potentially reducing parental conflict in divorce. In 1983,

I began a series of randomized trials of the mediation or litigation of child custody disputes. Recently, I completed a 12-year follow-up study of the families in this original work. The purpose of this chapter is to comment on the work of Sanders, not to review my own research, but I do want to make two general observations about my work and the field. First, my own research, together with the work of others, has demonstrated that relative to adversary settlement, mediation produces a number of benefits for children and for divorced families (Emery, 1994). This statement should be qualified immediately, however, because mediation is no panacea and divorce remains a significant stressor for children and for parents. Second, although "selling" mediation was something of a struggle at first, especially convincing skeptical members of the bar, mediation was embrace l rapidly—far more rapidly than I was prepared for. Today, divorce mediation s available in every state, and it is mandatory in several states and in many mc ·e counties or local jurisdictions. Lawyers are not opposing mediation; instea ., lawyers are rushing to learn to conduct mediation themselves. Divorce mediati)n also is used nationwide in the United Kingdom and in Australia, and it has spread ·idely through Canada and Western Europe. For example, I just returned from a s; eaking tour in Italy, where mediation—and divorce—both are relatively new, but he embrace of mediation seems much like what was happening in the United S ates 10 or 15 years ago.

The lesson I take away from this experience is that people \ ill embrace a new, effective alternative if we offer the right intervention at the right time. Two appealing aspects of mediation are: It is offered at a time when some intervention is needed, and if nothing else, mediation is more appealing than the alternative of adversary settlement; and mediation is offered at a critical time, when emotions are high and key family relationships are being renegotiated. A slight change in the family's trajectory at this point in time can have major implications for their relationships over many years to come. This is not just speculation—it is something I have demonstrated in my long–term follow-up research of randomized trials of mediation and adversary settlement.

OTHER AVENUES FOR HELPING COUPLES IN CONFLICT

I want to close by suggesting a few other promising avenues for helping families in conflict other than behavioral family intervention or mediation. Today, we hear a lot about two forms of couples intervention—marital education prior to marriage and marital therapy prior to divorce—an ironic pairing if there ever was one. Both efforts are well intentioned, and both may have some benefits. In my view, however, one intervention is offered too early and the other too late. Couples about to be married are not thinking of the realities of a long–term marriage. Instead, they are rightly preoccupied with the details of the wedding, dealing with two sets of families, and escaping on a honeymoon. Couples about to divorce typically have a made a decision (or at least one member of the couple has made a decision), and experiments in the 1950s had already shown that it is too late for couples therapy at that time.

When should we intervene? An experiment that I suggest, and one I hope to try, is to intervene to help couples with their relationship at the time their first child is born. We know this is a difficult time for the couples' relationship, even though parenting can be a joy; we know that very little advice is offered to couples at this time, for example, what to expect about sexuality; and we know that parents certainly are dealing with the reality of the long term when a child is born.

I believe that psychologists, sociologists, and other social scientists also have an important role to play in influencing even broader aspects of the social ecology in a way to contain couple conflict and promote positive family life. Examples include reforms to make acts of spousal violence illegal, and changes in divorce law that encourage parents to work cooperatively after divorce.

Even more broadly, I believe that social scientists can help to change our cultural views of marriage and parenting. In particular, I think we can help people to value marriage more by devaluing aspects of the couples' relationships. I think our cultural expectations of marriage have grown too large. Your partner or spouse cannot be your best friend, an incredible lover, a perfect parent, an easy room-mate, your therapist, your parent, your playmate, or your child—and anticipate and fulfill each of these roles based on your needs. But your partner can be your partner in the business of raising children, in the business of being a family. The business partnership is not just about family finances, but also about working together. I have come to believe that this partnership is a huge contribution to each of us as individuals, to children, and to society. I hope and believe that, by recognizing and embracing the value of the partnership aspect of marriage, social scientists will help to change the culture of marriage, and in so doing, help a great many parents, partners, and children.

REFERENCES

DuPaul, G. J., Barkley, R. A., & Connor, D. E. (1998). Stimulants. In R.A. Barkley (Ed.), *Attention-deficit hyperactivity disorder* (2nd ed., pp. 510-551). New York: Guilford.

Emery, R. E. (1992). Family conflict and its developmental implications: A conceptual analysis of deep meanings and systemic processes. In C. U. Shantz & W. W. Hartup (Eds.), *Conflict in child and adolescent development* (pp. 270-298). London: Cambridge University Press.

Emery, R. E. (1994). *Renegotiating family relationships: Divorce, child custody, and mediation.* New York: Guilford.

Emery, R. E., Fincham, F. D., & Cummings, E. M. (1992). Parenting in context: Systemic thinking about parental conflict and its influence on children. *Journal of Consulting and Clinical Psychology, 60,* 909-912.

Luborsky, L., Diguer, L., Seligman, D. A., Rosenthal, R., Krause, E. D., Johnson, S., Halperin, G., Bishop, M., Berman, J. S., & Schweizer, E. (1999). The researcher's own therapy allegiances: A "wild card" in comparisons of treatment efficacy. *Clinical Psychology: Science and Practice, 6,* 95-106.

Patterson, G. R. (1982). *Coercive family processes.* Eugene, OR: Castilia.

17

REVIEWING COUPLES IN CONFLICT

Chris Knoester and Tanya L. Afifi
Pennsylvania State University

Couple conflict has emerged as a central focus of research among family scholars—and for good reasons. As Bradbury, Rogge, and Lawrence (chap. 5, this volume) observed, strategies for dealing with conflict are at the heart of many theories of marriage, whereas conflict resolution is an important goal of most interventions aimed at improving marriages. Research findings substantiate couple conflict as an important factor for family outcomes. It is negatively associated with marital quality (Bradbury et al., chap. 5; Cummings, Goeke-Morey, & Papp, chap. 9; Johnson, chap. 7, this volume), personal well-being (Beach, chap. 6; Cordova, chap. 8; Johnson, chap. 7; Wilson & Daly, chap. 1, this volume), and child adjustment (Buchanan, Louca, & Waizenhofer, chap. 10; Conger, chap. 11; Cummings et al., chap. 9; Sanders, chap. 13, this volume). These associations suggest that couple conflict is a powerful source of emotional, behavioral, cognitive, and physiological problems for both individuals and their offspring (Cummings et al., chap. 9, this volume). Therefore, identifying the sources and risk factors that mark couple conflict may help direct interventions and contribute to improving personal well-being, child adjustment, and the quality of marriages.

This volume brings together diverse approaches to the study of the causes, effects, and prevention of couple conflict. The scholars represented here are drawn from a wide range of disciplines, including psychology, sociology, demography, and public policy. In addition, beyond this disciplinary diversity there are a variety of perspectives emphasized in analyzing couple conflict; these include evolutionary, feminist theory, behavioral therapy, developmental change, and family systems approaches. Despite the wide ranges in disciplinary representation, conceptual frameworks, and areas of emphasis, the chapters may be viewed as complementary reflections on the causes, effects, and prevention of couple conflict. Thus, although seemingly disparate chapters that employ varied approaches to studying couples in conflict, these chapters contribute valuable insights that can be organized around three major themes: the sources and risk factors associated with couple conflict, its effects, and techniques for preventing conflict and its detrimental consequences. Accordingly, we organize our concluding commentary around these three themes, and weave in the authors' observations as appropriate. Before proceeding, however, it is necessary that we say a few words about the definition of couple conflict.

DEFINING COUPLE CONFLICT

The term *couple conflict* has different meanings. These meanings, and the assumptions related to them, play a significant role in shaping conclusions about couple conflict. For example, Bradbury et al. (chap. 5, this volume) presented a very general definition of couple conflict: "social interactions in which the spouses hold incompatible goals . . . conflict arises when one spouse pursues a goal, or talks about pursuing that goal, and in so doing interferes with the goals the partner holds." Some couple conflict may not be overt (Beach, chap. 6, this volume). Johnson (chap. 7, this volume), however, argued that such a benign definition is misleading. Instead, he identified two distinct types of couple conflict that must be differentiated: common couple violence and patriarchal terrorism. Common couple violence refers to relatively infrequent arguments that sometimes escalate into violence. These episodes do not increase in severity over time, often involve reciprocal violence, and are generally gender-symmetric. Typically, the motive in common couple violence is simply to get one's way in a particular situation. In contrast, patriarchal terrorism results from a general motive to control one's partner, often involves frequent and escalating episodes of violence, usually is one-sided because of a history of domination, and is almost exclusively employed by husbands.

The implication of such definitional discrepancies is that scholars are likely to reach different conclusions about the causes, the effects, and the most effective techniques for preventing the harmful effects of couple conflict. Similarly, the assumptions behind the definitions of couple conflict are meaningful. This may be illustrated more clearly by comparing the assumptions of Wilson and Daly (chap. 1, this volume) with those of Gelles (chap. 14, this volume). Working from an evolutionary perspective, Wilson and Daly analyzed spousal homicide statistics from four different countries in an attempt to specify predictors that may be common to both lethal and nonlethal couple conflict. They assumed in this research that the predictors of spousal homicides coincide with the factors underlying nonlethal couple conflict. If this assumption is true, then lethal violence statistics may hold two advantages over nonlethal statistics: high face validity of conflict, and minor problems of biased reports. However, Gelles argued that this assumption is misleading. Instead of viewing couple conflict as ranging from minor to severe on a continuum, Gelles posited that a typology of conflict is more appropriate. As such, the underlying causes of conflict may vary depending on the type of conflict—a conclusion that is supported by Johnson's (chap. 7, this volume) work.

The results of defining couple conflict differently are apparent throughout our discussion of the causes, effects, and prevention of couple conflict. These discrepancies, and the assumptions behind them, account in part for the range of conclusions presented by the authors in this volume.

THE SOURCES OF COUPLE CONFLICT

One primary theme that runs through the chapters in this volume is an investigation into the causes and risk factors associated with couple conflict. This is an important theme, because if the sources and risk factors of couple conflict can be specified, then interventions aimed at eliminating the presence of couple conflict—or at least its harmful effects—can be better directed. The preceding chapters identified four potential sources of couple conflict: bioevolutionary gender differences and threats to monogamous unions, couple characteristics, male dominance, and interpersonal factors.

The Evolutionary Perspective

The evolutionary perspective of couple conflict is based on the premise that the current attributes of all living creatures evolved over time because these attributes contributed to the species' reproduction (Wilson & Daly, chap. 1, this volume). Belsky (chap. 2, this volume) provided a useful metaphor for this view by comparing creatures' basic drives to reproduce with the pull of gravity. He cautioned that although biology does not determine destiny, creatures' drives for reproductive fitness act as strong pulls that affect behavior—pulls analogous to the force of gravity.

Although Wilson and Daly focused on the differences between couple conflict in cohabiting versus sanctioned marriage unions, their discussion of the evolutionary perspective, augmented by Belsky's comments, suggests a number of sources of couple conflict. The authors noted that marriage is, in fact, a social institution that was invented and designed by humans for reproductive reasons. Although such a relationship is often beneficial to the people involved and society as a whole, the solidarity of marriage (and other similar) relationships is threatened by the innate drive of humans to reproduce and proliferate, but at the same time to invest solely in their own offspring. Conflict between partners may arise from the temptation by either partner to mate with another person, leave the relationship altogether, or free-ride on a partner's investment in the relationship. In addition, conflict may arise as a result of nepotism from relatives linked by blood or the presence of dependent children from prior unions.

Related to these factors is a major gender difference: According to the evolutionary perspective, males possess a greater inclination to pursue multiple sexual unions than do females. Presumably, this is because the reproductive fitness of males is compromised far more than that of females in monogamous relationships. Unbound by monogamy, males have the ability to produce substantially more offspring, because females' reproductive potential is limited by menstruation, pregnancy, lactation, and menopause.

Couple Characteristics

Other factors that put couples at risk of conflict include cohabitation, poverty, raising children, stepparenting, and the ages of partners (Buchanan et al., chap. 10; Cummings et al., chap. 9; Goldscheider, chap. 3; Wilson & Daly, chap. 1, this volume). Although the authors primarily acknowledged the presence of these factors as "risk markers," and not necessarily causes of couple conflict, the factors should also be considered as potential explanations of couple conflict. Regardless of whether these factors are only associated with couple conflict or are sources of couple conflict, it remains important to specify them. Interventions can then be directed at either treating the individuals with symptoms of high levels of couple conflict or addressing the known sources of couple conflict.

Wilson and Daly (chap. 1, this volume) focused their attention on the wide disparity in spousal homicide rates that occur in cohabiting versus married relationships. Evidence from four different countries clearly shows that being in a cohabiting relationship dramatically increases the risk of spousal homicide. The results of other surveys also suggest that nonlethal violence occurs at substantially higher rates in cohabiting unions (Anderson, 1997; Lupri, Grandin, & Brinkerhoff, 1994; Stets, 1991; Wilson, Johnson, & Daly, 1995). What remains unclear is *why* cohabitation increases the risk of spousal homicide and other forms of spousal violence.

Wilson and Daly proposed a number of explanations for the higher rates of spousal violence in cohabiting unions. Their first set of explanations displayed an emphasis on the uncertain nature of cohabiting relationships. They argued that the exit costs of leaving cohabiting relationships, as opposed to marriage relationships, are lower. With relatively low exit costs and obligations in cohabiting relationships, partners may be more inclined to have affairs, leave one's partner for another, or free-ride off of a partner's investment in the relationship—behaviors that are seen as quite natural from an evolutionary perspective. Such behavior frequently results in couple conflict, and sometimes lethal couple conflict. Although Wilson and Daly recognized this as one potential explanation for their findings, Belsky (chap. 2, this volume) asserted that it represents at least one reason why cohabitation is dangerous—especially for women and children.

The association between cohabitation and marital violence may be the result of selection factors, too. Wilson and Daly noted that cohabiting relationships are less likely to produce children than are marriage relationships, but cohabiting relationships are more likely to contain children from prior unions than are marriages. Having children of one's own may strengthen a relationship and reduce the likelihood of violence, according to an evolutionary perspective, as parents seek to invest in their own offspring. In contrast, the presence of children from one of the partners' prior unions may contribute to conflict because the nonbiological parent may be unwilling to invest in someone else's offspring—or even be mindful of them. Also, Wilson and Daly observed that partners in cohabiting relationships are less homogamous, in general, than are partners in registered marriages. Lack of homogamy predicts marital instability (Heaton, 1984; Lehrer & Chiswick, 1993) and may also contribute to couple conflict and the dissolution of relationships. Wilson and Daly's investigation of poverty and unemployment as selection factors that may help explain the discrepant spousal homicide rates did not find immediate support; however, poverty is mentioned as a correlate of both marital conflict and spousal homicide (Daly, Wiseman, & Wilson, 1997; Wilson et al., 1995).

Repetti (chap. 4, this volume) observed other selection factors that may explain why cohabiting relationships are more violent than marriage relationships. First, she noted that cohabiting relationships contain a much more heterogeneous group of relationships than do marriages. For example, cohabitation encompasses visiting unions, "on again-off again" relationships, and long-term committed relationships. Therefore, it may be very difficult to talk about cohabitation as a unitary phenomenon. Second, Repetti suggested that selection *out* of marriage may be a process influencing Wilson and Daly's findings. She argued that the average risk of homicide may be lower in marriage unions because they include a relatively large number of enduring relationships. The assumption is that violent marriages are less likely to last as long as nonviolent ones. The selection problem could be addressed by comparing rates of violence in cohabiting and marriage unions of *equal* duration. Finally, Repetti proposed that a similar selection process may act as a barrier *into* marriage unions. For instance, persons who are prone to commit violence may be less likely to marry than may nonviolent individuals, perhaps because their partners may be unwilling to enter into a more permanent, albeit potentially violent, relationship with them. Goldscheider (chap. 3, this volume) added that the rapid increases in cohabitation rates in recent years may have created additional stress for individuals. However, she predicted that as cohabitation becomes more institutionalized, conflict in these relationships may decrease.

Children also have the potential for influencing couple conflict. The presence of children born of both partners may work to reduce the likelihood of couple conflict. According to an evolutionary perspective, children in common create common cause and may strengthen relationships as well as reduce conflict (Belsky, chap. 2; Wilson & Daly, chap. 1, this volume). Alternatively, Cummings et al. (chap. 9, this volume) and Buchanan et al. (chap. 10, this volume) noted that children are often the source of couple conflict.

The impact of stepchildren on couple conflict appears more consistent; the presence of stepchildren is positively associated with couple conflict and may help explain the differences in spousal homicide rates between cohabiting and married unions (Wilson & Daly, chap. 1, this volume). Stepchildren are hypothesized to create problems because parents tend to invest only in their own biological offspring (Belsky, chap. 2; Wilson & Daly, chap. 1, this volume). Yet, Goldscheider (chap. 3, this volume) observed that problems may arise simply from the blending of complex family forms. Also, her comparison of fatherhood in Sweden and the United States suggests that at least some of the effects of stepparenting on couple conflict in the United States may be due to the fact that such parents tend to have lower incomes and to have experienced a family breakup during childhood. In Sweden, governmental support for stepparenting appears to make parenting, in these circumstances, less stressful than it is in the United States.

Goldscheider (chap. 3, this volume) went on to suggest that general increases in privacy may have allowed couple conflict to become more prevalent. Larger dwellings containing multiple rooms, decreases in household size and the number of adults present, and infrequent visitation due to the telephone may have increased the opportunities for couple conflict to take place behind closed doors.

Male Dominance

Male dominance figured prominently into Johnson's (chap. 7, this volume) distinction between common couple violence and patriarchal terrorism. The most severe type, patriarchal terrorism, is almost exclusively male violence, involves a motive to control one's partner, and stems from patriarchal ideas about relationships between men and women. Wilson and Daly (chap. 1, this volume) estimated that over 80% of the killings in their data resulted from male proprietary claims. By this, they meant that the men were either attempting to control their partners and/or were outraged because their feelings of entitlement were violated. Men's feelings of control, entitlement, and outrage were ostensibly precipitated by suspicions that their partners were either unfaithful and/or desired to end the relationship. Spousal homicides perpetrated by men generally occur when they overreact to such suspicions, whereas spousal homicides committed by women are typically acts of self-defense from their outraged and dominant male partners.

Interpersonal Factors

Beach (chap. 6, this volume) proposed that self-processes and self-evaluation maintenance are important sources of conflict. His work suggests that the nuances with which partners adjust their perceptions of both themselves and their partners are critical to determining whether potential conflicts are preempted or not. Repetti (chap. 4, this volume) stressed that breakdowns in cooperation are what matters. That is, conflict occurs when the normal, or expected, level of cooperation between partners in a relationship is not met. Still, Gelles (chap. 14, this volume) cautioned that the sources of couple conflict may vary, depending on the type of conflict. For example, Johnson (chap. 7, this volume) suggested that interpersonal factors such as poor communication and the lack of anger management may be important causes of common couple conflict. However, he pointed to patriarchal assumptions about the relationships between men and women as the root of more severe forms of couple conflict.

Although our discussion of the sources of couple is not exhaustive, it does summarize the risk markers of couple conflict offered by the authors in this volume. We turn now to investigating the effects of couple conflict.

THE EFFECTS OF COUPLE CONFLICT

A second major theme that emerges from the chapters in this volume centers on the effects of couple conflict. The authors identified negative outcomes for the children of conflictual couples, as well as for the couples themselves that require attention when designing intervention programs. In addition, the chapters in this volume examine the processes by which conflict affects children and the factors that may moderate the detrimental effects of couple conflict. Specifically, the preceding chapters identified (a) the effects of couple conflict on both adults and children, (b) variables that mediate and (c) moderate the relation between interparental conflict and child adjustment, and (d) factors other than conflict that may be pertinent when examining outcomes related to marital interaction.

The Effects of Couple Conflict on Adults and Children

Although the most extreme consequence of couple conflict for partners is homicide (Wilson & Daly, chap. 1, this volume), nonlethal couple violence also produces negative effects. These effects depend in large part on the type of couple violence committed (Johnson, chap. 7, this volume). As described earlier, common couple violence is typically used by both men and women in specific situations to get one's way. It occurs infrequently, and rarely escalates to more severe forms of violence. General survey studies indicate that there is little, if any, relation between common couple violence and marital satisfaction and stability. In contrast, patriarchal terrorism—the type of violence borne out of a man's need to completely control a woman—is associated with deep marital dissatisfaction and eventual marital dissolution. Thus, not only is common couple violence the less severe of the types, but its consequences are not as damaging as are those that result from patriarchal terrorism. Johnson recommended that conflict researchers distinguish between these two types of violence and examine their consequences separately.

In addition to the clearly negative effects of couple conflict on the partners themselves, the children of conflictual couples also suffer consequences associated with interparental conflict. Cummings, Goeke-Morey, and Papp (chap. 9, this volume) discussed the effects of marital conflict for children, and factors that might mediate the relation between such conflict and child adjustment. As Cummings and his colleagues pointed out, extant research indicates that children exposed to interparental conflict are more likely to experience internalizing problems such as anxiety, depression, and withdrawal. In addition, these children are also likely to exhibit externalizing behaviors including aggression and conduct problems.

Variables That Mediate the Effects of Couple Conflict

Although other research has frequently focused on the effects of current conflict on children, Cummings et al. (chap. 9, this volume) advocated a process-oriented approach to understanding the *mechanisms* by which repeated interparental conflict results in stable behavioral and cognitive patterns for children. From a process-oriented perspective, researchers can more fully describe how changes in children's day-to-day responses to conflict may result in long-term adjustment problems. For example, Cummings and his colleagues noted that psychological sensitization to conflict mediates the relation between couple conflict and child adjustment. Children are sensitized to marital conflict such that their responses depend not just on the immediately observed conflict, but also on their history with such conflict. The sensitization hypothesis posits that in response to the same conflict, children with greater exposure to conflict will exhibit more reactivity (distress, anger, aggression) than will children with less exposure to conflict.

Cummings et al. (chap. 9, this volume) further suggested that children's felt emotional security mediates the relationship between exposure to interparental conflict and children's adjustment. Emotional security represents the goal of children's functioning when they are exposed to family conflict. According to the emotional security hypothesis, children's reactions to marital conflict depend on the extent to which they perceive that conflict to threaten their emotional security within the family. Children who interpret a conflict to be very threatening to their emotional security will be more reactive to the conflict than will children who do not perceive the conflict in that way. In the latter case, the children will not react at all because their goal of feeling emotionally secure has not been threatened. Cummings et al. offered evidence supporting this model from research in which it was found that children's reduced emotional security, as it relates to their parent's marriage, mediates the association between negative marital conflict and children's adjustment problems. In contrast, children exposed to constructive marital conflict exhibit greater emotional security and, in turn, fewer adjustment problems.

Variables That Moderate the Effects of Couple Conflict

In addition to the mediating effects of children's emotional security, the authors of the preceding chapters identifed a number of variables that may determine the extent to which couple conflict affects children. As these authors noted, interparental conflict may not affect all children in the same way. Conflict type, affective tone, conflict resolution, children's perceptions of couple conflict, parenting practices, and demographic factors may moderate the consequences of couple conflict.

The authors of the preceding chapters specified conflict type as one moderator of the relation between interparental conflict and child adjustment. Conger (chap. 11, this volume) noted that the effects of couple conflict on children do not depend on the amount of conflict observed per se, but instead on the topic about which the parents engage in conflict. When the conflict is about childrearing, the negative consequences for the children are much greater than when parents engage in conflict about other topics. Similarly, Grych (chap. 12, this volume) reported that the combination of children's internalizing and externalizing behaviors depends on the type of conflict to which children are exposed. Specifically, Grych asserted that children who are exposed to their fathers' aggression toward their mothers are less well adjusted than are other children.

In an effort to distinguish between constructive and destructive conflict, Cummings and his colleagues (chap. 9, this volume) pointed to the affective tone of conflict. They presented evidence that conflict with negative affective tone has the most detrimental effects on children. Conger (chap. 11, this volume) also identified negative affective tone as a marker of destructive conflict—conflict that elicits more negative than positive emotional responses from children. In contrast, these authors categorized conflict with a positive or less negative affective tone as constructive—it elicits more positive than negative emotional responses from children. In fact, Cummings et al. suggested that conflict resolution may be critical to constructive conflict. Children are not as negatively affected by conflict that is resolved or that holds promise for resolution. The children may actually experience positive adjustment as a result of witnessing their parents resolve conflicts.

Although Conger (chap. 11, this volume) agreed with Cummings et al. that the affective tone of couple conflict has important consequences for children, he pointed out that the affective tone variable raises yet another issue related to the definition of conflict. In his work, Conger has typically equated conflict with negative affect. However, in light of Cummings et al.'s findings regarding the affective tone of conflict, Conger observed that this conceptualization of conflict is inaccurate. If conflict can have a less negative tone that ultimately has fewer detrimental effects on children, conflict and negative affect cannot be treated synonymously in conflict research. Accordingly, Conger suggested that conflict researchers use *disagreement* as the construct of interest, and assess the affective tone of disagreements.

Several of the authors in this volume noted that children's perceptions of marital conflict are just as predictive of children's internalizing and externalizing reactions as are the frequency and type of conflict. Cummings et al. (chap. 9, this volume) and Conger (chap. 11, this volume) hinted that children's interpretations of interparental conflict moderate the conflict-adjustment relation, and Grych (chap. 12, this volume) offered evidence in support of this assertion. His research indicates that children's perceptions of threat and blame stemming from interparental conflict are better predictors of children's adjustment than are their perceptions of the frequency, intensity, and resolution of the conflict. Specifically, children who perceive greater personal threat from interparental conflict (e.g., injury to a family member, family breakup), or who blame themselves for the conflict, exhibit more internalizing and externalizing problem behaviors.

A "spillover" effect may also moderate the relationship between marital conflict and child adjustment. The spillover hypothesis predicts that the distress that accompanies marital conflict spills over into parenting practices (Cummings et al., chap. 9, this volume). As a result of marital conflict, parents become less emotionally available, exhibit rejection or hostility toward their children, provide less monitoring of their children, and engage in inconsistent or harsh discipline. These changes in parenting practices, in turn, result in adjustment problems for the children. Conger (chap. 11, this volume) found support for the spillover hypothesis in his longitudinal study of rural families: Observed marital conflict predicts children's externalizing problems, but general marital distress does not. Conflict between parents predicts mothers' negative affect toward their children, which, in turn, predicts later externalizing behaviors in the children. In sum, the effect of marital conflict on parenting practices appears to be important in explaining the association between interparental conflict and child adjustment.

Finally, the conflict-adjustment relation may depend on demographic variables. Although family structure is frequently cited as a factor in predicting child outcomes, most research indicates that family structure does not moderate the relation between interparental conflict and adolescent adjustment (Buchanan et al., chap. 10, this volume). Interparental conflict influences child adjustment similarly in divorced and nondivorced families. According to Buchanan and her colleagues, however, conflict *does* have more negative consequences for children whose parents have joint custody or frequent visitation arrangements (chap. 10, this volume). Thus, Buchanan et al. suggested that conflict researchers must consider both family structure *and* the extent to which custody and visitation arrangements allow for children to maintain positive relationships with noncustodial parents when assessing the moderating effects of family structure. In addition to family structure, the authors in this volume proposed that children's gender may moderate the effect of interparental conflict on child adjustment. Specifically, Conger (chap. 11, this volume) reported that conflict about childrearing affects boys the most, whereas general interparental conflict has the most profound effects on girls. Furthermore, economic hardship may moderate the relationship between couple conflict and child adjustment. Consistent with the spillover hypothesis described by Cummings and his colleagues, Conger's Family Stress Model of economic hardship posits that financial distress disrupts parenting practices by creating more conflict between parents, which, in turn, negatively affects the children. Collectively, these authors demonstrated that couple conflict does not affect all couples or children equally, and that conflict researchers must look to mediating and moderating variables to truly grasp the relation between conflict and adjustment.

Beyond Couple Conflict

The authors in this volume pointed out that although couple conflict has important implications for families, researchers may do well to focus on other areas of marital or couple interaction. Recognizing that conflict dominates marital research, Bradbury, Rogge, and Lawrence (chap. 5, this volume) suggested that the focus on conflict may prevent researchers from fully understanding the effects of interparental interaction on couples and their children. Bradbury and his colleagues, as well as several other contributing authors, pointed to a number of shortcomings in conflict research.

First, the effect sizes relating couples' negative behaviors to their relational satisfaction are weak (Karney & Bradbury, 1995). As Bradbury et al. (chap. 5, this volume) noted, depending on the method used to calculate effect sizes, factors *other* than couple conflict account for between 75% and 90% of the variance in marital satisfaction. It seems plausible then that factors besides couple conflict may be the source of adjustment problems experienced by children in conflictual homes. Second, extant conflict research focuses on dyadic relationships. As Buchanan et al. (chap. 10, this volume) observed, most work examines relationships between children and each parent separately, and explores the consequences of conflict within each dyad. Buchanan et al. argued that to gain a deeper understanding of the consequences of interparental conflict for children, researchers must examine the entire family system. A family systems perspective is especially important in light of Buchanan et al.'s findings that interparental conflict triangulates children and makes them divide their loyalties. Finally, with a few notable exceptions (see Conger, chap. 11, this volume), much of the research examining the effects of couple conflict on the couple and their children is cross-sectional. Longitudinal and experimental research designs should provide better evidence about whether the associations between conflict and adjustment are causal or simply correlational.

In addition to highlighting some of the shortcomings of current conflict research, the authors of the preceding chapters proposed other strategies for examining the effects of couple conflict on families. For example, Repetti (chap. 4, this volume) suggested that conflict researchers frame conflict as an absence of cooperation between partners. By doing so, conflict researchers may identify new avenues for explaining the adjustment patterns of couples and their children. Relatedly, Bradbury and his colleagues (chap. 5, this volume) noted that a focus on social support in couples may be a fruitful perspective on marital interaction. Perhaps it is an absence of social support, rather than overt conflict, that predicts adjustment problems for couples and children.

The authors of the preceding chapters offered a well-rounded discussion of issues to consider when thinking about the effects of couple conflict. They pointed out the ways in which conflict affects couples and children, as well as shortcomings in the research on marital interaction and conflict. The future awaits further analysis of the relationship between conflict and adjustment as well as research grounded in alternative conceptualizations of conflict. We now turn to exploring the potential for preventing couple conflict and its deleterious consequences.

PREVENTING COUPLE CONFLICT AND ITS EFFECTS

A final theme among the preceding chapters is the exploration of strategies for preventing couple conflict and its harmful effects. With their differing approaches, the authors provided a thorough exploration of the prevention techniques currently in use, as well as ideas for additional prevention strategies. Specifically, the preceding chapters discussed new approaches to preventing conflict and its detrimental effects, prevention and intervention strategies targeted at violent couples, specific prevention techniques currently in use, and general guidelines for conflict prevention.

New Approaches

Several authors proposed that conflict prevention research may benefit from viewing conflict through a different lens than the one currently in use. First, Cordova (chap. 8, this volume) described the Marriage Checkup approach to intervening with conflictual couples and preventing eventual marital dissolution. The Marriage Checkup aims to "provide couples with information that they can use on their own to improve the quality and stability of their relationships." It differs from many other approaches to conflict prevention in that it focuses on those aspects of couples' relationships that are working, and attempts to build on those strengths while providing couples with information about the less functional aspects of their relationships in such a way that the they are motivated to change.

Whereas Cordova (chap. 8, this volume) offered a specific strategy for preventing couple conflict and marital dissolution, Repetti (chap. 4, this volume) and Bradbury et al. (chap. 5, this volume) posited that refocusing marital research, and redefining conflict, may provide new strategies for prevention. Repetti advocated examining the absence of partner cooperation instead of couple conflict (chap. 4, this volume). To better understand marital conflict, she suggested that it is necessary to understand the ways in which individuals attempt to meet their needs and achieve their goals while cooperating with another individual who is attempting to do the same. Prevention, in this framework, should focus on developing strategies that help partners build cooperation into their interactions with one another. Relatedly, Bradbury and his colleagues (chap. 5, this volume) proposed that marital research may benefit from a focus on social support as opposed to conflict per se. Perhaps conflict occurs once positive marital interaction has decayed—that is, once partners stop offering each other social support. Their finding that couples who exhibit social support are more likely to still be married 2 years later supports this claim. Clearly, programs aimed at increasing social support within couples hold promise for preventing marital dissatisfaction, instability, and dissolution.

The Self-Evaluation Maintenance model provides yet another possible avenue for preventing couple conflict and its deleterious consequences (Beach, chap. 6, this volume). This model posits that individuals hold self-representations about their abilities in particular life niches. Conflict arises when one partner who believes himself or herself to be an expert in one arena is outperformed by his or her partner in that arena. When partners are able to make adjustments to their self-representations, they can avoid reacting negatively to being outperformed by their partners. Prevention, from the perspective of this model, may take the form of encouraging partners to grant each other decision-making power in their respective areas of expertise, or encouraging and enabling individuals to develop more flexible self-representations.

Violent Couples

As the authors in this volume noted, the prevention and intervention challenges raised by couple violence are quite different from those used to prevent and alleviate the effects of verbal conflict. Johnson (chap. 7, this volume) and Gelles (chap. 14, this volume) agreed that couple violence intervention strategies must be tailored to specific types of violent offenders. According to Gelles, we cannot rely on interventions that focus on ratios of risk and protective factors; instead, we must recognize that the extent of violence and the psychological variables that contribute to it vary with offender types. For these different types of offenders, the sources of the violence vary, and so should the interventions. For example, patriarchal terrorism involves not just violence, but a variety of control tactics from explicit threats of murder or more violence to emotional abuse. Any intervention or prevention program must address the issues underlying perpetrators' needs to control their wives. Evidence suggests that preventing and intervening in this type of violence is difficult, at best. Programs designed to treat the perpetrators are not successful. Instead, intervention must focus on ensuring the safety of the victims (Johnson, chap. 7, this volume). In contrast to patriarchal terrorism, common couple violence has its roots in ineffective communication and anger management. Accordingly, programs such as anger management and couple therapy are most effective, and hold promise for preventing further violence (Johnson, chap. 7, this volume).

Current Techniques

Researchers and governmental bodies alike have attempted to address the incidence and consequences of both verbal conflict and couple violence. Targeted programs such as Sanders' Triple P-Positive Parenting Program (chap. 13, this volume) represent one such approach to preventing couple conflict. The Triple P program is a multilevel intervention based on principles of social learning theory, the public health model, and an ecological perspective. In general, this intervention program aims to prevent adjustment problems in children by fostering family environments characterized by low conflict levels and an absence of violence. Providing interventions at both universal and targeted levels, Triple P focuses on intervening at the point of parenting practices. Specifically, the core of the program centers on five parenting principles that translate to a number of specific parenting skills ranging from monitoring children's behavior to managing misbehavior to developing problem-solving and communication skills with one's partner. Controlled evaluations of the program indicate that parents can be trained to implement positive parenting strategies, and that they will do so in noncontrolled situations outside of their homes (Sanders, chap. 13, this volume).

In addition to specific programs like Triple P, approaches such as marriage education, counseling, and mediation are avenues for preventing couple conflict and its negative effects (Emery, chap. 16; Ooms, chap. 15, this volume). Marriage education and counseling are standard approaches for alleviating disagreements and conflicts between partners, and they have achieved moderate success. Mediation provides a particularly successful approach to resolving conflict between divorcing partners. Because divorce proceedings are typically adversarial and can exacerbate the conflict that led to the divorce, mediation provides an appealing alternative. Available in every state and mandatory in some, mediation allows divorcing couples to reach agreements about the specifics of their divorce more quickly and at less cost than do traditional divorce proceedings. Emery (chap. 16, this volume) noted that mediation produces a number of benefits for children and divorced families, possibly because couples are more likely to comply with mediated agreements than with court-ordered agreements (Ooms, chap. 15, this volume).

Just as researchers like Sanders attempt to prevent couple conflict and its negative effects, various governmental policies and programs aim to prevent couple violence and its seriously deleterious consequences. In fact, governmental responses to couple conflict focus almost exclusively on issues of couple violence, although there is growing interest in policy responses to nonviolent forms of couple conflict (Ooms, chap. 15, this volume). The primary goal of programs responding to couple violence is to assist women and children in escaping from dangerous situations. Funded by states and private foundations, these programs offer crisis hotlines, housing, food, clothing, shelter, and legal services. In addition to programs and policies that remove women and children from potentially lethal situations, policymakers are beginning to recognize the need to treat the perpetrators in an effort to prevent further violence (Ooms, chap. 15, this volume). Although many men are mandated into such batterer's programs, these interventions receive less attention and less funding than do programs designed to protect victims. Ooms noted that this trend is particularly distressing given that as many as one third of abuse victims return to their abusers. Furthermore, even if the victims to do not return to their abusers, the men are likely to abuse their next relational partner. As Johnson pointed out (chap. 7, this volume), these programs are only moderately successful, perhaps because they fail to recognize the different treatment needs of the perpetrators.

Recent changes in welfare eligibility have raised specific concerns about the consequences of changes in welfare for women who are the victims of domestic violence. Evidence suggests that 20% to 30% of all welfare recipients are victims of domestic violence, and that domestic abuse often begins or is exacerbated when women who are on welfare become employed (Ooms, chap. 15, this volume). It appears that their partners feel threatened by their increased autonomy and respond with violence. An amendment to the welfare reform legislation acknowledges these threats to the safety of women by allowing individual states to temporarily waive the new work requirement for receiving welfare while the women obtain assistance from domestic violence programs and shelters (Ooms, chap. 15, this volume).

General Guidelines

Beyond these specific prevention techniques, the contributing authors offered general strategies for preventing couple conflict and its negative effects. First, Goldscheider (chap. 3, this volume) observed that with increases in divorce and remarriage, fathers are less committed and involved with their children. Any success in increasing fathers' commitment to their children may ameliorate the negative consequences of conflict and divorce for children. Furthermore, Goldscheider suggested that increasing men's commitment to stepchildren—even formally through ceremony—may decrease the tensions and associated conflict related to stepchildren. Second, Goldscheider pointed out that the current U.S. system of governmental financial support drives men from their families. In contrast, the Swedish government provides financial support for families with children, allowing men to remain with their families even when they are unable to provide for the family. Goldscheider suggested that alleviating the financial burdens of raising a family may encourage men to remain connected to their families, avoiding the negative consequences of parental separation and divorce for children (chap. 3, this volume).

Finally, Gelles (chap. 14, this volume) and Emery (chap. 16, this volume) stressed the importance of timing in designing and implementing prevention and intervention programs. According to Gelles, interventions will only succeed if they occur at a time when individuals and couples are ready to change. Too many interventions target families who have not yet reached the point at which they are ready and able to change. For families that are resistant or are in the precontemplative stages of change, interventions need to focus on problem identification and consciousness raising more than on changing specific behaviors

(Gelles, chap. 14, this volume). For example, Emery (chap. 16, this volume) maintained that one reason for the great success of divorce mediation is that it is offered at a time in the divorce process when it is most needed— when emotions are running high and the primary task is renegotiating family relationships. Emery also asserted that intervening at critical times in couples' relationships can help to prevent conflict and divorce. One such time is when a couple has their first child.

Perhaps other strategies to prevent couple conflict and its detrimental effects may concentrate on the partners' willingness to compromise in disagreements or to change their behavior. Similarly, the incompatibility of partners' goals in life, their expectations for each other, or even their personality traits may be vital sources of their conflict. In terms of policy, perhaps a more proactive approach to preventing couple conflict is necessary. Sanders' (chap. 13, this volume) example of weekly televised parenting programs, Cordova's (chap. 8, this volume) outlines for regular marriage "checkups," Repetti's (chap. 4, this volume) emphasis on developing cooperation, and Bradbury et al.'s (chap. 5, this volume) focus on improving social support are a few examples of promising and creative advancements along these lines.

CONCLUSION

The authors in this volume provided informative observations about the sources, effects, and prevention of couple conflict. They identified evolutionary, couple, patriarchal, and interpersonal factors as potential sources of couple conflict. They noted that the consequences of couple conflict may range from temporary child adjustment problems (Cummings et al., chap. 9, this volume) to severe, sometimes even fatal, violence between partners (Wilson & Daly, chap. 1, this volume). Whatever the consequences, the effects of couple conflict may be moderated by conflict type (Conger, chap. 11; Grych, chap. 12; Johnson, chap. 7, this volume), affective tone (Conger, chap. 11; Cummings et al., chap. 9, this volume), conflict resolution (Cummings et al., chap. 9, this volume), children's perceptions (Conger, chap. 11; Cummings et al., chap. 9; Grych, chap. 12, this volume), parenting practices (Conger, chap. 11; Cummings et al., chap. 9, this volume), and various demographic variables (Buchanan et al., chap. 10; Conger, chap. 11, this volume). Finally, the authors recognized a variety of techniques for preventing couple conflict and its harmful effects. These techniques involve new approaches (Beach, chap. 6; Bradbury et al., chap. 5; Cordova, chap. 8; Repetti, chap. 4, this volume), specific strategies for dealing with violent couples (Gelles, chap. 14; Johnson, chap. 7, this volume), current policies and programs (Emery, chap. 16; Ooms, chap. 15; Sanders, chap. 13, this volume), and general guidelines for preventing couple conflict and its harmful effects (Emery, chap. 16; Gelles, chap. 14; Goldscheider, chap. 3, this volume).

These contributions notwithstanding, perhaps the most valuable insight emerging from these chapters is Bradbury's et al.'s (chap. 5, this volume) caution to reconsider the role of conflict in marriage. They critiqued the existing longitudinal research and prediction analyses of couple conflict, and suggested a number of shortcomings in this work. These include sampling problems, methodological challenges, weak effects, and inconsistent findings. In addition, they noted that although the results of treatment studies indicate that couples' problem-solving abilities may be improved, such change is not consistently related to marital satisfaction. These results are significant, because problem-solving training is frequently recommended as a solution to alleviate couple conflict. Furthermore, Bradbury et al. argued that couple conflict may be a reflection of the heightened distress that some couples face—not the cause of that distress. Finally, they observed that marital disagreements are relatively rare, and that most couples do not assess their future spouse's problem-solving abilities prior to marriage. This, too, suggests that couple conflict may not be as important as previously thought. In sum, these findings indicate that the influence of couple conflict may have been overemphasized in determining marital outcomes.

The possibility that couple conflict is not as important in predicting marital outcomes as once thought should encourage scholars to reevaluate their assumptions about couple conflict. Minimally, such a conclusion entails three corollaries. First, it is necessary to clarify the role of couple conflict for relationship outcomes. This involves improving sample representativeness, the precision of statistical models, the refinement of definitions, and the assessment of the contexts in which conflict occurs. Second, we need to continue to consider alternative explanations for the causes of the relationship and individual outcomes associated with couple conflict. The authors in this volume proposed a number of possibilities, including cooperation (Repetti, chap. 4, this volume), communication (Johnson, chap. 7, this volume), social support (Bradbury et al., chap. 5, this volume), and the willingness to redefine the self-representations of one's abilities (Beach, chap. 6, this volume). Finally, we need to consider rethinking and redirecting interventions designed to offset the harmful effects of couple conflict. If previous assumptions regarding the role of couple conflict for marital outcomes prove to be false, perhaps the solutions also lie elsewhere.

Just as partners in conflictual relationships are urged to change their behavior, perhaps present researchers need to modify their approaches and assumptions in studying couple conflict, also. Although this volume contains compelling arguments about the causes, consequences, and prevention of couple conflict, it remains unclear exactly why couple conflict matters, when it matters, how much it matters, and who it affects. Specifying these answers should continue to pose a formidable challenge for future research.

REFERENCES

Anderson, K. L. (1997). Gender, status, and domestic violence: An integration of feminist and family violence approaches. *Journal of Marriage and the Family, 59,* 655-669.

Daly, M., Wiseman, K. A., & Wilson, M. (1997). Women with children sired by previous partners incur excess risk of uxoricide. *Homicide Studies, 1,* 61-71.

Heaton, T. B. (1984). Religious homogamy and marital satisfaction reconsidered. *Journal of Marriage and the Family, 46,* 729-733.

Karney, B. R., & Bradbury, T. N. (1995). The longitudinal course of marital quality and stability: A review of theory, method, and research. *Psychological Bulletin, 118,* 3-34.

Lehrer, E. L., & Chiswick, C. U. (1993). Religion as a determinant of marital stability. *Demography, 30,* 385-401.

Lupri, E., Grandin, E., & Brinkerhoff, M. B. (1994). Socioeconomic status and male violence in the Canadian home: A reexamination. *Canadian Journal of Sociology, 19,* 7-73.

Stets, J. E. (1991). Cohabiting and marital aggression: The role of social isolation. *Journal of Marriage and the Family, 53,* 669-680.

Wilson, M., Johnson, H., & Daly, M. (1995). Lethal and nonlethal violence against wives. *Canadian Journal of Criminology, 37,* 331-361.

Author Index

Subject Index

*For Product Safety Concerns and Information please contact
our EU representative GPSR@taylorandfrancis.com Taylor & Francis
Verlag GmbH, Kaufingerstraße 24, 80331 München, Germany*

T - #0097 - 270225 - C0 - 229/152/16 - PB - 9780415647052 - Gloss Lamination